MARX'S CAPITAL

A Student Edition

AF539474

How, then, is the magnitude of this value to be measured? Plainly, by the quantity of the value-creating substance, the labour, contained in the article. The quantity of labour, however, is measured by its duration, and labour-time in its turn finds its standard in weeks, days, and hours.

Some people might think that if the value of a commodity is de[illegible] spent on it, the more idle and uns[illegible]ble would his commodity be, be[illegible]d in its production. The labour, how[illegible] value, is homogeneous human lab[illegible]rm labour-power. The total amo[illegible] embodied in the sum total of the values of all commodities produced by that society, counts here as one homogeneous mass of human labour-power, composed though it may be of innumerable individual units. Each of these units is the same as any other, so far as it has the character of the average labour-power of society, and takes effect as such; that is, so far as it requires for producing a commodity, no more time than is needed on an average, no more than is socially necessary. The labour-time socially necessary is that required to produce an article under the normal conditions of production, and with the average degree of skill and intensity prevalent at the time. The introduction of power-looms into England probably reduced by one-half the labour required to weave a given quantity of yarn into cloth. The hand-loom weavers, as a matter of fact, continued to require the same time as before; but for all that, the product of one hour of their labour represented after the change only half an hour's social labour, and consequently fell to one-half its former value.

We see then that that which determines the magnitude of the value of any article is the amount of labour socially necessary, or the labour-time socially necessary for its production. Each individual commodity, in this connexion, is to be considered as an average sample of its class. Commodities, therefore, in which equal quantities of labour are embodied, or which can be produced in the same time, have the same value. The value of one commodity is to the value of any other, as the labour-time necessary for the production of the one is to that necessary for the production of the other. As values, all commodities are only definite masses of congealed labour-time.

The value of a commodity would therefore remain constant, if the labour-time required for its production also remained constant. But the latter changes with every variation in the productiveness of labour. This productiveness is determined by various circumstances, amongst

MARX'S CAPITAL

A Student Edition

Edited and introduced by

C.J. Arthur

Marx's Capital: A Student Edition
Edited and introduced by C.J. Arthur

© Lawrence and Wishart 1992
© Aakar Books for South Asia 2014

First Published in India 2014
Reprinted 2019

ISBN 978-93-5002-259-7

Published in agreement with Lawrence and Wishart Limited, London for publication and sale only in South Asia

All rights reserved. No part of this book may be reproduced or transmitted, in any form or by any means, without prior permission of the publisher.

This edition is an edited and abridged version of the first volume of *Capital: A Critique of Political Economy* by Karl Marx, using the text of the English edition of 1887 which was translated from the third German edition by Samuel Moore and Edward Aveling, and edited by Friedrich Engels (first published by Lawrence and Wishart in 1954).

Published by
AAKAR BOOKS
28 E Pocket IV, Mayur Vihar Phase I
Delhi 110 091, India
aakarbooks@gmail.com
www.aakarbooks.com

Printed at
Sapra Brothers, Noida

Contents

PART III — THE PRODUCTION OF ABSOLUTE SURPLUS-VALUE

PART IV — PRODUCTION OF RELATIVE SURPLUS-VALUE

Editor's Introduction

Karl Marx was one of the intellectual giants of the modern epoch. While it is true that even without him we would still be arguing about capitalism and socialism, class struggle and revolution, it cannot be denied that in his work he established in large part the framework within which the discussion has been carried on. Furthermore, many of his own concepts have become common currency in the social sciences: 'class consciousness'; 'alienation', 'ideology'; 'exploitation'; 'mode of production'; 'relations of production'; 'commodity fetishism'; 'materialist conception of history'. Above all, Marx challenged the rationality of capitalist society. His 'critique of political economy' argued that capitalism was exploitative, inherently contradictory and systematically prone to crisis. That we still speak of capital and wage labour, that we can trace the booms and slumps in the economy since his day, means that Marx may still have much to teach us. Serious scholars, whether economists, historians or political scientists, know that if his work is not accepted or developed it must be refuted. In a word, he is unavoidable: anyone wishing to further their own education must take Marx's *Capital* seriously.

It was in 1867 that Marx brought out his masterpiece *Capital: A Critique of Political Economy*; to be precise, he brought out *Volume One: The Process of Production of Capital.* From the mass of his notes, Friedrich Engels brought out after his death two more volumes: *Volume Two* on circulation of capital, and *Volume Three* dealing with revenues such as rent. These are inferior in literary quality and coherence to *Volume One*. Karl Kautsky brought out a '*Volume Four*': *Theories of Surplus Value*, itself a mass of notes taking up three volumes. When people speak of Marx's *Capital* they usually have in mind simply *Volume One*. This is the book read by students, workers, social scientists, philosophers, historians and the educated public wishing to acquaint themselves with one of the great minds of the modern era. This is what is presented in our abridgement. The other volumes are read by economists of course; but they are relatively less known than the first volume. As Engels said in his Preface to the English Edition of 1887, *Volume One* 'is in great measure a whole in itself' and ranks 'as an independent work'. This was a verdict oft-repeated. Karl Korsch said that the book 'impresses us both in form and content as a finished and rounded whole', while Rosa Luxemburg asserted that it shows 'not a trace of theoretical incompleteness'. Moreover, it fully realises Marx's ambition to create an 'artistic whole' (as expressed in a letter to Engels 31 July 1865).

In the past it was undoubtedly true that people were discouraged from reading *Capital* by the text's formidable length and forest of footnotes. This is why we have issued this 'student edition'. We have done our best to retain the meat of the book, while making the way clear by judicious pruning of its sprawling branches. Of course, nothing can be done about the *theoretical* content. Marx presupposed a reader prepared to 'get stuck in'.

THE PRINCIPLE OF TOTALITY

Capital: Volume One is therefore a whole, not just a quarter of the complete theory, because the inner workings of capitalist production, which Marx laid bare in it, form the originating framework within which all other relations in this mode of production can be located. The later volumes are thus not of equal weight to the first, nor are they the conclusions to premises established here; rather, they are concretisations in more determinate form of the main relationships and tendencies established in the first volume.

Methodologically speaking, Marx can work in this way because, as the presentation itself shows, the capitalist mode of production has an organic unity. This means that knowledge of it must take the form of a *system* of related categories rather than a series of discrete investigations; moreover, in the theory, it is necessary to establish what is the hierarchy of determinations involved, and especially what lies at the heart of the matter – the principle that works itself out through the increasingly complex secondary and tertiary layers of the entire structure. Of course, it is equally necessary for theory to develop these further mediations, in order to show, in principle at least, how this fundamental dynamic grounds itself in its effects and thereby successfully reproduces the whole system.

But Marx's most significant problem clearly lay in disentangling from the bewilderingly complicated phenomena of modern economic life the essential features, which can be articulated in a few simple abstract categories (value, surplus-value, etc.). This he gives us here.

This means that the argument of *Capital* is pitched at a high level of generality throughout all three volumes, but especially *Volume One*.

New readers should not make the mistake of imagining that the discussion deals with very detailed movements and relationships of wages, prices and profits as they are determined in everyday life. When Marx formulates his law of value it is certainly intended to be the really fundamental regulator of everyday phenomena, but many further stages would be necessary to explain, even in principle, its concrete manifestation. This leads the more obtuse critic to wonder what use it is then, if it cannot be immediately 'applied', if it refers to relationships not visible on the surface of things. But no science, including social science, can dispense with such fundamental principles, 'abstracted', if you like, from contingent empirical phenomena.

It is clear that when Marx uses the metaphor 'laws of motion' he has Newton in mind. This should be taken quite seriously. No one ever *saw* a body moving at a constant speed in a straight line for ever. Such a body is always subject to disturbing influences, friction, air resistance, gravity and the like. But this did not stop Newton correctly considering such a law as the basic regulator of mechanical motion, and defending it against the Aristotelian assumption that bodies tend to a state of rest. Marx's law of value, explained in this volume, has much the same status. In its purity it is the principle underlying the most complex phenomena of capitalism, albeit that market prices never coincide with values, or profits with surplus-value. But Marx shows how one must understand the latter as a stage in generating the former.

Marx makes the point in *Volume Three* that there would be no need for science if the appearance of things directly coincided with their essence. He argues that the real relationships may be quite contrary to the way they appear; though that they appear so must itself be explained as well. Thus Marx's theory is explanatory because, instead of making observations of surface phenomena like costs and prices, it develops the inner structure of the observable relations. In so far as appearances are systematically misleading it is a *critical* science; for it undercuts moral and political positions rooted in these appearances; and conversely it represents in theory the standpoint of the proletariat.

THE PRINCIPLE OF SOCIAL FORM

It is important to understand, especially for those already acquainted with modern 'economics', that Marx's approach to his subject matter has very little in common with what is understood today by 'economics'. For example, Marx regards analysis of supply and demand curves as an entirely superficial problem compared with the theorisation of market exchange itself as a peculiar social form, and the divination of its long-run tendencies of development. Furthermore, the differential distribution of economic power in modern capitalism, which is glossed over and taken for granted in bourgeois economics, is precisely what Marx thinks requires investigation and explanation, in particular of course, the power of capital.

As early as 1847 Marx had adumbrated his basic approach to the understanding and critique of 'political economy', namely that 'economic categories are only the theoretical expressions, the abstractions, of the social relations of production' (*Poverty of Philosophy*). It was these '*social* relations of production' that Marx investigated. In his view, scientific study of the economy is not only about material transformations, for example the managing of scarce resources, or the correlation of inputs and outputs to determine technically consistent systems. Rather, such topics are to be subordinated to the understanding of how people relate to each other in particular, historically specific modes of production. Thus Marx's theory is not addressed primarily to 'economising' (a relation between people and things) nor to 'utility maximisation' (another, dubious relation between people and things) but to the 'social economy', through which labours are socially recognised, commensurated, allocated and exploited. It understands that technical methods are employed only within certain *social forms*: 'An African is an African. Only in certain relations does he become a slave. A mule is a machine for spinning cotton. Only in certain relations does it become *capital*.' (*Wage Labour and Capital*)

The specificity of the capitalist mode of production is, first, that the products of labour take the form of commodities for sale. The reason for this phenomenon is that labours are undertaken in private enterprises which are socially synthesised only through exchange in which products assume *the form of value*; this is not the only possible form of social synthesis, but it *is* the one determining almost all production in this society. Second, the immediate producers, the workers, have been deprived of means of production of their own and hence have nothing to sell but their labour-power; from this feature of the organisation of production arises the *capital relation* based on exploitation of wage-labour. Clearly this nexus is a *social* fact, not a natural one. In this way Marx can demonstrate that the Industrial Revolution was defined by the form of *capitalist* development. In general, Marx holds that it is the social form of the economy that is the key to understanding its movement, reproduction, development, limits and destiny.

THE PRINCIPLE OF HISTORICAL SPECIFICITY

Because social forms vary, there are no economic laws valid for each and every different form of society. Each socially specified mode of production has its own laws of motion. Marx's concern, as the very title of his work indicates, is with the capitalist mode of production; nothing he says here necessarily has any application to pre-capitalist, post-capitalist or, in general, non-capitalist societies. It is important, therefore, for theorists today to determine whether or not the mode of production has changed sufficiently to invalidate the laws Marx formulated. In 1859 Marx outlined a sketch of economic development listing the 'Asiatic, ancient, feudal, and modern bourgeois modes of production'. His topic is the last named only, as he puts it in his Preface: 'it is the ultimate aim of this work to reveal the economic law of motion of *modern* society' (my emphasis). History implies, in other words, an evolution of socio-economic forms of life. A Russian reviewer, quoted with approval by Marx, said that the value of Marx's book 'lies in the illumination of the special laws that regulate the origin, existence, development and death of a given social organism and its replacement by another, higher one.' We are now in a position to understand how Marx starts the exposition of his theory. We know that he must begin with that relationship which conditions the economy as a *whole*. We know that this relation must be *social* in form. We know that it must be historically *specific*, not just 'production in general'. Marx's chosen foundation is the relation of capital to wage-labour. Whereas in earlier modes of production land-ownership was the key element, nowadays it is industrial capital that is the dominant force, the overriding moment in the dynamic of the system. Thus in *Volume One* he concentrates entirely on this relation of production, leaving until later volumes such matters as rent, interest and commerce.

But capital is itself complex. Marx defines it as self-expanding value, so he must first thematise value in exchange (as distinguished from value in use) as it is borne by the mass of commodities circulating in the market place, then he must develop the logic of money from this, and finally reach the concept of capital. What Marx shows, then, in *Volume One*, is that capitalist production is a matter of producing value, surplus-value and capital itself; that this is at the same time a matter of the continual reproduction of its basic social form – the opposition of capital and wage-labour – within which the capitalist is compelled to accumulate and the workers are compelled to sell themselves; and finally that this in turn grounds the compulsion for the proletariat to unite itself as a class against capital, and to end wage-slavery.

On the basis of the method outlined above he can even risk already sketching out the destiny of the capitalist system, and reaffirming his judgement of nearly twenty years before – in the *Communist Manifesto* – that what capitalism produces above all else is its own gravediggers, a revolutionary proletariat.

HISTORICAL PRESUPPOSITIONS

Throughout *Capital* Marx has undertaken a systematic investigation of capitalism, its articulation as an ongoing system. But in the last part of the book he locates it historically. It has its origins and destiny. Capitalism is able to reproduce itself if its basic presuppositions, capital and wage-labour, are in place. But these are by no means 'givens' *historically*, however familiar they seem to us today. They are social forms taken on by labour and the means of production, which had to be historically produced. The most important single point here is that capital depends on the availability of labour-power. This requires the existence of a class without access to the means of production on their own account – thus forced to sell their services to capital in order to subsist. This separation of the producer from the means of production was by no means a natural, God-given fact; if anything was natural, it was the converse – an immediate unity of the producers with the land on which they subsisted. Marx therefore explains the real historical process of expropriation in Britain, whereby people were driven off the land, through such measures as the Enclosure Acts, the Highland 'clearances' and the like. It is noteworthy that the intervention of the state plays a role in forcing on the process.

Every country's history is different but in one way or another the traditional smallholder has been driven off the land to be made into a wage-labourer. How or when it happens is a historically specific matter.

COMMODITY FETISHISM

The main conceptual difficulties which lie in the way of the reader of *Capital* relate to the concepts of 'value' and 'surplus-value'. It is important to understand that Marx sharply distinguishes between use-value and exchange-value, and that the latter has a *purely social reality*. Daniel Defoe's Robinson Crusoe naturally took a great interest in the useful properties of the items salvaged from his ship, but it would have had no meaning whatsoever to 'value' them to see how much he was 'worth'. Nor does it make sense in any communal form of social production. It is only when the products of labour are treated by society as exchangeable commodities that they acquire value in the economic sense. Value does not inhere in them naturally like their mass. Just as a pawn is only an oddly shaped piece of wood outside the contest of the rules of chess, *within which* it acquires certain powers in relation to other pieces, so also does a product of labour acquire a certain value in relation to other such commodities within the rules of the 'exchange game'. To treat such powers as *naturally inherent* is to fetishise the commodity, says Marx.

At the same time, once the exchange system is in operation then the value of a commodity is perfectly *objective*, as against the hopes and wishes of individuals. Marx argues that the substance of value is 'abstract labour' and that its measure is 'socially necessary labour-time'. In principle, then, commodities exchange in proportions ultimately determined by the labour-time necessary to produce their kind.

In truth, what Marx does is to reduce a relation between products to another relation – between producers. But he points out that this theoretical achievement does not alter the fact that people have to conform to the laws of the market. Having set up the exchange system in which commodities have value relations to each other, we become its victim. It is not that the law of value *appears* like the law of gravity in its independence of human will. It really *is* effective over the agents concerned, whether they understand it or not, as long as private property and exchange exist. Commodity fetishism characterises not so much a confused consciousness as the form of appearance of the relations themselves (just as one distinguishes the hallucinations of a madman from the mirage everyone can 'see').

EXPLOITATION

It is clear from the outset that Marx's law of value is intended to be descriptive and explanatory: it shows *how the system works*. It has got nothing to do with any normative principle about how production and exchange *ought* to be carried on. (Marx's own prescription is that the market, and with it the law of value, should be abolished.)

It is not often so well understood that Marx stuck to this view even where surplus-value was concerned. It was not a question for him of complaining that appropriation of surplus-value broke the law of equivalent exchange. Rather, he undertakes to show how the capital relation ensures the systematic exploitation of the immediate producers *on the basis of the law itself*. So for him, it is not a matter of demanding 'fair wages' but of abolishing the wages system. Even those, like Smith and Ricardo, who advanced a labour theory of value, stumbled when it came to explaining surplus-value. If costs and prices were based on labour values, how could a surplus-value arise at all? Yet it obviously does; and forms the basis of profit, rent and interest. But this seems impossible if labour is paid for in full.

Marx solves the problem by pointing out that the expression 'value of labour' makes no sense. What workers sell is not their labour but their labour-power, their capacity to labour. Labour may be paid by the hour or by the piece, but Marx argues that the underlying determinant of the wage is the value of labour-power and that this is something distinct from labour itself.

There are two reasons Marx can advance for this conceptual innovation. First, the expression 'value of labour' has no sense because labour as the source of value can no more itself be valued than gravity which gives things weight can itself have a weight, or the wavelength of light which explains colour can itself be coloured. In logical terms, it is a category mistake to ask about the value of labour.

Second, a less abstract argument can be derived from considering the labour theory of value itself. What it envisages is that value is determined not by the *use* to which a thing is put, but in its conditions of *production*. For instance, it is no good my going to a furniture shop and telling the vendor I intend to use the goods for firewood. I have to pay compensation for all the work embodied in the commodity, even if it is no good for the use to which I intend to put it. In exactly the same way the value of what the worker sells must be determined not by the use to which the employer puts it but by its conditions of production. To produce a worker fit and ready for work involves the consumption of certain values, that is, means of subsistence. It is the quantity of labour embodied in these inputs which determines the value of labour-power, not the labour-time extorted out of it during the working day. One sees immediately that there is no necessary relationship between these two quantities. In Marx's favourite arithmetical illustration, suppose it takes six hours' labour a day to produce the workers' means of subsistence, and yet the employer gets twelve hours' labour a day out of them. Six hours of these twelve must go to create the counter-value of their wages. But this still leaves six hours' 'surplus labour' for the benefit of the capitalist, if he succeeds in realising it in the form of surplus-value. Unfortunately Marx often confuses the matter by using the expression 'unpaid labour', contrary to his own argument. In chapter eighteen he asserts that this 'popular expression' for surplus labour could not mislead anyone into thinking that the capitalist pays for labour. But it has.

The temptation to use the expression 'unpaid labour' has obvious political roots. It can even be justified theoretically in so far as 'surplus labour' is too general an expression. *All* exploitative modes of production rest on the 'pumping out' (*Volume Three*) of surplus labour. Marx explains the implications of this in *Volume One*: 'What distinguishes the various economic formations of society – the distinction for example between slavery and wage-labour – is the form in which this surplus labour is in each case extorted from the immediate producer, the worker.' The slave and the serf are obliged by force or customary obligations to work 'for nothing'. Yet capital claims to 'pay for' labour. Therefore Marx's interest (theoretical and practical) lies in the specific form in which surplus labour is appropriated in this case.

Marx did not discover that capitalism is exploitative. It does not require great intellect to see that the capitalists live off other people's labour. The theoretical problem resolved in the way just discussed is *how* it happens. Even those who had isolated labour as the sole source of value thought exploitation must be based on a failure to return to the labourers the full value of their labour. Marx grasped that surplus-value resulted, not from such a deduction, but from something, namely surplus labour, being added to the original values brought into play in the production process. This was how the value originally in the hands of the worker could be paid for in full, and yet surplus-value be appropriated by its purchaser.

DOMESTIC LABOUR AND HUMAN REPRODUCTION

Marx is a little too glib when he suggests that labour-power is a commodity like any other. Apart from the fact that normally it can only be hired and not bought outright, its conditions of production are not those of capitalist competition. As a consequence, it is impossible to establish the socially necessary labour-time for its production. Marx replies that, nonetheless, its value can be equated to the value of the means of subsistence required to sustain the worker and his or her family. Fair enough. But what is subsistence? Marx concedes that this notion has a 'historical and moral' component which does make a real difference to the value of labour-power. In the context of *Volume One*, perhaps, Marx does not need to develop this point because, however the value of labour-power is determined, the potentiality for the creation of surplus-value through exploitation remains. (It is worth noting that in chapter seventeen Marx points out that, given increased productivity, real wages can rise while the value of labour-power falls.)

Nevertheless, in view of much recent controversy on one aspect of the matter, we must dwell on the question a little longer. Some feminists have advanced the argument that Marx is at fault for neglecting the role of domestic labour in the production of labour-power. Surely this labour contributes to the *value* of labour-power?

Very often this criticism involves, in my view, a methodological confusion between normative discourse and explanatory discourse, and a conceptual confusion between use-value and exchange-value. Those who complain that Marx takes no account of domestic labour are simply shooting the messenger for bearing the bad news if, *in fact*, capitalism takes no account of it. Of course, capital gets the benefit of domestic labour in so far as the worker could not be fed and clothed without it; but it does not follow that any *value* has been appropriated, because the domestic economy is not subject to the value relations of the exchange system. It has a quite different social form. A worker does not 'shop around' among potential partners for domestic services, so to speak. From the point of view of capital the domestic economy is like a 'black box', which is linked into its system as a necessary part, but about the interior of which it knows nothing. Certain use-values go in (various subsistence goods), a different one comes out (namely labour-power); but from the point of view of value, all that can be said is that stability requires that the output supplied to capitalist factories must be valued as the equivalent of the inputs absorbed from the market in subsistence goods.

Incidentally, domestic labour is not a unique case. State-employed educators and doctors labour to maintain the quality of labour-power supplied to capital but they contribute nothing to its value. Like housework, the benefit of the labour comes to capital without having to be 'accounted for' in value terms. What makes the capitalist social formation complex is indeed the co-existence of different modes of production within it. Yet it is evident that the domestic mode of production, and the infrastructural industries (road-building and so forth) organised by the state, are functionally subordinated to the purely capitalist sector. At the same time, it could not sustain itself without them. This means that surplus labour may be indirectly appropriated from such sectors by capital, and be a pre-condition for its profitability, without appearing in the value of commodities in the way that labour directly regulated and exploited by capital does.

One can see in these cases how the tendency to slip from an explanatory theory of value to a normative one becomes almost irresistible. However, one should also reflect on the fact that for Marx it is production *for use* that is the 'ideal', not production *for profit*. That so-called women's work is for use anticipates socialism, whereas the 'value' society presently puts on work (formerly) mainly done by men Marx wants to abolish!

A second important point is that, as Marx's work is a *systematic* theory, everything must be dealt with in its due place, if the explanation is to be coherent instead of continually going backwards and forwards. The pure structure of capital is sex-blind, and at the level of abstraction Marx employs here he rightly pays only incidental attention to sex differences or gender relations. Strictly speaking, such matters (as unequal wages, domestic labour, the 'family wage') have their place when a much more concrete level of analysis is reached. Finally, it should be noted that in *Capital* Marx is concerned specifically with the capital relation. For a *full* account of the entire 'social economy', study of the role of the patriarchal family (and the bourgeois state) is a necessary supplement to the work he initiated. This is because Marx's ultimate objective was to establish in full the process whereby social reproduction occurs. How does capitalist society maintain and develop itself materially and socially? That is the problem. Through the operation of the law of value commodities are produced and distributed, and the capital relation which governs this is itself reproduced. We continually find that capital faces a propertyless mass of workers who must sell their labour-power to survive. However, to reproduce these people over generations it is not sufficient that the economy supply them with necessities; it is also the case that new generations must be born and reared; and this requires the family with its peculiar and historically mutable structure of sex roles, which can by no means be reduced to biological invariants. Marx, however, was silent in the main on the question of how the family, its structure, its history and its specific form of oppression, mesh with the capitalist system of production. Indeed, it has been suggested that it is the very 'invisibility' of these human and material processes which are carried on, in capitalist society, 'privately', that contributed to this oversight.

An important topic for further research is to elucidate the terms on which these spheres interact. Does the modern family passively reflect the social forms (e.g., the distinction between public and private) established by capital, and function according to its requirements (e.g., its demand for labour)? Or is there some independent dynamic of family organisation and function that is, or could be, recalcitrant to capital's logic?

PRINCIPLES OF ABRIDGEMENT

In reducing Marx's *Capital: Volume One* to a readable length the following principles were applied.

First and foremost – war on footnotes! The huge number of Marx's footnotes is notoriously intimidating. I have eliminated them all. For the most part they demonstrate Marx's exhaustive knowledge of the literature of political economy. But the general reader is not likely to be aware of the authors concerned. In the second place, they further extend the material evidence for some point already amply established in the text. Finally, there are the simple references to sources. Marx was the first social scientist to make comprehensive use of the facts made public in official reports such as those of the Children's Employment Commission (1863-67), those of H.M. Inspectors of Factories (1841-67), and the Public Health Reports (1860-65). On reflection, it seemed to me that only specialists would want to follow up the various sources cited by Marx. In this edition the text is not cluttered with footnote numbers in the hope that readers will be content with my assurance that Marx was absolutely scrupulous about documenting every fact and quotation he gave. In a handful of cases, where I thought an important point was made in a note, I have raised it to the text in brackets.

In the text itself, I have eliminated Marx's polemics against other writers – again, likely to be of interest only to specialists. I have cut a number of arithmetical illustrations. And I have eliminated a few of the less significant developments of his argument. Occasionally, this has involved cutting chapters from the original; the numbering of chapters has, however, been kept true to the full edition for obvious reasons. Finally, I have slimmed down the wealth of statistical and anecdotal information about the condition of the working class. It is true that Marx makes his point partly through the sheer weight of evidence he assembled. But there is more than enough here to convince anyone of the horrible sufferings of the British people caught up in the Industrial Revolution. The final chapter 'On Colonisation' is omitted here. It is neither a conclusion to the book, nor a transition to the second volume. The true climax of the book is chapter thirty-two on 'The Historical Tendency of Capitalist Accumulation', with its prediction of the downfall of capitalism.

The translation, based on the original of 1887, has been updated in a few places, but only the most necessary emendations have been made. (Perhaps I should point out that the word 'labourer' used in the text refers to workers in general, not just unskilled manual labourers.)

In sum, this edition provides the modern reader with everything of theoretical value in Marx's *Capital*, together with a wealth of historical material.

READING *CAPITAL*

Afraid that readers might find the work difficult, Marxists as different in their philosophy and politics as Karl Korsch and Louis Althusser, in introducing their editions of *Capital*, recommend reading it in an order other than that published. Korsch suggests starting at Part Three with 'The Labour Process'; Althusser, less radically, with Part Two. Both are inspired by a wish to direct the reader to Marx's descriptions of industrial development and class struggle before approaching the conceptual difficulties of value theory set out in the early chapters.

The danger in this procedure, in beginning in the middle of *Capital*, is that one is unlikely to read the chapters on industrial development without importing some sort of interpretive apparatus. If one omits value theory, one will inevitably import a 'technological determinism', and believe that the developments Marx outlines are due to some inner necessity of technological progress. It should be stressed that, in order to understand why technical change occurs, and why it occurs in the way that it does, it is necessary to have grasped the earlier exposition in this volume of the theory of value, of capital and of capitalist exploitation. The labour process, from its simple beginnings in cooperation to assembly lines and automation, is not neutral with regard to the social relations of production. The latter determine not only who benefits most from the system, but also the productive forces set in motion, and the inner organisation of factory life itself. Marx shows how the worker is not only legally subordinated to capital in the contract of employment, but becomes really subordinated to capital in that their every move is programmed in advance and they lose all control over their own activity.

My advice to the reader is therefore to begin at the beginning. But if you find the going rather difficult, then I suggest you begin again with Parts Three and Four. But it is critical to your understanding that you come back to the earlier chapters on commodities and capital in order to follow through Marx's elaboration of these concepts. It is essential to grasp the interaction of production, exchange and accumulation if the whole system is to be understood as an ongoing totality. You should find it well worth the while to master this remarkable, and hugely influential, book.

Christopher J. Arthur
Brighton, July 1992

From the Preface to the First German Edition

That every beginning is difficult holds in all sciences. To understand the first chapter, especially the section that contains the analysis of commodities, will, therefore, present the greatest difficulty. That which concerns more especially the analysis of the substance of value and the magnitude of value, I have, as much as it was possible, popularised. The value-form, whose fully developed shape is the money-form, is very elementary and simple. Nevertheless, the human mind has for more than 2,000 years sought in vain to get to the bottom of it, whilst on the other hand, to the successful analysis of much more composite and complex forms, there has been at least an approximation. Why? Because the body, as an organic whole, is more easy of study than are the cells of that body. In the analysis of economic forms, moreover, neither microscopes nor chemical reagents are of use. The force of abstraction must replace both. But in bourgeois society the commodity-form of the product of labour – or the value-form of the commodity – is the economic cell-form. To the superficial observer, the analysis of these forms seems to turn upon minutiae. It does in fact deal with minutiae, but they are of the same order as those dealt with in microscopic anatomy.

The physicist either observes physical phenomena where they occur in their most typical form and most free from disturbing influence, or, wherever possible, he makes experiments under conditions that assure the occurrence of the phenomenon in its normality. In this work I have to examine the capitalist mode of production, and the conditions of production and exchange corresponding to that mode. Up to the present time, their classic ground is England. That is the reason why England is used as the chief illustration in the development of my theoretical ideas. If, however, the German reader shrugs his shoulders at the condition of the English industrial and agricultural labourers, or in optimist fashion, comforts himself with the thought that in Germany things are not nearly so bad; I must plainly tell him, '*De te fabula narratur!*' ['It is of you the story is told!']

Intrinsically, it is not a question of the higher or lower degree of development of the social antagonisms that result from the natural laws of capitalist production. It is a question of these laws themselves, of these tendencies working with iron necessity towards inevitable results. The country that is more developed industrially only shows, to the less developed, the image of its own future.

The social statistics of Germany and the rest of Continental Western Europe are, in comparison with those of England, wretchedly compiled. But they raise the veil just enough to let us catch a glimpse of the Medusa head behind it. We should be appalled at the state of things at home, if, as in England, our governments and parliaments appointed periodically commissions of inquiry into economic conditions; if these commissions were armed with the same plenary powers to get at the truth; if it was possible to find for this purpose men as competent, as free from partisanship and respect of persons as are the English factory inspectors, her medical reporters on public health, her commissioners of inquiry into the exploitation of women and children, into housing and food.

For this reason, as well as others, I have given so large a space in this volume to the history, the details, and the results of English factory legislation. One nation can and should learn from others. And even when a society has got upon the right track for the discovery of the natural laws of its movement – and it is the ultimate aim of this work, to lay bare the economic law of motion of modern society – it can neither clear by bold leaps, nor remove by legal enactments, the obstacles offered by the successive phases of its normal development. But it can shorten and lessen the birth-pangs.

To prevent possible misunderstanding, a word. I show the capitalist and the landlord in no rosy light. But here individuals are dealt with only in so far as they are the personifications of economic categories, bearers of particular class-relations and class-interests. My standpoint, from which the evolution of the economic formation of society is viewed as a process of natural history, can less than any other make the individual responsible for relations whose creature he socially remains, however much he may subjectively raise himself above them.

Karl Marx, London, 25 July 1867

FROM THE AFTERWORD TO THE SECOND GERMAN EDITION

The appreciation which *Das Kapital* rapidly gained in wide circles of the German working class is the best reward of my labours. Herr Mayer, a Vienna manufacturer, who in economic matters represents the bourgeois point of view, in a pamphlet published during the Franco-German War aptly expounded the idea that the great capacity for theory, which used to be considered a hereditary German possession, had almost completely disappeared amongst the so-called educated classes in Germany, but that amongst its working class, on the contrary, that capacity was celebrating its revival.

To the present moment Political Economy, in Germany, is a foreign science. Gustav von Gülich in his *Historical Description of Commerce, Industry, etc.*, especially in the two first volumes published in 1830, has examined at length the historical circumstances that prevented, in Germany, the development of the capitalist mode of production, and consequently the development, in that country, of modern bourgeois society. Thus the soil whence Political Economy springs was wanting.

Since 1848 capitalist production has developed rapidly in Germany, and at the present time it is in the full bloom of speculation and swindling. But fate is still unpropitious to our professional economists. At the time when they were able to deal with Political Economy in a straightforward fashion, modern economic conditions did not actually exist in Germany. And as soon as these conditions did come into existence, they did so under circumstances that no longer allowed of their being really and impartially investigated within the bounds of the bourgeois horizon. In so far as Political Economy remains within that horizon, in so far, i.e. as the capitalist régime is looked upon as the absolutely final form of social production, instead of as a passing historical phase of its evolution, Political Economy can remain a science only so long as the class struggle is latent or manifests itself only in isolated and sporadic phenomena.

Let us take England. Its Political Economy belongs to the period in which the class struggle was as yet undeveloped. Its last great representative, Ricardo, in the end, consciously makes the antagonism of class interests, of wages and profits, of profits and rent, the starting point of his investigations; naïvely taking this antagonism for a social law of Nature. But by this start the science of bourgeois economy had reached the limits beyond which it could not pass. Already in the lifetime of Ricardo, and in opposition to him, it was met by criticism, in the person of Sismondi.

The succeeding period, from 1820 to 1830, was notable in England for scientific activity in the domain of Political Economy. It was the time as well of the vulgarising and extending of Ricardo's theory, as of the contest of that theory with the old school. Splendid tournaments were held. What was done then, is little known to the Continent generally, because the polemic is for the most part scattered through articles, in reviews, occasional literature and pamphlets. The unprejudiced character of this polemic – although the theory of Ricardo already serves, in exceptional cases, as a weapon of attack upon bourgeois economy – is explained by the circumstances of the time. On the one hand, modern industry itself was only just emerging from the age of childhood, as is shown by the fact that with the crisis of 1825 it for the first time opens the periodic cycle of its modern life. On the other hand, the class struggle between capital and labour is forced into the background, politically by the discord between the governments and the feudal aristocracy gathered around the Holy Alliance on the one hand, and the popular masses, led by the bourgeoisie, on the other; economically by the quarrel between industrial capital and aristocratic landed property – a quarrel that in France was concealed by the opposition between small and large landed property, and that in England broke out openly after the Corn Laws. The literature of Political Economy in England at this time calls to mind the stormy forward movement in France after Dr Quesnay's death, but only as a Saint Martin's summer reminds us of spring. With the year 1830 came the decisive crisis.

In France and in England the bourgeoisie had conquered political power. Thenceforth, the class struggle, practically as well as theoretically, took on more and more outspoken and threatening forms. It sounded the knell of scientific bourgeois economy. It was thenceforth no longer a question, whether this theorem or that was true, but whether it was useful to capital or harmful, expedient or inexpedient, politically dangerous or not. In place of disinterested inquirers, there were hired prizefighters; in place of genuine scientific research, the bad conscience and the evil intent of apologetic. Still, even the obtrusive pamphlets with which the Anti-Corn Law League, led by the manufacturers Cobden and Bright, deluged the world, have a historic interest, if no scientific one, on account of their polemic against the landed aristocracy. But since then the free-trade legislation, inaugurated by Sir Robert Peel, has deprived vulgar economy of this its last sting.

In Germany, therefore, the capitalist mode of production came to a head, after its antagonistic character had already, in France and England, shown itself in a fierce strife of classes. And meanwhile, moreover, the German proletariat had attained a much more clear class-consciousness than the German bourgeoisie. Thus, at the very moment when a bourgeois science of Political Economy seemed at last possible in Germany, it had in reality again become impossible.

The peculiar historical development of German society therefore forbids, in that country, all original work in bourgeois economy; but not the criticism of that economy. So far as such criticism represents a class, it can only represent the class whose vocation in history is the overthrow of the capitalist mode of production and the final abolition of all classes – the proletariat.

That the [dialectical] method employed in *Das Kapital* has been little understood, is shown by the various conceptions, contradictory one to another, that have been formed of it.

Of course the method of presentation must differ in form from that of inquiry. The latter has to appropriate the material in detail, to analyse its different forms of development, to trace out their inner connexion. Only after this work is done, can the actual movement be adequately described. If this is done successfully, if the life of the subject-matter is ideally reflected as in a mirror, then it may appear as if we had before us a mere a priori construction.

My dialectic method is not only different from the Hegelian, but is its direct opposite. To Hegel, the life-process of the human brain, i.e., the process of thinking, which, under the name of 'the Idea', he even transforms into an independent subject, is the demiurgos of the real world, and the real world is only the external, phenomenal form of 'the Idea'. With me, on the contrary, the ideal is nothing else than the material world reflected by the human mind, and translated into forms of thought.

The mystification which dialectic suffers in Hegel's hands, by no means prevents him from being the first to present its general form of working in a comprehensive and conscious manner. With him it is standing on its head. It must be turned right side up again, if you would discover the rational kernel within the mystical shell.

In its mystified form, dialectic became the fashion in Germany, because it seemed to transfigure and to glorify the existing state of things. In its rational form it is a scandal and abomination to bourgeoisdom and its doctrinaire professors, because it includes in its comprehension and affirmative recognition of the existing state of things, at the same time also, the recognition of the negation of that state, of its inevitable breaking up; because it regards every historically developed social form as in fluid movement, and therefore takes into account its transient nature not less than its momentary existence; because it lets nothing impose upon it, and is in its essence critical and revolutionary.

The contradictions inherent in the movement of capitalist society impress themselves upon the practical bourgeois most strikingly in the changes of the periodic cycle, through which modern industry runs, and whose crowning point is the universal crisis. That crisis is once again approaching, although as yet but in its preliminary stage; and by the universality of its theatre and the intensity of its action it will drum dialectics even into the heads of the mushroom-upstarts of the new, holy Prusso-German empire.

Karl Marx, London, 24 January 1873

PART I
COMMODITIES AND MONEY

CHAPTER 1

COMMODITIES

SECTION 1: THE TWO FACTORS OF A COMMODITY: USE-VALUE AND VALUE (THE SUBSTANCE OF VALUE AND THE MAGNITUDE OF VALUE)

The wealth of those societies in which the capitalist mode of production prevails, presents itself as an immense accumulation of commodities, its unit being a single commodity. Our investigation must therefore begin with the analysis of a commodity.

A commodity is, in the first place, an object outside us, a thing that by its properties satisfies human wants of some sort or another. The nature of such wants, whether, for instance, they spring from the stomach or from fancy, makes no difference. Neither are we here concerned to know how the object satisfies these wants, whether directly as means of subsistence, or indirectly as means of production.

Every useful thing, as iron, paper, etc., may be looked at from the two points of view of quality and quantity. It is an assemblage of many properties, and may therefore be of use in various ways. To discover the various uses of things is the work of history. So also is the establishment of socially-recognised standards of measure for the quantities of these useful objects. The diversity of these measures has its origin partly in the diverse nature of the objects to be measured, partly in convention.

The utility of a thing makes it a use-value. But this utility is not a thing of air. Being limited by the physical properties of the commodity, it has no existence apart from that commodity. A commodity, such as iron, corn, or a diamond, is therefore, so far as it is a material thing, a use-value, something useful. This property of a commodity is independent of the amount of labour required to appropriate its useful qualities. When treating of use-value, we always assume to be dealing with definite quantities, such as dozens of watches, yards of linen, or tons of iron. The use-values of commodities furnish the material for a special study, that of the commercial knowledge of commodities. Use-values become a reality only by use or consumption: they also constitute the substance of all wealth, whatever may be the social form of that wealth. In the form of society we are about to consider, they are, in addition, the material bearers of exchange-value.

Exchange-value, at first sight, presents itself as a quantitative relation, as the proportion in which values in use of one sort are exchanged for those of another sort, a relation constantly changing with time and place. Hence exchange-value appears to be something accidental and purely relative, and consequently an intrinsic value, i.e. an exchange-value that is inseparably connected with, inherent in commodities, seems a contradiction in terms. Let us consider the matter a little more closely.

A given commodity, e.g. a quarter of wheat, is exchanged for x blacking, y silk, or z gold, etc. – in short, for other commodities in the most different proportions. Instead of one exchange-value, the wheat has, therefore, a great many. But since x blacking, y silk, or z gold, etc., each represents the exchange-value of one quarter of wheat, x blacking, y silk, z gold, etc., must, as exchange-values, be replaceable by each other, or equal to each other. Therefore, first: the valid exchange-values of a given commodity express something equal; secondly, exchange-value, generally, is only the mode of expression, the phenomenal form, of something contained in it, yet distinguishable from it.

Let us take two commodities, e.g. corn and iron. The proportions in which they are exchangeable, whatever those proportions may be, can always be represented by an equation in which a given quantity of corn is equated to some quantity of iron: e.g., 1 quarter corn = x cwt iron. What does this equation tell us? It tells us that in two different things – in 1 quarter of corn and x cwt of iron, there exists in equal quantities something common to both. The two things must therefore be equal to a third, which in itself is neither the one nor the other. Each of them, so far as it is exchange-value, must therefore be reducible to this third.

This common 'something' cannot be either a geometrical, a chemical, or any other natural property of commodities. Such properties claim our attention only in so far as they affect the utility of those commodities, make them use-values. But the exchange of commodities is evidently an act characterised by a total abstraction from use-value. Then one use-value is just as good as another, provided only it be present in sufficient quantity. Or, as old Barbon says, 'one sort of wares are as good as another, if the values be equal. There is no difference or distinction in things of equal value . . . An hundred pounds' worth of lead or iron, is of as great value as one hundred pounds' worth of silver or gold.' As use-values, commodities are, above all, of different qualities, but as exchange-values they are merely different quantities, and consequently do not contain an atom of use-value.

If then we leave out of consideration the use-value of commodities, they have only one common property left, that of being products of labour. But even the product of labour itself has undergone a change in our hands. If we make abstraction from its use-value, we make abstraction at the same time from the material elements and shapes that make the product a use-value; we see in it no longer a table, a house, yarn, or any other useful thing. Its existence as a material thing is put out of sight. Neither can it any longer be regarded as the product of the labour of the joiner, the mason, the spinner, or of any other definite kind of productive labour. Along with the useful qualities of the products themselves, we put out of sight both the useful character of the various kinds of labour embodied in them, and the concrete forms of that labour; there is nothing left but what is common to them all; all are reduced to one and the same sort of labour, human labour in the abstract.

Let us now consider the residue of each of these products; it consists of the same unsubstantial reality in each, a mere congelation of homogeneous human labour, of labour-power expended without regard to the mode of its expenditure. All that these things now tell us is, that human labour-power has been expended in their production, that human labour is embodied in them. When looked at as crystals of this social substance, common to them all, they are – Values.

We have seen that when commodities are exchanged, their exchange-value manifests itself as something totally independent of their use-value. But if we abstract from their use-value, there remains their Value as defined above. Therefore, the common substance that manifests itself in the exchange-value of commodities, whenever they are exchanged, is their value. The progress of our investigation will show that exchange-value is the only form in which the value of commodities can manifest itself or be expressed. For the present, however, we have to consider the nature of value independently of this, its form.

A use-value, or useful article, therefore, has value only because human labour in the abstract has been embodied or materialised in it.

How, then, is the magnitude of this value to be measured? Plainly, by the quantity of the value-creating substance, the labour, contained in the article. The quantity of labour, however, is measured by its duration, and labour-time in its turn finds its standard in weeks, days, and hours.

Some people might think that if the value of a commodity is determined by the quantity of labour spent on it, the more idle and unskilful the labourer, the more valuable would his commodity be, because more time would be required in its production. The labour, however, that forms the substance of value, is homogeneous human labour, expenditure of one uniform labour-power. The total labour-power of society, which is embodied in the sum total of the values of all commodities produced by that society, counts here as one homogeneous mass of human labour-power, composed though it may be of innumerable individual units. Each of these units is the same as any other, so far as it has the character of the average labour-power of society, and takes effect as such; that is, so far as it requires for producing a commodity, no more time than is needed on an average, no more than is socially necessary. The labour-time socially necessary is that required to produce an article under the normal conditions of production, and with the average degree of skill and intensity prevalent at the time. The introduction of power-looms into England probably reduced by one-half the labour required to weave a given quantity of yarn into cloth. The hand-loom weavers, as a matter of fact, continued to require the same time as before; but for all that, the product of one hour of their labour represented after the change only half an hour's social labour, and consequently fell to one-half its former value.

We see then that that which determines the magnitude of the value of any article is the amount of labour socially necessary, or the labour-time socially necessary for its production. Each individual commodity, in this connexion, is to be considered as an average sample of its class. Commodities, therefore, in which equal quantities of labour are embodied, or which can be produced in the same time, have the same value. The value of one commodity is to the value of any other, as the labour-time necessary for the production of the one is to that necessary for the production of the other. As values, all commodities are only definite masses of congealed labour-time.

The value of a commodity would therefore remain constant, if the labour-time required for its production also remained constant. But the latter changes with every variation in the productiveness of labour. This productiveness is determined by various circumstances, amongst others, by the average amount of skill of the workmen, the state of science, and the degree of its practical application, the social organisation of production, the extent and capabilities of the means of production, and by physical conditions. For example, the same amount of labour in favourable seasons is embodied in 8 bushels of corn, and in unfavourable, only in four. The same labour extracts from rich mines more metal than from poor mines. Diamonds are of very rare occurrence on the earth's surface, and hence their discovery costs, on an average, a great deal of labour-time. Consequently much labour is represented in a small compass. Jacob doubts whether gold has ever been paid for at its full value. This applies still more to diamonds. According to Eschwege, the total produce of the Brazilian diamond mines for the eighty years, ending in 1823, had not realised the price of one-and-a-half years' average produce of the sugar and coffee plantations of the same country, although the diamonds cost much more labour, and therefore represented more value. With richer mines, the same quantity of labour would embody itself in more diamonds, and their value would fall. If we could succeed at a small expenditure of labour, in converting carbon into diamonds, their value might fall below that of bricks. In general, the greater the productiveness of labour, the less is the labour-time required for the production of an article, the less is the amount of labour crystallised in that article, and the less is its value; and vice versa, the less the productiveness of labour, the greater is the labour-time required for the production of an article, and the greater is its value. The value of a commodity, therefore, varies directly as the quantity, and inversely as the productiveness, of the labour incorporated in it.

A thing can be a use-value, without having value. This is the case whenever its utility to man is not due to labour. Such are air, virgin soil, natural meadows, etc. A thing can be useful, and the product of human labour, without being a commodity. Whoever directly satisfies his wants with the produce of his own labour, creates, indeed, use-values, but not commodities. In order to produce the latter, he must not only produce use-values, but use-values for others, social use-values. Lastly nothing can have value, without being an object of utility. If the thing is useless, so is the labour contained in it; the labour does not count as labour, and therefore creates no value.

SECTION 2. THE TWO-FOLD CHARACTER OF THE LABOUR EMBODIED IN COMMODITIES

At first sight a commodity presented itself to us as a complex of two things – use-value and exchange-value. Later on, we saw also that labour, too, possesses the same twofold nature; for, so far as it finds expression in value, it does not possess the same characteristics that belong to it as a creator of use-values. I was the first to point out and to examine critically this two-fold nature of the labour contained in commodities. As this point is the pivot on which a clear comprehension of Political Economy turns, we must go more into detail.

Let us take two commodities such as a coat and 10 yards of linen, and let the former be double the value of the latter, so that, if 10 yards of linen = W, the coat = 2W.

The coat is a use-value that satisfies a particular want. Its existence is the result of a special sort of productive activity, the nature of which is determined by its aim, mode of operation, subject, means, and result. The labour, whose utility is thus represented by the value in use of its product, or which manifests itself by making its product a use-value, we call useful labour. In this connexion we consider only its useful effect.

As the coat and the linen are two qualitatively different use-values, so also are the two forms of labour that produce them, tailoring and weaving. Were these two objects not qualitatively different, not produced respectively by labour of different quality, they could not stand to each other in the relation of commodities. Coats are not exchanged for coats, one use-value is not exchanged for another of the same kind.

To all the different varieties of values in use there correspond as many different kinds of useful labour, classified according to the order, genus, species, and variety to which they belong in the social division of labour. This division of labour is a necessary condition for the production of commodities, but it does not follow, conversely, that the production of commodities is a necessary condition for the division of labour. In the primitive Indian community there is social division of labour, without production of commodities. Or, to take an example nearer home, in every factory the labour is divided according to a system, but this division is not brought about by the operatives mutually exchanging their individual products. Only such products can become commodities with regard to each other, as result from different kinds of labour, each kind being carried on independently and for the account of private individuals.

To resume, then: In the use-value of each commodity there is contained useful labour, i.e. productive activity of a definite kind and exercised with a definite aim. Use-values cannot confront each other as commodities, unless the useful labour embodied in them is qualitatively different in each of them. In a community, the produce of which in general takes the form of commodities, i.e. in a community of commodity producers, this qualitative difference between the useful forms of labour that are carried on independently by individual producers, each on their own account, develops into a complex system, a social division of labour.

Anyhow, whether the coat be worn by the tailor or by his customer, in either case it operates as a use-value. Nor is the relation between the coat and the labour that produced it altered by the circumstance that tailoring may have become a special trade, an independent branch of the social division of labour. Wherever the want of clothing forced them to it, the human race made clothes for thousands of years, without a single man becoming a tailor. But coats and linen, like every other element of material wealth that is not the spontaneous produce of Nature, must invariably owe their existence to a special productive activity, exercised with a definite aim, an activity that appropriates particular nature-given materials to particular human wants. So far therefore as labour is a creator of use-value, is usefeul labour, it is a necessary condition, independent of all forms of society, for the existence of the human race; it is an eternal nature-imposed necessity, without which there can be no material exchanges between man and Nature, and therefore no life.

The use-values, coat, linen, etc., i.e. the bodies of commodities, are combinations of two elements – matter and labour. If we take away the useful labour expended upon them, a material substratum is always left, which is furnished by Nature without the help of man. The latter can work only as Nature does, that is by changing the form of matter. Nay more, in this work of changing the form he is constantly helped by natural forces. We see, then, that labour is not the only source of material wealth, of use-values produced by labour. As William Petty puts it, labour is its father and the earth its mother.

Let us now pass from the commodity considered as a use-value to the value of commodities.

By our assumption, the coat is worth twice as much as the linen. But this is a mere quantitative difference, which for the present does not concern us. We bear in mind, however, that if the value of the coat is double that of 10 yds of linen, 20 yds of linen must have the same value as one coat. So far as they are values, the coat and the linen are things of a like substance, objective expressions of essentially identical labour. But tailoring and weaving are, qualitatively, different kinds of labour. There are, however, states of society in which one and the same man does tailoring and weaving alternately, in which case these two forms of labour are mere modifications of the labour of the same individual, and no special and fixed functions of different persons; just as the coat which our tailor makes one day, and the trousers which he makes another day, imply only a variation in the labour of one and the same individual. Moreover, we see at a glance that, in our capitalist society, a given portion of human labour is, in accordance with the varying demand, at one time supplied in the form of tailoring, at another in the form of weaving. This change may possibly not take place without friction, but take place it must.

Productive activity, if we leave out of sight its special form, viz. the useful character of the labour, is nothing but the expenditure of human labour-power. Tailoring and weaving, though qualitatively different productive activities, are each a productive expenditure of human brains, nerves, and muscles, and in this sense are human labour. They are but two different modes of expending human labour-power. Of course, this labour-power, which remains the same under all its modifications, must have attained a certain pitch of development before it can be expended in a multiplicity of modes. But the value of a commodity represents human labour in the abstract, the expenditure of human labour in general. And just as in society, a general or a banker plays a great part, but mere man, on the other hand, a very shabby part, so here with mere human labour. It is the expenditure of simple labour-power, i.e., of the labour-power which, on an average, apart from any special development, exists in the organism of every ordinary individual. Simple average labour, it is true, varies in character in different countries and at different times, but in a particular society it is given. Skilled labour counts only as simple labour intensified, or rather, as multiplied simple labour, a given quantity of skilled labour being considered equal to a greater quantity of simple labour. Experience shows that this reduction is constantly being made. A commodity may be the product of the most skilled labour, but its value, by equating it to the product of simple unskilled labour, represents a definite quantity of the latter labour alone. (The reader must note that we are not speaking here of the wages or value that the labourer gets for a given labour-time, but of the value of the commodity in which that labour-time is materialised. Wages is a category that, as yet, has no existence at the present stage of our investigation.) The different proportions in which different sorts of labour are reduced to unskilled labour as their standard, are established by a social process that goes on behind the backs of the producers, and, consequently, appear to be fixed by custom. For simplicity's sake we shall henceforth account every kind of labour to be unskilled, simple labour; by this we do no more than save ourselves the trouble of making the reduction.

Just as, therefore, in viewing the coat and linen as values, we abstract from their different use-values, so it is with the labour represented by those values: we disregard the difference between its useful forms, weaving and tailoring. As the use-values, coat and linen, are combinations of special productive activities with cloth and yarn, while the values, coat and linen, are, on the other hand, mere homogeneous congelations of undifferentiated labour, so the labour embodied in these latter values does not count by virtue of its productive relation to cloth and yarn, but only as being expenditure of human labour-power. Tailoring and weaving are necessary factors in the creation of the use-values, coat and linen, precisely because these two kinds of labour are of different qualities; but only in so far as abstraction is made from their special qualities, only in so far as both possess the same quality of being human labour, do tailoring and weaving form the substance of the values of the same articles.

Coats and linen, however, are not merely values, but values of definite magnitude, and according to our assumption, the coat is worth twice as much as the ten yards of linen. Whence this difference in their values? It is owing to the fact that the linen contains only half as much labour as the coat, and consequently, that in the production of the latter, labour-power must have been expended during twice the time necessary for the production of the former.

While, therefore, with reference to use-value, the labour contained in a commodity counts only qualitatively, with reference to value it counts only quantitatively, and must first be reduced to human labour pure and simple. In the former case, it is a question of How and What, in the latter of How much? How long a time? Since the magnitude of the value of a commodity represents only the quantity of labour embodied in it, it follows that all commodities, when taken in certain proportions, must be equal in value.

If the productive power of all the different sorts of useful labour required for the production of a coat remains unchanged, the sum of the values of the coats produced increases with their number. If one coat represents x days' labour, two coats represent 2x days' labour, and so on. But assume that the duration of the labour necessary for the production of a coat becomes doubled or halved. In the first case, one coat is worth as much as two coats were before; in the second case, two coats are only worth as much as one was before, although in both cases one coat renders the same service as before, and the useful labour embodied in it remains of the same quality. But the quantity of labour spent on its production has altered.

An increase in the quantity of use-values is an increase of material wealth. With two coats two men can be clothed, with one coat only one man. Nevertheless, an increased quantity of material wealth may correspond to a simultaneous fall in the magnitude of its value. This antagonistic movement has its origin in the two-fold character of labour. Productive power has reference, of course, only to labour of some useful concrete form, the efficacy of any special productive activity during a given time being dependent on its productiveness. Useful labour becomes, therefore, a more or less abundant source of products, in proportion to the rise or fall of its productiveness. On the other hand, no change in this productiveness affects the labour represented by value. Since productive power is an attribute of the concrete useful forms of labour, of course it can no longer have any bearing on that labour, so soon as we make abstraction from those concrete useful forms. However then productive power may vary, the same labour, exercised during equal periods of time, always yields equal amounts of value. But it will yield, during equal periods of time, different quantities of values in use; more, if the productive power rise, fewer, if it fall. The same change in productive power, which increases the fruitfulness of labour, and, in consequence, the quantity of use-values produced by that labour, will diminish the total value of this increased quantity of use-values, provided such change shorten the total labour-time necessary for their production; and vice versa.

On the one hand, all labour is, speaking physiologically, an expenditure of human labour-power, and in its character of identical abstract human labour, it creates and forms the value of commodities. On the other hand, all labour is the expenditure of human labour-power in a special form and with a definite aim, and in this, its character of concrete useful labour, it produces use-values.

SECTION 3. THE FORM OF VALUE OR EXCHANGE-VALUE

Commodities come into the world in the shape of use-values, articles, or goods, such as iron, linen, corn etc. This is their plain, homely, bodily form. They are, however, commodities, only because they are something two-fold, both objects of utility, and, at the same time, depositories of value. They manifest themselves therefore as commodities, or have the form of commodities, only in so far as they have two forms, a physical or natural form, and a value-form.

The value of commodities is the very opposite of the coarse materiality of their substance, not an atom of matter enters into its composition. Turn and examine a single commodity, by itself, as we will, yet in so far as it remains an object of value, it seems impossible to grasp it. If, however, we bear in mind that the value of commodities has a purely social reality, and that they acquire this reality only in so far as they are expressions or embodiments of one identical social substance, viz., human labour, it follows as a matter of course, that value can only manifest itself in the social relation of commodity to commodity. In fact we started from exchange-value, or the exchange relation of commodities, in order to get at the value that lies hidden behind it. We must now return to this form under which value first appeared to us.

Everyone knows, if he knows nothing else, that commodities have a value-form common to them all, and presenting a marked contrast with the varied bodily forms of their use-values. I mean their money-form. Here, however, a task is set us, the performance of which has never yet even been attempted by bourgeois economy, the task of tracing the genesis of this money-form, of developing the expression of value implied in the value-relation of commodities, from its simplest, almost imperceptible outline, to the dazzling money-form. By doing this we shall, at the same time, solve the riddle presented by money.

The simplest value-relation is evidently that of one commodity to some one other commodity of a different kind. Hence the relation between the values of two commodities supplies us with the simplest expression of the value of a single commodity.

A. Elementary or Accidental Form of Value

x commodity A = y commodity B, or
x commodity A is worth y commodity B.
20 yards of linen = 1 coat, or
20 yards of linen are worth 1 coat.

1. The two poles of the expression of value. Relative form and equivalent form

The whole mystery of the form of value lies hidden in this elementary form. Its analysis, therefore, is our real difficulty.

Here two different kinds of commodities (in our example the linen and the coat) evidently play two different parts. The linen expresses its value in the coat; the coat serves as the material in which that value is expressed. The former plays an active, the latter a passive, part. The value of the linen is represented as relative value, or appears in relative form. The coat officiates as equivalent, or appears in equivalent form.

The relative form and the equivalent form are two intimately connected, mutually dependent and inseparable elements of the expression of value; but, at the same time, are mutually exclusive, antagonistic extremes – i.e. poles of the same expression. They are allotted respectively to the two different commodities brought into relation by that expression. It is not possible to express the value of linen in linen. 20 yards of linen = 20 yards of linen is no expression of value. On the contrary, such an equation merely says that 20 yards of linen are nothing else than 20 yards of linen, a definite quantity of the use-value linen. The value of the linen can therefore be expressed only relatively, i.e. in some other commodity. The relative form of the value of the linen presupposes, therefore, the presence of some other commodity – here the coat – under the form of an equivalent. On the other hand, the commodity that figures as the equivalent cannot at the same time assume the relative form. That second commodity is not the one whose value is expressed. Its function is merely to serve as the material in which the value of the first commodity is expressed.

No doubt the expression 20 yards of linen = 1 coat, or 20 yards of linen are worth 1 coat, implies the opposite relation: 1 coat = 20 yards of linen, or 1 coat is worth 20 yards of linen. But, in that case, I must reverse the equation, in order to express the value of the coat relatively; and, so soon as I do that, the linen becomes the equivalent instead of the coat. A single commodity cannot, therefore, simultaneously assume, in the same expression of value, both forms. The very polarity of these forms makes them mutually exclusive.

Whether, then, a commodity assumes the relative form, or the opposite equivalent form, depends entirely upon its accidental position in the expression of value – that is, upon whether it is the commodity whose value is being expressed or the commodity in which value is being expressed.

2. *The relative form of value*

(a) The nature and import of this form

In order to discover how the elementary expression of the value of a commodity lies hidden in the value-relation of two commodities, we must, in the first place, consider the latter entirely apart from its quantitative aspect. The usual mode of procedure is generally the reverse, and in the value-relation nothing is seen but the proportion between definite quantities of two different sorts of commodities that are considered equal to each other. It is apt to be forgotten that the magnitudes of different things can be compared quantitatively, only when those magnitudes are expressed in terms of the same unit. It is only as expressions of such a unit that they are of the same denomination, and therefore commensurable.

Whether 20 yards of linen = 1 coat or = 20 coats or = x coats – that is, whether a given quantity of linen is worth few or many coats, every such statement implies that the linen and coats, as magnitudes of value, are expressions of the same unit, things of the same kind. Linen = coat is the basis of the equation.

But the two commodities, whose identity of quality is thus assumed, do not play the same part. It is only the value of the linen that is expressed. And how? By its reference to the coat as its equivalent, as something that can be exchanged for it. In this relation the coat is the mode of existence of value, is value embodied, for only as such is it the same as the linen. On the other hand, the linen's own value comes to the front, receives independent expression, for it is only as being value that it is comparable with the coat as a thing of equal value, or exchangeable with the coat.

If we say that, as values, commodities are mere congelations of human labour, we reduce them by our analysis, it is true, to the abstraction, value; but we ascribe to this value no form apart from their bodily form. It is otherwise in the value-relation of one commodity to another. Here, the one stands forth in its character of value by reason of its relation to the other.

By making the coat the equivalent of the linen, we equate the labour embodied in the former to that in the latter. Now, it is true that the tailoring, which makes the coat, is concrete labour of a different sort from the weaving which makes the linen. But the act of equating it to the weaving, reduces the tailoring to that which is really equal in the two kinds of labour, to their common character of human labour. In this roundabout way, then, the fact is expressed, that weaving also, in so far as it weaves value, has nothing to distinguish it from tailoring, and, consequently, is abstract human labour. It is the expression of equivalence between different sorts of commodities that alone brings into relief the specific character of value-creating labour, and this it does by actually reducing the different varieties of labour embodied in the different kinds of commodities to their common quality of human labour in the abstract.

There is, however, something else required beyond the expression of the specific character of the labour of which the value of the linen consists. Human labour-power in motion, or human labour, creates value, but is not itself value. It becomes value only in its congealed state, when embodied in the form of some object. In order to express the value of the linen as a congelation of human labour, that value must be expressed as having objective existence, as being a something materially different from the linen itself, and yet a something common to the linen and all other commodities. The problem is already solved.

When occupying the position of equivalent in the equation of value, the coat ranks qualitatively as the equal of the linen, as something of the same kind, because it is value. In this position it is a thing in which we see nothing but value, or whose palpable bodily form represents value. Yet the coat itself, the body of the commodity, coat, is a mere use-value. A coat as such no more tells us it is value, than does the first piece of linen we take hold of. This shows that when placed in value-relation to the linen, the coat signifies more than when out of that relation, just as many a man strutting about in a gorgeous uniform counts for more than when in mufti.

In the production of the coat, human labour-power, in the shape of tailoring, must have been actually expended. Human labour is therefore accumulated in it. In this aspect the coat is a depository of value, but though worn to a thread, it does not let this fact show through. And as equivalent of the linen in the value equation, it exists under this aspect alone, counts therefore as embodied value, as a body that is value. *A*, for instance, cannot be 'your majesty' to *B*, unless at the same time majesty in B's eyes assumes the bodily form of A, and, what is more, with every new father of the people, changes its features, hair, and many other things besides.

Hence, in the value equation, in which the coat is the equivalent of the linen, the coat officiates as the form of value. The value of the commodity linen is expressed by the bodily form of the commodity coat, the value of one by the use-value of the other. As a use-value, the linen is something palpably different from the coat; as value, it is the same as the coat, and now has the appearance of a coat. Thus the linen acquires a value-form different from its physical form.

(b) Quantitative determination of relative value

Every commodity, whose value it is intended to express, is a useful object of given quantity, as 15 bushels of corn, or 100 lb of coffee. And a given quantity of any commodity contains a definite quantity of human labour. The value-form must therefore not only express value generally, but also value in definite quantity. Therefore, in the value-relation of commodity A to commodity B, of the linen to the coat, not only is the latter, as value in general, made the equal in quality of the linen, but a definite quantity of coat (1 coat) is made the equivalent of a definite quantity (20 yards) of linen.

The equation, 20 yards of linen = 1 coat, or 20 yards of linen are worth one coat, implies that the same quantity of value-substance (congealed labour) is embodied in both; that the two commodities have each cost the same amount of labour or the same quantity of labour-time. But the labour-time necessary for the production of 20 yards of linen or 1 coat varies with every change in the productiveness of weaving or tailoring. We have now to consider the influence of such changes on the quantitative aspect of the relative expression of value.

I. Let the value of the linen vary, that of the coat remaining constant. If, say in consequence of the exhaustion of flax-growing soil, the labour-time necessary for the production of the linen be doubled, the value of the linen will also be doubled. Instead of the equation, 20 yards of linen = 1 coat, we should have 20 yards of linen = 2 coats, since 1 coat would now contain only half the labour-time embodied in 20 yards of linen. If, on the other hand, in consequence, say, of improved looms, this labour-time be reduced by one-half, the value of the linen would fall by one-half. Consequently, we should have 20 yards of linen = ½ coat. The relative value of commodity A, i.e. its value expressed in commodity B, rises and falls directly as the value of A, the value of B being supposed constant.

II. Let the value of the linen remain constant, while the value of the coat varies. If, under these circumstances, in consequence, for instance, of a poor crop of wool, the labour-time necessary for the production of a coat becomes doubled, we have instead of 20 yards of linen = 1 coat, 20 yards of linen = ½ coat. If, on the other hand, the value of the coat sinks by one-half, then 20 yards of linen = 2 coats. Hence, if the value of commodity A remain constant, its relative value expressed in commodity B rises and falls inversely as the value of B.

If we compare the different cases in I. and II., we see that the same change of magnitude in relative value may arise from totally opposite causes. Thus, the equation, 20 yards of linen = 1 coat, becomes 20 yards of linen = 2 coats, either, because the value of the linen has doubled, or because the value of the coat has fallen by one-half; and it becomes 20 yards of linen = ½ coat, either, because the value of the linen has fallen by one-half, or because the value of the coat has doubled.

III. Let the quantities of labour-time respectively necessary for the production of the linen and the coat vary simultaneously in the same direction and in the same proportion. In this case 20 yards of linen continue equal to 1 coat, however much their values may have altered. Their change of value is seen as soon as they are compared with a third commodity, whose value has remained constant. If the values of all commodities rose or fell simultaneously, and in the same proportion, their relative values would remain unaltered. Their real change of value would appear from the diminished or increased quantity of commodities produced in a given time.

Thus real changes in the magnitude of value are neither unequivocally nor exhaustively reflected in their relative expression, that is, in the equation expressing the magnitude of relative value. The relative value of a commodity may vary, although its value remains constant. Its relative value may remain constant, although its value varies; and finally, simultaneous variations in the magnitude of value and in that of its relative expression by no means necessarily correspond in amount.

3. The equivalent form of value

We have seen that commodity A (the linen), by expressing its value in the use-value of a commodity differing in kind (the coat), at the same time impresses upon the latter a specific form of value, namely that of the equivalent. The commodity linen manifests its quality of having a value by the fact that the coat, without having assumed a value-form different from its bodily form, is equated to the linen. The fact that the latter therefore has a value is expressed by saying that the coat is directly exchangeable with it. Therefore, when we say that a commodity is in the equivalent form, we express the fact that it is directly exchangeable with other commodities.

When one commodity, such as a coat, serves as the equivalent of another, such as linen, and coats consequently acquire the characteristic property of being directly exchangeable with linen, we are far from knowing in what proportion the two are exchangeable. The value of the linen being given in magnitude, that proportion depends on the value of the coat. Whether the coat serves as the equivalent and the linen as relative value, or the linen as the equivalent and the coat as relative value, the magnitude of the coat's value is determined, independently of its value-form, by the labour-time necessary for its production. But whenever the coat assumes in the equation of value, the position of equivalent, its value acquires no quantitative expression; on the contrary, the commodity coat now figures only as a definite quantity of some article.

For instance, 40 yards of linen are worth – what? two coats. Because the commodity coat here plays the part of equivalent, because the use-value coat, as opposed to the linen, figures as an embodiment of value, therefore a definite number of coats suffices to express the definite quantity of value in the linen. Two coats may therefore express the quantity of value of 40 yards of linen, but they can never express the quantity of their own value. A superficial observation of this fact, namely, that in the equation of value, the equivalent figures exclusively as a simple quantity of some article, of some use-value, has misled Bailey, as also many others, both before and after him, into seeing, in the expression of value, merely a quantitative relation. The truth being, that when a commodity acts as equivalent, no quantitative determination of its value is expressed.

The first peculiarity that strikes us, in considering the form of the equivalent, is this: use-value becomes the form of manifestation, the phenomenal form of its opposite, value.

The bodily form of the commodity becomes its value-form. But, mark well, that this *quid pro quo* exists in the case of any commodity B, only when some other commodity A enters into a value-relation with it, and then only within the limits of this relation. Since no commodity can stand in the relation of equivalent to itself, and thus turn its own bodily shape into the expression of its own value, every commodity is compelled to choose some other commodity for its equivalent, and to accept the use-value, that is to say, the bodily shape of that other commodity as the form of its own value.

One of the measures that we apply to commodities as material substances, as use-values, will serve to illustrate this point. A sugar-loaf being a body, is heavy, and therefore has weight: but we can neither see nor touch this weight. We then take various pieces of iron, whose weight has been determined beforehand. The iron, as iron, is no more the form of manifestation of weight, than is the sugar-loaf.

Nevertheless, in order to express the sugar-loaf as so much weight, we put it into a weight-relation with the iron. In this relation, the iron officiates as a body representing nothing but weight. A certain quantity of iron therefore serves as the measure of the weight of the sugar, and represents, in relation to the sugar-loaf, weight embodied, the form of manifestation of weight. This part is played by the iron only within this relation, into which the sugar or any other body, whose weight has to be determined, enters with the iron. Were they not both heavy, they could not enter into this relation, and the one could therefore not serve as the expression of the weight of the other. When we throw both into the scales, we see in reality, that as weight they are both the same, and that, therefore, when taken in proper proportions, they have the same weight. Just as the substance iron, as a measure of weight, represents in relation to the sugar-loaf weight alone, so, in our expression of value, the material object, coat, in relation to the linen, represents value alone.

Here, however, the analogy ceases. The iron, in the expression of the weight of the sugar-loaf, represents a natural property common to both bodies, namely their weight; but the coat, in the expression of value of the linen, represents a non-natural property of both, something purely social, namely, their value.

Since the relative form of value of a commodity – the linen, for example – expresses the value of that commodity, as being something wholly different from its substance and properties, as being, for instance, coat-like, we see that this expression itself indicates that some social relation lies at the bottom of it. With the equivalent form it is just the contrary. The very essence of this form is that the material commodity itself – the coat – just as it is, expresses value, and is endowed with the form of value by Nature itself. Of course this holds good only so long as the value-relation exists, in which the coat stands in the position of equivalent to the linen. Since, however, the properties of a thing are not the result of its relations to other things, but only manifest themselves in such relations, the coat seems to be endowed with its equivalent form, its property of being directly exchangeable, just as much by Nature as it is endowed with the property of being heavy, or the capacity to keep us warm. Hence the enigmatical character of the equivalent form which escapes the notice of the bourgeois political economist, until this form, completely developed, confronts him in the shape of money. He then seeks to explain away the mystical character of gold and silver, by substituting for them less dazzling commodities, and by reciting, with ever renewed satisfaction, the catalogue of all possible commodities which at one time or another have played the part of equivalent. He has not the least suspicion that the most simple expression of value, such as 20 yds of linen = 1 coat, already propounds the riddle of the equivalent form for our solution.

The body of the commodity that serves as the equivalent, figures as the materialisation of human labour in the abstract, and is at the same time the product of some specifically useful concrete labour. This concrete labour becomes, therefore, the medium for expressing abstract human labour. If on the one hand the coat ranks as nothing but the embodiment of abstract human labour, so, on the other hand, the tailoring which is actually embodied in it, counts as nothing but the form under which that abstract labour is realised. In the expression of value of the linen, the utility of the tailoring consists, not in making clothes, but in making an object, which we at once recognise to be Value, and therefore to be a congelation of labour, but of labour indistinguishable from that realised in the value of the linen. In order to act as such a mirror of value, the labour of tailoring must reflect nothing besides its own abstract quality of being human labour generally.

In tailoring, as well as in weaving, human labour-power is expended. Both, therefore, possess the general property of being human labour, and may, therefore, in certain cases, such as in the production of value, have to be considered under this aspect alone. There is nothing mysterious in this. But in the expression of value there is a complete turn of the tables. For instance, how is the fact to be expressed that weaving creates the value of the linen, not by virtue of being weaving, as such, but by reason of its general property of being human labour? Simply by opposing to weaving that other particular form of concrete labour (in this instance tailoring), which produces the equivalent of the product of weaving. Just as the coat in its bodily form became a direct expression of value, so now does tailoring, a concrete form of labour, appear as the direct and palpable embodiment of human labour generally.

Hence, the second peculiarity of the equivalent form is, that concrete labour becomes the form under which its opposite, abstract human labour, manifests itself.

But because this concrete labour, tailoring in our case, ranks as, and is directly identified with, undifferentiated human labour, it also ranks as identical with any other sort of labour, and therefore with that embodied in the linen. Consequently, although, like all other commodity-producing labour, it is the labour of private individuals, yet, at the same time, it ranks as labour directly social in its character. This is the reason why it results in a labour directly exchangeable with other commodities. We have then a third peculiarity of the equivalent form, namely, that the labour of private individuals takes the form of its opposite, labour directly social in its form.

4. *The elementary form of value considered as a whole*

The elementary form of value of a commodity is contained in the equation, expressing its value-relation to another commodity of a different kind, or in its exchange-relation to the same. The value of commodity A is qualitatively expressed by the fact that commodity B is directly exchangeable with it. Its value is quantitatively expressed by the fact that a definite quantity of B is exchangeable with a definite quantity of A. In other words, the value of a commodity obtains independent and definite expression, by taking the form of exchange-value. When, at the beginning of this chapter, we said, in common parlance, that a commodity is both a use-value and an exchange-value, we were, accurately speaking, wrong. A commodity is a use-value or object of utility, and a value. It manifests itself as this two-fold thing, that it is, as soon as its value assumes an independent form – viz., the form of exchange-value. It never assumes this form when isolated, but only when placed in a value or exchange relation with another commodity of a different kind. When once we know this, such a mode of expression does no harm; it simply serves as an abbreviation.

A close scrutiny of the expression of the value of A in terms of B, contained in the equation expressing the value-relation of A to B, has shown us that, within that relation, the bodily form of A figures only as a use-value, the bodily form of B only as the form or aspect of value. The opposition or contrast existing internally in each commodity between use-value and value, is, therefore, made evident externally by two commodities being placed in such relation to each other, that the commodity whose value it is sought to express, figures directly as a mere use-value, while the commodity in which that value is to be expressed, figures directly as mere exchange-value. Hence the elementary form of value of a commodity is the elementary form in which the contrast contained in that commodity, between use-value and value, becomes apparent.

Every product of labour is, in all states of society, a use-value; but it is only at a definite historical epoch in a society's development that such a product becomes a commodity, viz., at the epoch when the labour spent on the production of a useful article becomes expressed as one of the objective qualities of that article, i.e. as its value. It therefore follows that the elementary value-form is also the primitive form under which a product of labour appears historically as a commodity, and that the gradual transformation of such products into commodities, proceeds *pari passu* with the development of the value-form.

We perceive, at first sight, the deficiencies of the elementary form of value: it is a mere germ, which must undergo a series of metamorphoses before it can ripen into the price-form.

The expression of the value of commodity A in terms of any other commodity B, merely distinguishes the value from the use-value of A, and therefore places A merely in a relation of exchange with a single different commodity, B; but it is still far from expressing A's qualitative equality, and quantitative proportionality, to all commodities. To the elementary relative value-form of a commodity, there corresponds the single equivalent form of one other commodity. Thus, in the relative expression of value of the linen, the coat assumes the form of equivalent, or of being directly exchangeable, only in relation to a single commodity, the linen.

Nevertheless, the elementary form of value passes by an easy transition into a more complete form. It is true that by means of the elementary form, the value of a commodity A, becomes expressed in terms of one, and only one, other commodity. But that one may be a commodity of any kind, coat, iron, corn, or anything else. Therefore, according as A is placed in relation with one or the other, we get for one and the same commodity, different elementary expressions of value. The number of such possible expressions is limited only by the number of the different kinds of commodities distinct from it. The isolated expression of A's value, is therefore convertible into a series, prolonged to any length, of the different elementary expressions of that value.

B. Total or Expanded Form of Value

z com. A = u com. B or = v com. C or = w com. D or = x com. E or = etc.
(20 yards of linen = 1 coat or = 10 lb tea or = 40 lb coffee or =
1 quarter corn or = 2 ounces gold or = ½ ton iron or = etc.)

1. The expanded relative form of value

The value of a single commodity, the linen, for example, is now expressed in terms of numberless other elements of the world of commodities. Every other commodity now becomes a mirror of the linen's value. It is thus, that for the first time, this value shows itself in its true light as a congelation of undifferentiated human labour. For the labour that creates it, now stands expressly revealed, as labour that ranks equally with every other sort of human labour, no matter what its form, whether tailoring, ploughing, mining, etc. and no matter, therefore, whether it is realised in coats, corn, iron, or gold. The linen, by virtue of the form of its value, now stands in a social relation, no longer with only one other kind of commodity, but with the whole world of commodities. As a commodity, it is a citizen of that world. At the same time, the interminable series of value equations implies, that as regards the value of a commodity, it is a matter of indifference under what particular form, or kind, of use-value it appears.

In the first form, 20 yds of linen = 1 coat, it might, for ought that otherwise appears, be pure accident, that these two commodities are exchangeable in definite quantities. In the second form, on the contrary, we perceive at once the background that determines, and is essentially different from, this accidental appearance. The value of the linen remains unaltered in magnitude, whether expressed in coats, coffee, or iron, or in numberless different commodities, the property of as many different owners. The accidental relation between two individual commodity-owners disappears. It becomes plain, that it is not the exchange of commodities which regulates the magnitude of their value; but, on the contrary, that it is the magnitude of their value which controls their exchange proportions.

2. *The particular equivalent form*

Each commodity, such as, coat, tea, corn, iron, etc. figures in the expression of value of the linen, as an equivalent, and, consequently, as a thing that is value. The bodily form of each of these commodities figures now as a particular equivalent form, one out of many. In the same way the manifold concrete useful kinds of labour, embodied in these different commodities, rank now as so many different forms of realisation, or manifestation, of undifferentiated human labour.

3. *Defects of the total or expanded form of value*

In the first place, the relative expression of value is incomplete because the series representing it is interminable. The chain of which each equation of value is a link, is liable at any moment to be lengthened by each new kind of commodity that comes into existence and furnishes the material for a fresh expression of value. In the second place, it is a many-coloured mosaic of disparate and independent expressions of value. And lastly, if, as must be the case, the relative value of each commodity in turn, becomes expressed in this expanded form, we get for each of them a relative value-form, different in every case, and consisting of an interminable series of expressions of value. The defects of the expanded relative value-form are reflected in the corresponding equivalent form. Since the bodily form of each single commodity is one particular equivalent form amongst numberless others, we have, on the whole, nothing but fragmentary equivalent forms, each excluding the others. In the same way, also, the special, concrete, useful kind of labour embodied in each particular equivalent, is presented only as a particular kind of labour, and therefore not as an exhaustive representative of human labour generally. The latter, indeed, gains adequate manifestation in the totality of its manifold, particular, concrete forms. But, in that case, its expression in an infinite series is ever incomplete and deficient in unity.

The expanded relative value-form is, however, nothing but the sum of the elementary relative expressions or equations of the first kind, such as

20 yards of linen = 1 coat
20 yards of linen = 10 lb of tea, etc.

Each of these implies the corresponding inverted equation,

1 coat = 20 yards of linen
10 lb of tea = 20 yards of linen, etc.

In fact, when a person exchanges his linen for many other commodities, and thus expresses its value in a series of other commodities, it necessarily follows, that the various owners of the latter exchange them for the linen, and consequently express the value of their various commodities in one and the same third commodity, the linen. If then, we reverse the series, 20 yards of linen = 1 coat or = 10 lb of tea, etc., that is to say, if we give expression to the converse relation already implied in the series, we get,

C. The General Form of Value

1 coat 10 lb of tea 40 lb of coffee 1 quarter of corn 2 ounces of gold ½ a ton of iron x com. A, etc.	} = 20 yards of linen

1. The altered character of the form of value

All commodities now express their value (1) in an elementary form, because in a single commodity; (2) with unity, because in one and the same commodity. This form of value is elementary and the same for all, therefore general.

The forms A and B were fit only to express the value of a commodity as something distinct from its use-value or material form.

The first form, A, furnishes such equations as the following: 1 coat = 20 yards of linen, 10 lb of tea = ½ a ton of iron. The value of the coat is equated to linen, that of the tea to iron. But to be equated to linen, and again to iron, is to be as different as are linen and iron. This form, it is plain, occurs practically only in the first beginning, when the products of labour are converted into commodities by accidental and occasional exchanges.

The second form, B, distinguishes, in a more adequate manner than the first, the value of a commodity from its use-value; for the value of the coat is there placed in contrast under all possible shapes with the bodily form of the coat; it is equated to linen, to iron, to tea, in short, to everything else, only not to itself, the coat. On the other hand, any general expression of value common to all is directly excluded; for, in the equation of value of each commodity, all other commodities now appear only under the form of equivalents. The expanded form of value comes into actual existence for the first time so soon as a particular product of labour, such as cattle, is no longer exceptionally, but habitually, exchanged for various other commodities.

The third and lastly developed form expresses the values of the whole world of commodities in terms of a single commodity set apart for the purpose, namely, the linen, and thus represents to us their values by means of their equality with linen. The value of every commodity is now, by being equated to linen, not only differentiated from its own use-value, but from all other use-values generally, and is, by that very fact, expressed as that which is common to all commodities. By this form, commodities are, for the first time, effectively brought into relation with one another as values, or made to appear as exchange-values.

The two earlier forms either express the value of each commodity in terms of a single commodity of a different kind, or in a series of many such commodities. In both cases, it is, so to say, the special business of each single commodity to find an expression for its value, and this it does without the help of the others. These others, with respect to the former, play the passive parts of equivalents. The general form of value, C, results from the joint action of the whole world of commodities, and from that alone. A commodity can acquire a general expression of its value only by all other commodities, simultaneously with it, expressing their values in the same equivalent; and every new commodity must follow suit. It thus becomes evident that, since the existence of commodities as values is purely social, this social existence can be expressed by the totality of their social relations alone, and consequently that the form of their value must be a socially recognised form.

All commodities being equated to linen now appear not only as qualitatively equal as values generally, but also as values whose magnitudes are capable of comparison. By expressing the magnitudes of their values in one and the same material, the linen, those magnitudes are also compared with each other. For instance, 10 lb of tea = 20 yards of linen, and 40 lb of coffee = 20 yards of linen. Therefore, 10 lb of tea = 40 lb of coffee. In other words, there is contained in 1 lb of coffee only one-fourth as much substance of value – labour – as is contained in 1 lb of tea.

The general form of relative value, embracing the whole world of commodities, converts the single commodity that is excluded from the rest, and made to play the part of equivalent – here the linen – into the universal equivalent. The bodily form of the linen is now the form assumed in common by the values of all commodities; it therefore becomes directly exchangeable with all and every one of them. The substance linen becomes the visible incarnation, the social chrysalis state of every kind of human labour. Weaving, which is the labour of certain private individuals producing a particular article, linen, acquires in consequence a social character, the character of equality with all other kinds of labour. The innumerable equations of which the general form of value is composed, equate in turn the labour embodied in the linen to that embodied in every other commodity, and they thus convert weaving into the general form of manifestation of undifferentiated human labour. In this manner the labour realised in the values of commodities is presented not only under its negative aspect, under which abstraction is made from every concrete form and useful property of actual work, but its own positive nature is made to reveal itself expressly. The general value-form is the reduction of all kinds of actual labour to their common character of being human labour generally, of being the expenditure of human labour-power.

The general value-form, which represents all products of labour as mere congelations of undifferentiated human labour, shows by its very structure that it is the social résumé of the world of commodities. That form consequently makes it indisputably evident that in the world of commodities the character possessed by all labour of being *human* labour constitutes its specific social character.

2. *The interdependent development of the relative form of value, and of the equivalent form*

The degree of development of the relative form of value corresponds to that of the equivalent form. But we must bear in mind that the development of the latter is only the expression and result of the development of the former.

The primary or isolated relative form of value of one commodity converts some other commodity into an isolated equivalent. The expanded form of relative value, which is the expression of the value of one commodity in terms of all other commodities, endows those other commodities with the character of particular equivalents differing in kind. And lastly, a particular kind of commodity acquires the character of universal equivalent, because all other commodities make it the material in which they uniformly express their value.

The antagonism between the relative form of value and the equivalent form, the two poles of the value-form, is developed concurrently with that form itself.

The first form, 20 yds of linen = one coat, already contains this antagonism, without as yet fixing it. According as we read this equation forwards or backwards, the parts played by the linen and the coat are different. In the one case the relative value of the linen is expressed in the coat, in the other case the relative value of the coat is expressed in the linen. In this first form of value, therefore, it is difficult to grasp the polar contrast.

Form B shows that only one single commodity at a time can completely expand its relative value, and that it acquires this expanded form only because, and in so far as, all other commodities are, with respect to it, equivalents. Here we cannot reverse the equations, as we can the equation 20 yds of linen = 1 coat, without altering its general charcter, and converting it from the expanded form of value into the general form of value.

Finally, the form C gives to the world of commodities a general social relative form of value, because, and in so far as, thereby all commodities, with the exception of one, are excluded from the equivalent form. A single commodity, the linen, appears therefore to have acquired the character of direct exchangeability with every other commodity because, and in so far as, this character is denied to every other commodity.

The commodity that figures as universal equivalent, is, on the other hand, excluded from the relative value-form. If the linen, or any other commodity serving as universal equivalent, were, at the same time, to share in the relative form of value, it would have to serve as its own equivalent. We should then have 20 yds of linen = 20 yds of linen; this tautology expresses neither value, nor magnitude of value. In order to express the relative value of the universal equivalent, we must rather reverse the form C. This equivalent has no relative form of value in common with other commodities, but its value is relatively expressed by a never ending series of other commodities.

Thus, the expanded form of relative value, or form B, now shows itself as the specific form of relative value for the equivalent commodity.

3. Transition from the general form of value to the money-form

The universal equivalent form is a form of value in general. It can, therefore, be assumed by any commodity. On the other hand, if a commodity be found to have assumed the universal equivalent form (form C), this is only because and in so far as it has been excluded from the rest of all other commodities as their equivalent, and that by their own act. And from the moment that this exclusion becomes finally restricted to one particular commodity, from that moment only, the general form of relative value of the world of commodities obtains real consistence and general social validity.

The particular commodity, with whose bodily form the equivalent form is thus socially identified, now becomes the money-commodity, or serves as money. It becomes the special social function of that commodity, and consequently its social monopoly, to play within the world of commodities the part of the universal equivalent. Amongst the commodities which, in form B, figure as particular equivalents of the linen, and, in form C, express in common their relative values in linen, this foremost place has been attained by one in particular – namely, gold. If, then, in form C we replace the linen by gold, we get,

D. The Money-form

20 yds of linen 1 coat 10 lb of tea 40 lb of coffee 1 qr of corn ½ a ton of iron *x* commodity A	} = 2 ounces of gold

In passing from form A to form B, and from the latter to form C, the changes are fundamental. On the other hand, there is no difference between forms C and D, except that, in the latter, gold has assumed the equivalent form in the place of linen. Gold is in form D, what linen was in form C – the universal equivalent. The progress consists in this alone, that the character of direct and universal exchangeability – in other words, that the universal equivalent form – has now, by social custom, become finally identified with the substance, gold.

Gold is now money with reference to all other commodities only because it was previously, with reference to them, a simple commodity. Like all other commodities, it was also capable of serving as an equivalent, either as simple equivalent in isolated exchanges, or as particular equivalent by the side of others. Gradually it began to serve, within varying limits, as universal equivalent. So soon as it monopolises this position in the expression of value for the world of commodities, it becomes the money commodity, and then, and not till then, does form D become distinct from form C, and the general form of value become changed into the money-form.

The elementary expression of the relative value of a single commodity, such as linen, in terms of the commodity, such as gold, that plays the part of money, is the price-form of that commodity. The price-form of the linen is therefore

20 yards of linen = 2 ounces of gold, or, if 2 ounces of gold when coined are £2, 20 yards of linen = £2.

The difficulty in forming a concept of the money-form, consists in clearly comprehending the universal equivalent form, and as a necessary corollary, the general form of value, form C. The latter is deducible from form B, the expanded form of value, the essential component element of which, we saw, is form A, 20 yards of linen = 1 coat or x commodity A = y commodity B. The simple commodity-form is therefore the germ of the money-form.

SECTION 4. THE FETISHISM OF COMMODITIES AND THE SECRET THEREOF

A commodity appears, at first sight, a very trivial thing, and easily understood. Its analysis shows that it is, in reality, a very queer thing, abounding in metaphysical subtleties and theological niceties. So far as it is a value in use, there is nothing mysterious about it, whether we consider it from the point of view that by its properties it is capable of satisfying human wants, or from the point that those properties are the product of human labour. It is as clear as noon-day, that man, by his industry, changes the forms of the materials furnished by Nature, in such a way as to make them useful to him. The form of wood, for instance, is altered, by making a table out of it. Yet, for all that, the table continues to be that common, everyday thing, wood. But, so soon as it steps forth as a commodity, it is changed into something transcendent. It not only stands with its feet on the ground, but, in relation to all other commodities, it stands on its head, and evolves out of its wooden brain grotesque ideas, far more wonderful than 'table-turning' ever was.

The mystical character of commodities does not originate, therefore, in their use-value. Just as little does it proceed from the nature of the determining factors of value. For, in the first place, however varied the useful kinds of labour, or productive activities, may be, it is a physiological fact, that they are functions of the human organism, and that each such function, whatever may be its nature or form, is essentially the expenditure of human brain, nerves, muscles, etc. Secondly, with regard to that which forms the ground-work for the quantitative determination of value, namely, the duration of that expenditure, or the quantity of labour, it is quite clear that there is a palpable difference between its quantity and quality. In all states of society, the labour-time that it costs to produce the means of subsistence, must necessarily be an object of interest to mankind, though not of equal interest in different stages of development. And lastly, from the moment that men in any way work for one another, their labour assumes a social form.

Whence, then, arises the enigmatical character of the product of labour, so soon as it assumes the form of commodities? Clearly from this form itself. The equality of all sorts of human labour is expressed objectively by their products all being equally values; the measure of the expenditure of labour-power by the duration of that expenditure, takes the form of the quantity of value of the products of labour; and finally, the mutual relations of the producers, within which the social character of their labour affirms itself, take the form of a social relation between the products.

A commodity is therefore a mysterious thing, simply because in it the social character of men's labour appears to them as an objective character stamped upon the product of that labour; because the relation of the producers to the sum total of their own labour is presented to them as a social relation, existing not between themselves, but between the products of their labour. This is the reason why the products of labour become commodities, social things whose qualities are at the same time perceptible and imperceptible by the senses. In the same way the light from an object is perceived by us not as the subjective excitation of our optic nerve, but as the objective form of something outside the eye itself. But, in the act of seeing, there is at all events, an actual passage of light from one thing to another, from the external object to the eye. There is a physical relation between physical things. But it is different with commodities. There, the existence of the things qua commodities, and the value-relation between the products of labour which stamps them as commodities, have absolutely no connexion with their physical properties and with the material relations arising therefrom. There it is a definite social relation between men, that assumes, in their eyes, the fantastic form of a relation between things. In order, therefore, to find an analogy, we must have recourse to the mist-enveloped regions of the religious world. In that world the productions of the human brain appear as independent beings endowed with life, and entering into relation both with one another and the human race. So it is in the world of commodities with the products of men's hands. This I call the fetishism which attaches itself to the products of labour, so soon as they are produced as commodities, and which is therefore inseparable from the production of commodities.

The fetishism of commodities has its origin, as the foregoing analysis has already shown, in the peculiar social character of the labour that produces them.

As a general rule, articles of utility become commodities, only because they are products of the labour of private individuals or groups of individuals who carry on their work independently of each other. The sum total of the labour of all these private individuals forms the aggregate labour of society. Since the producers do not come into social contact with each other until they exchange their products, the specific social character of each producer's labour does not show itself except in the act of exchange. In other words, the labour of the individual asserts itself as a part of the labour of society, only by means of the relations which the act of exchange establishes directly between the products, and indirectly, through them, between the producers. To the latter, therefore, the relations connecting the labour of one individual with that of the rest appear, not as direct social relations between individuals at work, but as what they really are, material relations between persons and social relations between things. It is only by being exchanged that the products of labour acquire, as values, one uniform social status, distinct from their varied forms of existence as objects of utility. This division of a product into a useful thing and a value becomes practically important, only when exchange has acquired such an extension that useful articles are produced for the purpose of being exchanged, and their character as values has therefore to be taken into account, beforehand, during production. From this moment the labour of the individual producer acquires socially a twofold character. On the one hand, it must, as a definite useful kind of labour, satisfy a definite social want, and thus hold its place as part and parcel of the collective labour of all, as a branch of a social division of labour that has sprung up spontaneously. On the other hand, it can satisfy the manifold wants of the individual producer himself, only in so far as the mutual exchangeability of all kinds of useful private labour is an established social fact, and therefore the private useful labour of each producer ranks on an equality with that of all others. The equalisation of the most different kinds of labour can be the result only of an abstraction from their inequalities, or of reducing them to their common denominator, viz. expenditure of human labour-power or human labour in the abstract. The twofold social character of the labour of the individual appears to him, when reflected in his brain, only under those forms which are impressed upon that labour in everyday practice by the exchange of products. In this way, the character that his own labour possesses of being socially useful takes the form of the condition, that the product must not only be useful, but useful for others, and the social character that his particular labour has of being the equal of all other particular kinds of labour, takes the form that all the physically different articles that are the products of labour, have one common quality, viz., that of having value.

Hence, when we bring the products of our labour into relation with each other as values, it is not because we see in these articles the material receptacles of homogeneous human labour. Quite the contrary: whenever, by an exchange, we equate as values our different products, by that very act, we also equate, as human labour, the different kinds of labour expended upon them. We are not aware of this, nevertheless we do it. Value, therefore, does not stalk about with a label describing what it is. It is value, rather, that converts every product into a social hieroglyphic. Later on, we try to decipher the hieroglyphic, to get behind the secret of our own social products; for to stamp an object of utility as a value, is just as much a social product as language. The recent scientific discovery, that the products of labour, so far as they are values, are but material expressions of the human labour spent in their production, marks, indeed, an epoch in the history of the development of the human race, but by no means dissipates the mist through which the social character of labour appears to us to be an objective character of the products themselves. The fact that in the particular form of production with which we are dealing, viz., the production of commodities, the specific social character of private labour carried on independently, consists in the equality of every kind of that labour, by virtue of its being human labour, which character, therefore, assumes in the product the form of value – this fact appears to the producers, notwithstanding the discovery above referred to, to be just as real and final, as the fact that, after the discovery by science of the component gases of air, the atmosphere itself remained unaltered.

What, first of all, practically concerns producers when they make an exchange, is the question, how much of some other product they get for their own? in what proportions the products are exchangeable? When these proportions have, by custom, attained a certain stability, they appear to result from the nature of the products, so that, for instance, one ton of iron and two ounces of gold appear as naturally to be of equal value as a pound of gold and a pound of iron in spite of their different physical and chemical qualities appear to be of equal weight. The character of having value, when once impressed upon products, obtains fixity only by reason of their acting and re-acting upon each other as quantities of value. These quantities vary continually, independently of the will, foresight and action of the producers. To them, their own social action takes the form of the action of objects, which rule the producers instead of being ruled by them. It requires a fully developed production of commodities before, from accumulated experience alone, the scientific conviction springs up, that all the different kinds of private labour, which are carried on independently of each other, and yet as spontaneously developed branches of the social division of labour, are continually being reduced to the quantitative proportions in which society requires them. And why? Because, in the midst of all the accidental and ever fluctuating exchange-relations between the products, the labour-time socially necessary for their production forcibly asserts itself like an over-riding law of Nature. The law of gravity thus asserts itself when a house falls about our ears. The determination of the magnitude of value by labour-time is therefore a secret, hidden under the apparent fluctuations in the relative values of commodities. Its discovery, while removing all appearance of mere accidentality from the determination of the magnitude of the values of products, yet in no way alters the mode in which that determination takes place.

Man's reflections on the forms of social life, and consequently, also, his scientific analysis of those forms, take a course directly opposite to that of their actual historical development. He begins, post festum, with the results of the process of development ready to hand before him. The characters that stamp products as commodities, and whose establishment is a necessary preliminary to the circulation of commodities, have already acquired the stability of natural, self-understood forms of social life, before man seeks to decipher, not their historical character, for in his eyes they are immutable, but their meaning. Consequently it was the analysis of the prices of commodities that alone led to the determination of the magnitude of value, and it was the common expression of all commodities in money that alone led to the establishment of their characters as values. It is, however, just this ultimate money-form of the world of commodities that actually conceals, instead of disclosing, the social character of private labour, and the social relations between the individual producers. When I state that coats or boots stand in a relation to linen, because it is the universal incarnation of abstract human labour, the absurdity of the statement is self-evident. Nevertheless, when the producers of coats and boots compare those articles with linen, or, what is the same thing, with gold or silver, as the universal equivalent, they express the relation between their own private labour and the collective labour of society in the same absurd form.

The categories of bourgeois economy consist of such like forms. They are forms of thought expressing with social validity the conditions and relations of a definite, historically determined mode of production, viz. the production of commodities. The whole mystery of commodities, all the magic and necromancy that surrounds the products of labour as long as they take the form of commodities, vanishes therefore, so soon as we come to other forms of production.

Since Robinson Crusoe's experiences are a favourite theme with political economists, let us take a look at him on his island. Moderate though he be, yet some few wants he has to satisfy, and must therefore do a little useful work of various sorts, such as making tools and furniture, taming goats, fishing and hunting. Of his prayers and the like we take no account, since they are a source of pleasure to him, and he looks upon them as so much recreation. In spite of the variety of his work, he knows that his labour, whatever its form, is but the activity of one and the same Robinson, and consequently, that it consists of nothing but different modes of human labour. Necessity itself compels him to apportion his time accurately between his different kinds of work. Whether one kind occupies a greater space in his general activity than another, depends on the difficulties, greater or less as the case may be, to be overcome in attaining the useful effect aimed at. This our friend Robinson soon learns by experience, and having rescued a watch, ledger, and pen and ink from the wreck, commences, like a true-born Briton, to keep a set of books. His stock-book contains a list of the objects of utility that belong to him, of the operations necessary for their production; and lastly, of the labour-time that definite quantities of those objects have, on an average, cost him. All the relations between Robinson and the objects that form this wealth of his own creation, are here so simple and clear as to be intelligible without exertion. And yet those relations contain all that is essential to the determination of value.

Let us now transport ourselves from Robinson's island bathed in light to the European middle ages shrouded in darkness. Here, instead of the independent man, we find everyone dependent, serfs and lords, vassals and suzerains, laymen and clergy. Personal dependence here characterises the social relations of production just as much as it does the other spheres of life organised on the basis of that production. But for the very reason that personal dependence forms the ground-work of society, there is no necessity for labour and its products to assume a fantastic form different from their reality. They take the shape, in the transactions of society, of services in kind and payments in kind. Here the particular and natural form of labour, and not, as in a society based on production of commodities, its general abstract form is the immediate social form of labour. Compulsory labour is just as properly measured by time, as commodity-producing labour; but every serf knows that what he expends in the service of his lord, is a definite quantity of his own personal labour-power. The tithe to be rendered to the priest is more matter of fact than his blessing. No matter, then, what we may think of the parts played by the different classes of people themselves in this society, the social relations between individuals in the performance of their labour, appear at all events as their own mutual personal relations, and are not disguised under the shape of social relations between the products of labour.

For an example of labour in common or directly associated labour, we have no occasion to go back to that spontaneously developed form which we find on the threshold of the history of all civilised races. We have one close at hand in the patriarchal industries of a peasant family, that produces corn, cattle, yarn, linen, and clothing for home use. These different articles are, as regards the family, so many products of its labour, but as between themselves, they are not commodities. The different kinds of labour, such as tillage, cattle tending, spinning, weaving and making clothes, which result in the various products, are in themselves, and such as they are, direct social functions, because functions of the family, which, just as much as a society based on the production of commodities, possesses a spontaneously developed system of division of labour. The distribution of the work within the family, and the regulation of the labour-time of the several members, depend as well upon differences of age and sex as upon natural conditions varying with the seasons. The labour-power of each individual, by its very nature, operates in this case merely as a definite portion of the whole labour-power of the family, and therefore, the measure of the expenditure of individual labour-power by its duration, appears here by its very nature as a social character of their labour.

Let us now picture to ourselves, by way of change, a community of free individuals, carrying on their work with the means of production in common, in which the labour-power of all the different individuals is consciously applied as the combined labour-power of the community. All the characteristics of Robinson's labour are here repeated, but with this difference, that they are social, instead of individual. Everything produced by him was exclusively the result of his own personal labour, and therefore simply an object of use for himself. The total product of our community is a social product. One portion serves as fresh means of production and remains social. But another portion is consumed by the members as means of subsistence. A distribution of this portion amongst them is consequently necessary. The mode of this distribution will vary with the productive organisation of the community, and the degree of historical development attained by the producers. We will assume, but merely for the sake of a parallel with the production of commodities, that the share of each individual producer in the means of subsistence is determined by his labour-time. Labour-time would, in that case, play a double part. Its apportionment in accordance with a definite social plan maintains the proper proportion between the different kinds of work to be done and the various wants of the community. On the other hand, it also serves as a measure of the portion of the common labour borne by each individual, and of his share in the part of the total product destined for individual consumption. The social relations of the individual producers, with regard both to their labour and to its products, are in this case perfectly simple and intelligible, and that with regard not only to production but also to distribution.

The religious world is but the reflex of the real world. And for a society based upon the production of commodities, in which the producers in general enter into social relations with one another by treating their products as commodities and values, whereby they reduce their individual private labour to the standard of homogeneous human labour – for such a society, Christianity with its *cultus* of abstract man, more especially in its bourgeois developments, Protestantism, Deism, etc., is the most fitting form of religion. In the ancient Asiatic and other ancient modes of production, we find that the conversion of products into commodities, and therefore the conversion of men into producers of commodities, holds a subordinate place, which, however, increases in importance as the primitive communities approach nearer and nearer to their dissolution. Trading nations, properly so called, exist in the ancient world only in its interstices, like the gods of Epicurus in the Intermundia, or like Jews in the pores of Polish society. Those ancient social organisms of production are, as compared with bourgeois society, extremely simple and transparent. But they are founded either on the immature development of man individually, who has not yet severed the umbilical cord that unites him with his fellowmen in a primitive tribal community, or upon direct relations of subjection. They can arise and exist only when the development of the productive power of labour has not risen beyond a low stage, and when, therefore, the social relations within the sphere of material life, between man and man, and between man and Nature, are correspondingly narrow. This narrowness is reflected in the ancient worship of Nature, and in the other elements of the popular religions. The religious reflex of the real world can, in any case, only then finally vanish, when the practical relations of everyday life offer to man none but perfectly intelligible and reasonable relations with regard to his fellowmen and to Nature.

The life-process of society, which is based on the process of material production, does not strip off its mystical veil until it is treated as production by freely associated men, and is consciously regulated by them in accordance with a settled plan. This, however, demands for society a certain material ground-work or set of conditions of existence which in their turn are the spontaneous product of a long and painful process of development.

Political Economy has indeed analysed, however incompletely, value and its magnitude, and has discovered what lies beneath these forms. But it has never once asked the question why labour is represented by the value of its product and labour-time by the magnitude of that value. These formulae, which bear it stamped upon them in unmistakable letters that they belong to a state of society, in which the process of production has the mastery over man, instead of being controlled by him, such formulae appear to the bourgeois intellect to be as much a self-evident necessity imposed by Nature as productive labour itself. Hence forms of social production that preceded the bourgeois form, are treated by the bourgeoisie in much the same way as the Fathers of the Church treated pre-Christian religions. (Truly comical is M. Bastiat, who imagines that the ancient Greeks and Romans lived by plunder alone. But when people plunder for centuries, there must always be something at hand for them to seize; the objects of plunder must be continually reproduced. It would thus appear that even Greeks and Romans had some process of production, consequently, an economy, which just as much constituted the material basis of their world, as bourgeois economy constitutes that of our modern world. Or perhaps Bastiat means, that a mode of production based on slavery is based on a system of plunder. In that case he treads on dangerous ground. If a giant thinker like Aristotle erred in his appreciation of slave labour, why should a dwarf economist like Bastiat be right in his appreciation of wage-labour? – I seize this opportunity of shortly answering an objection taken by a German paper in America, to my work, *Zur Kritik der Pol. Oekonomie, 1859*. In the estimation of that paper, my view that each special mode of production and the social relations corresponding to it, in short, that the economic structure of society, is the real basis on which the juridical and political superstructure is raised, and to which definite social forms of thought correspond; that the mode of production determines the character of the social, political, and intellectual life generally, all this is very true for our own times, in which material interests preponderate, but not for the middle ages, in which Catholicism, nor for Athens and Rome, where politics, reigned supreme. In the first place it strikes one as an odd thing for anyone to suppose that these well-worn phrases about the middle ages and the ancient world are unknown to anyone else. This much, however, is clear, that the middle ages could not live on Catholicism, nor the ancient world on politics. On the contrary, it is the mode in which they gained a livelihood that explains why here politics, and there Catholicism, played the chief part. For the rest, it requires but a slight acquaintance with the history of the Roman republic, for example, to be aware that its secret history is the history of its landed property. On the other hand, Don Quixote long ago paid the penalty for wrongly imagining that knight errantry was compatible with all economic forms of society.)

CHAPTER 2

EXCHANGE

It is plain that commodities cannot go to market and make exchanges of their own account. We must, therefore, have recourse to their guardians, who are also their owners. Commodities are things, and therefore without power of resistance against man. If they are wanting in docility he can use force; in other words, he can take possession of them. In order that these objects may enter into relation with each other as commodities, their guardians must place themselves in relation to one another, as persons whose will resides in those objects, and must behave in such a way that each does not appropriate the commodity of the other, and part with his own, except by means of an act done by mutual consent. They must therefore, mutually recognise in each other the rights of private proprietors. This juridical relation, which thus expresses itself in a contract, whether such contract be part of a developed legal system or not, is a relation between two wills, and is but the reflex of the real economic relation between the two. It is this economic relation that determines the subject-matter comprised in each such juridical act. The persons exist for one another merely as representatives of, and, therefore, as owners of, commodities. In the course of our investigation we shall find, in general, that the characters who appear on the economic stage are but the personifications of the economic relations that exist between them; it is as the bearers of these relations that they come into contact.

What chiefly distinguishes a commodity from its owner is the fact, that it looks upon every other commodity as but the form of appearance of its own value. A born leveller and a cynic, it is always ready to exchange not only soul, but body, with any and every other commodity, be the same more repulsive than Maritornes herself. The owner makes up for this lack in the commodity of a sense of the concrete, by his own five and more senses. His commodity possesses for himself no immediate use-value. Otherwise, he would not bring it to the market. It has use-value for others; but for himself its only direct use-value is that of being a bearer of exchange-value, and, consequently, a means of exchange. Therefore, he makes up his mind to part with it for commodities whose value in use is of service to him. All commodities are non-use-values for their owners, and use-values for their non-owners. Consequently, they must all change hands. But this change of hands is what constitutes their exchange, and the latter puts them in relation with each other as values, and realises them as values. Hence commodities must be realised as values before they can be realised as use-values.

On the other hand, they must show that they are use-values before they can be realised as values. For the labour spent upon them counts effectively, only in so far as it is spent in a form that is useful for others. Whether that labour is useful for others, and its product consequently capable of satisfying the wants of others, can be proved only by the act of exchange.

Every owner of a commodity wishes to part with it in exchange only for those commodities whose use-value satisfies some want of his. Looked at in this way, exchange is for him simply a private transaction. On the other hand, he desires to realise the value of his commodity, to convert it into any other suitable commodity of equal value, irrespective of whether his own commodity has or has not any use-value for the owner of the other. From this point of view, exchange is for him a social transaction of a general character. But one and the same set of transactions cannot be simultaneously for all owners of commodities both exclusively private and exclusively social and general.

Let us look at the matter a little closer. To the owner of a commodity, every other commodity is, in regard to his own, a particular equivalent, and consequently his own commodity is the universal equivalent for all the others. But since this applies to every owner, there is, in fact, no commodity acting as universal equivalent, and the relative value of commodities possesses no general form under which they can be equated as values and have the magnitude of their values compared. But a particular commodity cannot become the universal equivalent except by a social act. The social action therefore of all other commodities, sets apart the particular commodity in which they all represent their values. Thereby the bodily form of this commodity becomes the form of the socially recognised universal equivalent. To be the universal equivalent, becomes, by this social process, the specific function of the commodity thus excluded by the rest. Thus it becomes – money.

Money is a crystal formed of necessity in the course of the

exchanges, whereby different products of labour are practically equated to one another and thus by practice converted into commodities. The historical progress and extension of exchanges develops the contrast, latent in commodities, between use-value and value. The necessity for giving an external expression to this contrast for the purposes of commercial intercourse, urges on the establishment of an independent form of value, and finds no rest until it is once for all satisfied by the differentiation of commodities into commodities and money. At the same rate, then, as the conversion of products into commodities is being accomplished, so also is the conversion of one special commodity into money.

The direct barter of products attains the elementary form of the relative expression of value in one respect, but not in another. That form is x commodity A = y commodity B. The form of direct barter is x use-value A = y use-value B. The articles A and B in this case are not as yet commodities, but become so only by the act of barter. The first step made by an object of utility towards acquiring exchange-value is when it forms a non-use-value for its owner, and that happens when it forms a superfluous portion of some article required for his immediate wants. Objects in themselves are external to man, and consequently alienable by him. In order that this alienation may be reciprocal, it is only necessary for men, by a tacit understanding, to treat each other as private owners of those alienable objects, and by implication as independent individuals. But such a state of reciprocal independence has no existence in a primitive society based on property in common, whether such a society takes the form of a patriarchal family, an ancient Indian community, or a Peruvian Inca State. The exchange of commodities, therefore, first begins on the boundaries of such communities, at their points of contact with other similar communities, or with members of the latter. So soon, however, as products once become commodities in the external relations of a community, they also, by reaction, become so in its internal intercourse. The proportions in which they are exchangeable are at first quite a matter of chance. What makes them exchangeable is the mutual desire of their owners to alienate them. Meantime the need for foreign objects of utility gradually establishes itself. The constant repetition of exchange makes it a normal social act. In the course of time, therefore, some portion at least of the products of labour must be produced with a special view to exchange. From that moment the distinction becomes firmly established between the utility of an object for the purposes of consumption, and its utility for the purposes of exchange. Its use-value becomes distinguished from its exchange-value. On the other hand, the quantitative proportion in which the articles are exchangeable, becomes dependent on their production itself. Custom stamps them as values with definite magnitudes.

In the direct barter of products, each commodity is directly a means of exchange to its owner, and to all other persons an equivalent, but that only in so far as it has use-value for them. At this stage, therefore, the articles exchanged do not acquire a value-form independent of their own use-value, or of the individual needs of the exchangers. The necessity for a value-form grows with the increasing number and variety of the commodities exchanged. The problem and the means of solution arise simultaneously. Commodity-owners never equate their own commodities to those of others, and exchange them on a large scale, without different kinds of commodities belonging to different owners being exchangeable for, and equated as values to, one and the same special article. Such last-mentioned article, by becoming the equivalent of various other commodities, acquires at once, though within narrow limits, the character of a general social equivalent. This character comes and goes with the momentary social acts that called it into life. In turns and transiently it attaches itself first to this and then to that commodity. But with the development of exchange it fixes itself firmly and exclusively to particular sorts of commodities, and becomes crystallised by assuming the money-form. The particular kind of commodity to which it sticks is at first a matter of accident. Nevertheless there are two circumstances whose influence is decisive. The money-form attaches itself either to the most important articles of exchange from outside and these in fact are primitive and natural forms in which the exchange-value of home products finds expression; or else it attaches itself to the object of utility that forms, like cattle, the chief portion of indigenous alienable wealth. Nomad races are the first to develop the money-form, because all their worldly goods consist of moveable objects and are therefore directly alienable; and because their mode of life, by continually bringing them into contact with foreign communities, solicits the exchange of products. Man has often made man himself, under the form of slaves, serve as the primitive material of money, but has never used land for that purpose. Such an idea could only spring up in a bourgeois society already well developed. It dates from the last third of the seventeenth century, and the first attempt to put it in practice on a national scale was made a century afterwards, during the French bourgeois revolution.

In proportion as exchange bursts its local bonds, and the value of commodities more and more expands into an embodiment of human labour in the abstract, in the same proportion the character of money attaches itself to commodities that are by Nature fitted to perform the social function of a universal equivalent. Those commodities are the precious metals.

The truth of the proposition that, although gold and silver are not by Nature money, money is by Nature gold and silver, is shown by the fitness of the physical properties of these metals for the functions of money. Up to this point, however, we are acquainted only with one function of money, namely, to serve as the form of manifestation of the value of commodities, or as the material in which the magnitudes of their values are socially expressed. An adequate form of manifestation of value, a fit embodiment of abstract, undifferentiated, and therefore equal human labour, that material alone can be whose every sample exhibits the same uniform qualities. On the other hand, since the difference between the magnitudes of value is purely quantitative, the money-commodity must be susceptible of merely quantitative differences, must therefore be divisible at will, and equally capable of being re-united. Gold and silver possess these properties by Nature.

The use-value of the money-commodity becomes twofold. In addition to its special use-value as a commodity (gold, for instance, serving to stop teeth, to form the raw material of articles of luxury, etc.), it acquires a formal use-value, originating in its specific social function.

Since all commodities are merely particular equivalents of money, the latter being their universal equivalent, they, with regard to the latter as the universal commodity, play the parts of particular commodities.

We have seen that the money-form is but the reflex, thrown upon one single commodity, of the value relations between all the rest. That money is a commodity is therefore a new discovery only for those who, when they analyse it, start from its fully developed shape. The act of exchange gives to the commodity converted into money, not its value, but its specific value-form. By confounding these two distinct things some writers have been led to hold that the value of gold and silver is imaginary. The fact that money can, in certain functions, be replaced by mere symbols of itself, gave rise to that other mistaken notion, that it is itself a mere symbol. Nevertheless under this error lurked a presentiment that the money-form of an object is not an inseparable part of that object, but is simply the form under which certain social relations manifest themselves. In this sense every commodity is a symbol, since, in so far as it is value, it is only the material envelope of the human labour spent upon it. But if it be declared that the social characters assumed by objects, or the material forms assumed by the social qualities of labour under the regime of a definite mode of production, are mere symbols, it is in the same breath also declared that these characteristics are arbitrary fictions sanctioned by the so-called universal consent of mankind. This suited the mode of explanation in favour during the eighteenth century. Unable to account for the origin of the puzzling forms assumed by social relations between man and man, people sought to denude them of their strange appearance by ascribing to them a conventional origin.

It has already been remarked above that the equivalent form of a commodity does not imply the determination of the magnitude of its value. Therefore, although we may be aware that gold is money, and consequently directly exchangeable for all other commodities, yet that fact by no means tells how much 10 lb, for instance, of gold is worth. Money, like every other commodity, cannot express the magnitude of its value except relatively in other commodities. This value is determined by the labour-time required for its production, and is expressed by the quantity of any other commodity that costs the same amount of labour-time. Such quantitative determination of its relative value takes place at the source of its production by means of barter. When it steps into circulation as money, its value is already given. In the last decades of the seventeenth century it had already been shown that money is a commodity, but this step marks only the infancy of the analysis. The difficulty lies, not in comprehending that money is a commodity, but in discovering how, why, and by what means a commodity becomes money.

We have already seen, from the most elementary expression of value, x commodity A = y commodity B, that the object in which the magnitude of the value of another object is represented, appears to have the equivalent form independently of this relation, as a social property given to it by Nature. We followed up this false appearance to its final establishment, which is complete so soon as the universal equivalent form becomes identified with the bodily form of a particular commodity, and thus crystallised into the money-form. What appears to happen is, not that gold becomes money, in consequence of all other commodities expressing their values in it, but, on the contrary, that all other commodities universally express their values in gold, because it is money. The intermediate steps of the process vanish in the result and leave no trace behind. Commodities find their own value already completely represented, without any initiative on their part, in another commodity existing in company with them. These objects, gold and silver, just as they come out of the bowels of the earth, are forthwith the direct incarnation of all human labour. Hence the magic of money. In the form of society now under consideration, the behaviour of men in the social process of production is purely atomic. Hence their relations to each other in production assume a material character independent of their control and conscious individual action. These facts manifest themselves at first by products as a general rule taking the form of commodities. We have seen how the progressive development of a society of commodity-producers stamps one privileged commodity with the character of money. Hence the riddle presented by money is but the riddle presented by commodities; only it now strikes us in its most glaring form.

CHAPTER 3

MONEY, OR THE CIRCULATION OF COMMODITIES

SECTION 1. THE MEASURE OF VALUES

Throughout this work, I assume, for the sake of simplicity, gold as the money-commodity.

The first chief function of money is to supply commodities with the material for the expression of their values, or to represent their values as magnitudes of the same denomination, qualitatively equal, and quantitatively comparable. It thus serves as a *universal measure of value*. And only by virtue of this function does gold, the equivalent commodity *par excellence*, become money.

It is not money that renders commodities commensurable. Just the contrary. It is because all commodities, as values, are realised human labour, and therefore commensurable, that their values can be measured by one and the same special commodity, and the latter be converted into the common measure of their values, i.e., into money. Money as a measure of value is the phenomenal form that must of necessity be assumed by that measure of value which is immanent in commodities, labour-time.

The expression of the value of a commodity in gold – x commodity A = y money-commodity – is its money-form or price. A single equation, such as 1 ton of iron = 2 ounces of gold, now suffices to express the value of the iron in a socially valid manner. There is no longer any need for this equation to figure as a link in the chain of equations that express the values of all other commodities, because the equivalent commodity, gold, now has the character of money. The general form of relative value has resumed its original shape of simple or isolated relative value. On the other hand, the expanded expression of relative value, the endless series of equations, has now become the form peculiar to the relative value of the money-commodity. The series itself, too, is now given, and has social recognition in the prices of actual commodities. We have only to read the quotations of a price-list backwards, to find the magnitude of the value of money expressed in all sorts of commodities. But money itself has no price. In order to put it on an equal footing with all other commodities in this respect, we should be obliged to equate it to itself as its own equivalent.

The price or money-form of commodities is, like their form of value generally, a form quite distinct from their palpable bodily form; it is, therefore, a purely ideal or mental form. Although invisible, the value of iron, linen and corn has actual existence in these very articles: it is ideally made perceptible by their equality with gold, a relation that, so to say, exists only in their own heads. Their owner must, therefore, lend them his tongue, or hang a ticket on them, before their prices can be communicated to the outside world. Since the expression of the value of commodities in gold is a merely ideal act, we may use for this purpose imaginary or ideal money. Every trader knows, that he is far from having turned his goods into money, when he has expressed their value in a price or in imaginary money, and that it does not require the least bit of real gold, to estimate in that metal millions of pounds' worth of goods. When, therefore, money serves as a measure of value, it is employed only as imaginary or ideal money. This circumstance has given rise to the wildest theories. But, although the money that performs the functions of a measure of value is only ideal money, price depends entirely upon the actual substance that is money. The value, or in other words, the quantity of human labour contained in a ton of iron, is expressed in imagination by such a quantity of the money-commodity as contains the same amount of labour as the iron. According, therefore, as the measure of value is gold, silver, or copper, the value of the ton of iron will be expressed by very different prices, or will be represented by very different quantities of those metals respectively.

Commodities with definite prices present themselves under the form: a commodity A = x gold; b commodity B = z gold; c commodity C = y gold, etc., where a, b, c, represent definite quantities of the commodities A, B, C and x, z, y, definite quantities of gold. The values of these commodities are, therefore, changed in imagination into so many different quantities of gold. Hence, in spite of the confusing variety of the commodities themselves, their values become magnitudes of the same denomination, gold-magnitudes. They are now capable of being compared with each other and measured, and the want becomes technically felt of comparing them with some fixed quantity of gold as a unit measure. This unit, by subsequent division into aliquot parts, becomes itself the standard or scale. Before they become money, gold, silver, and copper already possess such standard measures in their standards of weight, so that, for example, a pound weight, while serving as the unit, is, on the one hand, divisible into ounces, and, on the other, may be combined to make up hundredweights. It is owing to this that in all metallic currencies, the names given to the standards of money or of price were originally taken from the pre-existing names of the standards of weight.

As *measure of Value*, and as *standard of price*, money has two entirely distinct functions to perform. It is the measure of value inasmuch as it is the socially recognised incarnation of human labour; it is the standard of price inasmuch as it is a fixed weight of metal. As the measure of value it serves to convert the values of all the manifold commodities into prices, into imaginary quantities of gold; as the standard of price it measures those quantities of gold. The measure of values measures commodities considered as values; the standard of price measures, on the contrary, quantities of gold by a unit quantity of gold, not the value of one quantity of gold by the weight of another. In order to make gold a standard of price, a certain weight must be fixed upon as the unit. In this case, as in all cases of measuring quantities of the same denomination, the establishment of an unvarying unit of measure is all-important. Hence, the less the unit is subject to variation, so much the better does the standard of price fulfil its office. But only in so far as it is itself a product of labour, and therefore potentially variable in value, can gold serve as a measure of value.

It is, in the first place, quite clear that a change in the value of gold does not, in any way, affect its function as a standard of price. No matter how this value varies, the proportions between the values of different quantities of the metal remain constant. However great the fall in its value, twelve ounces of gold still have twelve times the value of one ounce; and in prices, the only thing considered is the relation between different quantities of gold. Since, on the other hand, no rise or fall in the value of an ounce of gold can alter its weight, no alteration can take place in the weight of its aliquot parts. Thus gold always renders the same service as an invariable standard of price, however much its value may vary.

In the second place, a change in the value of gold does not interfere with its functions as a measure of value. The change affects all commodities simultaneously, and, therefore, *ceteris paribus*, leaves their relative values *inter se*, unaltered, although those values are now expressed in higher or lower gold-prices.

Let us now go back to the consideration of the price-form.

By degrees there arises a discrepancy between the current money-names of the various weights of the precious metal figuring as money, and the actual weights which those names originally represented.

Since the standard of money is on the one hand purely conventional, and must on the other hand find general acceptance, it is in the end regulated by law. A given weight of one of the precious metals, an ounce of gold, for instance, becomes officially divided into aliquot parts, with legally bestowed names, such as pound, dollar, etc. These aliquot parts, which thenceforth serve as units of money, are then subdivided into other aliquot parts with legal names, such as shilling, penny, etc. But, both before and after these divisions are made, a definite weight of metal is the standard of metallic money. The sole alteration consists in the subdivision and denomination.

The prices, or quantities of gold, into which the values of commodities are ideally changed, are therefore now expressed in the names of coins, or in the legally valid names of the subdivisions of the gold standard. Hence, instead of saying: A quarter of wheat is worth an ounce of gold; we say it is worth £3 17s. 10½d. In this way commodities express by their prices how much they are worth, and money serves as *money of account* whenever it is a question of fixing the value of an article in its money-form.

The name of a thing is something distinct from the qualities of that thing. I know nothing of a man, by knowing that his name is Jacob. In the same way with regard to money, every trace of a value-relation disappears in the names pound, dollar, franc, ducat, etc. The confusion caused by attributing a hidden meaning to these cabalistic signs is all the greater because these money-names express both the values of commodities, and, at the same time, aliquot parts of the weight of the metal that is the standard of money. On the other hand, it is absolutely necessary that value, in order that it may be distinguished from the varied bodily forms of commodities, should assume this material and unmeaning, but, at the same time, purely social form.

Price is the money-name of the labour realised in a commodity. Hence the expression of the equivalence of a commodity with the sum of money constituting its price is a tautology, just as in general the expression of the relative value of a commodity is a statement of the equivalence of two commodities. But although price being the exponent of the magnitude of a commodity's value, is the exponent of its exchange-ratio with money, it does not follow that the exponent of this exchange-ratio is necessarily the exponent of the magnitude of the commodity's value. Suppose two equal quantities of socially necessary labour to be respectively represented by 1 quarter of wheat and £2 (nearly ½ oz. of gold), £2 is the expression in money of the magnitude of the value of the quarter of wheat, or is its price. If now circumstances allow of this price being raised to £3, or compel it to be reduced to £1, then although £1 and £3 may be too small or too great properly to express the magnitude of the wheat's value, nevertheless they are its prices, for they are, in the first place, the form under which its value appears, i.e., money; and in the second place, the exponents of its exchange-ratio with money. If the conditions of production, in other words, if the productive power of labour remain constant, the same amount of social labour-time must, both before and after the change in price, be expended in the reproduction of a quarter of wheat. This circumstance depends neither on the will of the wheat producer, nor on that of the owners of other commodities.

Magnitude of value expresses a relation of social production, it expresses the connexion that necessarily exists between a certain article and the portion of the total labour-time of society required to produce it. As soon as magnitude of value is converted into price, the above necessary relation takes the shape of a more or less accidental exchange-ratio between a single commodity and another, the money-commodity. But this exchange-ratio may express either the real magnitude of that commodity's value, or the quantity of gold deviating from that value, for which, according to circumstances, it may be parted with. The possibility, therefore, of quantitative incongruity between price and magnitude of value, or the deviation of the former from the latter, is inherent in the price-form itself. This is no defect, but, on the contrary, admirably adapts the price-form to a mode of production whose inherent laws impose themselves only as the mean of apparently lawless irregularities that compensate one another.

The price-form, however, is not only compatible with the possibility of a quantitative incongruity between magnitude of value and price, i.e. between the former and its expression in money, but it may also conceal a qualitative inconsistency, so much so that although money is nothing but the value-form of commodities, price ceases altogether to express value. Objects that in themselves are no commodities, such as conscience, honour, etc., are capable of being offered for sale by their holders, and of thus acquiring, through their price, the form of commodities. Hence an object may have a price without having value. The price in that case is imaginary, like certain quantities in mathematics. On the other hand, the imaginary price-form may sometimes conceal either a direct or indirect real value-relation; for instance, the price of uncultivated land, which is without value, because no human labour has been incorporated in it.

SECTION 2. THE MEDIUM OF CIRCULATION

a) The Metamorphosis of Commodities

We saw in a former chapter that the exchange of commodities implies contradictory and mutually exclusive conditions. The differentiation of commodities into commodities and money does not sweep away these inconsistencies, but develops a *modus vivendi*, a form in which they can exist side by side. This is generally the way in which real contradictions are reconciled. For instance, it is a contradiction to depict one body as constantly falling towards another, and as, at the same time, constantly flying away from it. The ellipse is a form of motion which, while allowing this contradiction to go on, at the same time reconciles it.

In so far as exchange is a process, by which commodities are transferred from hands in which they are non-use-values, to hands in which they become use-values, it is a social circulation of matter. The product of one form of useful labour replaces that of another. When once a commodity has found a resting-place, where it can serve as a use-value, it falls out of the sphere of exchange into that of consumption. But the former sphere alone interests us at present. We have, therefore, now to consider exchange from a formal point of view; to investigate the change of form or metamorphosis of commodities which effectuates the social circulation of matter.

The comprehension of this change of form is, as a rule, very imperfect. The cause of this imperfection is, apart from indistinct notions of value itself, that every change of form in a commodity results from the exchange of two commodities, an ordinary one and the money-commodity. If we keep in view the material fact alone that a commodity has been exchanged for gold, we overlook the very thing that we ought to observe – namely, what has happened to the form of the commodity. We overlook the facts that gold, when a mere commodity, is not money, and that when other commodities express their prices in gold, this gold is but the money-form of those commodities themselves.

Commodities, first of all, enter into the process of exchange just as they are. The process then differentiates them into commodities and money, and thus produces an external opposition corresponding to the internal opposition inherent in them, as being at once use-values and values. Commodities as use-values now stand opposed to money as exchange-value. On the other hand, both opposing sides are commodities, unities of use-value and value. But this unity of differences manifests itself at two opposite poles, and at each pole in an opposite way. Being poles they are as necessarily opposite as they are connected. On the one side of the equation we have an ordinary commodity, which is in reality a use-value. Its value is expressed only ideally in its price, by which it is equated to its opponent, the gold, as to the real embodiment of its value. On the other hand, the gold, in its metallic reality, ranks as the embodiment of value, as money. Gold, as gold, is exchange-value itself. As to its use-value, that has only an ideal existence, represented by the series of expressions of relative value in which it stands face to face with all other commodities, the sum of whose uses makes up the sum of the various uses of gold. These antagonistic forms of commodities are the real forms in which the process of their exchange moves and takes place.

Let us now accompany the owner of some commodity – say, our old friend the weaver of linen – to the scene of action, the market. His 20 yards of linen has a definite price, £2. He exchanges it for the £2, and then, like a man of the good old stamp that he is, he parts with the £2 for a family Bible of the same price. The linen, which in his eyes is a mere commodity, a depository of value, he alienates in exchange for gold, which is the linen's value-form, and this form he again parts with for another commodity, the Bible, which is destined to enter his house as an object of utility and of edification to its inmates. The exchange becomes an accomplished fact by two metamorphoses of opposite yet supplementary character – the conversion of the commodity into money, and the re-conversion of the money into a commodity. The two phases of this metamorphosis are both of them distinct transactions of the weaver – selling, or the exchange of the commodity for money; buying, or the exchange of the money for a commodity; and, the unity of the two acts, selling in order to buy.

The result of the whole transaction, as regards the weaver, is this, that instead of being in possession of the linen, he now has the Bible;

instead of his original commodity, he now possesses another of the same value but of different utility. In like manner he procures his other means of subsistence and means of production. From his point of view, the whole process effectuates nothing more than the exchange of the product of his labour for the product of someone else's, nothing more than an exchange of products.

The exchange of commodities is therefore accompanied by the following changes in their form.

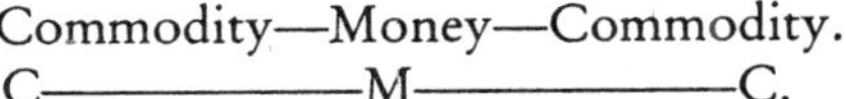
Commodity—Money—Commodity.
C————————M————————C.

The result of the whole process is, so far as concerns the objects themselves, C—C, the exchange of one commodity for another, the circulation of materialised social labour. When this result is attained, the process is at an end.

C—M. First metamorphosis, or sale

The leap taken by value from the body of the commodity, into the body of the gold, is, as I have elsewhere called it, the *salto mortale* of the commodity. If it falls short, then, although the commodity itself is not harmed, its owner decidedly is. The social division of labour causes his labour to be as one-sided as his wants are many-sided. This is precisely the reason why the product of his labour serves him solely as exchange-value. But it cannot acquire the properties of a socially recognised universal equivalent, except by being converted into money. That money, however, is in someone else's pocket. In order to entice the money out of that pocket, our friend's commodity must, above all things, be a use-value to the owner of the money. For this, it is necessary that the labour expended upon it, be of a kind that is socially useful, of a kind that constitutes a branch of the social division of labour. But division of labour is a system of production which has grown up spontaneously and continues to grow behind the backs of the producers. The commodity to be exchanged may possibly be the product of some new kind of labour, that pretends to satisfy newly arisen requirements, or even to give rise itself to new requirements. A particular operation, though yesterday, perhaps, forming one out of the many operations conducted by one producer in creating a given commodity, may today separate itself from this connexion, may establish itself as an independent branch of labour and send its incomplete product to market as an independent commodity. The circumstances may or may not be ripe for such a separation. Today the product satisfies a social want. Tomorrow the article may, either altogether or partially, be superseded by some other appropriate product. Moreover, although our weaver's labour may be a recognised branch of the social division of labour, yet that fact is by no means sufficient to guarantee the utility of his 20 yards of linen. If the community's want of linen, and such a want has a limit like every other want, should already be saturated by the products of rival weavers, our friend's product is superfluous, redundant, and consequently useless. Although people do not look a gift-horse in the mouth, our friend does not frequent the market for the purpose of making presents. But suppose his product turns out a real use-value, and thereby attracts money? The question arises, how much will it attract? No doubt the answer is already anticipated in the price of the article, in the exponent of the magnitude of its value. We leave out of consideration here any accidental miscalculation of value by our friend, a mistake that is soon rectified in the market. We suppose him to have spent on his product only that amount of labour-time that is on an average socially necessary. The price then, is merely the money-name of the quantity of social labour realised in his commodity. But without the leave, and behind the back, of our weaver, the old-fashioned mode of weaving undergoes a change. The labour-time that yesterday was without doubt socially necessary to the production of a yard of linen, ceases to be so today, a fact which the owner of the money is only too eager to prove from the prices quoted by our friend's competitors. Unluckily for him, weavers are not few and far between. Lastly, suppose that every piece of linen in the market contains no more labour-time than is socially necessary. In spite of this, all these pieces taken as a whole, may have had superfluous labour-time spent upon them. If the market cannot stomach the whole quantity at the normal price of two shillings a yard, this proves that too great a portion of the total labour of the community has been expended in the form of weaving. The effect is the same as if each individual weaver had expended more labour-time upon his particular product than is socially necessary. Here we may say, with the German proverb: caught together, hung together. All the linen in the market counts but as one article of commerce, of which each piece is only an aliquot part.

We see then, commodities are in love with money, but 'the course of true love never did run smooth.' The quantitative division of labour is brought about in exactly the same spontaneous and accidental manner as its qualitative division. The owners of commodities therefore find out, that the same division of labour that turns them into independent private producers, also frees the social process of production and the relations of the individual producers to each other within that process, from all dependence on the will of those producers, and that the seeming mutual independence of the individuals is supplemented by a system of general and mutual dependence through or by means of the products.

The division of labour converts the product of labour into a commodity, and thereby makes necessary its further conversion into money. At the same time it also makes the accomplishment of this transubstantiation quite accidental. Here, however, we are only concerned with the phenomenon in its integrity, and we therefore assume its progress to be normal. Moreover, if the conversion take place at all, that is, if the commodity be not absolutely unsaleable, its metamorphosis does take place although the price realised may be abnormally above or below the value.

The seller has his commodity replaced by gold, the buyer has his gold replaced by a commodity. The fact which here stares us in the face is that a commodity and gold, 20 yards of linen and £2, have changed hands and places, in other words, that they have been exchanged. But for what is the commodity exchanged? For the shape assumed by its own value, for the universal equivalent. And for what is the gold exchanged? For a particular form of its own use-value. Why does gold take the form of money face to face with the linen? Because the linen's price of £2, its denomination in money, has already equated the linen to gold in its character of money. A commodity strips off its original commodity-form on being alienated, i.e. on the instant its use-value actually attracts the gold, that before existed only ideally in its price. The realisation of a commodity's price, or of its ideal value-form, is therefore at the same time the realisation of the ideal use-value of money; the conversion of a commodity into money, is the simultaneous conversion of money into a commodity. The apparently single process is in reality a double one. From the pole of the commodity-owner it is a sale, from the opposite pole of the money-owner, it is a purchase. In other words, a sale is a purchase, C—M is also M—C.

Up to this point we have considered men in only one economic capacity, that of owners of commodities, a capacity in which they appropriate the produce of the labour of others, by alienating that of their own labour. Hence, for one commodity-owner to meet with another who has money, it is necessary, either, that the product of the labour of the latter person, the buyer, should be in itself money, should be gold, the material of which money consists, or that his product should already have changed its skin and have stripped off its original form of a useful object. In order that it may play the part of money, gold must of course enter the market at some point or other. This point is to be found at the source of production of the metal, at which place gold is bartered, as the immediate product of labour, for some other product of equal value. From that moment it always represents the realised price of some commodity. Apart from its exchange for other commodities at the source of its production, gold, in whose-soever hands it may be, is the transformed shape of some commodity alienated by its owner; it is the product of a sale or of the first metamorphosis C—M. Gold, as we saw, became ideal money, or a measure of values, in consequence of all commodities measuring their values by it, and thus contrasting it ideally with their natural shape as useful objects, and making it the shape of their value. It became real money, by the general alienation of commodities, by actually changing places with their natural forms as useful objects, and thus becoming in reality the embodiment of their values. When they assume this money-shape, commodities strip off every trace of their natural use-value, and of the particular kind of labour to which they owe their creation, in order to transform themselves into the uniform, socially recognised incarnation of homogeneous human labour. We cannot tell from the mere look of a piece of money, for what particular commodity it has been exchanged. Under their money-form all commodities look alike. Hence, money may be dirt, although dirt is not money. We will assume that the two gold pieces, in consideration of which our weaver has parted with his linen, are the metamorphosed shape of a quarter of wheat. The sale of the linen, C—M, is at the same time its purchase, M—C. But the sale is the first act of a process that ends with a transaction of an opposite nature, namely, the purchase of a Bible; the purchase of the linen, on the other hand, ends a movement that began with a transaction of an opposite nature, namely, with the sale of the wheat. C—M (linen—money), which is the first phase of C—M—C (linen—money—Bible), is also M—C (money—linen), the last phase of another movement C—M—C (wheat—money—linen). The first metamorphosis of one commodity, its transformation from a commodity into money, is therefore also invariably the second metamorphosis of some other commodity, the retransformation of the latter from money into a commodity.

M—C, or purchase. The second and concluding metamorphosis of a commodity

Because money is the metamorphosed shape of all other commodities, the result of their general alienation, for this reason it is alienable itself without restriction or condition. It reads all prices backwards, and thus, so to say, depicts itself in the bodies of all other commodities, which offer to it the material for the realisation of its own use-value. At the same time the prices, wooing glances cast at money by commodities, define the limits of its convertibility, by pointing to its quantity. Since every commodity, on becoming money, disappears as a commodity, it is impossible to tell from the money itself, how it got into the hands of its possessor, or what article has been changed into it. *Non olet*, from whatever source it may come. Representing on the one hand a sold commodity, it represents on the other a commodity to be bought.

M—C, a purchase, is, at the same time, C—M, a sale; the concluding metamorphosis of one commodity is the first metamorphosis of another. With regard to our weaver, the life of his commodity ends with the Bible, into which he has reconverted his £2. But suppose the seller of the Bible turns the £2 set free by the weaver into brandy M—C, the concluding phase of C—M—C (linen, money, Bible), is also C—M, the first phase of C—M—C (Bible, money, brandy). The producer of a particular commodity has that one article alone to offer; this he sells very often in large quantities, but his many and various wants compel him to split up the price realised, the sum of money set free, into numerous purchases. Hence a sale leads to many purchases of various articles. The concluding metamorphosis of a commodity thus constitutes an aggregation of first metamorphoses of various other commodities.

If we now consider the completed metamorphosis of a commodity, as a whole, it appears in the first place, that it is made up of two opposite and complementary movements, C—M and M—C. These two antithetical transmutations of a commodity are brought about by two antithetical social acts on the part of the owner, and these acts in their turn stamp the character of the economic parts played by him. As the person who makes a sale, he is a seller; as the person who makes a purchase, he is a buyer. But just as, upon every such transmutation of a commodity, its two forms, commodity-form and money-form, exist simultaneously but at opposite poles, so every seller has a buyer opposed to him, and every buyer a seller. While one particular commodity is going through its two transmutations in succession, from a commodity into money and from money into another commodity, the owner of the commodity changes in succession his part from that of seller to that of buyer. These characters of seller and buyer are therefore not permanent, but attach themselves in turns to the various persons engaged in the circulation of commodities.

The complete metamorphosis of a commodity, in its simplest form, implies four extremes, and three dramatis personae. First, a commodity comes face to face with money; the latter is the form taken by the value of the former, and exists in all its hard reality, in the pocket of the buyer. A commodity-owner is thus brought into contact with a possessor of money. So soon, now, as the commodity has been changed into money, the money becomes its transient equivalent-form, the use-value of which equivalent-form is to be found in the bodies of other commodities. Money, the final term of the first transmutation, is at the same time the starting-point for the second. The person who is a seller in the first transaction thus becomes a buyer in the second, in which a third commodity-owner appears on the scene as a seller.

The two phases, each inverse to the other, that make up the metamorphosis of a commodity constitute together a circular movement, a circuit: commodity-form, stripping off of this form, and return to the commodity-form. No doubt, the commodity appears here under two different aspects. At the starting-point it is not a use-value to its owner; at the finishing point it is. So, too, the money appears in the first phase as a solid crystal of value, a crystal into which the commodity eagerly solidifies, and in the second, dissolves into the mere transient equivalent-form destined to be replaced by a use-value.

The two metamorphoses constituting the circuit are at the same time two inverse partial metamorphoses of two other commodities. One and the same commodity, the linen, opens the series of its own metamorphoses, and completes the metamorphosis of another (the wheat). In the first phase or sale, the linen plays these two parts in its own person. But, then, changed into gold, it completes its own second and final metamorphosis, and helps at the same time to accomplish the first metamorphosis of a third commodity. Hence the circuit made by one commodity in the course of its metamorphoses is inextricably mixed up with the circuits of other commodities. The total of all the different circuits constitutes *the circulation of commodities*.

This circulation of commodities differs from the direct exchange of products (barter), not only in form, but in substance. Only consider the course of events. The weaver has, as a matter of fact, exchanged his linen for a Bible, his own commodity for that of some one else. But this is true only so far as he himself is concerned. The seller of the Bible, who prefers something to warm his inside, no more thought of exchanging his Bible for linen than our weaver knew that wheat had been exchanged for his linen. B's commodity replaces that of A, but A and B do not mutually exchange those commodities. It may, of course, happen that A and B make simultaneous purchases, the one from the other; but such exceptional transactions are by no means the necessary result of the general conditions of the circulation of commodities. We see here, on the one hand, how the exchange of commodities breaks through all local and personal bounds inseparable from direct barter, and develops the circulation of the products of social labour; and on the other hand, how it develops a whole network of social relations spontaneous in their growth and entirely beyond the control of the actors. It is only because the farmer has sold his wheat that the weaver is enabled to sell his linen, only because the weaver has sold his linen that our Hotspur is enabled to sell his Bible, and only because the latter has sold the water of everlasting life that the distiller is enabled to sell his *eau-de-vie*, and so on.

The process of circulation, therefore, does not, like direct barter of products, become extinguished upon the use-values changing places and hands. The money does not vanish on dropping out of the circuit of the metamorphosis of a given commodity. It is constantly being precipitated into new places in the arena of circulation vacated by other commodities. In the complete metamorphosis of the linen, for example, linen—money—Bible, the linen first falls out of circulation, and money steps into its place. Then the Bible falls out of circulation, and again money takes its place. When one commodity replaces another, the money-commodity always sticks to the hands of some third person. Circulation sweats money from every pore.

Nothing can be more childish than the dogma, that because every sale is a purchase, and every purchase a sale, therefore the circulation of commodities necessarily implies an equilibrium of sales and purchases. If this means that the number of actual sales is equal to the number of purchases, it is mere tautology. But its real purport is to prove that every seller brings his buyer to market with him. Nothing of the kind. The sale and the purchase constitute one identical act, an exchange between a commodity-owner and an owner of money, between two persons as opposed to each other as the two poles of a magnet. They form two distinct acts, of polar and opposite characters, when performed by one single person. Hence the identity of sale and purchase implies that the commodity is useless, if, on being thrown into the alchemistical retort of circulation, it does not come out again in the shape of money; if, in other words, it cannot be sold by its owner, and therefore be bought by the owner of the money. That identity further implies that the exchange, if it does take place, constitutes a period of rest, an interval, long or short, in the life of the commodity. Since the first metamorphosis of a commodity is at once a sale and a purchase, it is also an independent process in itself. The purchaser has the commodity, the seller has the money, i.e. a commodity ready to go into circulation at any time. No one can sell unless someone else purchases. But no one is forthwith bound to purchase, because he has just sold. Circulation bursts through all restrictions as to time, place, and individuals, imposed by direct barter, and this it effects by splitting up, into the antithesis of a sale and a purchase, the direct identity that in barter does exist between the alienation of one's own and the acquisition of some other man's product. To say that these two independent and antithetical acts have an intrinsic unity, are essentially one, is the same as to say that this intrinsic oneness expresses itself in an external antithesis. If the interval in time between the two complementary phases of the complete metamorphosis of a commodity become too great, if the split between the sale and the purchase become too pronounced, the intimate connexion between them, their oneness, asserts itself by producing – a crisis. The antithesis, use-value and value; the contradictions that private labour is bound to manifest itself as direct social labour, that a particularised concrete kind of labour has to pass for abstract human labour; the contradiction between the personification of objects and the representation of persons by things; all these antitheses and contradictions, which are immanent in commodities, assert themselves, and develop their modes of motion, in the antithetical phases of the metamorphosis of a commodity. These modes therefore imply the possibility, and no more than the possibility, of crises. The conversion of this mere possibility into a reality is the result of a long series of relations, that, from our present standpoint of simple circulation, have as yet no existence.

b) The Circulation of Money

The change of form, C—M—C, by which the circulation of the material products of labour is brought about, requires that a given value in the shape of a commodity shall begin the process, and shall, also in the shape of a commodity, end it. The movement of the commodity is therefore a circuit. On the other hand, the form of this movement precludes a circuit from being made by the money. The result is not the return of the money, but its continued removal further and further away from its starting-point. So long as the seller sticks fast to his money, which is the transformed shape of his commodity, that commodity is still in the first phase of its metamorphosis, and has completed only half its course. But so soon as he completes the process, so soon as he supplements his sale by a purchase, the money again leaves the hands of its possessor. It is true that if the weaver, after buying the Bible, sell more linen, money comes back into his hands. But this return is not owing to the circulation of the first 20 yards of linen; that circulation resulted in the money getting into the hands of the seller of the Bible. The return of money into the hands of the weaver is brought about only by the renewal or repetition of the process of circulation with a fresh commodity, which renewed process ends with the same result as its predecessor did. Hence the movement directly imparted to money by the circulation of commodities takes the form of a constant motion away from its starting-point, of a course from the hands of one commodity-owner into those of another.

The commodity is always in the hands of the seller; the money, as a means of purchase, always in the hands of the buyer. And money serves as a means of purchase by realising the price of the commodity. This realisation transfers the commodity from the seller to the buyer and removes the money from the hands of the buyer into those of the seller, where it again goes through the same process with another commodity. That this one-sided character of the money's motion arises out of the two-sided character of the commodity's motion, is a circumstance that is veiled over. The very nature of the circulation of commodities begets the opposite appearance. The first metamorphosis of a commodity is visibly, not only the money's movement, but also that of the commodity itself; in the second metamorphosis, on the contrary, the movement appears to us as the movement of the money alone. In the first phase of its circulation the commodity changes place with the money. Thereupon the commodity, under its aspect of a useful object, falls out of circulation into consumption. In its stead we have its value-shape – the money. It then goes through the second phase of its circulation, not under its own natural shape, but under the shape of money. The continuity of the movement is therefore kept up by the money alone, and the same movement that as regards the commodity consists of two processes of an antithetical character, is, when considered as the movement of the money, always one and the same process, a continued change of places with ever fresh commodities. Hence the result brought about by the circulation of commodities, namely, the replacing of one commodity by another, takes the appearance of having been effected not by means of the change of form of the commodities, but rather by the money acting as a medium of circulation, by an action that circulates commodities, to all appearance motionless in themselves, and transfers them from hands in which they are non-use-values, to hands in which they are use-values; and that in a direction constantly opposed to the direction of the money. The latter is continually withdrawing commodities from circulation and stepping into their places, and in this way continually moving further and further from its starting-point. Hence although the movement of the money is merely the expression of the circulation of commodities, yet the contrary appears to be the actual fact, and the circulation of commodities seems to be the result of the movement of the money.

Again, money functions as a means of circulation only because in it the values of commodities have independent reality. Hence its movement, as the medium of circulation, is, in fact, merely the movement of commodities while changing their forms. Thus the linen, for instance, first of all changes its commodity-form into its money-form. The second term of its first metamorphosis, C—M, the money-form, then becomes the first term of its final metamorphosis, M—C, its re-conversion into the Bible. But each of these two changes of form is accomplished by an exchange between commodity and money, by their *reciprocal displacement*. The same pieces of coin come into the seller's hand *as the alienated form of the commodity* and leave it as *the absolutely alienable form of the commodity*. They are displaced twice. The first metamorphosis of the linen puts these coins into the weaver's pocket, the second draws them out of it. The two inverse changes undergone by the same commodity are reflected in the displacement, twice repeated, but in opposite directions, of the same pieces of coin.

If, on the contrary, only one phase of the metamorphosis is gone through, if there are only sales or only purchases, then a given piece of money changes its place only once. Its second change of place always expresses the second metamorphosis of the commodity, its re-conversion from money. The frequent repetition of the displacement of the same coins reflects not only the series of metamorphoses that a single commodity has gone through, but also the intertwining of the innumerable metamorphoses in the world of commodities in general. It is a matter of course, that all this is applicable to the simple circulation of commodities alone, the only form that we are now considering.

Every commodity, when it first steps into circulation, and undergoes its first change of form, does so only to fall out of circulation again and to be replaced by other commodities. Money, on the contrary, as the medium of circulation, keeps continually within the sphere of circulation, and moves about in it. The question therefore arises, how much money this sphere constantly absorbs?

In a given country there take place every day at the same time, but in different localities, numerous one-sided metamorphoses of commodities, or, in other words, numerous sales and numerous purchases. The commodities are equated beforehand in imagination, by their prices, to definite quantities of money. And since, in the form of circulation now under consideration, money and commodities always come bodily face to face, one at the positive pole of purchase, the other at the negative pole of sale, it is clear that the amount of the means of circulation required, is determined beforehand by the sum of the prices of all these commodities. As a matter of fact, the money in reality represents the quantity or sum of gold ideally expressed beforehand by the sum of the prices of the commodities. The equality of these two sums is therefore self-evident. We know, however, that, the values of commodities remaining constant, their prices vary with the value of gold (the material of money), rising in proportion as it falls, and falling in proportion as it rises. Now if, in consequence of such a rise or fall in the value of gold, the sum of the prices of commodities fall or rise, the quantity of money in currency must fall or rise to the same extent. The change in the quantity of the circulating medium is, in this case, it is true, caused by the money itself, yet not in virtue of its function as a medium of circulation, but of its function as a measure of value. First, the price of the commodities varies inversely as the value of the money, and then the quantity of the medium of circulation varies directly as the price of the commodities. Exactly the same thing would happen if, for instance, instead of the value of gold falling, gold were replaced by silver as the measure of value, or if, instead of the value of silver rising, gold were to thrust silver out from being the measure of value. In the one case, more silver would be current than gold was before; in the other case, less gold would be current than silver was before. In each case the value of the material of money, i.e. the value of the commodity that serves as the measure of value, would have undergone a change, and therefore so, too, would the prices of commodities which express their values in money, and so, too, would the quantity of money current whose function it is to realise those prices. We have already seen, that the sphere of circulation has an opening through which gold (or the material of money generally) enters into it, as a commodity with a given value. Hence, when money enters on its functions as a measure of value, when it expresses prices, its value is already determined. If now its value fall, this fact is first evidenced by a change in the prices of those commodities that are directly bartered for the precious metals at the sources of their production. The greater part of all other commodities, especially in the imperfectly developed stages of civil society, will continue for a long time to be estimated by the former antiquated and illusory value of the measure of value. Nevertheless, one commodity infects another through their common value-relation, so that their prices, expressed in gold or in silver, gradually settle down into the proportions determined by their comparative values, until finally the values of all commodities are estimated in terms of the new value of the metal that constitutes money. This process is accompanied by the continued increase in the quantity of the precious metals, an increase caused by their streaming in to replace the articles directly bartered for them at their sources of production. In proportion therefore as commodities in general acquire their true prices, in proportion as their values become estimated according to the fallen value of the precious metal, in the same proportion the quantity of that metal necessary for realising those new prices is provided beforehand. A one-sided observation of the results that followed upon the discovery of fresh supplies of gold and silver, led some economists in the seventeenth, and particularly in the eighteenth century, to the false conclusion, that the prices of commodities had gone up in consequence of the increased quantity of gold and silver serving as means of circulation. Henceforth, we shall consider the value of gold to be given, as, in fact, it is momentarily whenever we estimate the price of a commodity.

On this supposition then, the quantity of the medium of circulation is determined by the sum of the prices that have to be realised. If now we further suppose the price of each commodity to be given, the sum of the prices clearly depends on the mass of commodities in circulation. It requires but little racking of brains to comprehend that if one quarter of wheat costs £2, 100 quarters will cost £200, 200 quarters £400, and so on, that consequently the quantity of money that changes place with the wheat, when sold, must increase with the quantity of that wheat.

If the mass of commodities remain constant, the quantity of circulating money varies with the fluctuations in the prices of those commodities. It increases and diminishes because the sum of the prices increases or diminishes in consequence of the change of price. To produce this effect, it is by no means requisite that the prices of all commodities should rise or fall simultaneously. A rise or a fall in the prices of a number of leading articles, is sufficient in the one case to increase, in the other to diminish, the sum of the prices of all commodities, and, therefore, to put more or less money in circulation. Whether the change in the price correspond to an actual change of value in the commodities, or whether it be the result of mere fluctuations in market-prices, the effect on the quantity of the medium of circulation remains the same.

Suppose the following articles to be sold or partially metamorphosed simultaneously in different localities: say, one quarter of wheat, 20 yards of linen, one Bible, and four gallons of brandy. If the price of each article be £2, and the sum of the prices to be realised be consequently £8, it follows that £8 in money must go into circulation. If, on the other hand, these same articles are links in the following chain of metamorphoses: 1 quarter of wheat—£2—20 yards of linen—£2—1 Bible—£2—4 gallons of brandy—£2, a chain that is already well known to us, in that case the £2 cause the different commodities to circulate one after the other, and after realising their prices successively, and therefore the sum of those prices, £8, they come to rest at last in the pocket of the distiller. The £2 thus make four moves. This repeated change of place of the same pieces of money corresponds to the double change in form of the commodities, to their motion in opposite directions through two stages of circulation, and to the interlacing of the metamorphoses of different commodities. These antithetic and complementary phases, of which the process of metamorphosis consists, are gone through, not simultaneously, but successively. Time is therefore required for the completion of the series. Hence the velocity of money is measured by the number of moves made by a given piece of money in a given time. Suppose the circulation of the four articles takes a day. The sum of the prices to be realised in the day is £8, the number of moves of the two pieces of money is four, and the quantity of money circulating is £2. Hence, for a given interval of time during the process of circulation, we have the following relation: the quantity of money functioning as the circulating medium is equal to the sum of the prices of the commodities divided by the number of moves made by coins of the same denomination. This law holds generally.

The total circulation of commodities in a given country during a given period is made up on the one hand of numerous isolated and simultaneous partial metamorphoses, sales which are at the same time purchases, in which each coin changes its place only once, or makes only one move; on the other hand, of numerous distinct series of metamorphoses partly running side by side, and partly coalescing with each other, in each of which series each coin makes a number of moves, the number being greater or less according to circumstances. The total number of moves made by all the circulating coins of one denomination being given, we can arrive at the average number of moves made by a single coin of that denomination, or at the average velocity of the circulation of money. The quantity of money thrown into circulation at the beginning of each day is of course determined by the sum of the prices of all the commodities circulating simultaneously side by side. But once in circulation, coins are, so to say, made responsible for one another. If the one increase its velocity, the other either retards its own, or altogether falls out of circulation; for the circulation can absorb only such a quantity of gold as when multiplied by the mean number of moves made by one single coin or element, is equal to the sum of the prices to be realised. Hence if the number of moves made by the separate pieces increase, the total number of those pieces in circulation diminishes. If the number of the moves diminish, the total number of pieces increases. Since the quantity of money capable of being absorbed by the circulation is given for a given mean velocity of currency, all that is necessary in order to abstract a given number of sovereigns from the circulation is to throw the same number of one-pound notes into it, a trick well known to all bankers.

Just as circulation of money, generally considered, is but a reflex of the circulation of commodities, or of the antithetical metamorphoses they undergo, so too the velocity of that circulation reflects the rapidity with which commodities change their forms, the continued interlacing of one series of metamorphoses with another, the hurried social interchange of matter, the rapid disappearance of commodities from the sphere of circulation, and the equally rapid substitution of fresh ones in their places. Hence, in the velocity of the currency we have the fluent unity of the antithetical and complementary phases, the unity of the conversion of the useful aspect of commodities into their value-aspect, and their re-conversion from the latter aspect to the former, or the unity of the two processes of sale and purchase. On the other hand, the retardation of circulation reflects the separation of these two processes into isolated antithetical phases, reflects the stagnation in the change of form, and therefore, in the social interchange of matter. The circulation itself, of course, gives no clue to the origin of this stagnation; it merely puts in evidence the phenomenon itself. The general public, who, simultaneously with the retardation of circulation, see money appear and disappear less frequently at the periphery of circulation, naturally attribute this retardation to a quantitative deficiency in the circulating medium.

The total quantity of money functioning during a given period as the circulating medium, is determined, on the one hand, by the sum of the prices of the circulating commodities, and on the other hand, by the rapidity with which the antithetical phases of the metamorphoses follow one another. On this rapidity depends what proportion of the sum of the prices can, on the average, be realised by each single coin. But the sum of the prices of the circulating commodities depends on the quantity, as well as on the prices, of the commodities. These three factors, however, state of prices, quantity of circulating commodities, and velocity of money-currency, are all variable. Hence, the sum of the prices to be realised, and consequently the quantity of the circulating medium depending on that sum, will vary with the numerous variations of these three factors in combination.

The law, that the quantity of the circulating medium is determined by the sum of the prices of the commodities circulating, and the average velocity of currency may also be stated as follows: given the sum of the values of commodities, and the average rapidity of their metamorphoses, the quantity of precious metal current as money depends on the value of that precious metal. The erroneous opinion that it is, on the contrary, prices that are determined by the quantity of the circulating medium, and that the latter depends on the quantity of the precious metals in a country; this opinion was based by those who first held it on the absurd hypothesis that commodities are without a price, and money without a value, when they first enter into circulation, and that, once in the circulation, an aliquot part of the medley of commodities is exchanged for an aliquot part of the heap of precious metals.

c) Coin and Symbols of Value

That money takes the shape of coin, springs from its function as the circulating medium. The weight of gold represented in imagination by the prices or money-names of commodities, must confront those commodities, within the circulation, in the shape of coins or pieces of gold of a given denomination. Coining, like the establishment of a standard of prices, is the business of the state. The different national uniforms worn at home by gold and silver as coins, and doffed again in the market of the world, indicate the separation between the internal or national spheres of the circulation of commodities, and their universal sphere.

The only difference, therefore, between coin and bullion, is one of shape, and gold can at any time pass from one form to the other. But no sooner does coin leave the mint, than it immediately finds itself on the high-road to the melting pot. During their currency, coins wear away, some more, others less. Name and substance, nominal weight and real weight, begin their process of separation. Coins of the same denomination become different in value, because they are different in weight. The weight of gold fixed upon as the standard of prices, deviates from the weight that serves as the circulating medium, and the latter thereby ceases any longer to be a real equivalent of the commodities whose prices it realises. The history of coinage during the middle ages and down into the eighteenth century, records the ever renewed confusion arising from this cause. The natural tendency of circulation to convert coins into a mere semblance of what they profess to be, into a symbol of the weight of metal they are officially supposed to contain, is recognised by modern legislation, which fixes the loss of weight sufficient to demonetise a gold coin, or to make it no longer legal tender.

The fact that the currency of coins itself effects a separation between their nominal and their real weight, creating a distinction between them as mere pieces of metal on the one hand, and as coins with a definite function on the other – this fact implies the latent possibility of replacing metallic coins by tokens of some other material, by symbols serving the same purposes as coins. The practical difficulties in the way of coining extremely minute quantities of gold or silver, and the circumstance that at first the less precious metal is used as a measure of value instead of the more precious, copper instead of silver, silver instead of gold, and that the less precious circulates as money until dethroned by the more precious – all these facts explain the parts historically played by silver and copper tokens as substitutes for gold coins. Silver and copper tokens take the place of gold in those regions of the circulation where coins pass from hand to hand most rapidly, and are subject to the maximum amount of wear and tear. This occurs where sales and purchases on a very small scale are continually happening. In order to prevent these satellites from establishing themselves permanently in the place of gold, positive enactments determine the extent to which they must be compulsorily received as payment instead of gold. The particular tracks pursued by the different species of coin in circulation, run naturally into each other. The tokens keep company with gold, to pay fractional parts of the smallest gold coin; gold is, on the one hand, constantly pouring into retail circulation, and on the other hand is as constantly being thrown out again by being changed into tokens.

The weight of metal in the silver and copper tokens is arbitrarily fixed by law. When in circulation, they wear away even more rapidly than gold coins. Hence their functions are totally independent of their weight, and consequently of all value. The function of gold as coin becomes completely independent of the metallic value of that gold. Therefore things that are relatively without value, such as paper notes, can serve as coins in its place. This purely symbolic character is to a certain extent masked in metal tokens. In paper money it stands out plainly.

We allude here only to inconvertible paper money issued by the state and having compulsory circulation. It has its immediate origin in the metallic currency. Money based upon credit implies on the other hand conditions, which, from our standpoint of the simple circulation of commodities, are as yet totally unknown to us. But we may affirm this much, that just as true paper money takes its rise in the function of money as the circulating medium, so money based upon credit takes root spontaneously in the function of money as the means of payment.

The state puts in circulation bits of paper on which their various denominations, say £1, £5, etc., are printed. In so far as they actually take the place of gold to the same amount, their movement is subject to the laws that regulate the currency of money itself. A law peculiar to the circulation of paper money can spring up only from the proportion in which that paper money represents gold. Such a law exists; stated simply, it is as follows: the issue of paper money must not exceed in amount the gold (or silver as the case may be) which would actually circulate if not replaced by symbols. Now the quantity of gold which the circulation can absorb constantly fluctuates about a given level. Still, the mass of the circulating medium in a given country never sinks below a certain minimum easily ascertained by actual experience. The fact that this minimum mass continually undergoes changes in its constituent parts, or that the pieces of gold of which it consists are being constantly replaced by fresh ones, causes of course no change either in its amount or in the continuity of its circulation. It can therefore be replaced by paper symbols. If, on the other hand, all the conduits of circulation were today filled with paper money to the full extent of their capacity for absorbing money, they might tomorrow be overflowing in consequence of a fluctuation in the circulation of commodities. There would no longer be any standard. If the paper money exceed its proper limit, which is the amount in gold coins of the like denomination that can actually be current, it would, apart from the danger of falling into general disrepute, represent only that quantity of gold, which, in accordance with the laws of the circulation of commodities, is required, and is alone capable of being represented by paper. If the quantity of paper money issued be double what it ought to be, then, as a matter of fact, £1 would be the money-name not of ¼ of an ounce, but of ⅛ of an ounce of gold. The effect would be the same as if an alteration had taken place in the function of gold as a standard of prices. Those values that were previously expressed by the price of £1 would now be expressed by the price of £2.

Paper money is a token representing gold or money. The relation between it and the values of commodities is this, that the latter are ideally expressed in the same quantities of gold that are symbolically represented by the paper. Only in so far as paper money represents gold, which like all other commodities has value, is it a symbol of value.

Finally, someone may ask why gold is capable of being replaced by tokens that have no value? But, as we have already seen, it is capable of being so replaced only in so far as it functions exclusively as coin, or as the circulating medium, and as nothing else. Now money has other functions besides this one, and the isolated function of serving as the mere circulating medium is not necessarily the only one attached to gold coin, although this is the case with those abraded coins that continue to circulate. Each piece of money is a mere coin, or means of circulation, only so long as it actually circulates. But this is just the case with that minimum mass of gold, which is capable of being replaced by paper money. That mass remains constantly within the sphere of circulation, continually functions as a circulating medium, and exists exclusively for that purpose. Its movement therefore represents nothing but the continued alternation of the inverse phases of the metamorphosis C—M—C, phases in which commodities confront their value forms, only to disappear again immediately. The independent existence of the exchange-value of a commodity is here a transient apparition, by means of which the commodity is immediately replaced by another commodity. Hence, in this process which continually makes money pass from hand to hand, the mere symbolical existence of money suffices. Its functional existence absorbs, so to say, its material existence. Being a transient and objective reflex of the prices of commodities, it serves only as a symbol of itself, and is therefore capable of being replaced by a token. One thing is, however, requisite; this token must have an objective social validity of its own, and this the paper symbol acquires by its forced currency. This compulsory action of the state can take effect only within that inner sphere of circulation which is co-terminous with the territories of the community, but it is also only within that sphere that money completely responds to its function of being the circulating medium, or becomes coin.

SECTION 3. MONEY

The commodity that functions as a measure of value, and, either in its own person or by a representative, as the medium of circulation, is money. Gold (or silver) is therefore money. It functions as money, on the one hand, when it has to be present in its own golden person. It is then the money-commodity, neither merely ideal, as in its function of a measure of value, nor capable of being represented, as in its function of circulating medium. On the other hand, it also functions as money, when by virtue of its function, whether that function be performed in person or by representative, it congeals into the sole form of value, the only adequate form of existence of exchange-value, in opposition to use-value, represented by all other commodities.

a) Hoarding

With the very earliest development of the circulation of commodities, there is also developed the necessity, and the passionate desire, to hold fast the product of the first metamorphosis. This product is the transformed shape of the commodity, or its gold-chrysalis. Commodities are thus sold not for the purpose of buying others, but in order to replace their commodity-form by their money-form. From being the mere means of effecting the circulation of commodities, this change of form becomes the end and aim. The changed form of the commodity is thus prevented from functioning as its unconditionally alienable form, or as its merely transient money-form. The money becomes petrified into a hoard, and the seller becomes a hoarder of money.

As the production of commodities further develops, every producer of commodities is compelled to make sure of the *nexus rerum* or the social pledge. His wants are constantly making themselves felt, and necessitate the continual purchase of other people's commodities, while the production and sale of his own goods require time, and depend upon circumstances. In order then to be able to buy without selling, he must have sold previously without buying. This operation, conducted on a general scale, appears to imply a contradiction. But the precious metals at the sources of their production are directly exchanged for other commodities. And here we have sales (by the owners of commodities) without purchases (by the owners of gold or silver). And subsequent sales, by other producers, not followed by purchases, merely bring about the distribution of the newly produced precious metals among all the owners of commodities. In this way, all along the line of exchange, hoards of gold and silver of varied extent are accumulated. With the possibility of holding and storing up exchange-value in the shape of a particular commodity, arises also the greed for gold. Along with the extension of circulation, increases the power of money, that absolutely social form of wealth ever ready for use. 'Gold is a wonderful thing! Whoever possesses it is lord of all he wants. By means of gold one can even get souls into Paradise.' (Columbus in his letter from Jamaica, 1503) Since gold does not disclose what has been transformed into it, everything, commodity or not, is convertible into gold. Everything becomes saleable and buyable. The circulation becomes the great social retort into which everything is thrown, to come out again as a gold-crystal. Just as every qualitative difference between commodities is extinguished in money, so money, on its side, like the radical leveller that it is, does away with all distinctions. But money itself is a commodity, an external object, capable of becoming the private property of any individual. Thus social power becomes the private power of private persons. The ancients therefore denounced money as subversive of the economic and moral order of things. Modern society, which, soon after its birth, pulled Plutus by the hair of his head from the bowels of the earth, greets gold as its Holy Grail, as the glittering incarnation of the very principle of its own life.

A commodity, in its capacity of a use-value, satisfies a particular want, and is a particular element of material wealth. But the value of a commodity measures the degree of its attraction for all other elements of material wealth, and therefore measures the social wealth of its owner. To a barbarian owner of commodities, and even to a West European peasant, value is the same as value-form, and therefore to him the increase in his hoard of gold and silver is an increase in value. It is true that the value of money varies, at one time in consequence of a variation in its own value, at another, in consequence of a change in the values of commodities. But this, on the one hand, does not prevent 200 ounces of gold from still containing more value than 100 ounces, nor, on the other hand, does it hinder the actual metallic form of this article from continuing to be the universal equivalent form of all other commodities, and the immediate social incarnation of all human labour. The desire after hoarding is in its very nature unsatiable. In its qualitative aspect, or formally considered, money has no bounds to its efficacy, i.e. it is the universal representative of material wealth, because it is directly convertible into any other commodity. But, at the same time, every actual sum of money is limited in amount, and, therefore, as a means of purchasing, has only a limited efficacy. This antagonism between the quantitative limits of money and its qualitative boundlessness, continually acts as a spur to the hoarder in his Sisyphus-like labour of accumulating. It is with him as it is with a conqueror who sees in every new country annexed, only a new boundary.

In order that gold may be held as money, and made to form a hoard, it must be prevented from circulating, or from transforming itself into a means of enjoyment. The hoarder, therefore, makes a sacrifice of the lusts of the flesh to his gold fetish. He acts in earnest up to the Gospel of abstention. On the other hand, he can withdraw from circulation no more than what he has thrown into it in the shape of commodities. The more he produces, the more he is able to sell. Hard work, saving, and avarice, are, therefore, his three cardinal virtues, and to sell much and buy little the sum of his political economy.

By the side of the gross form of a hoard, we find also its aesthetic form in the possession of gold and silver articles. This grows with the wealth of civil society. In this way there is created, on the one hand, a constantly extending market for gold and silver, unconnected with their functions as money, and, on the other hand, a latent source of supply, to which recourse is had principally in times of crisis and social disturbance.

b) Means of Payment

In the simple form of the circulation of commodities hitherto considered, we found a given value always presented to us in a double shape, as a commodity at one pole, as money at the opposite pole. The owners of commodities came therefore into contact as the respective representatives of what were already equivalents. But with the development of circulation, conditions arise under which the alienation of commodities becomes separated, by an interval of time, from the realisation of their prices. It will be sufficient to indicate the most simple of these conditions. One sort of article requires a longer, another a shorter time for its production. Again, the production of different commodities depends on different seasons of the year. One sort of commodity may be born on its own market place, another has to make a long journey to market. Commodity-owner no. 1 may therefore be ready to sell before no. 2 is ready to buy. When the same transactions are continually repeated between the same persons, the conditions of sale are regulated in accordance with the conditions of production. On the other hand, the use of a given commodity, of a house for instance, is sold (in common parlance, let) for a definite period. Here, it is only at the end of the term that the buyer has actually received the use-value of the commodity. He therefore buys it before he pays for it. The vendor sells an existing commodity, the purchaser buys as the mere representative of money, or rather of future money. The vendor becomes a creditor, the purchaser becomes a debtor. Since the metamorphosis of commodities, or the development of their value-form, appears here under a new aspect, money also acquires a fresh function; it becomes the means of payment.

The character of creditor, or of debtor, results here from the simple circulation. The change in the form of that circulation stamps buyer and seller with this new die. At first, therefore, these new parts are just as transient and alternating as those of seller and buyer, and are in turns played by the same actors. But the opposition is not nearly so pleasant, and is far more capable of crystallisation. The same characters can, however, be assumed independently of the circulation of commodities. The class struggles of the ancient world took the form chiefly of a contest between debtors and creditors, which in Rome ended in the ruin of the plebeian debtors. They were displaced by slaves. In the middle ages the contest ended with the ruin of the feudal debtors, who lost their political power together with the economic basis on which it was established. Nevertheless, the money relation of debtor and creditor that existed at these two periods reflected only the deeper-lying antagonism between the general economic conditions of existence of the classes in question.

Let us return to the circulation of commodities. The appearance of the two equivalents, commodities and money, at the two poles of the process of sale, has ceased to be simultaneous. The money functions now, first as a measure of value in the determination of the price of the commodity sold; the price fixed by the contract measures the obligation of the debtor, or the sum of money that he has to pay at a fixed date. Secondly, it serves as an ideal means of purchase. Although existing only in the promise of the buyer to pay, it causes the commodity to change hands. It is not before the day fixed for payment that the means of payment actually steps into circulation, leaves the hand of the buyer for that of the seller. The circulating medium was transformed into a hoard, because the process stopped short after the first phase, because the converted shape of the commodity, viz., the money, was withdrawn from circulation. The means of payment enters the circulation, but only after the commodity has left it. The money is no longer the means that brings about the process. It only brings it to a close, by stepping in as the absolute form of existence of exchange-value, or as the universal commodity. The seller turned his commodity into money, in order thereby to satisfy some want; the hoarder did the same in order to keep his commodity in its money-shape, and the debtor in order to be able to pay; if he does not pay, his goods will be sold by the sheriff. The value-form of commodities, money, is therefore now the end and aim of a sale, and that owing to a social necessity springing out of the process of circulation itself.

The buyer converts money back into commodities before he has turned commodities into money: in other words, he achieves the second metamorphosis of commodities before the first. The seller's commodity circulates, and realises its price, but only in the shape of a legal claim upon money. It is converted into a use-value before it has been converted into money. The completion of its first metamorphosis follows only at a later period.

The function of money as the means of payment implies a straight contradiction. In so far as the payments balance one another, money functions only ideally, as money of account, as a measure of value. In so far as actual payments have to be made, money does not serve as a circulating medium, as a mere transient agent in the interchange of products, but as the individual incarnation of social labour, as the independent form of existence of exchange-value, as the universal commodity. This contradiction comes to a head in those phases of industrial and commercial crises which are known as monetary crises. Such a crisis occurs only where the ever-lengthening chain of payments, and an artificial system of settling them, has been fully developed. Whenever there is a general and extensive disturbance of this mechanism, no matter what its cause, money becomes suddenly and immediately transformed, from its merely ideal shape of money of account, into hard cash. Profane commodities can no longer replace it. The use-value of commodities becomes valueless, and their value vanishes in the presence of its own independent form. On the eve of the crisis, the bourgeois, with the self-sufficiency that springs from intoxicating prosperity, declares money to be a vain imagination. Commodities alone are money. But now the cry is everywhere: money alone is a commodity! As the hart pants after fresh water, so pants his soul after money, the only wealth. In a crisis, the antithesis between commodities and their value-form, money, becomes heightened into an absolute contradiction. Hence, in such events, the form under which money appears is of no importance. The money famine continues, whether payments have to be made in gold or in credit money such as bank-notes.

Credit-money springs directly out of the function of money as a means of payment. Certificates of the debts owing for the purchased commodities circulate for the purpose of transferring those debts to others. On the other hand, to the same extent as the system of credit is extended, so is the function of money as a means of payment. In that character it takes various forms peculiar to itself under which it makes itself at home in the sphere of great commercial transactions. Gold and silver coin, on the other hand, are mostly relegated to the sphere of retail trade.

When the production of commodities has sufficiently extended itself, money begins to serve as the means of payment beyond the sphere of the circulation of commodities. It becomes the commodity that is the universal subject-matter of all contracts. Rents, taxes, and such like payments are transformed from payments in kind into money payments. To what extent this transformation depends upon the general conditions of production, is shown, to take one example, by the fact that the Roman Empire twice failed in its attempt to levy all contributions in money. The unspeakable misery of the French agricultural population under Louis XIV, a misery so eloquently denounced by Boisguillebert, Marshal Vauban, and others, was due not only to the weight of the taxes, but also to the conversion of taxes in kind into money taxes. In Asia, on the other hand, the fact that state taxes are chiefly composed of rents payable in kind depends on conditions of production that are reproduced with the regularity of natural phenomena. And this mode of payment tends in its turn to maintain the ancient form of production, It is one of the secrets of the conservation of the Ottoman Empire.

c) Universal Money

When money leaves the home sphere of circulation, it strips off the local garbs which it there assumes, of a standard of prices, of coin, of tokens, and of a symbol of value, and returns to its original form of bullion. In the trade between the markets of the world, the value of commodities is expressed so as to be universally recognised. Hence their independent value-form also, in these cases, confronts them under the shape of universal money. It is only in the markets of the world that money acquires to the full extent the character of the commodity whose bodily form is also the immediate social incarnation of human labour in the abstract. Its mode of existence in this sphere adequately corresponds to its concept.

Money of the world serves as the universal medium of payment, as the universal means of purchasing, and as the universally recognised embodiment of all wealth. Its function as a means of payment in the settling of international balances is its chief one.

PART II
THE TRANSFORMATION OF MONEY INTO CAPITAL

CHAPTER 4

THE GENERAL FORMULA FOR CAPITAL

The circulation of commodities is the starting-point of capital. The production of commodities, their circulation, and that more developed form of their circulation called commerce, these form the historical ground-work from which it rises. The modern history of capital dates from the creation in the sixteenth century of a world-embracing commerce and a world-embracing market.

If we abstract from the material substance of the circulation of commodities, that is, from the exchange of the various use-values, and consider only the economic forms produced by this process of circulation, we find its final result to be money: this final product of the circulation of commodities is the first form in which capital appears.

As a matter of history, capital, as opposed to landed property, invariably takes the form at first of money; it appears as moneyed wealth, as the capital of the merchant and of the usurer. But we have no need to refer to the origin of capital in order to discover that the first form of appearance of capital is money. We can see it daily under our very eyes. All new capital, to commence with, comes on the stage, that is, on the market, whether of commodities, labour, or money, even in our days, in the shape of money that by a definite process has to be transformed into capital.

The first distinction we notice between money that is money only, and money that is capital, is nothing more than a difference in their form of circulation.

The simplest form of the circulation of commodities is C—M—C, the transformation of commodities into money, and the change of the money back again into commodities; or selling in order to buy. But alongside of this form we find another specifically different form: M—C—M, the transformation of money into commodities, and the change of commodities back again into money; or buying in order to sell. Money that circulates in the latter manner is thereby transformed into, becomes capital, and is already potentially capital.

Now let us examine the circuit M—C—M a little closer. It consists, like the other, of two antithetical phases. In the first phase, M—C, or the purchase, the money is changed into a commodity. In the second phase, C—M, or the sale, the commodity is changed back again into money. The combination of these two phases constitutes the single movement whereby money is exchanged for a commodity, and the same commodity is again exchanged for money; whereby a commodity is bought in order to be sold, or, neglecting the distinction in form between buying and selling, whereby a commodity is bought with money, and then money is bought with a commodity. The result, in which the phases of the process vanish, is the exchange of money for money, M—M. If I purchase 2,000 lb of cotton for £100, and resell the 2,000 lb of cotton for £110, I have, in fact, exchanged £100 for £110, money for money.

Now it is evident that the circuit M—C—M would be absurd and without meaning if the intention were to exchange by this means two equal sums of money, £100 for £100. The miser's plan would be far simpler and surer; he sticks to his £100 instead of exposing it to the dangers of circulation. And yet, whether the merchant who has paid £100 for his cotton sells it for £110, or lets it go for £100, or even £50, his money has, at all events, gone through a characteristic and original movement, quite different in kind from that which it goes through in the hands of the peasant who sells corn, and with the money thus set free buys clothes. We have therefore to examine first the distinguishing characteristics of the forms of the circuits M—C—M and C—M—C, and in doing this the real difference that underlies the mere difference of form will reveal itself.

Let us see, in the first place, what the two forms have in common.

Both circuits are resolvable into the same two antithetical phases, C—M, a sale, and M—C, a purchase. In each of these phases the same material elements – a commodity, and money, and the same economic dramatis personae, a buyer and a seller – confront one another. Each circuit is the unity of the same two antithetical phases, and in each case this unity is brought about by the intervention of three contracting parties, of whom one only sells, another only buys, while the third both buys and sells.

What, however, first and foremost distinguishes the circuit C—M—C from the circuit M—C—M, is the inverted order of succession of the two phases. The simple circulation of commodities begins with a sale and ends with purchase, while the circulation of money as capital begins with a purchase and ends with a sale. In the one case both the starting-point and the goal are commodities, in the other they are money. In the first form the movement is brought about by the intervention of money, in the second by that of a commodity.

In the circulation C—M—C, the money is in the end converted into a commodity that serves as use-value; it is spent once for all. In the inverted form, M—C—M, on the contrary, the buyer lays out money in order that, as a seller, he may recover money. By the purchase of his commodity he throws money into circulation, in order to withdraw it again by the sale of the same commodity. He lets the money go, but only with the sly intention of getting it back again. The money, therefore, is not spent, it is merely advanced.

In the circuit C—M—C, the same piece of money changes its place twice. The seller gets it from the buyer and pays it away to another seller. The complete circulation, which begins with the receipt, concludes with the payment of money for commodities. It is the very contrary in the circuit M—C—M. Here it is not the piece of money that changes its place twice, but the commodity. The buyer takes it from the hands of the seller and passes it into the hands of another buyer. Just as in the simple circulation of commodities the double change of place of the same piece of money effects its passage from one hand into another, so here the double change of place of the same commodity brings about the reflux of the money to its point of departure.

Such reflux is not dependent on the commodity being sold for more than was paid for it. This circumstance influences only the amount of the money that comes back. The reflux itself takes place, so soon as the purchased commodity is resold, in other words, so soon as the circuit M—C—M is completed. We have here, therefore, a palpable difference between the circulation of money as capital, and its circulation as mere money.

The circuit C—M—C comes completely to an end, so soon as the money brought in by the sale of one commodity is abstracted again by the purchase of another.

If, nevertheless, there follows a reflux of money to its starting-point, this can only happen through a renewal or repetition of the operation. If I sell a quarter of corn for £3, and with this £3 buy clothes, the money, so far as I am concerned, is spent and done with. It belongs to the clothes merchant. If I now sell a second quarter of corn, money indeed flows back to me, not however as a sequel to the first transaction, but in consequence of its repetition. The money again leaves me, so soon as I complete this second transaction by a fresh purchase. Therefore, in the circuit C—M—C, the expenditure of money has nothing to do with its reflux. On the other hand, in M—C—M, the reflux of the money is conditioned by the very mode of its expenditure. Without this reflux, the operation fails, or the process is interrupted and incomplete, owing to the absence of its complementary and final phase, the sale.

The circuit C—M—C starts with one commodity, and finishes with another, which falls out of circulation and into consumption. Consumption, the satisfaction of wants, in one word, use-value, is its end and aim. The circuit M—C—M, on the contrary, commences with money and ends with money. Its leading motive, and the goal that attracts it, is therefore mere exchange-value.

In the simple circulation of commodities, the two extremes of the circuit have the same economic form. They are both commodities, and commodities of equal value. But they are also use-values differing in their qualities, as, for example, corn and clothes. The exchange of products, of the different materials in which the labour of society is embodied, forms here the basis of the movement. It is otherwise in the circulation M—C—M, which at first sight appears purposeless, because tautological. Both extremes have the same economic form. They are both money, and therefore are not qualitatively different use-values; for money is but the converted form of commodities, in which their particular use-values vanish. To exchange £100 for cotton, and then this same cotton again for £100, is merely a roundabout way of exchanging money for money, the same for the same, and appears to be an operation just as purposeless as it is absurd. One sum of money is distinguishable from another only by its amount. The character and tendency of the process M—C—M, is therefore not due to any qualitative difference between its extremes, both being money, but solely to their quantitative difference. More money is withdrawn from circulation at the finish than was thrown into it at the start. The cotton that was bought for £100 is perhaps resold for £100 + £10 or £110. The exact form of this process is therefore M—C—M′, where M′ = M + $\triangle$M = the original sum advanced, plus an increment. This increment or excess over the original value I call 'surplus-value'. The value originally advanced, therefore, not only remains intact while in circulation, but adds to itself a surplus-value or expands itself. It is this movement that converts it into capital.

Of course, it is also possible, that in C—M—C, the two extremes

C—C, say corn and clothes, may represent different quantities of value. The farmer may sell his corn above its value, or may buy the clothes at less than their value. He may, on the other hand, 'be done' by the clothes merchant. Yet, in the form of circulation now under consideration, such differences in value are purely accidental. The fact that the corn and the clothes are equivalents does not deprive the process of all meaning, as it does in M—C—M. The equivalence of their values is rather a necessary condition to its normal course.

The repetition or renewal of the act of selling in order to buy, is kept within bounds by the very object it aims at, namely, consumption or the satisfaction of definite wants, an aim that lies altogether outside the sphere of circulation. But when we buy in order to sell, we, on the contrary, begin and end with the same thing, money, exchange-value; and thereby the movement becomes interminable. No doubt, M becomes M+△M, £100 become £110. But when viewed in their qualitative aspect alone, £110 are the same as £100, namely money; and considered quantitatively, £110 is, like £100, a sum of definite and limited value. If now, the £110 be spent as money, they cease to play their part. They are no longer capital. Withdrawn from circulation, they become petrified into a hoard, and though they remained in that state till doomsday, not a single farthing would accrue to them. If, then, the expansion of value is once aimed at, there is just the same inducement to augment the value of the £110 as that of the £100; for both are but limited expressions for exchange-value, and therefore both have the same vocation to approach, by quantitative increase, as near as possible to absolute wealth. Momentarily, indeed, the value originally advanced, the £100 is distinguishable from the surplus-value of £10 that is annexed to it during circulation; but the distinction vanishes immediately. At the end of the process, we do not receive with one hand the original £100, and with the other, the surplus-value of £10. We simply get a value of £110, which is in exactly the same condition and fitness for commencing the expanding process, as the original £100 was. Money ends the movement only to begin it again. Therefore, the final result of every separate circuit, in which a purchase and consequent sale are completed, forms of itself the starting-point of a new circuit. The simple circulation of commodities – selling in order to buy – is a means of carrying out a purpose unconnected with circulation, namely, the appropriation of use-values, the satisfaction of wants. The circulation of money as capital is, on the contrary, an end in itself, for the expansion of value takes place only within this constantly renewed movement. The circulation of capital has therefore no limits.

As the conscious bearer of this movement, the possessor of money becomes a capitalist. His person, or rather his pocket, is the point from which the money starts and to which it returns. The expansion of value, which is the objective basis or main-spring of the circulation M—C—M, becomes his subjective aim, and it is only in so far as the appropriation of ever more and more wealth in the abstract becomes the sole motive of his operations, that he functions as a capitalist, that is, as capital personified and endowed with consciousness and a will. Use-values must therefore never be looked upon as the real aim of the capitalist, neither must the profit on any single transaction. The restless never-ending process of profit-making alone is what he aims at. This boundless greed after riches, this passionate chase after exchange-value, is common to the capitalist and the miser; but while the miser is merely a capitalist gone mad, the capitalist is a rational miser. The never-ending augmentation of exchange-value, which the miser strives after, by seeking to save his money from circulation, is attained by the more acute capitalist, by constantly throwing it afresh into circulation.

The independent form, i.e. the money-form, which the value of commodities assumes in the case of simple circulation, serves only one purpose, namely, their exchange, and vanishes in the final result of the movement. On the other hand, in the circulation M—C—M, both the money and the commodity represent only different modes of existence of value itself, the money its general mode, and the commodity its particular, or, so to say, disguised mode. It is constantly changing from one form to the other without thereby becoming lost, and thus assumes an automatically active character. If now we take in turn each of the two different forms which self-expanding value successively assumes in the course of its life, we then arrive at these two propositions: Capital is money: Capital is commodities. In truth, however, value is here the active factor in a process, in which, while constantly assuming the form in turn of money and commodities, it at the same time changes in magnitude, differentiates itself by throwing off surplus-value from itself; the original value, in other words, expands spontaneously. For the movement, in the course of which it adds surplus-value, is its own movement, its expansion, therefore, is automatic expansion. Because it is value, it has acquired the occult quality of being able to add value to itself. It brings forth living offspring, or, at the least, lays golden eggs.

Value, therefore, being the active factor in such a process, and assuming at one time the form of money, at another that of commodities, but through all these changes preserving itself and expanding, it requires some independent form, by means of which its identity may at any time be established. And this form it possesses only in the shape of money. It is under the form of money that value begins and ends, and begins again, every act of its own spontaneous generation. It began by being £100, it is now £110, and so on. But the money itself is only one of the two forms of value. Unless it takes the form of some commodity, it does not become capital. There is here no antagonism, as in the case of hoarding, between the money and commodities. The capitalist knows that all commodities, however scurvy they may look, or however badly they may smell, are in faith and in truth money, inwardly circumcised Jews, and what is more, a wonderful means whereby out of money to make more money.

In simple circulation, C—M—C, the value of commodities attained at the most a form independent of their use-values, i.e. the form of money; but that same value now in the circulation M—C—M, or the circulation of capital, suddenly presents itself as an independent substance, endowed with a motion of its own, passing through a life-process of its own, in which money and commodities are mere forms which it assumes and casts off in turn. Nay, more: instead of simply representing the relations of commodities, it enters now, so to say, into private relations with itself. It differentiates itself as original value from itself as surplus-value; as the father differentiates himself from himself *qua* the son, yet both are one and of one age: for only by the surplus-value of £10 does the £100 originally advanced become capital, and so soon as this takes place, so soon as the son, and by the son, the father, is begotten, so soon does their difference vanish, and they again become one, £110.

Value therefore now becomes value in process, money in process, and, as such, capital. It comes out of circulation, enters into it again, preserves and multiplies itself within its circuit, comes back out of it with expanded bulk, and begins the same round ever afresh. M—M′, money which begets money, such is the description of Capital from the mouths of its first interpreters, the Mercantilists.

Buying in order to sell, or, more accurately, buying in order to sell dearer, M—C—M′, appears certainly to be a form peculiar to one kind of capital alone, namely, merchants' capital. But industrial capital too is money that is changed into commodities, and by the sale of these commodities, is re-converted into more money. The events that take place outside the sphere of circulation, in the interval between the buying and selling, do not affect the form of this movement. Lastly, in the case of interest-bearing capital, the circulation of M—C—M′

appears abridged. We have its result without the intermediate stage, in the form M—M′, '*en style lapidaire*' so to say, money that is worth more money, value that is greater than itself.

M—C—M′ is therefore in reality the general formula of capital as it appears prima facie within the sphere of circulation.

CHAPTER 5

Contradictions in the General Formula of Capital

The form which circulation takes when money becomes capital, is opposed to all the laws we have hitherto investigated bearing on the nature of commodities, value and money, and even of circulation itself. What distinguishes this form from that of the simple circulation of commodities is the inverted order of succession of the two antithetical processes, sale and purchase. How can this purely formal distinction between these processes change their character as it were by magic?

But that is not all. This inversion has no existence for two out of the three persons who transact business together. As capitalist, I buy commodities from A and sell them again to B, but as a simple owner of commodities, I sell them to B and then purchase fresh ones from A. A and B see no difference between the two sets of transactions. They are merely buyers or sellers. And I on each occasion meet them as a mere owner of either money or commodities, as a buyer or a seller, and, what is more, in both sets of transactions, I am opposed to A only as a buyer and to B only as a seller, to the one only as money, to the other only as commodities, and to neither of them as capital or a capitalist, or as representative of anything that is more than money or commodities, or that can produce any effect beyond what money and commodities can. For me the purchase from A and the sale to B are part of a series. But the connexion between the two acts exists for me alone. A does not trouble himself about my transaction with B, nor does B about my business with A. And if I offered to explain to them the meritorious nature of my action in inverting the order of succession, they would probably point out to me that I was mistaken as to that order of succession, and that the whole transaction, instead of beginning with a purchase and ending with a sale, began, on the contrary, with a sale and was concluded with a purchase. In truth, my first act, the purchase, was from the standpoint of A, a sale, and my second act, the sale, was from the standpoint of B, a purchase. Not content with that, A and B would declare that the whole series was superfluous and nothing but Hokus Pokus; that for the future A would buy direct from B, and B sell direct to A. Thus the whole transaction would be reduced to a single act forming an isolated, non-complemented phase in the ordinary circulation of commodities, a mere sale from A's point of view, and from B's, a mere purchase. The inversion, therefore, of the order of succession, does not take us outside the sphere of the simple circulation of commodities, and we must rather look, whether there is in this simple circulation anything permitting an expansion of the value that enters into circulation, and, consequently, a creation of surplus-value.

Let us take the process of circulation in a form under which it presents itself as a simple and direct exchange of commodities. This is always the case when two owners of commodities buy from each other, and on the settling day the amounts mutually owing are equal and cancel each other. The money in this case is money of account and serves to express the value of the commodities by their prices, but is not, itself, in the shape of hard cash, confronted with them. So far as regards use-values, it is clear that both parties may gain some advantage. Both part with goods that, as use-values, are of no service to them, and receive others that they can make use of. And there may also be a further gain. A, who sells wine and buys corn, possibly produces more wine, with given labour-time, than farmer B could, and B on the other hand, more corn than wine-grower A could. A, therefore, may get, for the same exchange-value, more corn, and B more wine, than each would respectively get without any exchange by producing his own corn and wine. With reference, therefore, to use-value, there is good ground for saying that exchange is a transaction by which both sides gain. It is otherwise with exchange-value.

Abstractedly considered, that is, apart from circumstances not immediately flowing from the laws of the simple circulation of commodities, there is in an exchange nothing (if we except the replacing of one use-value by another) but a metamorphosis, a mere change in the form of the commodity. This change of form no more implies, taken alone, a change in the quantity of value, than does the change of a £5 note into sovereigns, half sovereigns and shillings. So far therefore as the circulation of commodities effects a change in the form alone of their values, and is free from disturbing influences, it must be the exchange of equivalents. Little as Vulgar-Economy knows about the nature of value, yet whenever it wishes to consider the phenomena of circulation in their purity, it assumes that supply and demand are equal, which amounts to this, that their effect is nil. If therefore, as regards the use-values exchanged, both buyer and seller may possibly gain something, this is not the case as regards the exchange-values. Here we must rather say, 'Where equality exists there can be no gain.' It is true, commodities may be sold at prices deviating from their values, but these deviations are to be considered as infractions of the laws of the exchange of commodities, which in its normal state is an exchange of equivalents, consequently, no method for increasing value.

Hence, we see that behind all attempts to represent the circulation of commodities as a source of surplus-value, there lurks a *quid pro quo*, a mixing up of use-value and exchange-value. For instance, Condillac says: 'It is not true that on an exchange of commodities we give value for value. On the contrary, each of the two contracting parties in every case, gives a less for a greater value. . . . If we really exchanged equal values, neither party could make a profit. And yet, they both gain, or ought to gain. Why? The value of a thing consists solely in its relation to our wants. What is more to the one is less to the other, and vice versa.' Still, Condillac's argument is frequently used by modern economists, more especially when the point is to show, that the exchange of commodities in its developed form, commerce, is productive of surplus-value. For instance, 'Commerce . . . adds value to products, for the same products in the hands of consumers, are worth more than in the hands of producers, and it may strictly be considered an act of production.' But commodities are not paid for twice over, once on account of their use-value, and again on account of their value. And though the use-value of a commodity is more serviceable to the buyer than to the seller, its money-form is more serviceable to the seller. Would he otherwise sell it? We might therefore just as well say that the buyer performs 'strictly an act of production', by converting stockings, for example, into money.

If commodities, or commodities and money, of equal exchange-value, and consequently equivalents, are exchanged, it is plain that no one abstracts more value from, than he throws into, circulation. There is no creation of surplus-value. And, in its normal form, the circulation of commodities demands the exchange of equivalents. But in actual practice, the process does not retain its normal form. Let us, therefore, assume an exchange of non-equivalents.

In any case the market for commodities is only frequented by owners of commodities, and the power which these persons exercise over each other is no other than the power of their commodities. The material variety of these commodities is the material incentive to the act of exchange, and makes buyers and sellers mutually dependent, because none of them possess the object of his own wants, and each holds in his hand the object of another's wants. Besides these material differences of their use-values, there is only one other difference between commodities, namely, that between their bodily form and the form into which they are converted by sale, the difference between commodities and money. And consequently the owners of commodities are distinguishable only as sellers, those who own commodities, and buyers, those who own money.

Suppose then, that by some inexplicable privilege, the seller is enabled to sell his commodities above their value, what is worth £100 for £110, in which case the price is nominally raised 10 per cent. The seller therefore pockets a surplus-value of £10. But after he has sold he becomes a buyer. A third owner of commodities comes to him now as seller, who in this capacity also enjoys the privilege of selling his commodities 10 per cent too dear. Our friend gained £10 as a seller only to lose it again as a buyer. The net result is, that all owners of commodities sell their goods to one another at 10 per cent above their value, which comes precisely to the same as if they sold them at their true value. Such a general and nominal rise of prices has the same effect as if the values had been expressed in weight of silver instead of in weight of gold. The nominal prices of commodities would rise, but the real relation between their values would remain unchanged.

Let us make the opposite assumption, that the buyer has the privilege of purchasing commodities under their value. In this case it is no longer necessary to bear in mind that he in his turn will become a seller. He was so before he became buyer; he had already lost 10 per cent in selling before he gained 10 per cent as buyer. Everything is just as it was.

The creation of surplus-value, and therefore the conversion of money into capital, can consequently be explained neither on the assumption that commodities are sold above their value, nor that they are bought below their value.

A may be clever enough to get the advantage of B or C without their being able to retaliate. A sells wine worth £40 to B, and obtains from him in exchange corn to the value of £50. A has converted his £40 into £50, has made more money out of less, and has converted his commodities into capital. Let us examine this a little more closely. Before the exchange we had £40 worth of wine in the hands of A, and

£50 worth of corn in those of B, a total of £90. After the exchange we have still the same total value of £90. The value in circulation has not increased by one iota, it is only distributed differently between A and B. What is a loss of value to B is surplus-value to A; what is 'minus' to one is 'plus' to the other. The same change would have taken place, if A, without the formality of an exchange, had directly stolen the £10 from B. The sum of the values in circulation can clearly not be augmented by any change in their distribution.

Turn and twist then as we may, the fact remains unaltered. If equivalents are exchanged, no surplus-value results, and if non-equivalents are exchanged, still no surplus-value. Circulation, or the exchange of commodities, begets no value.

The reason is now therefore plain why, in analysing the standard form of capital, the form under which it determines the economic organisation of modern society, we entirely left out of consideration its most popular, and, so to say, antediluvian forms, merchants' capital and money-lenders' capital.

The circuit M—C—M′, buying in order to sell dearer, is seen most clearly in genuine merchants' capital. But the movement takes place entirely within the sphere of circulation. Since, however, it is impossible, by circulation alone, to account for the conversion of money into capital, for the formation of surplus-value, it would appear, that merchants' capital is an impossibility, so long as equivalents are exchanged, that, therefore, it can only have its origin in the two-fold advantage gained, over both the selling and the buying producers, by the merchant who parasitically shoves himself in between them. It is in this sense that Franklin says, 'war is robbery, commerce is generally cheating.' If the transformation of merchants' money into capital is to be explained otherwise than by the producers being simply cheated, a long series of intermediate steps would be necessary, which, at present, when the simple circulation of commodities forms our only assumption, are entirely wanting.

What we have said with reference to merchants' capital applies still more to money-lenders' capital. In merchants' capital, the two extremes, the money that is thrown upon the market, and the augmented money that is withdrawn from the market, are at least connected by a purchase and a sale, in other words by the movements of the circulation. In money-lenders' capital the form M—C—M′ is reduced to two extremes without a mean, M—M′, money exchanged for more money, a form that is incompatible with the nature of money, and therefore remains inexplicable from the standpoint of the circulation of commodities. Hence Aristotle:

> The usurer is most rightly hated, because money itself is the source of his gain, and is not used for the purposes for which it was invented. For it originated for the exchange of commodities, but interest makes out of money, more money. Hence its name (*tokos* interest and offspring). For the begotten are like those who beget them. But interest is money of money, so that, of all modes of making a living, this is the most contrary to Nature.

In the course of our investigation, we shall find that both merchants' capital and interest-bearing capital are derivative forms, and at the same time it will become clear why these two forms appear in the course of history before the modern standard form of capital.

We have shown that surplus-value cannot be created by circulation, and therefore that in its formation, something must take place in the background, which is not apparent in the circulation itself. But can surplus-value possibly originate anywhere else than in circulation, which is the sum total of all the mutual relations of commodity-owners, as far as they are determined by their commodities? Apart from circulation, the commodity-owner is in relation only with his own commodity. So far as regards value, that relation is limited to this, that the commodity contains a quantity of his own labour, that quantity being measured by a definite social standard. This quantity is expressed by the value of the commodity, and since the value is reckoned in money of account, this quantity is also expressed by the price, which we will suppose to be £10. But his labour is not represented both by the value of the commodity, and by a surplus over that value, not by a price of £10 that is also a price of £11, not by a value that is greater than itself. The commodity owner can, by his labour, create value, but not self-expanding value. He can increase the value of his commodity by adding fresh labour, and therefore more value to the value in hand, by making, for instance, leather into boots. The same material has now more value, because it contains a greater quantity of labour. The boots have therefore more value than the leather, but the value of the leather remains what it was; it has not expanded itself, has not, during the making of the boots, annexed surplus-value. It is therefore impossible that outside the sphere of circulation, a producer of commodities can, without coming into contact with other commodity-owners, expand value, and consequently convert money or commodities into capital.

It is therefore impossible for capital to be produced by circulation, and it is equally impossible for it to originate apart from circulation. It must have its origin both in circulation and yet not in circulation.

We have, therefore, got a double result.

The conversion of money into capital has to be explained on the basis of the laws that regulate the exchange of commodities, in such a way that the starting-point is the exchange of equivalents. Our friend, Moneybags, who as yet is only an embryo capitalist, must buy his commodities at their value, must sell them at their value, and yet at the end of the process must withdraw more value from circulation than he threw into it at starting. His development into a full-grown capitalist must take place both within the sphere of circulation and without it. These are the conditions of the problem.

CHAPTER 6

THE BUYING AND SELLING OF LABOUR-POWER

The change of value that occurs in the case of money intended to be converted into capital, cannot take place in the money itself, since in its function of means of purchase and of payment, it does no more than realise the price of the commodity it buys or pays for; and, as hard cash, it is value petrified, never varying. Just as little can it originate in the second act of circulation, the resale of the commodity, which does no more than transform the article from its bodily form back again into its money-form. The change must, therefore, take place in the commodity bought by the first act, M—C, but not in its value, for equivalents are exchanged, and the commodity is paid for at its full value. We are, therefore, forced to the conclusion that the change originates in the use-value, as such, of the commodity, i.e. in its consumption. In order to be able to extract value from the consumption of a commodity, our friend, Moneybags, must be so lucky as to find, within the sphere of circulation, in the market, a commodity, whose use-value possesses the peculiar property of being a source of value, whose actual consumption, therefore, is itself an embodiment of labour, and, consequently, a creation of value. The possessor of money does find on the market such a special commodity in capacity for labour, or labour-power.

By labour-power or capacity for labour is to be understood the aggregate of those mental and physical capabilities existing in a human being, which he exercises whenever he produces a use-value of any description.

But in order that our owner of money may be able to find labour-power offered for sale as a commodity, various conditions must first be fulfilled. The exchange of commodities of itself implies no other relations of dependence than those which result from its own nature. On this assumption, labour-power can appear upon the market as a commodity, only if, and so far as, its possessor, the individual whose labour-power it is, offers it for sale, or sells it, as a commodity. In order that he may be able to do this, he must have it at his disposal, must be the untrammelled owner of his capacity for labour, i.e. of his person. He and the owner of money meet in the market, and deal with each other as on the basis of equal rights, with this difference alone, that one is buyer, the other seller; both, therefore, equal in the eyes of the law. The continuance of this relation demands that the owner of the labour-power should sell it only for a definite period, for if he were to sell it rump and stump, once for all, he would be selling himself, converting himself from a free man into a slave, from an owner of a commodity into a commodity. He must constantly look upon his labour-power as his own property, his own commodity, and this he can only do by placing it at the disposal of the buyer temporarily, for a definite period of time. By this means can he avoid renouncing his rights of ownership over it.

The second essential condition to the owner of money finding labour-power in the market as a commodity is this – that the labourer instead of being in the position to sell commodities in which his labour is incorporated, must be obliged to offer for sale as a commodity that very labour-power, which exists only in his living self.

In order that a man may be able to sell commodities other than labour-power, he must of course have the means of production, as raw material, implements, etc. No boots can be made without leather. He requires also the means of subsistence. Nobody – not even 'a musician of the future' – can live upon future products, or upon use-values in an unfinished state; and ever since the first moment of his appearance on the world's stage, man always has been, and must still be a consumer, both before and while he is producing. In a society where all products assume the form of commodities, these commodities must be sold after they have been produced, it is only after their sale that they can serve in satisfying the requirements of their producer. The time necessary for their sale is superadded to that necessary for their production.

For the conversion of his money into capital, therefore, the owner of money must meet in the market with the free labourer, free in the double sense, that as a free man he can dispose of his labour-power as his own commodity, and that on the other hand he has no other commodity for sale, is short of everything necessary for the realisation of his labour-power.

The question why this free labourer confronts him in the market, has no interest for the owner of money, who regards the labour market as a branch of the general market for commodities. And for the present it interests us just a little. We cling to the fact theoretically, as he does practically. One thing, however, is clear – Nature does not produce on the one side owners of money or commodities, and on the other men possessing nothing but their own labour-power. This relation has no natural basis, neither is its social basis one that is common to all historical periods. It is clearly the result of a past historical development, the product of many economic revolutions, of the extinction of a whole series of older forms of social production.

So too, the economic categories, already discussed by us, bear the stamp of history. Definite historical conditions are necessary that a product may become a commodity. It must not be produced as the immediate means of subsistence of the producer himself. Had we gone further, and inquired under what circumstances all, or even the majority of products take the form of commodities, we should have found that this can only happen with production of a very specific kind, capitalist production. Such an inquiry, however, would have been foreign to the analysis of commodities. Production and circulation of commodities can take place, although the great mass of the objects produced are intended for the immediate requirements of their producers, are not turned into commodities, and consequently social production is not yet by a long way dominated in its length and breadth by exchange-value. The appearance of products as commodities presupposes such a development of the social division of labour, that the separation of use-value from exchange-value, a separation which first begins with barter, must already have been completed. But such a degree of development is common to many forms of society, which in other respects present the most varying historical features. On the other hand, if we consider money, its existence implies a definite stage in the exchange of commodities. The particular functions of money which it performs, either as the mere equivalent of commodities, or as means of circulation, or means of payment, as hoard or as universal money, point, according to the extent and relative preponderance of the one function or the other, to very different stages in the process of social production. Yet we know by experience that a circulation of commodities relatively primitive, suffices for the production of all these forms. Otherwise with capital. The historical conditions of its existence are by no means given with the mere circulation of money and commodities. It can spring into life, only when the owner of the means of production and subsistence meets in the market with the free labourer selling his labour-power. And this one historical condition comprises a world's history. Capital, therefore, announces from its first appearance a new epoch in the process of social production.

We must now examine more closely this peculiar commodity, labour-power. Like all others it has a value. How is that value determined?

The value of labour-power is determined, as in the case of every other commodity, by the labour-time necessary for the production, and consequently also the reproduction, of this special article. So far as it has value, it represents no more than a definite quantity of the average labour of society incorporated in it. Labour-power exists only as a capacity, or power of the living individual. Its production consequently presupposes his existence. Given the individual, the production of labour-power consists in his reproduction of himself or his maintenance. For his maintenance he requires a given quantity of the means of subsistence. Therefore the labour-time requisite for the production of labour-power reduces itself to that necessary for the production of those means of subsistence; in other words, the value of labour-power is the value of the means of subsistence necessary for the maintenance of the labourer. Labour-power, however, becomes a reality only by its exercise; it sets itself in action only by working. But thereby a definite quantity of human muscle, nerve, brain, etc. is wasted, and these require to be restored. This increased expenditure demands a larger income. If the owner of labour-power works today, tomorrow he must again be able to repeat the same process in the same conditions as regards health and strength. His means of subsistence must therefore be sufficient to maintain him in his normal state as a labouring individual. His natural wants, such as food, clothing, fuel, and housing, vary according to the climatic and other physical conditions of his country. On the other hand, the number and extent of his so-called necessary wants, as also the modes of satisfying them, are themselves the product of historical development, and depend therefore to a great extent on the degree of civilisation of a country, more particularly on the conditions under which, and consequently on the habits and degree of comfort in which, the class of free labourers has been formed. In contradistinction therefore to the case of other commodities, there enters into the determination of the value of labour-power a historical and moral element. Nevertheless, in a given country, at a given period, the average quantity of the means of subsistence necessary for the labourer is practically known.

The labour-power withdrawn from the market by wear and tear and death, must be continually replaced by, at the very least, an equal amount of fresh labour-power. Hence the sum of the means of subsistence necessary for the production of labour-power must include the means necessary for the labourer's substitutes, i.e. his children, in order that this race of peculiar commodity-owners may perpetuate its appearance in the market.

In order to modify the human organism, so that it may acquire skill and handiness in a given branch of industry, and become labour-power of a special kind, a special education or training is requisite, and this, on its part, costs an equivalent in commodities of a greater or less amount. This amount varies according to the more or less complicated character of the labour-power. The expenses of this education (excessively small in the case of ordinary labour-power), enter *pro tanto* into the total value spent in its production.

The value of labour-power resolves itself into the value of a definite quantity of the means of subsistence. It therefore varies with the value of these means or with the quantity of labour requisite for their production.

The minimum limit of the value of labour-power is determined by the value of the commodities, without the daily supply of which the labourer cannot renew his vital energy, consequently by the value of those means of subsistence that are physical indispensable. If the price of labour-power fall to this minimum, it falls below its value, since under such circumstances it can be maintained and developed only in a crippled state. But the value of every commodity is determined by the labour-time requisite to turn it out so as to be of normal quality.

One consequence of the peculiar nature of labour-power as a commodity is, that its use-value does not, on the conclusion of the contract between the buyer and seller, immediately pass into the hands of the former. Its value, like that of every other commodity, is already fixed before it goes into circulation, since a definite quantity of social labour has been spent upon it; but its use-value consists in the subsequent exercise of its force. The alienation of labour-power and its actual appropriation by the buyer, its employment as a use-value, are separated by an interval of time. But in those cases in which the formal alienation by sale of the use-value of a commodity, is not simultaneous with its actual delivery to the buyer, the money of the latter usually functions as means of payment. In every country in which the capitalist mode of production reigns, it is the custom not to pay for labour-power before it has been exercised for the period fixed by the contract, as for example, the end of each week. In all cases, therefore, the use-value of the labour-power is advanced to the capitalist: the labourer allows the buyer to consume it before he receives payment of the price; he everywhere gives credit to the capitalist. That this credit is no mere fiction, is shown not only by the occasional loss of wages on the bankruptcy of the capitalist but also by a series of more enduring consequences. Nevertheless, whether money serves as a means of purchase or as a means of payment, this makes no alteration in the nature of the exchange of commodities. The price of the labour-power is fixed by the contract, although it is not realised till later, like the rent of a house. The labour-power is sold, although it is only paid for at a later period. It will, therefore, be useful, for a clear comprehension of the relation of the parties, to assume provisionally, that the possessor of labour-power, on the occasion of each sale, immediately receives the price stipulated to be paid for it.

We now know how the value paid by the purchaser to the possessor of this peculiar commodity, labour-power, is determined. The use-value which the former gets in exchange, manifests itself only in the actual usufruct, in the consumption of the labour-power. The money-owner buys everything necessary for this purpose, such as raw material, in the market, and pays for it at its full value. The consumption of labour-power is at one and the same time the production of commodities and of surplus-value. The consumption of labour-power is completed, as in the case of every other commodity, outside the limits of the market or of the sphere of circulation. Accompanied by Mr Moneybags and by the possessor of labour-power, we therefore take leave for a time of this noisy sphere, where everything takes place on the surface and in view of all men, and follow them both into the hidden abode of production, on whose threshold there stares us in the face 'No admittance except on business'. Here we shall see, not only how capital produces, but how capital is produced. We shall at last force the secret of profit-making.

This sphere that we are deserting, within whose boundaries the sale and purchase of labour-power goes on, is in fact a very Eden of the innate rights of man. There alone rule Freedom, Equality, Property and Bentham. Freedom, because both buyer and seller of a commodity, say of labour-power, are constrained only by their own free will. They contract as free agents, and the agreement they come to is but the form in which they give legal expression to their common will. Equality, because each enters into relation with the other, as with a simple owner of commodities, and they exchange equivalent for equivalent. Property, because each disposes only of what is his own. And Bentham, because each looks only to himself. The only force that brings them together and puts them in relation with each other, is the selfishness, the gain and the private interests of each. Each looks to himself only, and no one troubles himself about the rest, and just because they do so, do they all, in accordance with the pre-established harmony of things, or under the auspices of an all-shrewd providence, work together to their mutual advantage, for the common weal and in the interest of all.

On leaving this sphere of simple circulation or of exchange of commodities, which furnishes the 'Free-trader Vulgaris' with his views and ideas, and with the standard by which he judges a society based on capital and wages, we think we can perceive a change in the physiognomy of our dramatis personae. He, who before was the money-owner, now strides in front as capitalist; the possessor of labour-power follows as his labourer. The one with an air of importance, smirking, intent on business; the other, timid and holding back, like one who is bringing his own hide to market and has nothing to expect but – a hiding.

PART III
THE PRODUCTION OF ABSOLUTE SURPLUS-VALUE

CHAPTER 7

THE LABOUR-PROCESS AND THE PROCESS OF PRODUCING SURPLUS-VALUE

SECTION 1. THE LABOUR-PROCESS OR THE PRODUCTION OF USE-VALUES

The capitalist buys labour-power in order to use it; and labour-power in use is labour itself. The purchaser of labour-power consumes it by setting the seller of it to work. By working, the latter becomes actually, what before he only was potentially, labour-power in action, a labourer. In order that his labour may re-appear in a commodity, he must, before all things, expend it on something useful, on something capable of satisfying a want of some sort. Hence, what the capitalist sets the labourer to produce, is a particular use-value, a specified article. The fact that the production of use-values, or goods, is carried on under the control of a capitalist and on his behalf does not alter the general character of that production. We shall, therefore, in the first place, have to consider the labour-process independently of the particular form it assumes under given social conditions.

Labour is, in the first place, a process in which both man and Nature participate, and in which man of his own accord starts, regulates, and controls the material re-actions between himself and Nature. He opposes himself to Nature as one of her own forces, setting in motion arms and legs, head and hands, the natural forces of his body, in order to appropriate Nature's productions in a form adapted to his own wants. By thus acting on the external world and changing it, he at the same time changes his own nature. He develops his slumbering powers and compels them to act in obedience to his sway. We are not now dealing with those primitive instinctive forms of labour that remind us of the mere animal. An immeasurable interval of time separates the state of things in which a man brings his labour-power to market for sale as a commodity, from that state in which human labour was still in its first instinctive stage. We presuppose labour in a form that stamps it as exclusively human. A spider conducts operations that resemble those of a weaver, and a bee puts to shame many an architect in the construction of her cells. But what distinguishes the worst architect from the best of bees is this, that the architect raises his structure in imagination before he erects it in reality. At the end of every labour-process, we get a result that already existed in the imagination of the labourer at its commencement. He not only effects a change of form in the material on which he works, but he also realises a purpose of his own that gives the law to his modus operandi, and to which he must subordinate his will. And this subordination is no mere momentary act. Besides the exertion of the bodily organs, the process demands that, during the whole operation, the workman's will be steadily in consonance with his purpose. This means close attention. The less he is attracted by the nature of the work, and the mode in which it is carried on, and the less, therefore, he enjoys it as something which gives play to his bodily and mental powers, the more close his attention is forced to be.

The elementary factors of the labour-process are (1) the personal activity of man, i.e. work itself, (2) the subject of that work, and (3) its instruments.

An instrument of labour is a thing, or a complex of things, which the labourer interposes between himself and the subject of his labour, and which serves as the conductor of his activity. He makes use of the mechanical, physical, and chemical properties of some substances in order to make other substances subservient to his aims. Leaving out of consideration such ready-made means of subsistence as fruits, in gathering which a man's own limbs serve as the instruments of his labour, the first thing of which the labourer possesses himself is not the subject of labour but its instrument. Thus Nature becomes one of the organs of his activity, one that he annexes to his own bodily organs, adding stature to himself in spite of the Bible. As the earth is his original larder, so too it is his original tool house. It supplies him, for instance, with stones for throwing, grinding, pressing, cutting, etc. The earth itself is an instrument of labour, but when used as such in agriculture implies a whole series of other instruments and a comparatively high development of labour. No sooner does labour undergo the least development, than it requires specially prepared instruments. Thus in the oldest caves we find stone implements and weapons. In the earliest period of human history domesticated animals, i.e. animals which have been bred for the purpose, and have undergone modifications by means of labour, play the chief part as instruments of labour along with specially prepared stones, wood, bones, and shells. The use and fabrication of instruments of labour, although existing in the germ among certain species of animals, is specifically characteristic of the human labour-process, and Franklin therefore defines man as a tool-making animal. Relics of bygone instruments of labour possess the same importance for the investigation of extinct economic forms of society, as do fossil bones for the determination of extinct species of animals. It is not the articles made, but how they are made, and by what instruments, that enables us to distinguish different economic epochs. Instruments of labour not only supply a standard of the degree of development to which human labour has attained, but they are also indicators of the social conditions under which that labour is carried on. Among the instruments of labour, those of a mechanical nature, which, taken as a whole, we may call the bone and muscles of production, offer much more decided characteristics of a given epoch of production, than those which, like pipes, tubs, baskets, jars, etc., serve only to hold the materials for labour, which latter class, we may in a general way, call the vascular system of production. The latter first begins to play an important part in the chemical industries.

In a wider sense we may include among the instruments of labour, in addition to those things that are used for directly transferring labour to its subject, and which therefore, in one way or another, serve as conductors of activity, all such objects as are necessary for carrying on the labour-process. These do not enter directly into the process, but without them it is either impossible for it to take place at all, or possible only to a partial extent. Once more we find the earth to be a universal instrument of this sort, for it furnishes a locus standi to the labourer and a field of employment for his activity. Among instruments that are the result of previous labour and also belong to this class, we find workshops, canals, roads, and so forth.

In the labour-process, therefore, man's activity, with the help of the instruments of labour, effects an alteration, designed from the commencement, in the material worked upon. The process disappears in the product; the latter is a use-value, Nature's material adapted by a change of form to the wants of man. Labour has incorporated itself with its subject: the former is materialised, the latter transformed. That which in the labourer appeared as movement, now appears in the product as a fixed quality without motion. The blacksmith forges and the product is a forging.

If we examine the whole process from the point of view of its result, the product, it is plain that both the instruments and the subject of labour, are means of production, and that the labour itself is productive labour. (This method of determining, from the standpoint of the labour-process alone, what is productive labour, is by no means directly applicable to the case of the capitalist process of production.)

Though a use-value, in the form of a product, issues from the labour-process, yet other use-values, products of previous labour, enter into it as means of production. The same use-value is both the product of a previous process, and a means of production in a later process. Products are therefore not only results, but also essential conditions of labour.

With the exception of the extractive industries, in which the material for labour is provided immediately by Nature, such as mining, hunting, fishing, and agriculture (so far as the latter is confined to breaking up virgin soil), all branches of industry manipulate raw material, objects already filtered through labour, already products of labour. Such is seed in agriculture. Animals and plants, which we are accustomed to consider as products of Nature, are in their present form, not only products of, say last year's labour, but the result of a gradual transformation, continued through many generations, under man's superintendence, and by means of his labour. But in the great majority of cases, instruments of labour show even to the most superficial observer, traces of the labour of past ages.

A product, though ready for immediate consumption, may yet serve as raw material for a further product, as grapes when they become the raw material for wine. On the other hand, labour may give us its product in such a form, that we can use it only as raw material, as in the case with cotton, thread, and yarn. Such a raw material, though itself a product, may have to go through a whole series of different processes: in each of these in turn, it serves, with constantly varying form, as raw material, until the last process of the series leaves it a perfect product, ready for individual consumption, or for use as an instrument of labour.

Hence we see that whether a use-value is to be regarded as raw material, as instrument of labour, or as product, this is determined entirely by its function in the labour-process, by the position it there occupies: as this varies, so does its character.

Whenever therefore a product enters as a means of production into a new labour-process, it thereby loses its character of product, and becomes a mere factor in the process. A spinner treats spindles only as implements for spinning, and flax only as the material that he spins. Of course it is impossible to spin without material and spindles; and therefore the existence of these things as products, at the commencement of the spinning operation, must be presumed: but in the process itself, the fact that they are products of previous labour, is a matter of utter indifference; just as in the digestive process, it is of no importance whatever that bread is the produce of the previous labour of the farmer, the miller, and the baker. On the contrary, it is generally by their imperfections as products, that the means of production in any process assert themselves in their character of products. A blunt knife or weak thread forcibly remind us of Mr A, the cutler, or Mr B, the spinner. In the finished product the labour by means of which it has acquired its useful qualities is not palpable, has apparently vanished.

A machine which does not serve the purpose of labour is useless. In addition, it falls a prey to the destructive influence of natural forces. Iron rusts and wood rots. Yarn with which we neither weave nor knit is cotton wasted. Living labour must seize upon these things and rouse them from their death-sleep, change them from mere possible use-values into real and effective ones. Bathed in the fire of labour, appropriated as part and parcel of labour's organism, and, as it were, made alive for the performance of their functions in the process, they are in truth consumed, but consumed with a purpose, as elementary constituents of use-values, of new products, ever ready as means of subsistence for individual consumption, or as means of production for some new labour-process.

If then, on the one hand, finished products are not only results, but also necessary conditions, of the labour-process, on the other hand, their assumption into that process, their contact with living labour, is the sole means by which they can be made to retain their character of use-values, and be utilised.

Labour uses up its material factors, its subject and its instruments, consumes them, and is therefore a process of consumption. Such productive consumption is distinguished from individual consumption by this, that the latter uses up products, as means of subsistence for the living individual; the former, as means whereby alone, labour, the labour-power of the living individual, is enabled to act. The product, therefore, of individual consumption, is the consumer himself; the result of productive consumption is a product distinct from the consumer.

In so far then as its instruments and subjects are themselves products, labour consumes products in order to create products, or in other words, consumes one set of products by turning them into means of production for another set. But, just as in the beginning, the only participators in the labour-process were man and the earth, which latter exists independently of man, so even now we still employ in the process many means of production, provided directly by Nature, that do not represent any combination of natural substances with human labour.

The labour-process, resolved as above into its simple elementary factors, is human action with a view to the production of use-values, appropriation of natural substances to human requirements; it is the necessary condition for effecting exchange of matter between man and Nature; it is the everlasting Nature-imposed condition of human existence, and therefore is independent of every social phase of that existence, or rather, is common to every such phase. It was, therefore, not necessary to represent our labourer in connexion with other labourers; man and his labour on one side, Nature and its materials on the other, sufficed. As the taste of the porridge does not tell you who grew the oats, no more does this simple process tell you of itself what are the social conditions under which it is taking place, whether under the slave-owner's brutal lash, or the anxious eye of the capitalist, whether Cincinnatus carries it on in tilling his modest farm or a savage in killing wild animals with stones.

Let us now return to our would-be capitalist. We left him just after he had purchased, in the open market, all the necessary factors of the labour-process; its objective factors, the means of production, as well as its subjective factor, labour-power. With the keen eye of an expert, he has selected the means of production and the kind of labour-power best adapted to his particular trade, be it spinning, bootmaking, or any other kind. He then proceeds to consume the commodity, the labour-power that he has just bought, by causing the labourer, the impersonation of that labour-power, to consume the means of production by his labour. The general character of the labour-process is evidently not changed by the fact that the labourer works for the capitalist instead of for himself; moreover, the particular methods and operations employed in bootmaking or spinning are not immediately changed by the intervention of the capitalist. He must begin by taking the labour-power as he finds it in the market, and consequently be satisfied with labour of such a kind as would be found in the period immediately preceding the rise of capitalists. Changes in the methods of production by the subordination of labour to capital, can take place only at a later period, and therefore will have to be treated of in a later chapter.

The labour-process, turned into the process by which the capitalist consumes labour-power, exhibits two characteristic phenomena. First, the labourer works under the control of the capitalist to whom his labour belongs; the capitalist taking good care that the work is done in a proper manner, and that the means of production are used with intelligence, so that there is no unnecessary waste of raw material, and no wear and tear of the implements beyond what is necessarily caused by the work.

Secondly, the product is the property of the capitalist and not that of the labourer, its immediate producer. Suppose that a capitalist pays for a day's labour-power at its value; then the right to use that power for a day belongs to him, just as much as the right to use any other commodity, such as a horse that he has hired for the day. To the purchaser of a commodity belongs its use, and the seller of labour-power, by giving his labour, does no more, in reality, than part with the use-value that he has sold. From the instant he steps into the workshop, the use-value of his labour-power, and therefore also its use, which is labour, belongs to the capitalist. By the purchase of labour-power, the capitalist incorporates labour, as a living ferment, with the lifeless constituents of the product. From his point of view, the labour-process is nothing more than the consumption of the commodity purchased, i.e. of labour-power; but this consumption cannot be effected except by supplying the labour-power with the means of production. The labour-process is a process between things that the capitalist has purchased, things that have become his property. The product of this process belongs, therefore, to him, just as much as does the wine which is the product of a process of fermentation completed in his cellar.

SECTION 2. THE PRODUCTION OF SURPLUS-VALUE

The product appropriated by the capitalist is a use-value, as yarn, for example, or boots. But, although boots are, in one sense, the basis of all social progress, and our capitalist is a decided 'progressist', yet he does not manufacture boots for their own sake. Use-value is, by no means, the thing '*qu'on aime pour lui-même*' in the production of commodities. Use-values are only produced by capitalists, because, and in so far as, they are the material substratum, the depositories of exchange-value. Our capitalist has two objects in view: in the first place, he wants to produce a use-value that has a value in exchange, that is to say, an article destined to be sold, a commodity; and secondly, he desires to produce a commodity whose value shall be greater than the sum of the values of the commodities used in its production, that is, of the means of production and the labour-power, that he purchased with his good money in the open market. His aim is to produce not only a use-value, but a commodity also; not only use-value, but value; not only value, but at the same time surplus-value.

It must be borne in mind, that we are now dealing with the production of commodities, and that, up to this point, we have only considered one aspect of the process. Just as commodities are, at the same time, use-values and values, so the process of producing them must be a labour-process, and at the same time, a process of creating value.

Let us now examine production as a creation of value.

We know that the value of each commodity is determined by the quantity of labour expended on and materialised in it, by the working-time necessary, under given social conditions, for its production. This rule also holds good in the case of the product that accrued to our capitalist, as the result of the labour-process carried on for him. Assuming this product to be 10 lb of yarn, our first step is to calculate the quantity of labour realised in it.

For spinning the yarn, raw material is required; suppose in this case 10 lb of cotton. We have no need at present to investigate the value of this cotton, for our capitalist has, we will assume, bought it at its full value, say of ten shillings. In this price the labour required for the production of the cotton is already expressed in terms of the average labour of society. We will further assume that the wear and tear of the spindle, which, for our present purpose, may represent all other instruments of labour employed, amounts to the value of two shillings. If, then, twenty-four hours' labour, or two working days, are required to produce the quantity of gold represented by twelve shillings, we have here, to begin with, two days' labour already incorporated in the yarn.

We must not let ourselves be misled by the circumstance that the cotton has taken a new shape while the substance of the spindle has to a certain extent been used up. By the general law of value, if the value of 40 lb of yarn = the value of 40 lb of cotton plus the value of a whole spindle, i.e. if the same working-time is required to produce the commodities on either side of this equation, then 10 lb of yarn are an equivalent for 10 lb of cotton, together with one-fourth of a spindle. In the case we are considering the same working-time is materialised in the 10 lb of yarn on the one hand, and in the 10 lb of cotton and the fraction of a spindle on the other. Therefore, whether value appears in cotton, in a spindle, or in yarn, makes no difference in the amount of that value. The spindle and cotton, instead of resting quietly side by side, join together in the process, their forms are altered, and they are turned into yarn; but their value is no more affected by this fact than it would be if they had been simply exchanged for their equivalent in yarn.

The labour required for the production of the cotton, the raw material of the yarn, is part of the labour necessary to produce the yarn, and is therefore contained in the yarn. The same applies to the labour embodied in the spindle, without whose wear and tear the cotton could not be spun.

Hence, in determining the value of the yarn, or the labour-time required for its production, all the special processes carried on at various times and in different places, which were necessary, first to produce the cotton and the wasted portion of the spindle, and then with the cotton and spindle to spin the yarn, may together be looked on as different and successive phases of one and the same process. The whole of the labour in the yarn is past labour; and it is a matter of no importance that the operations necessary for the production of its constituent elements were carried on at times which, referred to the present, are more remote than the final operation of spinning. If a definite quantity of labour, say thirty days, is requisite to build a house, the total amount of labour incorporated in it is not altered by the fact that the work of the last day is done twenty-nine days later than that of the first. Therefore the labour contained in the raw material and the instruments of labour can be treated just as if it were labour expended in an earlier stage of the spinning process, before the labour of actual spinning commenced.

The values of the means of production, i.e. the cotton and the spindle, which values are expressed in the price of twelve shillings, are therefore constituent parts of the value of the yarn, or, in other words, of the value of the product.

Two conditions must nevertheless be fulfilled. First, the cotton and spindle must concur in the production of a use-value; they must in the present case become yarn. Value is independent of the particular use-value by which it is borne, but it must be embodied in a use-value of some kind. Secondly, the time occupied in the labour of production must not exceed the time really necessary under the given social conditions of the case. Therefore, if no more than 1 lb of cotton be requisite to spin 1 lb of yarn, care must be taken that no more than this weight of cotton is consumed in the production of 1 lb of yarn; and similarly with regard to the spindle. Though the capitalist have a hobby, and use a gold instead of steel spindle, yet the only labour that counts for anything in the value of the yarn is that which would be required to produce a steel spindle, because no more is necessary under the given social conditions.

We now know what portion of the value of the yarn is owing to the cotton and the spindle. It amounts to twelve shillings or the value of two days' work. The next point for our consideration is, what portion of the value of the yarn is added to the cotton by the labour of the spinner.

We have now to consider this labour under a very different aspect from that which it had during the labour-process; there, we viewed it solely as that particular kind of human activity which changes cotton into yarn; there, the more the labour was suited to the work, the better the yarn, other circumstances remaining the same. The labour of the spinner was then viewed as specifically different from other kinds of productive labour, different on the one hand in its special aim, viz., spinning, different, on the other hand, in the special character of its operations, in the special nature of its means of production and in the special use-value of its product. For the operation of spinning, cotton and spindles are a necessity, but for making rifled cannon they would be of no use whatever. Here, on the contrary, where we consider the labour of the spinner only so far as it is value-creating, i.e. a source of value, his labour differs in no respect from the labour of the man who bores cannon, or (what here more nearly concerns us), from the labour of the cotton-planter and spindle-maker incorporated in the means of production. It is solely by reason of this identity, that cotton planting, spindle making and spinning are capable of forming the component parts, differing only quantitatively from each other, of one whole, namely, the value of the yarn. Here, we have nothing more to do with the quality, the nature and the specific character of the labour, but merely with its quantity. And this simply requires to be calculated. We proceed upon the assumption that spinning is simple, unskilled labour, the average labour of a given state of society. Hereafter we shall see that the contrary assumption would make no difference.

While the labourer is at work, his labour constantly undergoes a transformation: from being motion, it becomes an object without motion; from being the labourer working, it becomes the thing produced. At the end of one hour's spinning, that act is represented by a definite quantity of yarn; in other words, a definite quantity of labour, namely that of one hour, has become embodied in the cotton.

We say labour, i.e. the expenditure of his vital force by the spinner, and not spinning labour, because the special work of spinning counts here only so far as it is the expenditure of labour-power in general, and not in so far as it is the specific work of the spinner.

In the process we are now considering it is of extreme importance that no more time be consumed in the work of transforming the cotton into yarn than is necessary under the given social conditions. If under normal, i.e. average social conditions of production, *a* pounds of cotton ought to be made into *b* pounds of yarn by one hour's labour, then a day's labour does not count as 12 hours' labour unless 12*a* pounds of cotton have been made into 12*b* pounds of yarn; for in the creation of value, the time that is socially necessary alone counts.

Not only the labour, but also the raw material and the product now appear in quite a new light, very different from that in which we viewed them in the labour-process pure and simple. The raw material serves now merely as an absorbent of a definite quantity of labour. By this absorption it is in fact changed into yarn, because it is spun, because labour-power in the form of spinning is added to it; but the product, the yarn, is now nothing more than a measure of the labour absorbed by the cotton. If in one hour 1⅔ lb of cotton can be spun into 1⅔ lb of yarn, then 10 lb of yarn indicate the absorption of 6 hours' labour. Definite quantities of product, these quantities being determined by experience, now represent nothing but definite quantities of labour, definite masses of crystallised labour-time. They are nothing more than the materialisation of so many hours or so many days of social labour.

We are here no more concerned about the facts, that the labour is the specific work of spinning, that its subject is cotton and its product yarn, than we are about the fact that the subject itself is already a product and therefore raw material. If the spinner, instead of spinning, were working in a coal mine, the subject of his labour, the coal, would be supplied by Nature; nevertheless, a definite quantity of extracted coal, a hundredweight for example, would represent a definite quantity of absorbed labour.

We assumed, on the occasion of its sale, that the value of a day's labour-power is three shillings, and that six hours' labour is incorporated in that sum; and consequently that this amount of labour is requisite to produce the necessaries of life daily required on an average by the labourer. If now our spinner by working for one hour, can convert 1⅔ lb of cotton into 1⅔ lb of yarn, it follows that in six hours he will convert 10 lb of cotton into 10 lb of yarn. Hence, during the spinning process, the cotton absorbs six hours' labour. The same quantity of labour is also embodied in a piece of gold of the value of three shillings. Consequently by the mere labour of spinning, a value of three shillings is added to the cotton.

Let us now consider the total value of the product, the 10 lb of yarn. Two and a half days' labour has been embodied in it, of which two days were contained in the cotton and in the substance of the spindle worn away, and half a day was absorbed during the process of spinning. This two and a half days' labour is also represented by a piece of gold of the value of fifteen shillings. Hence, fifteen shillings is an adequate price for the 10 lb of yarn, or the price of one pound is eighteen pence.

Our capitalist stares in astonishment. The value of the product is exactly equal to the value of the capital advanced. The value so advanced has not expanded, no surplus-value has been created, and consequently money has not been converted into capital. The price of the yarn is fifteen shillings, and fifteen shillings were spent in the open market upon the constituent elements of the product, or, what amounts to the same thing, upon the factors of the labour-process; ten shillings were paid for the cotton, two shillings for the substance of the spindle worn away, and three shillings for the labour-power. The swollen value of the yarn is of no avail, for it is merely the sum of the values formerly existing in the cotton, the spindle, and the labour-power: out of such a simple addition of existing values, no surplus-value can possibly arise. These separate values are now all concentrated in one thing; but so they were also in the sum of fifteen shillings, before it was split up into three parts, by the purchase of the commodities.

There is in reality nothing very strange in this result. The value of one pound of yarn being eighteen pence, if our capitalist buys 10 lb of yarn in the market, he must pay fifteen shillings for it. It is clear that, whether a man buys his house ready built, or gets it built for him, in neither case will the mode of acquisition increase the amount of money laid out on the house.

Our capitalist, who is at home in his vulgar economy, exclaims: 'Oh! but I advanced my money for the express purpose of making more money.' The way to hell is paved with good intentions, and he might just as easily have intended to make money, without producing at all. He threatens all sorts of things. He won't be caught napping again. In future he will buy the commodities in the market, instead of manufacturing them himself. But if all his brother capitalists were to do the same, where would he find his commodities in the market? And his money he cannot eat. He tries persuasion. 'Consider my abstinence; I might have played ducks and drakes with the 15 shillings; but instead of that I consumed it productively, and made yarn with it.' Very well, and by way of reward he is now in possession of good yarn instead of a bad conscience; and as for playing the part of a miser, it would never do for him to relapse into such bad ways as that; we have seen before to what results such asceticism leads. Besides, where nothing is, the king has lost his rights; whatever may be the merit of his abstinence, there is nothing wherewith specially to remunerate it, because the value of the product is merely the sum of the values of the commodities that were thrown into the process of production. Let him therefore console himself with the reflection that virtue is its own reward. But no, he becomes importunate. He says: 'The yarn is of no use to me: I produced it for sale.' In that case let him sell it, or, still better, let him for the future produce only things for satisfying his personal wants, a remedy that his physician MacCulloch has already prescribed as infallible against an epidemic of over-production. He now gets obstinate. 'Can the labourer,' he asks, 'merely with his arms and legs, produce commodities out of nothing? Did I not supply him with the materials, by means of which, and in which alone, his labour could be embodied? And as the greater part of society consists of such ne'er-do-wells, have I not rendered society incalculable service by my instruments of production, my cotton and my spindle, and not only society, but the labourer also, whom in addition I have provided with the necessaries of life? And am I to be allowed nothing in return for all this service?' Well, but has not the labourer rendered him the equivalent service of changing his cotton and spindle into yarn? Moreover, there is here no question of service. A service is nothing more than the useful effect of a use-value, be it of a commodity, or be it of labour. But here we are dealing with exchange-value. The capitalist paid to the labourer a value of three shillings, and the labourer gave him back an exact equivalent in the value of three shillings, added by him to the cotton: he gave him value for value. Our friend, up to this time so purse-proud, suddenly assumes the modest demeanour of his own workman, and exclaims: 'Have I myself not worked? Have I not performed the labour of superintendence and of overlooking the spinner? And does not this labour, too, create value?' His overlooker and his manager try to hide their smiles. Meanwhile, after a hearty laugh, he re-assumes his usual mien. Though he chanted to us the whole creed of the economists, in reality, he says, he would not give a brass farthing for it. He leaves this and all such like subterfuges and juggling tricks to the professors of Political Economy, who are paid for it. He himself is a practical man; and though he does not always consider what he says outside his business, yet in his business he knows what he is about.

Let us examine the matter more closely. The value of a day's labour-power amounts to three shillings, because on our assumption half a day's labour is embodied in that quantity of labour-power, i.e. because the means of subsistence that are daily required for the production of labour-power, cost half a day's labour. But the past labour that is embodied in the labour-power, and the living labour that it can call into action; the daily cost of maintaining it, and its daily expenditure in work, are two totally different things. The former determines the exchange-value of the labour-power, the latter is its use-value. The fact that half a day's labour is necessary to keep the labourer alive during 24 hours, does not in any way prevent him from working a whole day. Therefore, the value of labour-power, and the value which that labour-power creates in the labour-process, are two entirely different magnitudes; and this difference of the two values was what the capitalist had in view, when he was purchasing the labour-power. The useful qualities that labour-power possesses, and by virtue of which it makes yarn or boots, were to him nothing more than a *conditio sine qua non*; for in order to create value, labour must be expended in a useful manner. What really influenced him was the specific use-value which this commodity possesses of being *a source not only of value, but of more value than it has itself*. This is the special service that the capitalist expects from labour-power and in this transaction he acts in accordance with the 'eternal laws' of the exchange of commodities. The seller of labour-power, like the seller of any other commodity, realises its exchange-value, and parts with its use-value. He cannot take the one without giving the other. The use-value of labour-power, or in other words, labour, belongs just as little to its seller, as the use-value of oil after it has been sold belongs to the dealer who has sold it. The owner of the money has paid the value of a day's labour-power; his, therefore, is the use of it for a day; a day's labour belongs to him. The circumstance, that on the one hand the daily sustenance of labour-power costs only half a day's labour, while on the other hand the very same labour-power can work during a whole day, that consequently the value which its use during one day creates, is double what he pays for that use, this circumstance is, without doubt, a piece of good luck for the buyer, but by no means an injury to the seller.

Our capitalist foresaw this state of things, and that was the cause of his laughter. The labourer therefore finds, in the workshop, the means of production necessary for working, not only during six, but during twelve hours. Just as during the six hours' process our 10 lb of cotton absorbed six hours' labour, and became 10 lb of yarn, so now, 20 lb of cotton will absorb twelve hours' labour and be changed into 20 lb of yarn. Let us now examine the product of this prolonged process. There is now materialised in this 20 lb of yarn the labour of five days, of which four days are due to the cotton and the lost steel of the spindle, the remaining day having been absorbed by the cotton during the spinning process. Expressed in gold, the labour of five days is thirty shillings. This is therefore the price of the 20 lb of yarn, giving, as before, eighteen pence as the price of a pound. But the sum of the values of the commodities that entered into the process amounts to 27 shillings. The value of the yarn is 30 shillings. Therefore the value of the product is greater than the value advanced for its production; 27 shillings have been transformed into 30 shillings; a surplus-value of three shillings has been created. The trick has at last succeeded; money has been converted into capital.

Every condition of the problem is satisfied, while the laws that regulate the exchange of commodities, have been in no way violated. Equivalent has been exchanged for equivalent. For the capitalist as buyer paid for each commodity, for the cotton, the spindle and the labour-power, its full value. He then did what is done by every purchaser of commodities; he consumed their use-value. The consumption of the labour-power, which was also the process of producing commodities, resulted in 20 lb of yarn, having a value of 30 shillings. The capitalist, formerly a buyer, now returns to market as a seller, of commodities. He sells his yarn at eighteen pence a pound, which is its exact value. Yet for all that he withdraws three shillings more from circulation than he originally threw into it. This metamorphosis, this conversion of money into capital, takes place both within the sphere of circulation and also outside it; within the circulation, because conditioned by the purchase of the labour-power in the market; outside the circulation, because what is done within it is only a stepping-stone to the production of surplus-value, a process which is entirely confined to the sphere of production.

By turning his money into commodities that serve as the material elements of a new product, and as factors in the labour-process, by incorporating living labour with their dead substance, the capitalist at the same time converts value, i.e. past, materialised, and dead labour into capital, into value big with value, a live monster that is fruitful and multiplies.

If we now compare the two processes of producing value and of creating surplus-value, we see that the latter is nothing but the continuation of the former beyond a definite point. If on the one hand the process be not carried beyond the point, where the value paid by the capitalist for the labour-power is replaced by an exact equivalent, it is simply a process of producing value; if, on the other hand, it be continued beyond that point, it becomes a process of creating surplus-value.

If we proceed further, and compare the process of producing value with the labour-process, pure and simple, we find that the latter consists of the useful labour, the work, that produces use-values. Here we contemplate the labour as producing a particular article; we view it under its qualitative aspect alone, with regard to its end and aim. But viewed as a value-creating process, the same labour-process presents itself under its quantitative aspect alone. Here it is a question merely of the time occupied by the labourer in doing the work; of the period during which the labour-power is usefully expended. Here, the commodities that take part in the process, do not count any longer as necessary adjuncts of labour-power in the production of a definite, useful object. They count merely as depositories of so much absorbed or materialised labour; that labour, whether previously embodied in the means of production, or incorporated in them for the first time during the process by the action of labour-power, counts in either case only according to its duration; it amounts to so many hours or days as the case may be.

Moreover, only so much of the time spent in the production of any article is counted, as, under the given social conditions, is necessary. The consequences of this are various. In the first place, it becomes necessary that the labour should be carried on under normal conditions. If a self-acting mule is the implement in general use for spinning, it would be absurd to supply the spinner with a distaff and spinning wheel. The cotton too must not be such rubbish as to cause extra waste in being worked, but must be of suitable quality. Otherwise the spinner would be found to spend more time in producing a pound of yarn than is socially necessary, in which case the excess of time would create neither value nor money. But whether the material factors of the process are of normal quality or not, depends not upon the labourer, but entirely upon the capitalist. Then again, the labour-power itself must be of average efficacy. In the trade in which it is being employed, it must possess the average skill, handiness and quickness prevalent in that trade, and our capitalist took good care to buy labour-power of such normal goodness. This power must be applied with the average amount of exertion and with the usual degree of intensity; and the capitalist is as careful to see that this is done, as that his workmen are not idle for a single moment. He has bought the use of the labour-power for a definite period, and he insists upon his rights. He has no intention of being robbed. Lastly, and for this purpose our friend has a penal code of his own, all wasteful consumption of raw material or instruments of labour is strictly forbidden, because what is so wasted, represents labour superfluously expended, labour that does not count in the product or enter into its value.

(This is one of the circumstances that makes production by slave labour such a costly process. The labourer here is, to use a striking expression of the ancients, distinguishable only as *instrumentum vocale*, from an animal as *instrumentum semi-vocale*, and from an implement as *instrumentum mutum*. But he himself takes care to let both beast and implement feel that he is none of them, but is a man. He convinces himself with immense satisfaction, that he is a different being, by treating the one unmercifully and damaging the other *con amore*. Hence the principle, universally applied in this method of production, only to employ the rudest and heaviest implements and such as are difficult to damage owing to their sheer clumsiness. In the slave-states bordering on the Gulf of Mexico, down to the date of the civil war, ploughs constructed on old Chinese models, which turned up the soil like a hog or a mole, instead of making furrows, were alone to be found. In his *Sea Board Slave States*, Olmsted tells us:

> I am here shown tools that no man in his senses, with us, would allow a labourer, for whom he was paying wages, to be encumbered with; and the excessive weight and clumsiness of which, I would judge, would make work at least ten per cent greater than with those ordinarily used with us. And I am assured that, in the careless and clumsy way they must be used by the slaves, anything lighter or less rude could not be furnished them with good economy, and that such tools as we constantly give our labourers and find our profit in giving them, would not last out a day in a Virginia cornfield – much lighter and more free from stones though it be than ours. So, too, when I ask why mules are so universally substituted for horses on the farm, the first reason given, and confessedly the most conclusive one, is that horses cannot bear the treatment that they always must get from negroes; horses are always soon foundered or crippled by them, while mules will bear cudgelling, or lose a meal or two now and

then, and not be materially injured, and they do not take cold or get sick, if neglected or overworked. But I do not need to go further than to the window of the room in which I am writing, to see at almost any time, treatment of cattle that would ensure the immediate discharge of the driver by almost any farmer owning them in the North.)

We now see, that the difference between labour, considered on the one hand as producing utilities, and on the other hand, as creating value, a difference which we discovered by our analysis of a commodity, resolves itself into a distinction between two aspects of the process of production.

The process of production, considered on the one hand as the unity of the labour-process and the process of creating value, is production of commodities; considered on the other hand as the unity of the labour-process and the process of producing surplus-value, it is the capitalist process of production, or capitalist production of commodities.

We stated, on a previous page, that in the creation of surplus-value it does not in the least matter, whether the labour appropriated by the capitalist be simple unskilled labour of average quality or more complicated skilled labour. All labour of a higher or more complicated character than average labour is expenditure of labour-power of a more costly kind, labour-power whose production has cost more time and labour, and which therefore has a higher value, than unskilled or simple labour-power. This power being of higher value, its consumption is labour of a higher class, labour that creates in equal times proportionally higher values than unskilled labour does. Whatever difference in skill there may be between the labour of a spinner and that of a jeweller, the portion of his labour by which the jeweller merely replaces the value of his own labour-power does not in any way differ in quality from the additional portion by which he creates surplus-value. In the making of jewellery, just as in spinning, the surplus-value results only from a quantitative excess of labour, from a lengthening-out of one and the same labour-process, in the one case, of the process of making jewels, in the other of the process of making yarn.

But on the other hand, in every process of creating value, the reduction of skilled labour to average social labour, for example one day of skilled to six days of unskilled labour, is unavoidable. We therefore save ourselves a superfluous operation, and simplify our analysis, by the assumption, that the labour of the workman employed by the capitalist is unskilled average labour. (The distinction between skilled and unskilled labour rests in part on pure illusion, or, to say the least, on distinctions that have long since ceased to be real, and that survive only by virtue of a traditional convention; in part on the helpless condition of some groups of the working class, a condition that prevents them from exacting equally with the rest the value of their labour-power.)

CHAPTER 8

CONSTANT CAPITAL AND VARIABLE CAPITAL

The various factors of the labour-process play different parts in forming the value of the product.

The labourer adds fresh value to the subject of his labour by expending upon it a given amount of additional labour, no matter what the specific character and utility of that labour may be. On the other hand, the values of the means of production used up in the process are preserved, and present themselves afresh as constituent parts of the value of the product; the values of the cotton and the spindle, for instance, reappear again in the value of the yarn. The value of the means of production is therefore preserved, by being transferred to the product. This transfer takes place during the conversion of those means into a product, or in other words, during the labour-process. It is brought about by labour; but how?

The labourer does not perform two operations at once, one in order to add value to the cotton, the other in order to preserve the value of the means of production, or, what amounts to the same thing, to transfer to the yarn, to the product, the value of the cotton on which he works, and part of the value of the spindle with which he works. But, by the very act of adding new value, he preserves their former values. Since, however, the addition of new value to the subject of his labour, and the preservation of its former value, are two entirely distinct results, produced simultaneously by the labourer, during one operation, it is plain that this twofold nature of the result can be explained only by the twofold nature of his labour; at one and the same time, it must in one character create value, and in another character preserve or transfer value.

Now, in what matter does every labourer add new labour and consequently new value? Evidently, only by labouring productively in a particular way; the spinner by spinning, the weaver by weaving, the smith by forging. But, while thus incorporating labour generally, that is value, it is by the particular form alone of the labour, by the spinning, the weaving and the forging respectively, that the means of production, the cotton and spindle, the yarn and loom, and the iron and anvil become constituent elements of the product, of a new use-value. Each use-value disappears, but only to reappear under a new form in a new use-value. Now, we saw, when we were considering the process of creating value, that, if a use-value be effectively consumed in the production of a new use-value, the quantity of labour expended in the production of the consumed article forms a portion of the quantity of labour necessary to produce the new use-value; this portion is therefore labour transferred from the means of production to the new product. Hence the labourer preserves the values of the consumed means of production, or transfers them as portions of its value to the product, not by virtue of his additional labour, abstractedly considered, but by virtue of the particular useful character of that labour, by virtue of its special productive form. In so far then as labour is such specific productive activity, in so far as it is spinning, weaving, or forging, it raises, by mere contact, the means of production from the dead, makes them living factors of the labour-process, and combines with them to form the new products.

If the special productive labour of the workman were not spinning, he could not convert the cotton into yarn, and therefore could not transfer the values of the cotton and spindle to the yarn. Suppose the same workman were to change his occupation to that of a joiner, he would still by a day's labour add value to the material he works upon. Consequently, we see, first, that the addition of new value takes place not by virtue of his labour being spinning in particular, or joinering in particular, but because it is labour in the abstract, a portion of the total labour of society; and we see next, that the value added is of a given definite amount, not because his labour has a special utility, but because it is exerted for a definite time. On the one hand, then, it is by virtue of its general character, as being expenditure of human labour-power in the abstract, that spinning adds new value to the values of the cotton and the spindle; and on the other hand, it is by virtue of its special character, as being a concrete, useful process, that the same labour of spinning both transfers the values of the means of production to the product, and preserves them in the product. Hence at one and the same time there is produced a two-fold result.

By the simple addition of a certain quantity of labour, new value is added, and by the quality of this added labour, the original values of the means of production are preserved in the product. This twofold effect, resulting from the twofold character of labour, may be traced in various phenomena.

Let us assume, that some invention enables the spinner to spin as much cotton in 6 hours as he was able to spin before in 36 hours. His labour is now six times as effective as it was, for the purposes of useful production. The product of 6 hours' work has increased six-fold, from 6 lb to 36 lb. But now the 36 lb of cotton absorb only the same amount of labour as formerly did the 6 lb. One-sixth as much new labour is absorbed by each pound of cotton, and consequently, the value added by the labour to each pound is only one-sixth of what it formerly was. On the other hand, in the product, in the 36 lb of yarn, the value transferred from the cotton is six times as great as before. By the 6 hours' spinning, the value of the raw material preserved and transferred to the product is six times as great as before, although the new value added by the labour of the spinner to each pound of the very same raw material is one-sixth what it was formerly. This shows that the two properties of labour, by virtue of which it is enabled in one case to preserve value, and in the other to create value, are essentially different. On the one hand, the longer the time necessary to spin a given weight of cotton into yarn, the greater is the new value added to the material; on the other hand, the greater the weight of the cotton spun in a given time, the greater is the value preserved, by being transferred from it to the product.

Let us now assume that the productiveness of the spinner's labour, instead of varying, remains constant, that he therefore requires the same time as he formerly did, to convert one pound of cotton into yarn, but that the exchange-value of the cotton varies, either by rising to six times its former value or falling to one-sixth of that value. In both these cases, the spinner puts the same quantity of labour into a pound of cotton, and therefore adds as much value, as he did before the change in the value: he also produces a given weight of yarn in the same time as he did before. Nevertheless, the value that he transfers from the cotton to the yarn is either one-sixth of what it was before the variation or, as the case may be, six times as much as before. The same result occurs when the value of the instruments of labour rises or falls, while their useful efficacy in the process remains unaltered.

Again, if the technical conditions of the spinning process remain unchanged, and no change of value takes place in the means of production, the spinner continues to consume in equal working-time equal quantities of raw material, and equal quantities of machinery of unvarying value. The value that he preserves in the product is directly proportional to the new value that he adds to the product. In two weeks he incorporates twice as much labour, and therefore twice as much value, as in one week, and during the same time he consumes twice as much material, and wears out twice as much machinery, of double the value in each case; he therefore preserves, in the product of two weeks, twice as much value as in the product of one week. So long as the conditions of production remain the same, the more value the labourer adds by fresh labour, the more value he transfers and preserves; but he does so merely because this addition of new value takes place under conditions that have not varied and are independent of his own labour. Of course, it may be said in one sense, that the labourer preserves old value always in proportion to the quantity of new value that he adds. Whether the value of cotton rise from one shilling to two shillings, or fall to sixpence, the workman invariably preserves in the product of one hour only one half as much value as he preserves in two hours. In like manner, if the productiveness of his own labour varies by rising or falling, he will in one hour spin either more or less cotton, as the case may be, than he did before, and will consequently preserve in the product of one hour, more or less value of cotton; but, all the same, he will preserve by two hours' labour twice as much value as he will by one.

Value exists only in articles of utility, in objects: we leave out of consideration its purely symbolical representation by tokens. (Man himself, viewed as the impersonation of labour-power, is a natural object, a thing, although a living conscious thing, and labour is the manifestation of this power residing in him.) If therefore an article loses its utility, it also loses its value. The reason why means of production do not lose their value, at the same time that they lose their use-value, is this: they lose in the labour-process the original form of their use-value, only to assume in the product the form of a new use-value. But, however important it may be to value, that it should have some object of utility to embody itself in, yet it is a matter of complete indifference what particular object serves this purpose; this we saw when treating of the metamorphosis of commodities. Hence it follows that in the labour-process the means of production transfer their value to the product only so far as along with their use-value they lose also their exchange-value. They give up to the product that value alone which they themselves lose as means of production. But in this respect the material factors of the labour-process do not all behave alike.

The coal burnt under the boiler vanishes without leaving a trace; so, too, the tallow with which the axles of wheels are greased. Dye stuffs and other auxiliary substances also vanish but reappear as properties of the product. Raw material forms the substance of the product, but only after it has changed its form. Hence raw material and auxiliary substances lose the characteristic form with which they are clothed on entering the labour-process. It is otherwise with the instruments of labour. Tools, machines, workshops, and vessels, are of use in the labour-process, only so long as they retain their original shape, and are ready each morning to renew the process with their shape unchanged. And just as during their lifetime, that is to say, during the continued labour-process in which they serve, they retain their shape independent of the product, so, too, they do after their death. The corpses of machines, tools, workshops, etc. are always separate and distinct from the product they helped to turn out. It we now consider the case of any instrument of labour during the whole period of its service, from the day of its entry into the workshop, till the day of its banishment into the lumber room, we find that during this period its use-value has been completely consumed, and therefore its exchange-value completely transferred to the product. For instance, if a spinning machine lasts for ten years, it is plain that during that working period its total value is gradually transferred to the product of the ten years. The lifetime of an instrument of labour, therefore, is spent in the repetition of a greater or less number of similar operations. Its life may be compared with that of a human being. Every day brings a man 24 hours nearer to his grave: but how many days he has still to travel on that road, no man can tell accurately by merely looking at him. This difficulty, however, does not prevent life insurance offices from drawing, by means of the theory of averages, very accurate, and at the same time very profitable conclusions. So it is with the instruments of labour. It is known by experience how long on the average a machine of a particular kind will last. Suppose its use-value in the labour-process to last only six days. Then, on the average, it loses each day one-sixth of its use-value, and therefore parts with one-sixth of its value to the daily product. The wear and tear of all instruments, their daily loss of use-value, and the corresponding quantity of value they part with to the product, are accordingly calculated upon this basis.

It is thus strikingly clear, that means of production never transfer more value to the product than they themselves lose during the labour-process by the destruction of their own use-value. If such an instrument has no value to lose, if, in other words, it is not the product of human labour, it transfers no value to the product. It helps to create use-value without contributing to the formation of exchange-value. In this class are included all means of production supplied by Nature without human assistance, such as land, wind, water, metals in situ, and timber in virgin forests.

Yet another interesting phenomenon here presents itself. Suppose a machine to be worth £1,000, and to wear out in 1,000 days. Then one thousandth part of the value of the machine is daily transferred to the day's product. At the same time, though with diminishing vitality, the machine as a whole continues to take part in the labour-process. Thus it appears, that one factor of the labour-process, a means of production, continually enters as a whole into that process, while it enters into the process of the formation of value by fractions only. The difference between the two processes is here reflected in their material factors, by the same instrument of production taking part as a whole in the labour-process, while at the same time as an element in the formation of value, it enters only by fractions.

We have seen that the means of production transfer value to the new product, so far only as during the labour-process they lose value in the shape of their old use-value. The maximum loss of value that they can suffer in the process, is plainly limited by the amount of the original value with which they came into the process, or in other words, by the labour-time necessary for their production. Therefore, the means of production can never add more value to the product than they themselves possess independently of the process in which they assist. However useful a given kind of raw material, or a machine, or other means of production may be, though it may cost £150, or, say, 500 days' labour, yet it cannot, under any circumstances, add to the value of the product more than £150. Its value is determined not by the labour-process into which it enters as a means of production, but by that out of which it has issued as a product. In the labour-process it only serves as a mere use-value, a thing with useful properties, and could not, therefore, transfer any value to the product, unless it possessed such value previously.

While productive labour is changing the means of production into constituent elements of a new product, their value undergoes a metempsychosis. It deserts the consumed body, to occupy the newly created one. But this transmigration takes place, as it were, behind the back of the labourer. He is unable to add new labour, to create new value, without at the same time preserving old values, and this, because the labour he adds must be of a specific useful kind; and he cannot do work of a useful kind, without employing products as the means of production of a new product, and thereby transferring their value to the new product. The property therefore which labour-power in action, living labour, possesses of preserving value, at the same time that it adds it, is a gift of Nature which costs the labourer nothing, but which is very advantageous to the capitalist inasmuch as it preserves the existing value of his capital. So long as trade is good, the capitalist is too much absorbed in money-grubbing to take notice of this gratuitous gift of labour. A violent interruption of the labour-process by a crisis makes him sensitively aware of it.

As regards the means of production, what is really consumed is their use-value, and the consumption of this use-value by labour results in the product. There is no consumption of their value, and it would therefore be inaccurate to say that it is reproduced. It is rather preserved; not by reason of any operation it undergoes itself in the process; but because the article in which it originally exists, vanishes, it is true, but vanishes into some other article. Hence, in the value of the product, there is a reappearance of the value of the means of production, but there is, strictly speaking, no reproduction of that value. That which is produced is a new use-value in which the old exchange-value reappears.

It is otherwise with the subjective factor of the labour-process, with labour-power in action. While the labourer, by virtue of his labour being of a specialised kind that has a special object, preserves and transfers to the product the value of the means of production, he at the same time, by the mere act of working, creates each instant an additional or new value. Suppose the process of production to be stopped just when the workman has produced an equivalent for the value of his own labour-power, when, for example, by six hours' labour, he has added a value of three shillings. This value is the surplus of the total value of the product, over the portion of its value that is due to the means of production. It is the only original bit of value formed during this process, the only portion of the value of the product created by this process. Of course, we do not forget that this new value only replaces the money advanced by the capitalist in the purchase of the labour-power, and spent by the labourer on the necessaries of life. With regard to the money spent, the new value is merely a reproduction; but, nevertheless, it is an actual, and not, as in the case of the value of the means of production, only an apparent, reproduction. The substitution of one value for another is here effected by the creation of new value.

We know, however, from what has gone before, that the

labour-process may continue beyond the time necessary to reproduce and incorporate in the product a mere equivalent for the value of the labour-power. Instead of the six hours that are sufficient for the latter purpose, the process may continue for twelve hours. The action of labour-power, therefore, not only reproduces its own value, but produces value over and above it. This surplus-value is the difference between the value of the product and the value of the elements consumed in the formation of that product, in other words, of the means of production and the labour-power.

By our explanation of the different parts played by the various factors of the labour-process in the formation of the product's value, we have, in fact, disclosed the characters of the different functions allotted to the different elements of capital in the process of expanding its own value. The surplus of the total value of the product, over the sum of the values of its constituent factors, is the surplus of the expanded capital over the capital originally advanced. The means of production on the one hand, labour-power on the other, are merely the different modes of existence which the value of the original capital assumed when from being money it was transformed into the various factors of the labour-process. That part of capital then, which is represented by the means of production, by the raw material, auxiliary material and the instruments of labour, does not, in the process of production, undergo any quantitative alteration of value. I therefore call it the constant part of capital, or, more shortly, *constant capital.*

On the other hand, that part of capital represented by labour-power, does, in the process of production, undergo an alteration of value. It both reproduces the equivalent of its own value, and also produces an excess, a surplus-value, which may itself vary, may be more or less according to circumstances. This part of capital is continually being transformed from a constant into a variable magnitude. I therefore call it the variable part of capital, or, shortly, *variable capital.* The same elements of capital which, from the point of view of the labour-process, present themselves respectively as the objective and subjective factors, as means of production and labour-power, present themselves, from the point of view of the process of creating surplus-value, as constant and variable capital.

The definition of constant capital given above by no means excludes the possibility of a change of value in its elements. Suppose the price of cotton to be one day sixpence a pound, and the next day, in consequence of a failure of the cotton crop, a shilling a pound. Each pound of the cotton bought at sixpence, and worked up after the rise in value, transfers to the product a value of one shilling; and the cotton already spun before the rise, and perhaps circulating in the market as yarn, likewise transfers to the product twice its original value. It is plain, however, that these changes of value are independent of the increment or surplus-value added to the value of the cotton by the spinning itself. If the old cotton had never been spun, it could, after the rise, be resold at a shilling a pound instead of at sixpence. Further, the fewer the processes the cotton has gone through, the more certain is this result. We therefore find that speculators make it a rule when such sudden changes in value occur, to speculate in that material on which the least possible quantity of labour has been spent: to speculate, therefore, in yarn rather than in cloth, in cotton itself, rather than in yarn. The change of value in the case we have been considering, originates, not in the process in which the cotton plays the part of a means of production, and in which it therefore functions as constant capital, but in the process in which the cotton itself is produced. The value of a commodity, it is true, is determined by the quantity of labour contained in it, but this quantity is itself limited by social conditions. If the time socially necessary for the production of any commodity alters – and a given weight of cotton represents, after a bad harvest, more labour than after a good one – all previously existing commodities of the same class are affected, because they are, as it were, only individuals of the species, and their value at any given time is measured by the labour socially necessary, i.e. by the labour necessary for their production under the then existing social conditions.

As the value of the raw material may change, so, too, may that of the instruments of labour, of the machinery, etc. employed in the process; and consequently that portion of the value of the product transferred to it from them, may also change. If in consequence of a new invention, machinery of a particular kind can be produced by a diminished expenditure of labour, the old machinery becomes depreciated more or less, and consequently transfers so much less value to the product. But here again, the change in value originates outside the process in which the machine is acting as a means of production. Once engaged in this process, the machine cannot transfer more value than it possesses apart from the process.

Just as a change in the value of the means of production, even after they have commenced to take a part in the labour-process, does not alter their character as constant capital, so, too, a change in the proportion of constant to variable capital does not affect the respective functions of these two kinds of capital. The technical conditions of the labour-process may be revolutionised to such an extent that where formerly ten men using ten implements of small value worked up a relatively small quantity of raw material, one man may now, with the aid of one expensive machine, work up one hundred times as much raw material. In the latter case we have an enormous increase in the constant capital, that is represented by the total value of the means of production used, and at the same time a great reduction in the variable capital, invested in labour-power. Such a revolution, however, alters only the quantitative relation between the constant and the variable capital, or the proportions in which the total capital is split up into its constant and variable constituents; it has not in the least degree affected the essential difference between the two.

CHAPTER 9

THE RATE OF SURPLUS-VALUE

The surplus-value generated in the process of production by C, the capital advanced, or in other words, the self-expansion of the value of the capital C, presents itself for our consideration in the first place as a surplus, as the amount by which the value of the product exceeds the value of its constituent elements.

The capital C is made up of two components, one, the sum of money c laid out upon the means of production, and the other, the sum of money v expended upon the labour-power; c represents the portion that has become constant capital, and v the portion that has become variable capital. At first then, C = c+v: for example, if £500 is the capital advanced, its components may be such that the £500 = £410 const. + £90 var. When the process of production is finished, we get a commodity whose value = (c+v)+s, where s is the surplus-value; or taking our former figures, the value of this commodity may be (£410 const. + £90 var.) + £90 surpl. The original capital has now changed from C to C′, from £500 to £590. The difference is s or a surplus-value of £90. Since the value of the constituent elements of the product is equal to the value of the advanced capital, it is mere tautology to say that the excess of the value of the product over the value of its constituent elements, is equal to the expansion of the capital advanced or to the surplus-value produced.

Nevertheless, we must examine that tautology a little more closely. The two things compared are the value of the product and the value of its constituents consumed in the process of production. Now we have seen how that portion of the constant capital which consists of the instruments of labour, transfers to the production only a fraction of its value, while the remainder of that value continues to reside in those instruments. Since this remainder plays no part in the formation of value, we may at present leave it on one side. Throughout this book therefore, by constant capital advanced for the production of value we always mean, unless the context is repugnant thereto, the value of the means of production actually consumed in the process, and that value alone.

This being so, let us return to the formula C = c+v, which we saw was transformed into C′ = (c+v)+s, C becoming C′. We know that the value of the constant capital is transferred to, and merely reappears in the product. The new value actually created in the process, the value produced, or value-product, is therefore not the same as the value of the product; it is not, as it would at first sight appear (c+v)+s or £410 const. + £90 var. + £90 surpl.; but v+s or £90 var. + £90 surpl., not £590 but £180. If c = 0, or in other words, if there were branches of industry in which the capitalist could dispense with all means of production made by previous labour, employing only labour-power and materials supplied by Nature, in that case, there would be no constant capital to transfer to the product. This component of the value of the product, i.e. the £410 in our example, would be eliminated, but the sum of £180, the amount of new value created, or the value produced, which contains £90 of surplus-value, would remain just as great as if c represented the highest value imaginable. We should have C = (0+v) = v or C′ the expanded capital = v+s and therefore C′−C = s as before. On the other hand, if s = 0, or in other words, if the labour-power, whose value is advanced in the form of variable capital, were to produce only its equivalent, we should have C = c+v or C′ the value of the product = (c+v)+0 or C = C′. The capital advanced would, in this case, not have expanded its value.

From what has gone before, we know that surplus-value is purely the result of a variation in the value of v, of that portion of the capital which is transformed into labour-power; consequently, v+s = v+v′ or v plus an increment of v. But the fact that it is v alone that varies, and the conditions of that variation, are obscured by the circumstance that in consequence of the increase in the variable component of the capital, there is also an increase in the sum total of the advanced capital. It was originally £500 and becomes £590. Therefore in order that our investigation may lead to accurate results, we must make abstraction from that portion of the value of the product in which constant capital alone appears, and consequently must equate the constant capital to zero or make c = 0. This is merely an application of a mathematical rule, employed whenever we operate with constant and variable magnitudes, related to each other by the symbols of addition and subtraction only.

A further difficulty is caused by the original form of the variable capital. In our example, C′ = £410 const. + £90 var. + £90 surpl.; but £90 is a given and therefore a constant quantity; hence it appears absurd to treat it as variable. But in fact, the term £90 var. is here merely a symbol to show that this value undergoes a process. The portion of the capital invested in the purchase of labour-power is a definite quantity of materialised labour, a constant value like the value of the labour-power purchased. But in the process of production the place of the £90 is taken by the labour-power in action, dead labour is replaced by living labour, something stagnant by something flowing, a constant by a variable. The result is the reproduction of v plus an increment of v. From the point of view then of capitalist production, the whole process appears as the spontaneous variation of the originally constant value, which is transformed into labour-power. Both the process and its result appear to be owing to this value. If, therefore, such expressions as '£90 variable capital,' or 'so much self-expanding value', appear contradictory, this is only because they bring to the surface a contradiction immanent in capitalist production.

At first sight it appears a strange proceeding, to equate the constant capital to zero. Yet it is what we do every day. If, for example, we wish to calculate the amount of England's profits from the cotton industry, we first of all deduct the sums paid for cotton to the United States, India, Egypt and other countries; in other words, the value of the capital that merely reappears in the value of the product, is put = 0.

Of course the ratio of surplus-value not only to that portion of the capital from which it immediately springs, and whose change of value it represents, but also to the sum total of the capital advanced is economically of very great importance. We shall, therefore, in the third book, treat of this ratio exhaustively. In order to enable one portion of a capital to expand its value by being converted into labour-power, it is necessary that another portion be converted into means of production. In order that variable capital may perform its function, constant capital must be advanced in proper proportion, a proportion given by the special technical conditions of each labour-process. The circumstance, however, that retorts and other vessels are necessary to a chemical process, does not compel the chemist to notice them in the result of his analysis. If we look at the means of production in their relation to the creation of value, and to the variation in the quantity of value, apart from anything else, they appear simply as the material in which labour-power, the value-creator, incorporates itself. Neither the nature, nor the value of this material is of any importance. The only requisite is that there be a sufficient supply to absorb the labour expended in the process of production. That supply once given, the material may rise or fall in value, or even be, as land and the sea, without any value in itself; but this will have no influence on the creation of value or on the variation in the quantity of value.

In the first place then we equate the constant capital to zero. The capital advanced is consequently reduced from c+v to v, and instead of the value of the product (c+v)+s we have now the value produced (v+s). Given the new value produced = £180, which sum consequently represents the whole labour expended during the process, then subtracting from it £90, the value of the variable capital, we have remaining £90, the amount of the surplus-value. This sum of £90 or s expresses the absolute quantity of surplus-value produced. The relative quantity produced, or the increase per cent of the variable capital, is determined, it is plain, by the ratio of the surplus-value to the variable capital, or is expressed by $^{s}/_{v}$. In our example this ratio is $^{90}/_{90}$, which gives an increase of 100 per cent. This relative increase in the value of the variable capital, or the relative magnitude of the surplus-value, I call 'the rate of surplus-value'.

We have seen that the labourer, during one portion of the labour-process, produces only the value of his labour-power, that is, the value of his means of subsistence. Now since his work forms part of a system, based on the social division of labour, he does not directly produce the actual necessaries which he himself consumes; he produces instead a particular commodity, yarn for example, whose value is equal to the value of those necessaries or of the money with which they can be bought. The portion of his day's labour devoted to this purpose, will be greater or less, in proportion to the value of the necessaries that he daily requires on an average, or, what amounts to the same thing, in proportion to the labour-time required on an average to produce them. If the value of those necessaries represent on an average the expenditure of six hours' labour, the workman must on an average work for six hours to produce that value. If instead of working for the capitalist, he worked independently on his own account, he would, other things being equal, still be obliged to labour for the same number of hours, in order to produce the value of his labour-power, and thereby to gain the means of subsistence necessary for his conservation or continued reproduction. But as we have seen, during that portion of his day's labour in which he produces the value of his labour-power, say three shillings, he produces only an equivalent for the value of his labour-power already advanced by the capitalist; the new value created only replaces the variable capital advanced. It is owing to this fact that the production of the new value of three shillings takes the semblance of a mere reproduction. That portion of the working day, then, during which this reproduction takes place, I call necessary labour-time and the labour expended during that time I call necessary labour. Necessary, as regards the labourer, because independent of the particular social form of his labour; necessary, as regards capital, and the world of capitalists, because on the continued existence of the labourer depends their existence also.

During the second period of the labour-process, that in which his labour is no longer necessary labour, the workman, it is true, labours, expends labour-power; but his labour, being no longer necessary labour, he creates no value for himself. He creates surplus-value which, for the capitalist, has all the charms of a creation out of nothing. This portion of the working-day, I name *surplus* labour-time, and to the labour expended during that time, I give the name of *surplus-labour*. It is every bit as important, for a correct understanding of surplus-value, to conceive it as a mere congelation of surplus labour-time, as nothing but materialised surplus-labour, as it is, for a proper comprehension of value, to conceive it as a mere congelation of so many hours of labour, as nothing but materialised labour. The essential difference between the various economic forms of society, between, for instance a society based on slave-labour and one based on wage-labour, lies only in the mode in which this surplus-labour is in each case extracted from the actual producer, the labourer.

Since, on the one hand, the values of the variable capital and of the labour-power purchased by that capital are equal, and the value of this labour-power determines the necessary portion of the working day; and since, on the other hand, the surplus-value is determined by the surplus portion of the working day, it follows that surplus-value bears the same ratio to variable capital that surplus-labour does to necessary labour, or in other words, the rate of surplus-value $^{s}/_{v} = \frac{\text{surplus–labour}}{\text{necessary labour}}$ Both ratios, $^{s}/_{v}$ and $\frac{\text{surplus–labour}}{\text{necessary labour}}$ express the same thing in different ways; in the one case by reference to materialised, incorporated labour, in the other by reference to living, fluent labour.

The rate of surplus-value is therefore an exact expression for the degree of exploitation of labour-power by capital, or of the labourer by the capitalist.

CHAPTER 10

THE WORKING DAY

SECTION 1. THE LIMITS OF THE WORKING DAY

We started with the supposition that labour-power is bought and sold at its value. Its value, like that of all other commodities, is determined by the working-time necessary to its production. If the production of the average daily means of subsistence of the labourer takes up 6 hours, he must work, on the average, 6 hours every day, to produce his daily labour-power, or to reproduce the value received as the result of its sale. The necessary part of his working day amounts to 6 hours, and is, therefore, *caeteris paribus*, a given quantity. But with this, the extent of the working day itself is not yet given.

Let us assume that the line A B represents the length of the necessary working-time, say 6 hours. If the labour be prolonged 1, 3, or 6 hours beyond A B, we have 3 other lines:

6 1	6 3	6 6
Working day(i)	Working day(ii)	Working day(iii)
A——B—C.	A——B——C.	A———B———C

representing three different working days of 7, 9, and 12 hours. The extension BC of the line AB represents the length of the surplus-labour. As the working day is AB+BC or AC, it varies with the variable quantity BC. Since AB is constant, the ratio of BC to AB can always be calculated. In working day (i) it is $\frac{1}{6}$, in working day (ii), $\frac{3}{6}$, in working day (iii), $\frac{6}{6}$ of AB. Since, further, the ratio

$$\frac{\text{surplus working-time}}{\text{necessary working-time}}$$

determines the rate of the surplus-value, the latter is given by the ratio of BC to AB. It amounts in the three different working days respectively to 16⅔, 50 and 100 per cent. On the other hand, the rate of surplus-value alone would not give us the extent of the working day. If this rate, e.g. were 100 per cent, the working day might be of 8, 10,

12, or more hours. It would indicate that the two constituent parts of the working day, necessary-labour and surplus-labour time, were equal in extent, but not how long each of these two constituent parts was.

The working day is thus not a constant, but a variable quantity. One of its parts, certainly, is determined by the working-time required for the reproduction of the labour-power of the labourer himself. But its total amount varies with the duration of the surplus-labour. The working day is, therefore, determinable, but is, *per se*, indeterminate.

Although the working day is not a fixed, but a fluent quantity, it can, on the other hand, only vary within certain limits. The minimum limit is, however, not determinable; of course, if we make the extension line BC or the surplus-labour = 0, we have a minimum limit, i.e. the part of the day which the labourer must necessarily work for his own maintenance. On the basis of capitalist production, however, this necessary labour can form a part only of the working day; the working day itself can never be reduced to this minimum. On the other hand, the working day has a maximum limit. It cannot be prolonged beyond a certain point. This maximum limit is conditioned by two things. First, by the physical bounds of labour-power. Within the 24 hours of the natural day a man can expend only a definite quantity of his vital force. A horse, in like manner, can only work from day to day, eight hours. During part of the day this force must rest, sleep; during another part the man has to satisfy other physical needs, to feed, wash, and clothe himself. Besides these purely physical limitations, the extension of the working day encounters moral ones. The labourer needs time for satisfying his intellectual and social wants, the extent and number of which are conditioned by the general state of social advancement. The variation of the working day fluctuates, therefore, within physical and social bounds. But both these limiting conditions are of a very elastic nature, and allow the greatest latitude. So we find working days of 8, 10, 12, 14, 16, 18 hours, i.e. of the most different lengths.

The capitalist has bought the labour-power at its day-rate. To him its use-value belongs during one working day. He has thus acquired the right to make the labourer work for him during one day. But what is a working day?

At all events, less than a natural day. By how much? The capitalist has his own views of this *ultima Thule*, the necessary limit of the working day. As capitalist, he is only capital personified. His soul is the soul of capital. But capital has one single life impulse, the tendency to create value and surplus-value, to make its constant factor, the means of production, absorb the greatest possible amount of surplus-labour.

Capital is dead labour, that, vampire-like, only lives by sucking living labour, and lives the more, the more labour it sucks. The time during which the labourer works is the time during which the capitalist consumes the labour-power he has purchased of him.

We see then, that, apart from extremely elastic bounds, the nature of the exchange of commodities itself imposes no limit to the working day, no limit to surplus-labour. The capitalist maintains his rights as a purchaser when he tries to make the working day as long as possible, and to make, whenever possible, two working days out of one. On the other hand, the peculiar nature of the commodity sold implies a limit to its consumption by the purchaser, and the labourer maintains his right as seller when he wishes to reduce the working day to one of definite normal duration. There is here, therefore, an antimony, right against right, both equally bearing the seal of the law of exchanges. Between equal rights force decides. Hence is it that in the history of capitalist production the determination of what is a working day, presents itself as the result of a struggle, a struggle between collective capital, i.e. the class of capitalists, and collective labour, i.e. the working class.

SECTION 2. THE GREED FOR SURPLUS-LABOUR

Capital has not invented surplus-labour. Wherever a part of society possesses the monopoly of the means of production, the labourer, free or not free, must add to the working-time necessary for his own maintenance an extra working-time in order to produce the means of subsistence for the owners of the means of production, whether this proprietor be the Athenian aristocrat, Etruscan theocrat, civis Romanus, Norman baron, American slave-owner, Wallachian Boyar, modern landlord or capitalist. It is, however, clear that in any given economic formation of society, where not the exchange-value but the use-value of the product predominates, surplus-labour will be limited by a given set of wants which may be greater or less, and that here no boundless thirst for surplus-labour arises from the nature of the production itself. Hence in antiquity overwork becomes horrible only when the object is to obtain exchange-value in its specific independent money-form; in the production of gold and silver. Compulsory working to death is here the recognised form of overwork. Still these are exceptions in antiquity. But as soon as people, whose production still moves within the lower forms of slave-labour, *corvee*-labour, etc. are drawn into the whirlpool of an international market dominated by the capitalistic mode of production, the sale of their products for export becoming their principal interest, the civilised horrors of overwork are grafted on the barbaric horrors of slavery, serfdom, etc. Hence the negro labour in the southern States of the American Union preserved something of a patriarchal character, so long as production was chiefly directed to immediate local consumption. But in proportion, as the export of cotton became of vital interest to these states, the overworking of the negro and sometimes the using up of his life in seven years of labour became a factor in a calculated and calculating system. It was no longer a question of obtaining from him a certain quantity of useful products. It was now a question of production of surplus-labour itself.

English Factory Acts curb the passion of capital for a limitless draining of labour-power by forcibly limiting the working day by state regulations, made by a state that is ruled by capitalist and landlord. Apart from the working-class movement that daily grew more threatening, the limiting of factory labour was dictated by the same necessity which spread guano over the English fields. The same blind eagerness for plunder that in the one case exhausted the soil, had, in the other, torn up by the roots the living force of the nation. Periodical epidemics speak on this point as clearly as the diminishing military standard in Germany and France.

The Factory Act of 1850 now in force (1867) allows for the average working day 10 hours, i.e. for the first 5 days 12 hours from 6 a.m. to 6 p.m., including half an hour for breakfast, and an hour for dinner, and thus leaving 10½ working hours, and 8 hours for Saturday, from 6 a.m. to 2 p.m., of which half an hour is subtracted for breakfast. 60 working hours are left, 10½ for each of the first 5 days, 7½ for the last. Certain guardians of these laws are appointed, Factory Inspectors, directly under the Home Secretary, whose reports are published half-yearly, by order of Parliament. They give regular and official statistics of the capitalistic greed for surplus-labour.

Let us listen, for a moment, to the Factory Inspectors.

> The fraudulent mill-owner begins work a quarter of an hour (sometimes more, sometimes less) before 6 a.m., and leaves off a quarter of an hour (sometimes more, sometimes less) after 6 p.m. He takes 5 minutes from the beginning and from the end of the half hour nominally allowed for breakfast, and 10 minutes at the beginning and end of the hour nominally allowed for dinner. He works for a quarter of an hour (sometimes more,

> sometimes less) after 2 p.m. on Saturday. Thus his gain is 5 hours and 40 minutes weekly, which multiplied by 50 working weeks in the year (allowing two for holidays and occasional stoppages) is equal to 27 working days.
>
> Five minutes a day's increased work, multiplied by weeks, are equal to two and a half days of produce in the year.
>
> An additional hour a day gained by small instalments before 6 a.m., after 6 p.m., and at the beginning and end of the times nominally fixed for meals, is nearly equivalent to working 13 months in the year.
>
> The profit to be gained by it (over-working in violation of the Act) appears to be, to many, a greater temptation than they can resist; they calculate upon the chance of not being found out; and when they see the small amount of penalty and costs, which those who have been convicted have had to pay, they find that if they should be detected there will still be a considerable balance of gain. . . . In cases where the additional time is gained by a multiplication of small thefts in the course of the day, there are insuperable difficulties to the inspectors making out a case.

These 'small thefts' of capital from the labourer's meal and recreation time, the factory inspectors also designate as 'petty pilferings of minutes', 'snatching a few minutes', or, as the labourers technically called them, 'nibbling and cribbling at meal-times'.

It is evident that in this atmosphere the formation of surplus-value by surplus-labour, is no secret. 'If you allow me', said a highly respectable master to me, 'to work only ten minutes in the day over-time, you put one thousand a year in my pocket'. 'Moments are the elements of profit.'

Nothing is from this point of view more characteristic than the designation of the workers who work full time as 'full-timers', and the children under 13 who are only allowed to work six hours as 'half-timers'. The worker is here nothing more than personified labour-time. All individual distinctions are merged in those of 'full-timers' and 'half-timers'.

SECTION 3. BRANCHES OF ENGLISH INDUSTRY WITHOUT LEGAL LIMITS TO EXPLOITATION

We have hitherto considered the tendency to the extension of the working day, the were-wolf's hunger for surplus-labour in a department where the monstrous exactions, not surpassed, says an English bourgeois economist, by the cruelties of the Spaniards to the American red-skins, caused capital at last to be bound by the chains of legal regulations. Now let us cast a glance at certain branches of production in which the exploitation of labour is either free from fetters to this day, or was so yesterday.

Mr Broughton Charlton, county magistrate, declared, as chairman of a meeting held at the Assembly Rooms, Nottingham, on 14 January 1860,

> that there was an amount of privation and suffering among that portion of the population connected with the lace trade unknown in other parts of the kingdom, indeed, in the civilized world.... Children of nine or ten years are dragged from their squalid beds at two, three, or four o'clock in the morning and compelled to work for a bare subsistence until ten, eleven, or twelve at night, their limbs wearing away, their frames dwindling, their faces whitening, and their humanity absolutely sinking into a stone-like torpor, utterly horrible to contemplate.... We are not surprised that Mr Mallett, or any other manufacturer, should stand forward and protest against discussion.... The system, as the Rev. Montagu Valpy describes it, is one of unmitigated slavery, socially, physically, morally, and spiritually.... What can be thought of a town which holds a public meeting to petition that the period of labour for men shall be diminished to eighteen hours a day? ... We declaim against the Virginian and Carolinian cotton-planters. Is their black-market, their lash, and their barter of human flesh more detestable than this slow sacrifice of humanity which takes place in order that veils and collars may be fabricated for the benefit of capitalists?

The potteries of Staffordshire have, during the last 22 years, been the subject of three parliamentary inquiries. The result is embodied in Mr Scriven's Report of 1841 to the Children's Employment Commissioners, in the report of Dr Greenhow of 1860 published by order of the medical officer of the Privy Council (*Public Health, Third Report*, 112-113), lastly, in the report of Mr Longe of 1862 in the *First Report of the Children's Employment Commission, of the 13th June, 1863*. For my purpose it is enough to take, from the reports of 1860 and 1863, some depositions of the exploited children themselves. From the children we may form an opinion as to the adults, especially the girls and women, and that in a branch of industry by the side of which cotton-spinning appears an agreeable and healthful occupation.

William Wood, nine years old, was seven years and ten months when he began to work. He 'ran moulds' (carried ready-moulded articles into the drying-room, afterwards bringing back the empty mould) from the beginning. He came to work every day in the week at 6 a.m., and left off about 9 p.m. 'I work till nine o'clock at night six days in the week. I have done so seven or eight weeks.' 15 hours of labour for a child seven years old! J. Murray, twelve years of age, says:

I turn jigger, and run moulds. I come at six. Sometimes I come at four. I worked all night last night, till six o'clock this morning. I have not been in bed since the night before last. There were eight or nine other boys working last night. All but one have come this morning. I get three shillings and sixpence. I do not get any more for working at night. I worked two nights last week.

Fernyhough, a boy of ten: 'I have not always an hour (for dinner). I have only half an hour sometimes; on Thursday, Friday, and Saturday.'

Dr Greenhow states that the average duration of life in the pottery districts of Stoke-on-Trent, and Wolstanton is extraordinarily short. Although in the district of Stoke, only 36.6 per cent and in Wolstanton only 30.4 per cent of the adult male population above 20 are employed in the potteries, among the men of that age in the first district more than half, in the second, nearly of the whole deaths are the result of pulmonary diseases among the potters. Dr Boothroyd, a medical practitioner at Hanley, says: 'Each successive generation of potters is more dwarfed and less robust than the preceding one.' In like manner another doctor, Mr M'Bean: 'Since he began to practise among the potters 25 years ago, he had observed a marked degeneration especially shown in diminution of stature and breadth.'

Dr J.T. Arledge, senior physician of the North Staffordshire Infirmary, says:

The potters as a class, both men and women, represent a degenerated population, both physically and morally. They are, as a rule, stunted in growth, ill-shaped, and frequently ill-formed in the chest; they become prematurely old, and are certainly short-lived; they are phlegmatic and bloodless, and exhibit their debility of constitution by obstinate attacks of dyspepsia, and disorders of the liver and kidneys, and by rheumatism. But of all diseases they are especially prone to chest-disease, to pneumonia, phthisis, bronchitis, and asthma. One form would appear peculiar to them, and is known as potter's asthma, or potter's consumption. Scrofula attacking the glands, or bones, or other parts of the body, is a disease of two-thirds or more of the potters . . . That the 'degenerescence' of the population of this district is not even greater than it is, is due to the constant recruiting from the adjacent country, and intermarriages with more healthy races.

Mr Charles Parsons, late house surgeon of the same institution, writes in a letter to Commissioner Longe, amongst other things:

I can only speak from personal observation and not from statistical data, but I do not hesitate to assert that my indignation has been aroused again and again at the sight of poor children whose health has been sacrificed to gratify the avarice of either parents or employers.

He enumerates the causes of the diseases of the potters, and sums them up in the phrase 'long hours'. The report of the Commission trusts that

> a manufacture which has assumed so prominent a place in the whole world, will not long be subject to the remark that its great success is accompanied with the physical deterioration, widespread bodily suffering, and early death of the workpeople . . . by whose labour and skill such great results have been achieved.

And all that holds of the potteries in England is true of those in Scotland.

The manufacture of lucifer matches dates from 1833, from the discovery of the method of applying phosphorus to the match itself. Since 1845 this manufacture has rapidly developed in England, and has extended especially amongst the thickly populated parts of London as well as in Manchester, Birmingham, Liverpool, Bristol, Norwich, Newcastle and Glasgow. With it has spread the form of lockjaw, which a Vienna physician in 1845 discovered to be a disease peculiar to lucifer-matchmakers. Half the workers are children under thirteen, and young persons under eighteen. The manufacture is on account of its unhealthiness and unpleasantness in such bad odour that only the most miserable part of the labouring class, half-starved widows and so forth, deliver up their children to it, 'the ragged, half-starved, untaught children'.

Of the witnesses that Commissioner White examined (1863), 270 were under 18, 50 under 10, 10 only 8, and 5 only 6 years old. A range of the working day from 12 to 14 or 15 hours, night-labour, irregular meal-times, meals for the most part taken in the very workrooms that are pestilent with phosphorus. Dante would have found the worst horrors of his Inferno surpassed in this manufacture.

In the manufacture of paper-hangings the coarser sorts are printed by machine; the finer by hand (block-printing). The most active business months are from the beginning of October to the end of April. During this time the work goes on fast and furious without intermission from six a.m. to ten p.m. or further into the night.

J. Leach deposes: 'Last winter six out of nineteen girls, were away from ill-health at one time from over-work. I have to bawl at them to keep them awake.' W. Duffy: 'I have seen when the children could none of them keep their eyes open for the work; indeed, none of us could.' J. Lightbourne: 'Am 13 . . . We worked last winter till 9 (evening), and the winter before till 10. I used to cry with sore feet every night last winter.' G. Apsden:

> That boy of mine . . . when he was seven years old I used to carry him on my back to and fro through the snow, and he used to have 16 hours a day . . . I have often knelt down to feed him as he stood by the machine, for he could not leave it or stop.

Smith, the managing partner of a Manchester factory:

> We [he means his 'hands' who work for 'us'] work on, with no stoppage for meals, so that day's work of 10½ hours is finished by 4.30 p.m., and all after that is over-time. [Does this Mr Smith take no meals himself during 10½ hours?] We [this same Smith] seldom leave off working before 6 p.m. [he means leave off the consumption of 'our' labour-power machines], so that we [iterum Crispinus] are really working over-time the whole year round. . . . For all these, children and adults alike (152 children and young persons and 140 adults), the average work for the last 18 months has been at the very least 7 days, 5 hours, or 78½ hours a week. For the six weeks ending May 2nd this year (1862), the average was higher – 8 days or 84 hours a week.

Still this same Mr Smith, who is so extremely devoted to the *pluralis majestatis*, adds with a smile, 'Machine-work is not great.' So the employers in the block-printing say: 'Hand labour is more healthy than machine-work.' On the whole, manufacturers declare with indignation against the proposal 'to stop the machines at least during meal-times.' A clause says Mr Otley, manager of a wall-paper factory in the Borough,

> which allowed work between, say 6 a.m. and 9 p.m. . . . would suit us [!] very well, but the factory hours, 6 a.m. to 6 p.m., are not suitable. Our machine is always stopped for dinner. [What generosity!] There is no waste of paper and colour to speak of.

'But', he adds sympathetically, 'I can understand the loss of time not being liked.' The report of the Commission opines with *naïveté* that the fear of some 'leading firms' of losing time, i.e. the time for appropriating the labour of others, and thence losing profit is not a sufficient reason for allowing children under 13, and young persons under 18, working 12 to 16 hours per day, to lose their dinner, nor for giving it to them as coal and water are supplied to the steam-engine, soap to wool, oil to the wheel – as merely auxiliary material to the instruments of labour, during the process of production itself.

From the motley crowd of labourers of all callings, ages, sexes, that press on us more busily than the souls of the slain on Ulysses, on whom – without referring to the Blue Books under their arms – we see at a glance the mark of over-work, let us take two more figures whose striking contrast proves that before capital all men are alike – a milliner and a blacksmith.

In the last week of June 1863, all the London daily papers published a paragraph with the 'sensational' heading, 'Death from simple over-work'. It dealt with the death of the milliner, Mary Anne Walkley, 20 years of age, employed in a highly-respectable dressmaking establishment, exploited by a lady with the pleasant name of Elise. The old, often-told story, was once more recounted. The girl worked, on an average, 16½ hours, during the season often 30 hours, without a break, whilst her failing labour-power was revived by occasional supplies of sherry, port, or coffee. It was just now the height of the season. It was necessary to conjure up in the twinkling of an eye the gorgeous dresses for the noble ladies bidden to the ball in honour of the newly-imported Princess of Wales. Mary Anne Walkley had worked without intermission for 26½ hours, with 60 other girls, 30 in one room, that only afforded ⅓ of the cubic feet of air required for them. At night, they slept in pairs in one of the stifling holes into which the bedroom was divided by partitions of board. And this was one of the best millinery establishments in London. Mary Anne Walkley fell ill on the Friday, died on Sunday, without, to the astonishment of Madame Elise, having previously completed the work in hand. The doctor, Mr Keys, called too late to the death-bed, duly bore witness before the coroner's jury that 'Mary Anne Walkley had died from long hours of work in an over-crowded work-room, and a too small and badly-ventilated bedroom.' In order to give the doctor a lesson in good manners, the coroner's jury thereupon brought in a verdict that 'the deceased had died of apoplexy, but there was reason to fear that her death had been accelerated by over-work in an over-crowded work-room, etc.' 'Our white slaves,' cried the *Morning Star*, the organ of the Free-traders, Cobden and Bright, 'our white slaves, who are toiled into the grave, for the most part silently pine and die.'

> It is not only in dressmaker's rooms that working to death is the order of the day, but in a thousand other places; in every place I had almost said, where 'a thriving business' has to be done. . . . We will take the blacksmith as a type. If the poets were true, there is no man so hearty, so merry, as the blacksmith; he rises early and strikes his sparks before the sun; he eats and drinks and sleeps as no other man. Working in moderation, he is, in fact, in one of the best of human positions, physically speaking. But we follow him into the city or town, and we see the stress of work on that strong man, and what then is his position in the death-rate of his country. In Marylebone, blacksmiths die at the rate of 31 per thousand per annum, or 11 above the mean of the male adults of the country in its entirety. The occupation, instinctive almost as a portion of

human art, unobjectionable as a branch of human industry, is made by mere excess of work, the destroyer of the man. He can strike so many blows per day, walk so many steps, breathe so many breaths, produce so much work, and live an average, say of fifty years; he is made to strike so many more blows, to walk so many more steps, to breathe so many more breaths per day, and to increase altogether a fourth of his life. He meets the effort; the result is, that producing for a limited time a fourth more work, he dies at 37 for 50 (Dr Richardson).

SECTION 4. DAY AND NIGHT WORK. THE RELAY SYSTEM

Constant capital, the means of production, considered from the standpoint of the creation of surplus-value, only exist to absorb labour, and with every drop of labour a proportional quantity of surplus-labour. While they fail to do this, their mere existence causes a relative loss to the capitalist, for they represent during the time they lie fallow, a useless advance of capital. And this loss becomes positive and absolute as soon as the intermission of their employment necessitates additional outlay at the recommencement of work. The prolongation of the working day beyond the limits of the natural day, into the night, only acts as a palliative. It quenches only in a slight degree the vampire thirst for the living blood of labour. To appropriate labour during all the 24 hours of the day is, therefore, the inherent tendency of capitalist production. But as it is physically impossible to exploit the same individual labour-power constantly during the night as well as the day, to overcome this physical hindrance an alternation becomes necessary between the workpeople whose powers are exhausted by day, and those who are used up by night. This alternation may be effected in various ways; for example it may be so arranged that part of the workers are one week employed on day-work, the next week on night-work. It is well known that this relay system, this alternation of two sets of workers, held full sway in the full-blooded youth-time of the English cotton manufacture, and that at the present time it still flourishes, among others, in the cotton spinning of the Moscow district. This 24 hours' process of production exists today as a system in many of the branches of industry of Great Britain that are still 'free', in the blast-furnaces, forges, plate-rolling mills, and other metallurgical establishments in England, Wales, and Scotland. The working-time here includes, besides the 24 hours of the 6 working days, a great part also of the 24 hours of Sunday. The workers consist of men and women, adults and children of both sexes. The ages of the children and young persons run through all intermediate grades, from 8 (in some cases from 6) to 18.

Mr J. Ellis, one of the firm of Messrs John Brown & Co., steel and iron works, employing about 3,000 men and boys, part of whose operations, namely, iron and heavier steel work, goes on night and day by relays, states 'that in the heavier steel work one or two boys are employed to a score or two men'. Their concern employs upwards of 500 boys under 18, of whom about one third or 170 are under the age of 13. With reference to the proposed alteration of the law, Mr Ellis says:

> I do not think it would be very objectionable to require that no person under the age of 18 should work more than 12 hours in the 24. But we do not think that any line could be drawn over the age of 12, at which boys could be dispensed with for night-work. But we would sooner be prevented from employing boys under the age of 13, or even so high as 14, at all, than not be allowed to employ boys that we do have at night. Those boys who work in the day sets must take their turn in the night sets also, because the men could not work in the night sets only; it would ruin their health. . . . We think, however, that night-work in alternate weeks is no harm. [Messrs Naylor & Vickers, on the other hand, in conformity with the interest of their business, considered that periodically changed night-labour might possibly do more harm than continual night-labour.] We find the men who do it, as well [healthy] as the others who do other work only by day. . . . Our objections to not allowing boys under 18 to work at night, would be on account of the increase of expense, but this is the only reason. [What cynical *naïveté*!] We think that the increase would be more than the trade, with due regard to its being successfully carried out, could fairly bear. [What mealy-mouthed phraseology!] Labour is scarce here, and might fall short if there were such a regulation.

i.e. Ellis, Brown & Co. might fall into the fatal perplexity of being obliged to pay labour-power its full value.

The Cyclops Steel and Iron Works of Messrs Cammel & Co., are conducted on the same large scale as those of the above-mentioned John Brown & Co. The managing director had handed in his evidence to the Government Commissioner Mr White in writing. Later he found it convenient to suppress the MS when it had been returned to him for revision. Mr White, however, has a good memory. He remembered quite clearly that for the Messrs Cyclops the forbidding of the night-labour of children and young persons 'would be impossible, it would be tantamount to stopping their works', and yet their business employs little more than 6 per cent of boys under 18, and less than 1 per cent under 13.

On the same subject Mr E.F. Sanderson, of the firm of Sanderson

Bros & Co., steel rolling-mills and forges, Attercliffe, says:

> Great difficulty would be caused by preventing boys under 18 from working at night. The chief would be the increase of cost from employing men instead of boys. I cannot say what this would be, but probably it would not be enough to enable the manufacturers to raise the price of steel, and consequently it would fall on them, as of course the men [what queer-headed folk!] would refuse to pay it.

Mr Sanderson does not know how much he pays the children, but

> perhaps the younger boys get from 4s. to 5s. a week. . . . The boys' work is of a kind for which the strength of the boys is generally ['generally,' of course not always] quite sufficient, and consequently there would be no gain in the greater strength of the men to counterbalance the loss, or it would be only in the few cases in which the metal is heavy. The men would not like so well not to have boys under them, as men would be less obedient. Besides, boys must begin young to learn the trade. Leaving day-work alone open to boys would not answer this purpose.

And why not? Why could not boys learn their handicraft in the day-time? Your reason?

> Owing to the men working days and nights in alternate weeks, the men would be separated half the time from their boys, and would lose half the profit which they make from them. The training which they give to an apprentice is considered as part of the return for the boys' labour, and thus enables the man to get it at a cheaper rate. Each man would want half of this profit.

In other words, Messrs Sanderson would have to pay part of the wages of the adult men out of their own pockets instead of by the night-work of the boys. Messrs Sanderson's profit would thus fall to some extent, and this is the good Sandersonian reason why boys cannot learn their handicraft in the day. In addition to this, it would throw night-labour on those who worked instead of the boys, which they would not be able to stand. The difficulties in fact would be so great that they would very likely lead to the giving up of night-work altogether, and 'as far as the work itself is concerned', says E.F. Sanderson, 'this would suit as well, but –'. But Messrs Sanderson have something else to make besides steel. Steel-making is simply a pretext for surplus-value making. The smelting furnaces, rolling-mills, etc., the buildings, machinery, iron, coal, etc. have something more to do than transform themselves into steel. They are there to absorb surplus-labour, and naturally absorb more in 24 hours than in 12. In fact they give, by grace of God and law, the Sandersons a cheque on the working-time of a certain number of hands for all the 24 hours of the day, and they lose their character as capital, are therefore a pure loss for the Sandersons, as soon as their function of absorbing labour is interrupted.

> But then there would be the loss from so much expensive machinery, lying idle half the time, and to get through the amount of work which we are able to do on the present system, we should have to double our premises and plant, which would double the outlay.

But why should these Sandersons pretend to a privilege not enjoyed by the other capitalists who only work during the day, and whose buildings, machinery, raw material, therefore lie 'idle' during the night? E.F. Sanderson answers in the name of all the Sandersons:

> It is true that there is this loss from machinery lying idle in those manufactories in which work only goes on by day. But the use of furnaces would involve a further loss in our case. If they were kept up there would be a waste of fuel [instead of, as now, a waste of the living substance of the workers], and if they were not, there would be loss of time in laying the fires and getting the heat up [whilst the loss of sleeping time, even to children of 8 is a gain of working-time for the Sanderson tribe], and the furnaces themselves would suffer from the changes of temperature. [Whilst those same furnaces suffer nothing from the day and night change of labour.]

SECTION 5. THE STRUGGLE FOR A NORMAL WORKING DAY

'What is a working day? What is the length of time during which capital may consume the labour-power whose daily value it buys? How far may the working day be extended beyond the working-time necessary for the reproduction of labour-power itself?' It has been seen that to these questions capital replies: the working day contains the full 24 hours, with the deduction of the few hours of repose without which labour-power absolutely refuses its services again. Hence it is self-evident that the labourer is nothing else, his whole life through, than labour-power, that therefore all his disposable time is by nature and law labour-time, to be devoted to the self-expansion of capital. Time for education, for intellectual development, for the fulfilling of social functions and for social intercourse, for the free play of his bodily and mental activity, even the rest time of Sunday (and that in a country of Sabbatarians!) – moonshine! But in its blind unrestrainable passion, its were-wolf hunger for surplus-labour, capital oversteps not only the moral, but even the merely physical maximum bounds of the working day. It usurps the time for growth, development, and healthy maintenance of the body. It steals the time required for the consumption of fresh air and sunlight. It higgles over a mealtime, incorporating it where possible with the process of production itself, so that food is given to the labourer as to a mere means of production, as coal is supplied to the boiler, grease and oil to the machinery. It reduces the sound sleep needed for the restoration, reparation, refreshment of the bodily powers to just so many hours of torpor as the revival of an organism, absolutely exhausted, renders essential. It is not the normal maintenance of the labour-power which is to determine the limits of the working-day; it is the greatest possible daily expenditure of labour-power, no matter how diseased, compulsory, and painful it may be, which is to determine the limits of the labourers' period of repose. Capital cares nothing for the length of life of labour-power. All that concerns it is simply and solely the maximum of labour-power that can be rendered fluent in a working day. It attains this end by shortening the extent of the labourer's life, as a greedy farmer snatches increased produce from the soil by robbing it of its fertility.

The capitalistic mode of production (essentially the production of surplus-value, the absorption of surplus-labour), produces thus, with the extension of the working day, not only the deterioration of human labour-power by robbing it of its normal, moral and physical, conditions of development and function. It produces also the premature exhaustion and death of this labour-power itself. It extends the labourer's time of production during a given period by shortening his actual lifetime.

But the value of the labour-power includes the value of the commodities necessary for the reproduction of the worker, or for the keeping up of the working class. If then the unnatural extension of the working day, that capital necessarily strives after in its unmeasured passion for self-expansion, shortens the length of life of the individual labourer, and therefore the duration of his labour-power, the forces used up have to be replaced at a more rapid rate and the sum of the expenses for the reproduction of labour-power will be greater; just as in a machine the part of its value to be reproduced every day is greater the more rapidly the machine is worn out. It would seem therefore that the interest of capital itself points in the direction of a normal working day.

The slave-owner buys his labourer as he buys his horse. If he loses his slave, he loses capital that can only be restored by new outlay in the slave-mart. But

> the rice-grounds of Georgia, or the swamps of the Mississippi may be fatally injurious to the human constitution; but the waste of human life which the cultivation of these districts necessitates, is not so great that it cannot be repaired from the teeming preserves of Virginia and Kentucky. Considerations of economy, moreover, which, under a natural system, afford some security for humane treatment by identifying the master's interest with the slave's preservation, when once trading in slaves is practised, become reasons for racking to the uttermost the toil of the slave; for, when his place can at once be supplied from foreign preserves, the duration of his life becomes a matter of less moment than its productiveness while it lasts. It is accordingly a maxim of slave management, in slave-importing countries, that the most effective economy is that which takes out of the human chattel in the shortest space of time the utmost amount of exertion it is capable of putting forth. It is in tropical culture, where annual profits often equal the whole capital of plantations, that negro life is most recklessly sacrificed. It is the agriculture of the West Indies, which has been for centuries prolific of fabulous wealth, that has engulfed millions of the African race. It is in Cuba, at this day, whose revenues are reckoned by millions, and whose planters are princes, that we see in the service class, the coarsest fare, the most exhausting and unremitting toil, and even the absolute destruction of a portion of its numbers every year. (Cairnes, *The Slave Power*, pp. 110–11.)

For slave-trade read labour market, for Kentucky and Virginia, Ireland and the agricultural districts of England, Scotland, and Wales, for Africa, Germany. We heard how over-work thinned the ranks of the bakers in London. Nevertheless, the London labour market is always over-stocked with German and other candidates for death in the bakeries. Pottery, as we saw, is one of the shortest-lived industries. Is there any want therefore of potters? Josiah Wedgwood, the inventor of modern pottery, himself originally a common workman, said in 1785 before the House of Commons that the whole trade employed from 15,000 to 20,000 people. In the year 1861 the population alone of the town centres of this industry in Great Britain numbered 101,302. 'The cotton trade has existed for ninety years. . . . It has existed for three generations of the English race, and I believe I may safely say that during that period it has destroyed nine generations of factory operatives.' (Ferrand's Speech in the House of Commons, 27 April, 1863.)

No doubt in certain epochs of feverish activity the labour market shows significant gaps. In 1834, for example. But then the manufacturers proposed to the Poor Law Commissioners that they should send the 'surplus-population' of the agricultural districts to the north, with the explanation 'that the manufacturers would absorb and use it up.'

> Agents were appointed with the consent of the Poor Law Commissioners. . . . An office was set up in Manchester, to which lists were sent of those workpeople in the agricultural districts wanting employment, and their names were registered in books. The manufacturers attended at these offices, and selected such persons as they chose; when they had selected such persons as their 'wants required', they gave instructions to have them forwarded to Manchester, and they were sent, ticketed like bales of goods, by canals, or with carriers, others tramping on the road, and many of them were found on the way lost and half-starved. This system had grown up into a regular trade. This House will hardly believe it, but I tell them, that this traffic in human flesh was as well kept up, they were in effect as regularly sold to these [Manchester] manufacturers as slaves are sold to the cotton-grower in the United States. . . . In 1860, 'the cotton trade was at its zenith'. . . . The manufacturers again found that they were short of hands. . . . They applied to the 'flesh agents', as they are called. Those agents sent to the southern downs of England, to the pastures of Dorsetshire, to the glades of Devonshire, to the people tending kine in Wiltshire, but they sought in vain. The surplus-population was 'absorbed'.

The *Bury Guardian* said, on the completion of the French treaty, that '10,000 additional hands could be absorbed by Lancashire, and that 30,000 or 40,000 will be needed.' After the 'flesh agents and sub-agents' had in vain sought through the agricultural districts, 'a deputation came up to London, and waited on the right hon. gentleman [Mr Villiers, President of the Poor Law Board] with a view of obtaining poor children from certain union houses for the mills of Lancashire.'

What experience shows to the capitalist generally is a constant excess of population, i.e. an excess in relation to the momentary requirements of surplus-labour-absorbing capital, although this excess is made up of generations of human beings stunted, short-lived, swiftly replacing each other, plucked, so to say, before maturity. And indeed, experience shows to the intelligent observer with what swiftness and grip the capitalist mode of production, dating, historically speaking, only from yesterday, has seized the vital power of the people by the very root – shows how the degeneration of the industrial population is only retarded by the constant absorption of primitive and physically uncorrupted elements from the country – shows how even the country labourers, in spite of fresh air and the principle of natural selection, that works so powerfully amongst them, and only permits the survival of the strongest, are already beginning to die off. Capital that has such good reasons for denying the sufferings of the legions of workers that surround it is in practice moved as much and as little by the sight of the coming degradation and final depopulation of the human race, as by the probable fall of the earth into the sun. In every stock-jobbing swindle everyone knows that some time or other the crash must come, but everyone hopes that it may fall on the head of his neighbour, after he himself has caught the shower of gold and placed it in safety. *Après moi le déluge!* is the watchword of every capitalist and of every capitalist nation. Hence Capital is reckless of the health or length of life of the labourer, unless under compulsion from society. To the outcry as to the physical and mental degradation, the premature death, the torture of over-work, it answers: Ought these to trouble us since they increase our profits? But looking at things as a whole, all this does not, indeed, depend on the good or ill will of the individual capitalist. Free competition brings out the inherent laws of capitalist production, in the shape of external coercive laws having power over every individual capitalist.

We therefore find for example, that in the beginning of 1863, 26 firms owning extensive potteries in Staffordshire, amongst others, Josiah Wedgwood & Sons, petition in a memorial for 'some legislative enactment'. Competition with other capitalists permits them no voluntary limitation of working-time for children etc.

> Much as we deplore the evils before mentioned, it would not be possible to prevent them by any scheme of agreement between the manufacturers. . . . Taking all these points into consideration, we have come to the conviction that some legislative enactment is wanted. (*Children's Employment Comm.* Rep. 1, 1863, p. 322.)

Most recently a much more striking example offers. The rise in the price of cotton during a period of feverish activity, had induced the manufacturers in Blackburn to shorten, by mutual consent, the working-time in their mills during a certain fixed period. This period terminated about the end of November 1871. Meanwhile, the wealthier manufacturers, who combined spinning with weaving, used the diminution of production resulting from this agreement to extend their own business and thus to make great profits at the expense of the small employers. The latter thereupon turned in their extremity to the operatives, urged them earnestly to agitate for the nine hours' system, and promised contributions in money to this end.

SECTION 6. THE ENGLISH FACTORY ACTS, 1833 TO 1864

After capital had taken centuries in extending the working day to its normal maximum limit, and then beyond this to the limit of the natural day of twelve hours, there followed on the birth of machinism and modern industry in the last third of the eighteenth century, a violent encroachment like that of an avalanche in its intensity and extent. All bounds of morals and nature, age and sex, day and night, were broken down. Even the ideas of day and night, of rustic simplicity in the old statutes became so confused that an English judge, as late as 1860, needed a quite Talmudic sagacity to explain 'judicially' what was day and what was night. Capital celebrated its orgies.

As soon as the working class, stunned at first by the noise and turmoil of the new system of production, recovered, in some measure, its senses, its resistance began, and first in the native land of machinism, in England. For 30 years however, the concessions conquered by the workpeople were purely nominal. Parliament passed five Labour Laws between 1802 and 1833, but was shrewd enough not to vote a penny for their carrying out, for the requisite officials, etc.

They remained a dead letter. 'The fact is that prior to the Act of 1833, young persons and children were worked all night, all day, or both *ad libitum*.'

A normal working day for modern industry only dates from the Factory Act of 1833, which included cotton, wool, flax, and silk factories. Nothing is more characteristic of the spirit of capital than the history of the English Factory Acts from 1833 to 1864.

The Act of 1833 declares the ordinary factory working day to be from 5.30 a.m. to 8.30 p.m., and within these limits, a period of fifteen hours, it is lawful to employ young persons, (i.e. persons between thirteen and eighteen years of age), at any time of the day, provided no one individual young person should work more than twelve hours in any one day, except in certain cases especially provided for. The sixth section of the Act provided: 'That there shall be allowed in the course of every day not less than one and a half hours for meals to every such person restricted as hereinbefore provided.' The employment of children under nine, with exceptions mentioned later, was forbidden; the work of children between nine and thirteen was limited to eight hours a day, night-work, i.e. according to this Act, work between 8.30 p.m. and

5.30 a.m., was forbidden for all persons between nine and eighteen.

The law-makers were so far from wishing to trench on the freedom of capital to exploit adult labour-power, or, as they called it, 'the freedom of labour', that they created a special system in order to prevent the Factory Acts from having a consequence so outrageous.

'The great evil of the factory system as at present conducted', says the first report of the Central Board of the Commission of 28 June 1833

> has appeared to us to be that it entails the necessity of continuing the labour of children to the utmost length of that of the adults. The only remedy for this evil, short of the limitation of the labour of adults, which would, in our opinion, create an evil greater than that which is sought to be remedied, appears to be the plan of working double sets of children.

Under the name of System of Relays, this 'plan' was therefore carried out, so that e.g. from 5.30 a.m. until 1.30 in the afternoon, one set of children between nine and thirteen, and from 1.30 p.m. to 8.30 in the evening another set were 'put to', etc.

In order to reward the manufacturers for having, in the most barefaced way, ignored all the Acts as to children's labour passed during the last 22 years, the pill was yet further gilded for them. Parliament decreed that after 1 March 1834, no child under eleven, after 1 March 1835, no child under twelve, and after 1 March 1836, no child under thirteen, was to work more than eight hours in a factory. This 'liberalism', so full of consideration for 'capital', was the more noteworthy as Dr Farre, Sir A. Carlisle, Sir B. Brodie, Sir C. Bell, Mr Guthrie, etc., in a word, the most distinguished physicians and surgeons in London, had declared in their evidence before the House of Commons, that there was danger in delay. Dr Farre expressed himself still more coarsely. 'Legislation is necessary for the prevention of death, in any form in which it can be prematurely inflicted, and certainly this [the factory method] must be viewed as a most cruel mode of inflicting it.'

That same 'reformed' Parliament, which in its delicate consideration for the manufacturers, condemned children under 13, for years to come, to 72 hours of work per week in the Factory Hell, on the other hand, in the Emancipation Act, which also administered freedom drop by drop, forbade the planters, from the outset, to work any negro slave more than 45 hours a week.

But in no wise conciliated, capital now began a noisy agitation that went on for several years. It turned chiefly on the age of those who, under the name of children, were limited to eight hours' work, and were subject to a certain amount of compulsory education. According to capitalistic anthropology, the age of childhood ended at ten, or at the outside, at eleven. The more nearly the time approached for the coming into full force of the Factory Act, the fatal year 1836, the more wildly raged the mob of manufacturers. They managed, in fact, to intimidate the government to such an extent that in 1835 it proposed to lower the limit of the age of childhood from 13 to 12. In the meantime the pressure from without grew more threatening. Courage failed the House of Commons. It refused to throw children of 13 under the Juggernaut Car of capital for more than eight hours a day, and the Act of 1833 came into full operation. It remained unaltered until June 1844.

In the ten years during which it regulated factory work, first in part, and then entirely, the official reports of the factory inspectors teem with complaints as to the impossibility of putting the Act into force. As the law of 1833 left it optional with the lords of capital during the 15 hours from 5.30 a.m. to 8.30 p.m. to make every 'young person', and 'every child' begin, break off, resume, or end his twelve or eight hours at any moment they liked, and also permitted them to assign to different persons different times for meals, these gentlemen soon discovered a new 'system of relays', by which the labour-horses were not changed at fixed stations, but were constantly re-harnessed at changing stations. We do not pause longer on the beauty of this system, as we shall have to return to it later. But this much is clear at the first glance: that this system annulled the whole Factory Act, not only in the spirit, but in the letter. How could factory inspectors, with this complex book-keeping in respect of each individual child or young person, enforce the legally determined work-time and the granting of the legal mealtimes? In a great many of the factories, the old brutalities soon blossomed out again unpunished. In an interview with the Home Secretary (1844), the factory inspectors demonstrated the impossibility of any control under the newly invented relay system. In the meantime, however, circumstances had greatly changed. The factory hands, especially since 1838, had made the Ten Hours' Bill their economic, as they had made the Charter their political, election-cry. Some of the manufacturers, even, who had managed their factories in conformity with the Act of 1833, overwhelmed Parliament with memorials on the immoral competition of their false brethren whom greater impudence, or more fortunate local circumstances, enabled to break the law. Moreover, however much the individual manufacturer might give the rein to his old lust for gain, the spokesmen and political leaders of the manufacturing class ordered a change of front and of speech towards the workpeople. They had entered upon the contest for the repeal of the Corn Laws, and needed the workers to help them to victory. They promised, therefore, not only a double-sized loaf of bread, but the enactment of the Ten Hours' Bill in the Free-trade millennium. Thus they still less dared to oppose a measure intended only to make the law of 1833 a reality. Threatened in their holiest interest, the rent of land, the Tories thundered with philanthropic indignation against the 'nefarious practices' of their foes.

This was the origin of the additional Factory Act of 7 June 1844. It came into effect on 10 September 1844. It places under protection a new category of workers, viz., the women over 18. They were placed in every respect on the same footing as the young persons, their work-time limited to twelve hours, their night-labour forbidden, etc. For the first time, legislation saw itself compelled to control directly and officially the labour of adults. In the Factory Report of 1844–1845, it is said with irony: 'No instances have come to my knowledge of adult women having expressed any regret at their *rights* being thus far interfered with.' The working-time of children under 13 was reduced to 6½, and in certain circumstances to 7 hours a day.

To get rid of the abuses of the 'spurious relay system', the law established besides others the following important regulations: 'That the hours of work of children and young persons shall be reckoned from the time when any child or young person shall begin to work in the morning.' So that if A, e.g., begins work at 8 in the morning, and B at 10, B's workday must nevertheless end at the same hour as A's. 'The time shall be regulated by a public clock,' for example, the nearest railway clock, by which the factory clock is to be set. The occupier is to hang up a 'legible' printed notice stating the hours for the beginning and ending of work and the times allowed for the several meals. Children beginning work before 12 noon may not be again employed after 1 p.m. The afternoon shift must therefore consist of other children than those employed in the morning. Of the hour and a half for mealtimes,

> one hour thereof at the least shall be given before three of the clock in the afternoon . . . and at the same period of the day. No child or young person shall be employed more than five hours before 1 p.m. without an interval for meal-time of at least 30 minutes. No child or young person [or female] shall be employed or allowed to remain in any room in which any manufacturing process is then [i.e. at mealtimes] carried on.

It has been seen that these minutiae, which, with military uniformity, regulate by stroke of the clock the times, limits, pauses of the work, were not at all the products of Parliamentary fancy. They developed gradually out of circumstances as natural laws of the modern mode of production. Their formulation, official recognition, and proclamation by the state were the result of a long struggle of classes. One of their first consequences was that in practice the working day of the adult males in factories became subject to the same limitations, since in most processes of production the cooperation of the children, young persons, and women is indispensable. On the whole, therefore, during the period from 1844 to 1847, the twelve hours' working day became general and uniform in all branches of industry under the Factory Act.

The manufacturers, however, did not allow this 'progress' without a compensating 'retrogression'. At their instigation the House of Commons reduced the minimum age for exploitable children from nine to eight, in order to assure that additional supply of factory children which is due to capitalists, according to divine and human law.

The years 1846–47 are epoch-making in the economic history of England. The Repeal of the Corn Laws, and of the duties on cotton and other raw material; Free trade proclaimed as the guiding star of legislation; in a word, the arrival of the millennium. On the other hand, in the same years, the Chartist movement and the ten hours' agitation reached their highest point. They found allies in the Tories panting for revenge. Despite the fanatical opposition of the army of perjured Free-traders, with Bright and Cobden at their head, the Ten Hours' Bill, struggled for so long, went through Parliament.

The new Factory Act of 8 June 1847, enacted that on 1 July 1847, there should be a preliminary shortening of the working day for 'young persons' (from 13 to 18), and all females to eleven hours, but that on 1 May 1848 there should be a definite limitation of the working day to ten hours. In other respects, the Act only amended and completed the Acts of 1833 and 1844.

Capital now entered upon a preliminary campaign in order to hinder the Act from coming into full force on 1 May 1848. And the workers themselves, under the pretence that they had been taught by experience, were to help in the destruction of their own work. The moment was cleverly chosen.

It must be remembered, too, that there has been more than two years of

> great suffering (in consequence of the terrible crisis of 1846–47) among the factory operatives, from many mills having worked short time, and many being altogether closed. A considerable number of the operatives must therefore be in very narrow circumstances; many, it is to be feared, in debt; so that it might fairly have been presumed that at the present time they would prefer working the longer time, in order to make up for past losses, perhaps to pay off debts, or get their furniture out of pawn, or replace that sold, or to get a new supply of clothes for themselves and their families.

The manufacturers tried to aggravate the natural effect of these circumstances by a general reduction of wages by ten per cent. This was done, so to say, to celebrate the inauguration of the new Free-trade era. Then followed a further reduction of 8.3 per cent as soon as the working day was shortened to eleven, and a reduction of double that amount as soon as it was finally shortened to ten hours. Wherever, therefore, circumstances allowed it, a reduction of wages of at least 25 per cent took place. Under such favourably prepared conditions the agitation among the factory workers for the repeal of the Act of 1847 was begun. Neither lies, bribery, nor threats were spared in this attempt. But all was in vain. Concerning the half-dozen petitions in which workpeople were made to complain of 'their oppression by the Act', the petitioners themselves declared under oral examination, that their signatures had been extorted from them. They felt themselves oppressed, but not exactly by the Factory Act. But if the manufacturers did not succeed in making the workpeople speak as they wished, they themselves shrieked all the louder in press and Parliament in the name of the workpeople. They denounced the Factory Inspectors as a kind of revolutionary commissioners like those of the French National Convention ruthlessly sacrificing the unhappy factory workers to their humanitarian crotchet. This manoeuvre also failed. Factory Inspector Leonard Horner conducted in his own person, and through his sub-inspectors, many examinations of witnesses in the factories of Lancashire. About 70 per cent of the workpeople examined declared in favour of ten hours, a much smaller percentage in favour of eleven, and an altogether insignificant minority for the old twelve hours.

Another 'friendly' dodge was to make the adult males work 12 to 15 hours, and then to blazon abroad this fact as the best proof of what the proletariat desired in its heart of hearts. But the 'ruthless' Factory Inspector Leonard Horner was again to the fore. The majority of the 'over-times' declared:

> They would much prefer working ten hours for less wages, but that they had no choice; that so many were out of employment (so many spinners getting very low wages by having to work as piecers, being unable to do better), that if they refused to work the longer time, others would immediately get their places, so that it was a question with them of agreeing to work the longer time, or of being thrown out of employment altogether.

The preliminary campaign of capital thus came to grief, and the Ten Hours' Act came into force on 1 May 1848. But meanwhile the fiasco of the Chartist party whose leaders were imprisoned, and whose organisation was dismembered, had shaken the confidence of the English working class in its own strength. Soon after this the June insurrection in Paris and its bloody suppression united, in England as on the Continent, all fractions of the ruling classes, landlords and capitalists, stock-exchange wolves and shopkeepers, Protectionists and Free-traders, government and opposition, priests and freethinkers, young whores and old nuns, under the common cry for the salvation of Property, Religion, the Family and Society. The working class was everywhere proclaimed, placed under a ban, under a virtual law of suspects. The manufacturers had no need any longer to restrain themselves. They broke out in open revolt not only against the Ten Hours' Act, but against the whole of the legislation that since 1833 had aimed at restricting in some measure the 'free' exploitation of labour-power. It was a pro-slavery rebellion in miniature, carried on for over two years with a cynical recklessness, a terrorist energy all the cheaper because the rebel capitalist risked nothing except the skin of his 'hands'.

To understand that which follows we must remember that the Factory Acts of 1833, 1844, and 1847 were all three in force so far as the one did not amend the other: that not one of these limited the working day of the male worker over 18, and that since 1833 the 15 hours from 5.30 a.m. to 8.30 p.m. had remained the legal 'day', within the limits of which at first the 12, and later the 10 hours' labour of young persons and women had to be performed under the prescribed conditions.

The manufacturers began by here and there discharging a part of, in many cases half of, the young persons and women employed by them, and then, for the adult males, restoring the almost obsolete night-work. The Ten Hours' Act, they cried, leaves no other alternative.

Their second step dealt with the legal pauses for meals. Let us hear the Factory Inspectors.

> Since the restriction of the hours of work to ten, the factory occupiers maintain, although they have not yet practically gone the whole length, that supposing the hours of work to be from 9 a.m. to 7 p.m. they fulfil the provisions of the statutes by allowing an hour before 9 a.m. and half an hour after 7 p.m. [for meals]. In some cases they now allow an hour, or half an hour for dinner, insisting at the same time, that they are not bound to allow any part of the hour and a half in the course of the factory working day.

The manufacturers maintained therefore that the scrupulously strict provisions of the Act of 1844 with regard to meal-times only gave the operatives permission to eat and drink before coming into, and after leaving the factory, i.e. at home. And why should not the workpeople eat their dinner before 9 in the morning? The crown lawyers, however, decided that the prescribed mealtimes 'must be in the interval during the working-hours, and that it will not be lawful to work for 10 hours continuously, from 9 a.m. to 7 p.m., without any interval'.

After these pleasant demonstrations, Capital preluded its revolt by a step which agreed with the letter of the law of 1844, and was therefore legal.

The Act of 1844 certainly prohibited the employment after 1 p.m. of such children, from eight to thirteen, as had been employed before noon. But it did not regulate in any way the 6½ hours' work of the children whose work-time began at 12 midday or later. Children of eight might, if they began work at noon, be employed from 12 to 1, 1 hour; from 2 to 4 in the afternoon, 2 hours; from 5 to 8.30 in the evening, 3½ hours; in all, the legal 6½ hours. Or better still. In order to make their work coincide with that of the adult male labourers up to 8.30 p.m., the manufacturers only had to give them no work till 2 in the afternoon; they could then keep them in the factory without intermission till 8.30 in the evening.

> And it is now expressly admitted that the practice exists in England from the desire of mill-owners to have their machinery at work for more than 10 hours a-day, to keep the children at work with male adults after all the young persons and women have left, and until 8.30 p.m. if the factory-owners choose.

Workmen and factory inspectors protested on hygienic and moral grounds, but Capital answered:

> My deeds upon my head! I crave the law.
> The penalty and forfeit of my bond.

In fact, according to statistics laid before the House of Commons on 26 July 1850, in spite of all protests, on 15 July 1850, 3,742 children were subjected to this 'practice' in 257 factories. Still, this was not enough. The lynx eye of Capital discovered that the Act of 1844 did not allow five hours' work before midday without a pause of at least 30 minutes for refreshment, but prescribed nothing of the kind for work after midday. Therefore, it claimed and obtained the enjoyment not only of making children of eight drudge without intermission from 2 to 8.30 p.m., but also of making them hunger during that time.

Ay, his heart,
So says the bond.

This Shylock-clinging to the letter of the law of 1844, so far as it regulated children's labour, was but to lead up to an open revolt against the same law, so far as it regulated the labour of 'young persons and women'. It will be remembered that the abolition of the 'false relay system' was the chief aim and object of that law. The masters began their revolt with the simple declaration that the sections of the Act of 1844 which prohibited the *ad libitum* use of young persons and women in such short fractions of the day of 15 hours as the employer chose, were 'comparatively harmless' so long as the work-time was fixed at twelve hours. But under the Ten Hours' Act they were 'a grievous hardship'. They informed the inspectors in the coolest manner that they should place themselves above the letter of the law, and reintroduce the old system on their own account. They were acting in the interests of the ill-advised operatives themselves,

> in order to be able to pay them higher wages. This was the only possible plan by which to maintain, under the Ten Hours' Act, the industrial supremacy of Great Britain. Perhaps it may be a little difficult to detect irregularities under the relay system; but what of that? Is the great manufacturing interest of this country to be treated as a secondary matter in order to save some little trouble to Inspectors and Sub-Inspectors of Factories?

All these shifts naturally were of no avail. The Factory Inspectors appealed to the Law Courts. But soon such a cloud of dust in the way of petitions from the masters overwhelmed the Home Secretary, Sir George Grey, that in a circular of 5 August 1848 he recommends the inspectors not

> to lay information against mill-owners for a breach of the letter of the Act, or for employment of young persons by relays in cases in which there is no reason to believe that such young persons have been actually employed for a longer period than that sanctioned by law.

Hereupon, Factory Inspector J. Stuart allowed the so-called relay system during the 15 hours of the factory day throughout Scotland, where it soon flourished again as of old. The English Factory

Inspectors, on the other hand, declared that the Home Secretary had no power dictatorially to suspend the law, and continued their legal proceedings against the pro-slavery rebellion.

But what was the good of summoning the capitalists when the Courts, in this case the country magistrates – Cobbett's 'Great Unpaid' – acquitted them? In these tribunals, the masters sat in judgment on themselves. An example. One Eskrigge, cotton-spinner, of the firm of Kershaw, Leese, & Co., had laid before the Factory Inspector of his district the scheme of a relay system intended for his mill. Receiving a refusal, he at first kept quiet. A few months later, an individual named Robinson, also a cotton-spinner, and if not his Man Friday, at all events related to Eskrigge, appeared before the borough magistrates of Stockport on a charge of introducing the identical plan of relays invented by Eskrigge. Four Justices sat, among them three cotton-spinners, at their head this same inevitable Eskrigge. Eskrigge acquitted Robinson, and now was of opinion that what was right for Robinson was fair for Eskrigge. Supported by his own legal decision, he introduced the system at once into his own factory. Of course, the composition of this tribunal was in itself a violation of the law. These judicial farces, exclaims Inspector Howell,

> urgently call for a remedy – either that the law should be so altered as to be made to conform to these decisions, or that it should be administered by a less fallible tribunal, whose decisions would conform to the law . . . when these cases are brought forward. I long for a stipendiary magistrate.

The crown lawyers declared the masters' interpretation of the Act of 1848 absurd. But the Saviours of Society would not allow themselves to be turned from their purpose. Leonard Horner reports,

> Having endeavoured to enforce the Act . . . by ten prosecutions in seven magisterial divisions, and having been supported by the magistrates in one case only . . . I considered it useless to prosecute more for this evasion of the law. That part of the Act of 1848 which was framed for securing uniformity in the hours of work . . . is thus no longer in force in my district (Lancashire). Neither have the sub-inspectors or myself any means of satisfying ourselves, when we inspect a mill working by shifts, that the young persons and women are not working more than 10 hours a-day. . . . In a return of 30 April . . . of mill-owners working by shifts, the number amounts to 114, and has been for some time rapidly increasing. In general, the time of working the mill is extended to 13½ hours, from 6 a.m. to 7.30 p.m. . . . in some instances it amounts to 15 hours, from 5.30 a.m. to 8.30 p.m.

Already in December 1848 Leonard Horner had a list of 65 manufacturers and 29 overlookers who unanimously declared that no system of supervision could, under this relay system, prevent enormous over-work. Now, the same children and young persons were shifted from the spinning-room to the weaving-room, now, during 15 hours, from one factory to another. How was it possible to control a system which,

> under the guise of relays, is some one of the many plans for shuffling 'the hands' about in endless variety, and shifting the hours of work and of rest for different individuals throughout the day, so that you may never have one complete set of hands working together in the same room at the same time.

But altogether independently of actual over-work, this so-called relay system was an offspring of capitalistic fantasy, such as Fourier, in his humorous sketches of *Courtes Séances*, has never surpassed, except that the 'attraction of labour' was changed into the attraction of capital. Look, for example, at those schemes of the masters which the 'respectable' press praised as models of 'what a reasonable degree of care and method can accomplish'. The *personnel* of the workpeople was sometimes divided into from 12 to 14 categories, which themselves constantly changed and rechanged their constituent parts. During the 15 hours of the factory day, capital dragged in the labourer now for 30 minutes, now for an hour, and then pushed him out again, to drag him into the factory and to thrust him out afresh, hounding him hither and thither, in scattered shreds of time, without ever losing hold of him until the full 10 hours' work was done. As on the stage, the same persons had to appear in turns in the different scenes of the different acts. But as an actor during the whole course of the play belongs to the stage, so the operatives, during 15 hours, belonged to the factory, without reckoning the time for going and coming. Thus the hours of rest were turned into hours of enforced idleness, which drove the youths to the pot-house, and the girls to the brothel. At every new trick that the capitalist, from day to day, hit upon for keeping his machinery going 12 or 15 hours without increasing the number of his hands, the worker had to swallow his meals now in this fragment of time, now in that. At the time of the ten hours' agitation, the masters cried out that the working mob petitioned in the hope of obtaining 12 hours' wages for 10 hours' work. Now they reversed the medal. They paid 10 hours' wages for 12 to 15 hours' lordship over labour-power. This was the gist of the matter, this the masters' interpretation of the 10 hours' law! These were the same unctuous Free-traders, perspiring with the love of humanity, who for full 10 years, during the Anti-Corn Law agitation, had preached to the operatives, by a reckoning of pounds, shillings, and pence, that with free importation of corn, and with the means possessed by English industry, 10 hours' labour would be quite enough to enrich the capitalists. This revolt of capital, after two years was at last crowned with victory by a decision of one of the four highest Courts of Justice in England, the Court of Exchequer, which in a case brought before it on 8 February 1850, decided that the manufacturers were certainly acting against the sense of the Act of 1844, but that this Act itself contained certain words that rendered it meaningless. By this decision, the Ten Hours' Act was abolished. A crowd of masters, who until then had been afraid of using the relay system for young persons and women, now took it up heart and soul.

But on this apparently decisive victory of capital, followed at once a revulsion. The workpeople had hitherto offered a passive, although inflexible and unremitting resistance. They now protested in Lancashire and Yorkshire in threatening meetings. The pretended Ten Hours' Act was thus simple humbug, Parliamentary cheating, had never existed! The Factory Inspectors urgently warned the Government that the antagonism of classes had arrived at an incredible tension. Some of the masters themselves murmured: 'On account of the contradictory decisions of the magistrates, a condition of things altogether abnormal and anarchical obtains. One law holds in Yorkshire, another in Lancashire; one law in one parish of Lancashire, another in its immediate neighbourhood. The manufacturer in large towns could evade the law, the manufacturer in country districts could not find the people necessary for the relay system, still less for the shifting of hands from one factory to another,' etc. And the first birthright of capital is equal exploitation of labour-power by all capitalists.

Under these circumstances a compromise between masters and men was effected that received the seal of Parliament in the additional Factory Act of 5 August 1850. The working day for 'young persons and women' was raised from 10 to 10½ hours for the first five days of the week, and shortened to 7½ on the Saturday. The work was to go on between 6 a.m. and 6 p.m. with pauses of not less than 1½ hours for mealtimes, these mealtimes to be allowed at one and the same time for all, and conformably to the conditions of 1844. By this an end was put to the relay system once for all. For children's labour, the Act of 1844 remained in force.

One set of masters, this time as before, secured to itself special seigneurial rights over the children of the proletariat. These were the silk manufacturers. In 1833 they had howled out in threatening fashion, 'if the liberty of working children of any age for 10 hours a day were taken away, it would stop their works.' It would be impossible for them to buy a sufficient number of children over 13. They extorted the privilege they desired. The pretext was shown on subsequent investigation to be a deliberate lie. It did not, however, prevent them, during 10 years, from spinning silk 10 hours a day out of the blood of little children who had to be placed upon stools for the performance of their work. The Act of 1844 certainly 'robbed' them of the 'liberty' of employing children under 11 longer than 6½ hours a day. But it secured to them, on the other hand, the privilege of working children between 11 and 13, 10 hours a day, and of annulling in their case the education made compulsory for all other factory children. This time the pretext was 'the delicate texture of the fabric in which they were employed, requiring a lightness of touch, only to be acquired by their early introduction to these factories'. The children were slaughtered out-and-out for the sake of their delicate fingers, as in Southern Russia the horned cattle for the sake of their hide and tallow. At length, in 1850, the privilege granted in 1844 was limited to the departments of silk-twisting and silk-winding. But here, to make amends to capital bereft of its 'freedom', the work-time for children from 11 to 13 was raised from 10 to 10½ hours. Pretext: 'Labour in silk mills was lighter than in mills for other fabrics, and less likely in other respects also to be prejudicial to health.' Official medical inquiries proved afterwards that, on the contrary, 'the average death-rate is exceedingly high in the silk districts and amongst the female part of the population is higher even than it is in the cotton districts of Lancashire.' Despite the protests of the Factory Inspector, renewed every 6 months, the mischief continues to this hour.

The Act of 1850 changed the 15 hours' time from 6 a.m. to 8.30 p.m., into the 12 hours from 6 a.m. to 6 p.m. for 'young persons and women' only. It did not, therefore, affect children who could always be employed for half an hour before and 2½ hours after this period, provided the whole of their labour did not exceed 6½ hours. Whilst the bill was under discussion, the Factory Inspectors laid before Parliament statistics of the infamous abuses due to this anomaly. To no purpose. In the background lurked the intention of screwing up, during prosperous years, the working day of adult males to 15 hours by the aid of the children. The experience of the three following years showed that such an attempt must come to grief against the resistance of the adult male operatives. The Act of 1850 was therefore finally completed in 1853 by forbidding the 'employment of children in the morning before and in the evening after young persons and women'. Henceforth with a few exceptions the Factory Act of 1850 regulated the working day of all workers in the branches of industry that come under it. Since the passing of the first Factory Act half a century had elapsed.

Factory legislation for the first time went beyond its original sphere in the Printworks' Act of 1845. The displeasure with which capital received this new 'extravagance' speaks through every line of the Act. It limits the working day for children from 8 to 13, and for women to 16 hours, between 6 a.m. and 10 p.m., without any legal pause for mealtimes. It allows males over 13 to be worked at will day and night. It is a Parliamentary abortion.

However, the principle had triumphed with its victory in those great branches of industry which form the most characteristic creation of the modern mode of production. Their wonderful development from 1853 to 1860, hand-in-hand with the physical and moral regeneration of the factory workers, struck the most purblind. The masters from whom the legal limitation and regulation had been wrung step by step after a civil war of half a century, themselves referred ostentatiously to the contrast with the branches of exploitation still 'free'. The Pharisees of 'Political Economy' now proclaimed the discernment of the necessity of a legally fixed working day as a characteristic new discovery of their 'science'. It will be easily understood that after the factory magnates had resigned themselves and become reconciled to the inevitable, the power of resistance of capital gradually weakened, whilst at the same time the power of attack of the working class grew with the number of its allies in the classes of society not immediately interested in the question. Hence the comparatively rapid advance since 1860.

The dye-works and bleach-works all came under the Factory Act of 1850 in 1860; lace and stocking manufactures in 1861.

In consequence of the first report of the Commission on the employment of children (1863) the same fate was shared by the manufacturers of all earthenwares (not merely pottery), lucifer-matches, percussion-caps, cartridges, carpets, fustian-cutting, and many processes included under the name of 'finishing'. In the year 1863 bleaching in the open air and baking were placed under special Acts, by which, in the former, the labour of young persons and women during the night (from eight in the evening to six in the morning), and in the latter, the employment of journeymen bakers under 18, between nine in the evening and five in the morning were forbidden. We shall return to the later proposals of the same Commission, which threatened to deprive of their 'freedom' all the important branches of English industry, with the exception of agriculture, mines, and the means of transport.

SECTION 7. THE STRUGGLE FOR THE NORMAL WORKING DAY. CONCLUSION

The reader will bear in mind that the production of surplus-value, or the extraction of surplus-labour, is the specific end and aim, the sum and substance, of capitalist production, quite apart from any changes in the mode of production, which may arise from the subordination of labour to capital. He will remember that as far as we have at present gone, only the independent labourer, and therefore only the labourer legally qualified to act for himself, enters as a vendor of a commodity into a contract with the capitalist. If, therefore, in our historical sketch, on the one hand, modern industry; on the other, the labour of those who are physically and legally minors, play important parts, the former was to us only a special department, and the latter only a specially striking example of labour exploitation. Without, however, anticipating the subsequent development of our inquiry, from the mere connexion of the historic facts before us, it follows:

First. The passion of capital for an unlimited and reckless extension of the working day is first gratified in the industries earliest revolutionised by water-power, steam, and machinery, in those first creations of the modern mode of production, cotton, wool, flax, and silk spinning, and weaving. The changes in the material mode of production and the corresponding changes in the social relations of the producers gave rise first to an extravagance beyond all bounds, and then in opposition to this, called forth a control on the part of society which legally limits, regulates, and makes uniform the working day and its pauses. This control appears, therefore, during the first half of the nineteenth century simply as exceptional legislation. As soon as this primitive dominion of the new mode of production was conquered, it was found that, in the meantime, not only had many other branches of production been made to adopt the same factory system, but that manufactures with more or less obsolete methods, such as potteries, glass-making, etc. that old-fashioned handicrafts, like baking, and, finally, even that the so-called domestic industries, such as nail-making, had long since fallen as completely under capitalist exploitation as the factories themselves. Legislation was, therefore, compelled to gradually get rid of its exceptional character, or where, as in England, it proceeds after the manner of the Roman Casuists, to declare any house in which work was done to be a factory.

Second. The history of the regulation of the working day in certain branches of production, and the struggle still going on in others in regard to this regulation, prove conclusively that the isolated labourer, the labourer as 'free' vendor of his labour-power, when capitalist production has once attained a certain stage, succumbs without any power of resistance. The creation of a normal working day is, therefore, the product of a protracted civil war, more or less dissembled, between the capitalist class and the working class. As the contest takes place in the arena of modern industry, it first breaks out in the home of that industry – England. The English factory workers were the champions, not only of the English, but of the modern working class generally, as their theorists were the first to throw down the gauntlet to the theory of capital. (Robert Owen, soon after 1810, not only maintained the necessity of a limitation of the working day in theory, but actually introduced the ten hours' day into his factory at New Lanark. This was laughed at as a communistic utopia; so were his 'combination of children's education with productive labour' and the cooperative societies of working-men, first called into being by him. Today, the first utopia is a Factory Act, the second figures as an official phrase in all Factory Acts, the third is already being used as a cloak for reactionary humbug.)

In the United States of North America, every independent movement of the workers was paralysed so long as slavery disfigured a part of the Republic. Labour cannot emancipate itself in the white skin where in the black it is branded. But out of the death of slavery a new life at once arose. The first fruit of the Civil War was the eight hours' agitation, that ran with the seven-leagued boots of the locomotive from the Atlantic to the Pacific, from New England to California. The General Congress of Labour at Baltimore (16 August 1866) declared:

> The first and great necessity of the present, to free the labour of this country from capitalistic slavery, is the passing of a law by which eight hours shall be the normal working day in all States of the American Union. We are resolved to put forth all our strength until this glorious result is attained.

At the same time, the Congress of the International Working Men's Association at Geneva, on the proposition of the London General Council, resolved that 'the limitation of the working day is a preliminary condition without which all further attempts at improvement and emancipation must prove abortive . . . the Congress proposes eight hours as the legal limit of the working day.'

Thus the movement of the working class on both sides of the Atlantic, that had grown instinctively out of the conditions of production themselves, endorsed the words of the English Factory Inspector, R.J. Saunders: 'Further steps towards a reformation of society can never be carried out with any hope of success, unless the hours of labour be limited, and the prescribed limit strictly enforced.'

It must be acknowledged that our labourer comes out of the process of production other than he entered. In the market he stood as owner of the commodity 'labour-power' face to face with other owners of commodities, dealer against dealer. The contract by which he sold to the capitalist his labour-power proved, so to say, in black and white that he disposed of himself freely. The bargain concluded, it is discovered that he was no 'free agent', that the time for which he is free to sell his labour-power is the time for which he is forced to sell it, that in fact the vampire will not lose its hold on him so long as there is a muscle, a nerve, a drop of blood to be exploited. For 'protection' against 'the serpent of their agonies', the labourers must put their heads together, and, as a class, compel the passing of a law, an all-powerful social barrier that shall prevent the very workers from selling, by voluntary contract with capital, themselves and their families into slavery and death. In place of the pompous catalogue of the 'inalienable rights of man' comes the modest Magna Charta of a legally limited working day, which shall make clear when the time which the worker sells is ended, and when his own begins.

CHAPTER 11

RATE AND MASS OF SURPLUS-VALUE

In this chapter, as hitherto, the value of labour-power, and therefore the part of the working day necessary for the reproduction or maintenance of that labour-power, are supposed to be given, constant magnitudes.

This premised, with the rate, the mass is at the same time given of the surplus-value that the individual labourer furnishes to the capitalist in a definite period of time. If, e.g., the necessary labour amounts to 6 hours daily, expressed in a quantum of gold = 3 shillings, then 3 shillings is the daily value of one labour-power or the value of the capital advanced in the buying of one labour-power. If, further, the rate of surplus-value be 100 per cent, this variable capital of 3 shillings produces a mass of surplus-value of 3 shillings, or the labourer supplies daily a mass of surplus-labour equal to 6 hours.

The mass of the surplus-value produced is therefore equal to the surplus-value which the working day of one labourer supplies multiplied by the number of labourers employed. But as further the mass of surplus-value which a single labourer produces, the value of labour-power being given, is determined by the rate of the surplus-value, this law follows: the mass of the surplus-value produced is equal to the amount of the variable capital advanced, multiplied by the rate of surplus-value; in other words: it is determined by the compound ratio between the number of labour-powers exploited simultaneously by the same capitalist and the degree of exploitation of each individual labour-power.

Diminution of the variable capital may therefore be compensated by a proportionate rise in the degree of exploitation of labour-power, or the decrease in the number of the labourers employed by a proportionate extension of the working day. Within certain limits therefore the supply of labour exploitable by capital is independent of the supply of labourers. On the contrary, a fall in the rate of surplus-value leaves unaltered the mass of the surplus-value produced, if the amount of the variable capital, or number of the labourers employed, increases in the same proportion.

The absolute limit of the average working day – this being by nature always less than 24 hours – sets an absolute limit to the compensation of a reduction of variable capital by a higher rate of surplus-value, or of the decrease of the number of labourers exploited by a higher degree of exploitation of labour-power. This palpable law is of importance for the clearing up of many phenomena, arising from a tendency (to be worked out later on) of capital to reduce as much as possible the number of labourers employed by it, or its variable constituent transformed into labour-power, in contradiction to its other tendency to produce the greatest possible mass of surplus-value.

If the limit of the working day is given, and also the limit of its necessary constituent, the mass of value and surplus-value that an individual capitalist produces, is clearly exclusively dependent on the mass of labour that he sets in motion. But this, under the conditions supposed above, depends on the mass of labour-power, or the number of labourers whom he exploits, and this number in its turn is determined by the amount of the variable capital advanced. With a given rate of surplus-value, and a given value of labour-power, therefore, the masses of surplus-value produced vary directly as the amounts of the variable capitals advanced. Now we know that the capitalist divides his capital into two parts. One part he lays out in means of production. This is the constant part of his capital. The other part he lays out in living labour-power. This part forms his variable capital. On the basis of the same mode of social production, the division of capital into constant and variable differs in different branches of production, and within the same branch of production, too, this relation changes with changes in the technical conditions and in the social combinations of the processes of production.

The law demonstrated above now therefore takes this form: the masses of value and of surplus-value produced by different capitals – the value of labour-power being given and its degree of exploitation being equal – vary directly as the amounts of the variable constituents of these capitals, i.e. as their constituents transformed into living labour-power.

This law clearly contradicts all experience based on appearance. Everyone knows that a cotton spinner, who, reckoning the percentage on the whole of his applied capital, employs much constant and little variable capital, does not, on account of this, pocket less profit or surplus-value than a baker, who relatively sets in motion much variable and little constant capital. For the solution of this apparent contradiction, many intermediate terms are as yet wanted, as from the standpoint of elementary algebra many intermediate terms are wanted to understand that $^0/_0$ may represent an actual magnitude.

The labour which is set in motion by the total capital of a society, day in, day out, may be regarded as a single collective working day. If, e.g., the number of labourers is a million, and the average working day of a labourer is ten hours, the social working day consists of ten million hours. With a given length of this working day, whether its limits are fixed physically or socially, the mass of surplus-value can only be increased by increasing the number of labourers, i.e. of the labouring population. The growth of population here forms the mathematical limit to the production of surplus-value by the total social capital. On the contrary, with a given amount of population, this limit is formed by the possible lengthening of the working day. It will, however, be seen in the following chapter that this law only holds for the form of surplus-value dealt with up to the present.

From the treatment of the production of surplus-value so far, it follows that not every sum of money, or of value, is at pleasure transformable into capital. To effect this transformation, in fact, a certain minimum of money or of exchange-value must be presupposed in the hands of the individual possessor of money or commodities. The minimum of variable capital is the cost price of a single labour-power, employed the whole year through, day in, day out, for the production of surplus-value. If this labourer were in possession of his own means of production, and were satisfied to live as a labourer, he need not work beyond the time necessary for the reproduction of his means of subsistence, say eight hours a day. He would, besides, only require the means of production sufficient for eight working-hours. The capitalist, on the other hand, who makes him do, besides these eight hours, say four hours' surplus-labour, requires an additional sum of money for furnishing the additional means of production. On our supposition, however, he would have to employ two labourers in order to live, on the surplus-value appropriated daily, as well as, and no better than a labourer, i.e. to be able to satisfy his necessary wants. In this case the mere maintenance of life would be the end of his production, not the increase of wealth; but this latter is implied in capitalist production. That he may live only twice as well as an ordinary labourer, and besides turn half of the surplus-value produced into capital, he would have to raise, with the number of labourers, the minimum of the capital advanced eight times. Of course he can, like his labourer, take to work himself, participate directly in the process of production, but he is then only a hybrid between capitalist and labourer, a 'small master'. A certain stage of capitalist production necessitates that the capitalist be able to devote the whole of the time during which he functions as a capitalist, i.e. as personified capital, to the appropriation and therefore control of the labour of others, and to the selling of the products of this labour. The guilds of the middle ages therefore tried to prevent by force the transformation of the master of a trade into a capitalist, by limiting the number of labourers that could be employed by one master within a very small maximum. The possessor of money or commodities actually turns into a capitalist in such cases only where the minimum sum advanced for production greatly exceeds the maximum of the middle ages. Here, as in natural science, is shown the correctness of the law discovered by Hegel (in his *Logic*), that merely quantitative differences beyond a certain point pass into qualitative changes.

The minimum of the sum of value that the individual possessor of money or commodities must command, in order to metamorphose himself into a capitalist, changes with the different stages of development of capitalist production, and is at given stages different in different spheres of production, according to their special and technical conditions. Certain spheres of production demand, even at the very outset of capitalist production, a minimum of capital that is not as yet found in the hands of single individuals. This gives rise partly to state subsidies to private persons, as in France in the time of Colbert, and as in many German states up to our own epoch; partly to the formation of societies with legal monopoly for the exploitation of certain branches of industry and commerce, the forerunners of our modern joint-stock companies.

Within the process of production, as we have seen, capital acquired the command over labour, i.e. over functioning labour-power or the labourer himself. Personified capital, the capitalist takes care that the labourer does his work regularly and with the proper degree of intensity.

Capital further developed into a coercive relation, which compels the working class to do more work than the narrow round of its own life-wants prescribes. As a producer of the activity of others, as a pumper-out of surplus-labour and exploiter of labour-power, it surpasses in energy, disregard of bounds, recklessness and efficiency, all earlier systems of production based on directly compulsory labour.

At first, capital subordinates labour on the basis of the technical conditions in which it historically finds it. It does not, therefore, change immediately the mode of production. The production of surplus-value – in the form hitherto considered by us – by means of simple extension of the working day, proved, therefore, to be independent of any change in the mode of production itself. It was not less active in the old-fashioned bakeries than in the modern cotton factories.

If we consider the process of production from the point of view of the simple labour-process, the labourer stands in relation to the means of production, not in their quality as capital, but as the mere means and material of his own intelligent productive activity. In tanning for example, he deals with the skins as his simple object of labour. It is not the capitalist whose skin he tans. But it is different as soon as we deal with the process of production from the point of view of the process of creation of surplus-value. The means of production are at once changed into means for the absorption of the labour of others. It is now no longer the labourer that employs the means of production, but the means of production that employ the labourer. Instead of being consumed by him as material elements of his productive activity, they consume him as the ferment necessary to their own life-process, and the life-process of capital consists only in its movement as value constantly expanding, constantly multiplying itself. Furnaces and workshops that stand idle by night, and absorb no living labour, are 'a mere loss' to the capitalist. Hence, furnaces and workshops constitute lawful claims upon the night-labour of the workpeople. The simple transformation of money into the material factors of the process of production, into means of production, transforms the latter into a title and a right to the labour and surplus-labour of others.

PART IV
Production of Relative Surplus-value

CHAPTER 12

THE CONCEPT OF RELATIVE SURPLUS-VALUE

That portion of the working day which merely produces an equivalent for the value paid by the capitalist for his labour-power, has, up to this point, been treated by us as a constant magnitude, and such in fact it is, under given conditions of production and at a given stage in the economic development of society. Beyond this, his necessary labour-time, the labourer, we saw, could continue to work for 2, 3, 4, 6, etc. hours. The rate of surplus-value and the length of the working day depended on the magnitude of this prolongation. Though the necessary labour-time was constant, we saw, on the other hand, that the total working day was variable. Now suppose we have a working day whose length, and whose apportionment between necessary labour and surplus-labour, are given. Let the whole line ac, a——b—c represent, for example, a working day of 12 hours; the portion of ab 10 hours of necessary labour, and the portion bc 2 hours of surplus-labour. How now can the production of surplus-value be increased, i.e. how can the surplus-labour be prolonged, without, or independently of, any prolongation of ac?

Although the length of ac is given, bc appears to be capable of prolongation, if not by extension beyond its end c, which is also the end of the working-day ac, yet, at all events, by pushing back its starting-point b in the direction of a. Assume that b′–b in the line a b′ bc is equal to half of bc

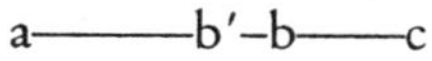

a———b′–b——c

or to one hour's labour-time. If now, in ac, the working day of 12 hours, we move the point b to b′, bc becomes b′c; the surplus-labour increases by one half, from 2 hours to 3 hours, although the working-day remains as before at 12 hours. This extension of the surplus labour-time from bc to b′c, from 2 hours to 3 hours, is, however, evidently impossible, without a simultaneous contraction of the necessary labour-time from ab into ab′, from 10 hours to 9 hours. The prolongation of the surplus-labour would correspond to a shortening of the necessary labour; or a portion of the labour-time previously consumed, in reality, for the labourer's own benefit, would be converted into labour-time for the benefit of the capitalist. There would be an alteration, not in the length of the working day, but in its division into necessary labour-time and surplus labour-time.

On the other hand, it is evident that the duration of the surplus-labour is given when the length of the working day, and the value of labour-power, are given. The value of labour-power, i.e. the labour-time requisite to produce labour-power, determines the labour-time necessary for the reproduction of that value. If one working-hour be embodied in sixpence, and the value of a day's labour-power be five shillings, the labourer must work 10 hours a day, in order to replace the value paid by capital for his labour-power, or to produce an equivalent for the value of his daily necessary means of subsistence. Given the value of these means of subsistence, the value of his labour-power is given; and given the value of his labour-power, the duration of his necessary labour-time is given. The duration of the surplus-labour, however, is arrived at, by subtracting the necessary labour-time from the total working day. Ten hours subtracted from twelve, leave two, and it is not easy to see how, under the given conditions, the surplus-labour can possibly be prolonged beyond two hours. No doubt the capitalist can, instead of five shillings, pay the labourer four shillings and sixpence or even less. For the reproduction of this value of four shillings and sixpence, nine hours' labour-time would suffice; and consequently three hours of surplus-labour, instead of two, would accrue to the capitalist, and the surplus-value would rise from one shilling to eighteen pence. This result, however, would be obtained only by lowering the wages of the labourer below the value of his labour-power. With the four shillings and sixpence which he produces in nine hours, he commands one-tenth less of the necessaries of life than before, and consequently the proper reproduction of his labour-power is crippled. The surplus-labour would in this case be prolonged only by an overstepping of its normal limits; its domain would be extended only by a usurpation of part of the domain of necessary labour-time. Despite the important part which this method plays in actual practice, we are excluded from considering it in this place, by our assumption that all commodities, including labour-power, are bought and sold at their full value. Granted this, it follows that the labour-time necessary for the production of labour-power, or for the reproduction of its value, cannot be lessened by a fall in the labourer's wages below the value of his labour-power, but only by a fall in this value itself. Given the length of the working day, the prolongation of the surplus-labour must of necessity originate in the curtailment of the necessary labour-time; the latter cannot arise from the former. In the example we have taken, it is necessary that the value of labour-power should actually fall by one-tenth, in order that the necessary labour-time may be diminished by one-tenth, i.e. from ten hours to nine, and in order that the surplus-labour may consequently be prolonged from two hours to three.

Such a fall in the value of labour-power implies, however, that the same necessaries of life which were formerly produced in ten hours, can now be produced in nine hours. But this is impossible without an increase in the productiveness of labour. For example, suppose a shoe-maker, with given tools, makes in one working day of twelve hours, one pair of boots. If he must make two pairs in the same time, the productiveness of his labour must be doubled; and this cannot be done, except by an alteration in his tools or in his mode of working, or in both. Hence, the conditions of production, i.e. his mode of production, and the labour-process itself, must be revolutionised. By increase in the productiveness of labour, we mean, generally, an alteration in the labour-process, of such a kind as to shorten the labour-time socially necessary for the production of a commodity, and to endow a given quantity of labour with the power of producing a greater quantity of use-value. Hitherto in treating of surplus-value, arising from a simple prolongation of the working day, we have assumed the mode of production to be given and invariable. But when surplus-value has to be produced by the conversion of necessary labour into surplus-labour, it by no means suffices for capital to take over the labour-process in the form under which it has been historically handed down, and then simply to prolong the duration of that process. The technical and social conditions of the process, and consequently the very mode of production must be revolutionised, before the productiveness of labour can be increased. By that means alone can the value of labour-power be made to sink, and the portion of the working day necessary for the reproduction of that value be shortened.

The surplus-value produced by prolongation of the working day I call *absolute surplus-value*. On the other hand, the surplus-value arising from the curtailment of the necessary labour-time, and from the corresponding alteration in the respective lengths of the two components of the working day, I call *relative surplus-value*.

In order to effect a fall in the value of labour-power, the increase in the productiveness of labour must seize upon those branches of industry, whose products determine the value of labour-power, and consequently either belong to the class of customary means of subsistence, or are capable of supplying the place of those means. But the value of a commodity is determined, not only by the quantity of labour which the labourer directly bestows upon that commodity, but also by the labour contained in the means of production. For instance, the value of a pair of boots depends, not only on the cobbler's labour, but also on the value of the leather, wax, thread, etc. Hence, a fall in the value of labour-power is also brought about by an increase in the productivenesss of labour and by a corresponding cheapening of commodities in those industries which supply the instruments of labour and the raw material, that form the material elements of the constant capital required for producing the necessaries of life. But an increase in the productiveness of labour in those branches of industry which supply neither the necessaries of life, nor the means of production for such necessaries, leaves the value of labour-power undisturbed.

The cheapened commodity, of course, causes only a *pro tanto* fall in the value of labour-power, a fall proportional to the extent of that commodity's employment in the reproduction of labour-power. Shirts, for instance, are a necessary means of subsistence, but are only one out of many. The totality of the necessaries of life consists, however, of various commodities, each the product of a distinct industry; and the value of each of those commodities enters as a component part into the value of labour-power. This latter value decreases with the decrease of the labour-time necessary for its reproduction; the total decrease being the sum of all the different curtailments of labour-time effected in those various and distinct industries. This general result is treated, here, as if it were the immediate result directly aimed at in each individual case. Whenever an individual capitalist cheapens shirts, for instance, by increasing the productiveness of labour, he by no means necessarily aims at reducing the value of labour-power and shortening, *pro tanto*, the necessary labour-time. But it is only in so far as he ultimately contributes to this result, that he assists in raising the general rate of surplus-value. The general and necessary tendencies of capital must be distinguished from their forms of manifestation.

It is not our intention to consider here the way in which the laws, immanent in capitalist production, manifest themselves in the movements of individual masses of capital, where they assert themselves as coercive laws of competition, and are brought home to the mind and consciousness of the individual capitalist as the directing motives of his operations. But this much is clear; a scientific analysis of competition is not possible before we have a conception of the inner nature of capital, just as the apparent motions of the heavenly bodies are not intelligible to any but him, who is acquainted with their real motions, motions which are not directly perceptible by the senses. Nevertheless, for the better comprehension of the production of relative surplus-value, we may add the following remarks, in which we assume nothing more than the results we have already obtained.

If one hour's labour is embodied in sixpence, a value of six shillings will be produced in a working day of 12 hours. Suppose, that with the prevailing productiveness of labour, 12 articles are produced in these 12 hours. Let the value of the means of production used up in each article be sixpence. Under these circumstances, each article costs one shilling: sixpence for the value of the means of production, and sixpence for the value newly added in working with those means. Now let some one capitalist contrive to double the productiveness of labour, and to produce in the working day of 12 hours, 24 instead of 12 such articles. The value of the means of production remaining the same, the value of each article will fall to ninepence, made up of sixpence for the value of the means of production and threepence for the value newly added by the labour. Despite the doubled productiveness of labour, the day's labour creates, as before, a new value of six shillings and no more, which, however, is now spread over twice as many articles. Of this value each article now has embodied in it one-twenty-fourth, instead of one-twelfth, threepence instead of sixpence; or, what amounts to the same thing, only half an hour's instead of a whole hour's labour-time, is now added to the means of production while they are being transformed into each article. The individual value of these articles is now below their social value; in other words, they have cost less labour-time than the great bulk of the same article produced under the average social conditions. Each article costs, on an average, one shilling, and represents two hours of social labour; but under the altered mode of production it costs only ninepence, or contains only 1½ hours' labour. The real value of a commodity is, however, not its individual value, but its social value; that is to say, the real value is not measured by the labour-time that the article in each individual case costs the producer, but by the labour-time socially required for its production. If therefore, the capitalist who applies the new method, sells his commodity at its social value of one shilling, he sells it for threepence above its individual value, and thus realises an extra surplus-value of threepence. On the other hand, the working day of 12 hours is, as regards him, now represented by 24 articles instead of 12. Hence, in order to get rid of the product of one working day, the demand must be double what it was, i.e. the market must become twice as extensive. Other things being equal, his commodities can command a more extended market only by a diminution of their prices. He will therefore sell them above their individual but under their social value, say at tenpence each. By this means he still squeezes an extra surplus-value of one penny out of each. This augmentation of surplus-value is pocketed by him, whether his commodities belong or not to the class of necessary means of subsistence that participate in determining the general value of labour-power. Hence, independently of this latter circumstance, there is a motive for each individual capitalist to cheapen his commodities, by increasing the productiveness of labour.

Nevertheless, even in this case, the increased production of surplus-value arises from the curtailment of the necessary labour-time, and from the corresponding prolongation of the surplus-labour. The exceptionally productive labour operates as intensified labour; it creates in equal periods of time greater values than average social labour of the same kind.

Hence the capitalist who applies the improved method of production appropriates to surplus-labour a greater portion of the working day than the other capitalists in the same trade. He does individually what the whole body of capitalists engaged in producing relative surplus-value do collectively. On the other hand, however, this extra surplus-value vanishes so soon as the new method of production has become general, and has consequently caused the difference between the individual value of the cheapened commodity and its social value to vanish. The law of the determination of value by labour-time, a law which brings under its sway the individual capitalist who applies the new method of production, by compelling him to sell his goods under their social value, this same law, acting as a coercive law of competition, forces his competitors to adopt the new method. The general rate of surplus-value is, therefore, ultimately affected by the whole process only when the increase in the productiveness of labour has seized upon those branches of production that are connected with, and has cheapened those commodities that form part of, the necessary means of subsistence, and are therefore elements of the value of labour-power.

The value of commodities is in inverse ratio to the productiveness of labour. And so, too, is the value of labour-power, because it depends on the values of commodities. Relative surplus-value is, on the contrary, directly proportional to that productiveness. It rises with rising and falls with falling productiveness. The value of money being assumed to be constant, an average social working day of twelve hours always produces the same new value, six shillings, no matter how this sum may be apportioned between surplus-value and wages. But if, in consequence of increased productiveness, the value of the necessaries of life fall, and the value of a day's labour-power be thereby reduced from five shillings to three, the surplus-value increases from one shilling to three. Ten hours were necessary for the reproduction of the value of the labour-power; now only six are required. Four hours have been set free, and can be annexed to the domain of surplus-labour. Hence there is immanent in capital an inclination and constant tendency, to heighten the productiveness of labour, in order to cheapen commodities, and by such cheapening to cheapen the labourer himself.

The value of a commodity is, in itself, of no interest to the capitalist. What alone interests him, is the surplus-value that dwells in it, and is realisable by sale. Realisation of the surplus-value necessarily carries with it the refunding of the value that was advanced. Now, since relative surplus-value increases in direct proportion to the development of the productiveness of labour, while, on the other hand, the value of commodities diminishes in the same proportion; since one and the same process cheapens commodities, and augments the surplus-value contained in them; we have here the solution of the riddle: why does the capitalist, whose sole concern is the production of exchange-value, continually strive to depress the exchange-value of commodities?

The shortening of the working day is, therefore, by no means what is aimed at, in capitalist production, when labour is economised by increasing its productiveness. It is only the shortening of the labour-time necessary for the production of a definite quantity of commodities, that is aimed at. The fact that the workman, when the productiveness of his labour has been increased, produces, say ten times as many commodities as before, and thus spends one-tenth as much labour-time on each, by no means prevents him from continuing to work twelve hours as before, nor from producing in those twelve hours 1,200 articles instead of 120. The object of all development of the productiveness of labour, within the limits of capitalist production, is to shorten that part of the working day, during which the workman must labour for his own benefit, and by that very shortening, to lengthen the other part of the day, during which he is at liberty to work gratis for the capitalist. How far this result is also attainable, without cheapening commodities, will appear from an examination of the particular modes of producing relative surplus-value, to which examination we now proceed.

CHAPTER 13

Cooperation

Capitalist production only then really begins, as we have already seen, when each individual capital employs simultaneously a comparatively large number of labourers; when consequently the labour-process is carried on on an extensive scale and yields, relatively, large quantities of products. A greater number of labourers working together, at the same time, in one place (or, if you will, in the same field of labour), in order to produce the same sort of commodity under the mastership of one capitalist, constitutes, both historically and logically, the starting-point of capitalist production. With regard to the mode of production itself, manufacture, in its strict meaning, is hardly to be distinguished, in its earliest stages, from the handicraft trades of the guilds, otherwise than by the greater number of workmen simultaneously employed by one and the same individual capital. The workshop of the mediaeval master handicraftsman is simply enlarged.

Nevertheless, within certain limits, a modification takes place. The labour realised in value is labour of an average social quality; is consequently the expenditure of average labour-power. Any average magnitude, however, is merely the average of a number of separate magnitudes all of one kind, but differing as to quantity. In every industry, each individual labourer, be he Peter or Paul, differs from the average labourer. These individual differences, or 'errors' as they are called in mathematics, compensate one another, and vanish, whenever a certain minimum number of workmen are employed together. The celebrated sophist and sycophant, Edmund Burke, goes so far as to make the following assertion, based on his practical observations as a farmer; that 'in so small a platoon' as that of five farm labourers, all individual differences in the labour vanish, and that consequently any given five adult farm labourers taken together, will in the same time do as much work as any other five. But, however that may be, it is clear, that the collective working day of a large number of workmen simultaneously employed, divided by the number of these workmen, gives one day of average social labour. Thus the laws of the production of value are only fully realised for the individual producer when he produces as a capitalist, and employs a number of workmen together, whose labour, by its collective nature, is at once stamped as average social labour.

Even without an alteration in the system of working, the simultaneous employment of a large number of labourers effects a revolution in the material conditions of the labour-process. The buildings in which they work, the storehouses for the raw material, the implements and utensils used simultaneously or in turns by the workmen; in short, a portion of the means of production, are now consumed in common. On the one hand, the exchange-value of these means of production is not increased; for the exchange-value of a commodity is not raised by its use-value being consumed more thoroughly and to greater advantage. On the other hand, they are used in common, and therefore on a larger scale than before. A room where twenty weavers work at twenty looms must be larger than the room of a single weaver with two assistants. But it costs less labour to build one workshop for twenty persons than to build ten to accommodate two weavers each; thus the value of the means of production that are concentrated for use in common on a large scale does not increase in direct proportion to the expansion and to the increased useful effect of those means. When consumed in common, they give up a smaller part of their value to each single product; partly because the total value they part with is spread over a greater quantity of products, and partly because their value, though absolutely greater, is, having regard to their sphere of action in the process, relatively less than the value of isolated means of production. Owing to this, the value of a part of the constant capital falls, and in proportion to the magnitude of the fall, the total value of the commodity also falls. The effect is the same as if the means of production had cost less. The economy in their application is entirely owing to their being consumed in common by a large number of workmen. Moreover, this character of being necessary conditions of social labour, a character that distinguishes them from the dispersed and relatively more costly means of production of isolated, independent labourers, or small masters, is acquired even when the numerous workmen assembled together do not assist one another, but merely work side by side. A portion of the instruments of labour acquires this social character before the labour-process itself does so.

When numerous labourers work together side by side, whether in one and the same process, or in different but connected processes, they are said to cooperate, or to work in cooperation.

Just as the offensive power of a squadron of cavalry, or the defensive power of a regiment of infantry, is essentially different from the sum of the offensive or defensive powers of the individual cavalry or infantry soldiers taken separately, so the sum total of the mechanical forces exerted by isolated workmen differs from the social force that is developed, when many hands take part simultaneously in one and the same undivided operation, such as raising a heavy weight, turning a winch, or removing an obstacle. In such cases the effect of the combined labour could either not be produced at all by isolated individual labour, or it could only be produced by a great expenditure of time, or on a very dwarfed scale. Not only have we here an increase in the productive power of the individual, by means of cooperation, but the creation of a new power, namely, the collective power of masses.

Apart from the new power that arises from the fusion of many forces into one single force, mere social contact begets in most industries an emulation and a stimulation of the animal spirits that heighten the efficiency of each individual workman. Hence it is that a dozen persons working together will, in their collective working day of 144 hours, produce far more than twelve isolated men each working twelve hours, or than one man who works twelve days in succession. The reason for this is that man is, if not as Aristotle contends, a political, at all events a social animal.

Although a number of men may be occupied together at the same time on the same, or the same kind of work, yet the labour of each, as a part of the collective labour, may correspond to a distinct phase of the labour-process, through all whose phases, in consequence of cooperation, the subject of their labour passes with greater speed. For instance, if a dozen masons place themselves in a row, so as to pass stones from the foot of a ladder to its summit, each of them does the same thing; nevertheless, their separate acts form connected parts of one total operation; they are particular phases, which must be gone through by each stone; and the stones are thus carried up quicker by the 24 hands of the row of men than they could be if each man went separately up and down the ladder with his burden. The object is carried over the same distance in a shorter time. Again, a combination of labour occurs whenever a building, for instance, is taken in hand on different sides simultaneously; although here also the cooperating masons are doing the same, or the same kind of work. The twelve masons, in their collective working day of 144 hours, make much more progress with the building than one mason could make working for twelve days, or 144 hours. The reason is that a body of men working in concert has hands and eyes both before and behind, and is, to a certain degree, omnipresent. The various parts of the work progress simultaneously.

In the above instances we have laid stress upon the point that the men do the same, or the same kind of work, because this, the most simple form of labour in common, plays a great part in cooperation, even in its most fully developed stage. If the work be complicated, then the mere number of the men who cooperate allows of the various operations being apportioned to different hands, and, consequently, of being carried on simultaneously. The time necessary for the completion of the whole work is thereby shortened.

In many industries, there are critical periods, determined by the nature of the process, during which certain definite results must be obtained. For instance, if a flock of sheep has to be shorn, or a field of wheat to be cut and harvested, the quantity and quality of the product depends on the work being begun and ended within a certain time. In these cases, the time that ought to be taken by the process is prescribed, just as it is in herring fishing. A single person cannot carve a working day of more than, say twelve hours, out of the natural day, but 100 men cooperating extend the working day to 1,200 hours. The shortness of the time allowed for the work is compensated for by the large mass of labour thrown upon the field of production at the decisive moment. The completion of the task within the proper time depends on the simultaneous application of numerous combined working days; the amount of useful effect depends on the number of labourers; this number, however, is always smaller than the number of isolated labourers required to do the same amount of work in the same period. It is owing to the absence of this kind of cooperation that, in the western part of the United States, quantities of corn, and in those parts of East India where English rule has destroyed the old communities, quantities of cotton, are yearly wasted.

On the one hand, cooperation allows of the work being carried on over an extended space; it is consequently imperatively called for in certain undertakings, such as draining, constructing dykes, irrigation works, and the making of canals, roads and railways. On the other hand, while extending the scale of production, it renders possible a relative contraction of the arena. This contraction of arena simultaneous with, and arising from, extension of scale, whereby a number of useless expenses are cut down, is owing to the conglomeration of labourers, to the aggregation of various processes, and to the concentration of the means of production.

The combined working day produces, relatively to an equal sum of isolated working days, a greater quantity of the use-values, and, consequently, diminishes the labour-time necessary for the production of a given useful effect. Whether the combined working day, in a given case, acquires this increased productive power, because it heightens the mechanical force of labour, or extends its sphere of action over a greater space, or contracts the field of production relatively to the scale of production, or at the critical moment sets large masses of labour to work, or excites emulation between individuals and raises their animal spirits, or impresses on the similar operations carried on by a number of men the stamp of continuity and many-sidedness, or performs simultaneously different operations, or economises the means of production by use in common, or lends to individual labour the character of average social labour – whichever of these be the cause of the increase, the special productive power of the combined working day, is under all circumstances, the social productive power of labour, or the productive power of social labour. This power is due to cooperation itself. When the labourer cooperates systematically with others, he strips off the fetters of his individuality, and develops the capabilities of his species.

As a general rule, labourers cannot cooperate without being brought together: their assemblage in one place is a necessary condition of their cooperation. Hence wage-labourers cannot cooperate, unless they are employed simultaneously by the same capital, the same capitalist, and unless therefore their labour-powers are bought simultaneously by him. The total value of these labour-powers, or the amount of the wages of these labourers for a day, or a week, as the case may be, must be ready in the pocket of the capitalist, before the workmen are assembled for the process of production. The payment of 300 workmen at once, though only for one day, requires a greater outlay of capital, than does the payment of a smaller number of men, week by week, during a whole year. Hence the number of the labourers that cooperate, or the scale of cooperation, depends, in the first instance, on the amount of capital that the individual capitalist can spare for the purchase of labour-power; in other words, on the extent to which a single capitalist has command over the means of subsistence of a number of labourers.

And as with the variable, so it is with the constant capital. For example, the outlay on raw material is 30 times as great for the capitalist who employs 300 men, as it is for each of the 30 capitalists who employ 10 men. The value and quantity of the instruments of labour used in common do not, it is true, increase at the same rate as the number of workmen, but they do increase very considerably. Hence, concentration of large masses of the means of production in the hands of individual capitalists is a material condition for the cooperation of wage-labourers, and the extent of the cooperation or the scale of production, depends on the extent of this concentration.

We saw in a former chapter, that a certain minimum amount of capital was necessary, in order that the number of labourers simultaneously employed, and, consequently, the amount of surplus-value produced, might suffice to liberate the employer himself from manual labour, to convert him from a small master into a capitalist, and thus formally to establish capitalist production. We now see that a certain minimum amount is a necessary condition for the conversion of numerous isolated and independent processes into one combined social process.

We also saw that at first, the subjection of labour to capital was only a formal result of the fact, that the labourer, instead of working for himself, works for and consequently under the capitalist. By the cooperation of numerous wage-labourers, the sway of capital develops into a requisite for carrying on the labour-process itself, into a real requisite of production. That a capitalist should command on the field of production, is now as indispensable as that a general should command on the field of battle.

All combined labour on a large scale requires, more or less, a directing authority, in order to secure the harmonious working of the individual activities, and to perform the general functions that have their origin in the action of the combined organism, as distinguished from the action of its separate organs. A single violin player is his own conductor; an orchestra requires a separate one. The work of directing, superintending, and adjusting, becomes one of the functions of capital, from the moment that the labour under the control of capital, becomes cooperative. Once a function of capital, it acquires special characteristics.

The directing motive, the end and aim of capitalist production, is to extract the greatest possible amount of surplus-value, and consequently to exploit labour-power to the greatest possible extent. As the number of the cooperating labourers increases, so too does their resistance to the domination of capital, and with it, the necessity for capital to overcome this resistance by counterpressure. The control exercised by the capitalist is not only a special function, due to the nature of the social labour-process, and peculiar to that process, but it is, at the same time, a function of the exploitation of a social labour-process, and is consequently rooted in the unavoidable antagonism between the exploiter and the living and labouring raw material he exploits.

Again, in proportion to the increasing mass of the means of production, now no longer the property of the labourer, but of the capitalist, the necessity increases for some effective control over the proper application of those means. Moreover, the cooperation of wage-labourers is entirely brought about by the capital that employs them. Their union into one single productive body and the establishment of a connexion between their individual functions are matters foreign and external to them, are not their own act, but the act of the capital that brings and keeps them together. Hence the connexion existing between their various labours appears to them, ideally, in the shape of a preconceived plan of the capitalist, in the shape of the powerful will of another, who subjects their activity to his aims. If, then, the control of the capitalist is in substance twofold by reason of the twofold nature of the process of production itself – which, on the one hand, is a social process for producing use-values, on the other, a process for creating surplus-value – in form that control is despotic. As cooperation extends its scale, this despotism takes forms peculiar to itself. Just as at first the capitalist is relieved from actual labour so soon as his capital has reached that minimum amount with which capitalist production, as such, begins, so now, he hands over the work of direct and constant supervision of the individual workmen, and groups of workmen, to a special kind of wage-labourer. An industrial army of workmen, under the command of a capitalist, requires, like a real army, officers (managers), and sergeants (foremen, overlookers), who, while the work is being done, command in the name of the capitalist. The work of supervision becomes their established and exclusive function. When comparing the mode of production of isolated peasants and artisans with production by slave-labour, the political economist counts this labour of superintendence among the *faux frais* of production. But, when considering the capitalist mode of production, he, on the contrary, treats the work of control made necessary by the cooperative character of the labour-process as identical with the different work of control, necessitated by the capitalist character of that process and the antagonism of interests between capitalist and labourer. It is not because he is a leader of industry that a man is a capitalist; on the contrary, he is a leader of industry because he is a capitalist. The leadership of industry is an attribute of capital, just as in feudal times the functions of general and judge, were attributes of landed property.

The labourer is the owner of his labour-power until he has done bargaining for its sale with the capitalist; and he can sell no more than what he has – i.e. his individual, isolated labour-power. This state of things is in no way altered by the fact that the capitalist, instead of buying the labour-power of one man, buys that of 100, and enters into separate contracts with 100 unconnected men instead of with one. He is at liberty to set the 100 men to work, without letting them cooperate. He pays them the value of 100 independent labour-powers, but he does not pay for the combined labour-power of the hundred. Being independent of each other, the labourers are isolated persons, who enter into relations with the capitalist, but not with one another. This cooperation begins only with the labour-process, but they have then ceased to belong to themselves. On entering that process, they become incorporated with capital. As cooperators, as members of a working organism, they are but special modes of existence of capital. Hence, the productive power developed by the labourer when working in cooperation, is the productive power of capital. This power is developed gratuitously, whenever the workmen are placed under given conditions, and it is capital that places them under such conditions. Because this power costs capital nothing, and because, on the other hand, the labourer himself does not develop it before his labour belongs to capital, it appears as a power with which capital is endowed by Nature – a productive power that is immanent in capital.

CHAPTER 14

Division of Labour and Manufacture

SECTION 1. TWO-FOLD ORIGIN OF MANUFACTURE

That cooperation which is based on division of labour assumes its typical form in manufacture, and is the prevalent characteristic form of the capitalist process of production throughout the manufacturing period properly so called. That period, roughly speaking, extends from the middle of the sixteenth to the last third of the eighteenth century.

Manufacture takes its rise in two ways:

(1) By the assemblage, in one workshop under the control of a single capitalist, of labourers belonging to various independent handicrafts, but through whose hands a given article must pass on its way to completion. A carriage, for example, was formerly the product of the labour of a great number of independent artificers, such as wheelwrights, harness-makers, tailors, locksmiths, upholsterers, turners, fringe-makers, glaziers, painters, polishers, gilders, etc. In the manufacture of carriages, however, all these different artificers are assembled in one building where they work into one another's hands. It is true that a carriage cannot be gilt before it has been made. But if a number of carriages are being made simultaneously, some may be in the hands of the gilders while others are going through an earlier process. So far, we are still in the domain of simple cooperation, which finds its materials ready to hand in the shape of men and things. But very soon an important change takes place. The tailor, the locksmith, and the other artificers, being now exclusively occupied in carriage-making, each gradually loses, through want of practice, the ability to carry on, to its full extent, his old handicraft. But, on the other hand, his activity now confined in one groove assumes the form best adapted to the narrowed sphere of action. At first, carriage manufacture is a combination of various independent handicrafts. By degrees, it becomes the splitting up of carriage-making into its various

detail processes, each of which crystallises into the exclusive function of a particular workman, the manufacture as a whole being carried on by the men in conjunction. In the same way, cloth manufacture, as also a whole series of other manufactures, arose by combining different handicrafts together under the control of a single capitalist.

(2) Manufacture also arises in a way exactly the reverse of this – namely, by one capitalist employing simultaneously in one workshop a number of artificers, who all do the same, or the same kind of work, such as making paper, type, or needles. This is cooperation in its most elementary form. Each of these artificers (with the help, perhaps, of one or two apprentices), makes the entire commodity, and he consequently performs in succession all the operations necessary for its production. He still works in his old handicraft-like way. But very soon external circumstances cause a different use to be made of the concentration of the workmen on one spot, and of the simultaneousness of their work. An increased quantity of the article has perhaps to be delivered within a given time. The work is therefore redistributed. Instead of each man being allowed to perform all the various operations in succession, these operations are changed into disconnected, isolated ones, carried on side by side; each is assigned to a different artificer, and the whole of them together are performed simultaneously by the cooperating workmen. This accidental repartition gets repeated, develops advantages of its own, and gradually ossifies into a systematic division of labour. The commodity, from being the individual product of an independent artificer, becomes the social product of a union of artificers, each of whom performs one, and only one, of the constituent partial operations. The same operations which, in the case of a papermaker belonging to a German Guild, merged one into the other as the successive acts of one artificer, became in the Dutch paper manufacture so many partial operations carried on side by side by numerous co-operating labourers. The needlemaker of the Nuremberg Guild was the cornerstone on which the English needle manufacture was raised. But while in Nuremberg that single artificer performed a series of perhaps 20 operations one after another, in England it was not long before there were 20 needle-makers side by side, each performing one alone of those 20 operations, and in consequence of further experience, each of those 20 operations was again split up, isolated, and made the exclusive function of a separate workman.

The mode in which manufacture arises, its growth out of handicrafts, is therefore twofold. On the one hand, it arises from the union of various independent handicrafts, which become stripped of their independence and specialised to such an extent as to be reduced to mere supplementary partial processes in the production of one particular commodity. On the other hand, it arises from the co-operation of artificers of one handicraft; it splits up that particular handicraft into its various detail operations, isolating, and making these operations independent of one another up to the point where each becomes the exclusive function of a particular labourer. On the one hand, therefore, manufacture either introduces division of labour into a process of production, or further develops that division; on the other hand, it unites together handicrafts that were formerly separate. But whatever may have been its particular starting-point, its final form is invariably the same – a productive mechanism whose parts are human beings.

For a proper understanding of the division of labour in manufacture, it is essential that the following points be firmly grasped. First, the decomposition of a process of production into its various successive steps coincides, here, strictly with the resolution of a handicraft into its successive manual operations. Whether complex or simple, each operation has to be done by hand, retains the character of a handicraft, and is therefore dependent on the strength, skill, quickness, and sureness, of the individual workman in handling his tools. The handicraft continues to be the basis. This narrow technical basis excludes a really scientific analysis of any definite process of industrial production, since it is still a condition that each detail process gone through by the product must be capable of being done by hand and of forming, in its way, a separate handicraft. It is just because handicraft skill continues, in this way, to be the foundation of the process of production, that each workman becomes exclusively assigned to a partial function, and that for the rest of his life, his labour-power is turned into the organ of this detail function.

Secondly, this division of labour is a particular sort of cooperation, and many of its disadvantages spring from the general character of cooperation, and not from this particular form of it.

SECTION 2. THE DETAIL LABOURER AND HIS IMPLEMENTS

If we now go more in detail, it is, in the first place, clear that a labourer who all his life performs one and the same simple operation, converts his whole body into the automatic, specialised implement of that operation. Consequently, he takes less time in doing it than the artificer who performs a whole series of operations in succession. But the collective labourer, who constitutes the living mechanism of manufacture, is made up solely of such specialised detail labourers. Hence, in comparison with the independent handicraft, more is produced in a given time, or the productive power of labour is increased. Moreover, when once this fractional work is established as the exclusive function of one person, the methods it employs become perfected. The workman's continued repetition of the same simple act, and the concentration of his attention on it, teach him by experience how to attain the desired effect with the minimum of exertion. But since there are always several generations of labourers living at one time, and working together at the manufacture of a given article, the technical skill, the tricks of the trade thus acquired, become established, and are accumulated and handed down. Manufacture, in fact, produces the skill of the detail labourer, by reproducing, and systematically driving to an extreme within the workshop, the naturally developed differentiation of trades which it found ready to hand in society at large. On the other hand, the conversion of fractional work into the life calling of one man, corresponds to the tendency shown by earlier societies, to make trades hereditary; either to petrify them into castes, or whenever definite historical conditions beget in the individual a tendency to vary in a manner incompatible with the nature of castes, to ossify them into guilds. Castes and guilds arise from the action of the same natural law that regulates the differentiation of plants and animals into species and varieties, except that, when a certain degree of development has been reached, the heredity of castes and the exclusiveness of guilds are ordained as a law of society.

An artificer, who performs one after another the various fractional operations in the production of a finished article, must at one time change his place, at another his tools. The transition from one operation to another interrupts the flow of his labour, and creates, so to say, gaps in his working day. These gaps close up so soon as he is tied to one and the same operation all day long; they vanish in proportion as the changes in his work diminish. The resulting increased productive power is owing either to an increased expenditure of labour-power in a given time – i.e. to an increased intensity of labour – or to a decrease in the amount of labour-power unproductively consumed. The extra expenditure of power demanded by every transition from rest to motion, is made up for by prolonging the duration of the normal velocity when once acquired. On the other hand, constant labour of one uniform kind disturbs the intensity and flow of a man's animal spirits, which find recreation and delight in mere change of activity.

The productiveness of labour depends not only on the proficiency of the workman, but on the perfection of his tools. Tools of the same kind, such as knives, drills, gimlets, hammers, etc. may be employed in different processes; and the same tool may serve various purposes in a single process. But so soon as the different operations of a labour-process are disconnected the one from the other, and each fractional operation acquires in the hands of the detail labourer a suitable and peculiar form, alterations become necessary in the implements that previously served more than one purpose. The direction taken by this change is determined by the difficulties experienced in consequence of the unchanged form of the implement. Manufacture is characterised by the differentiation of the instruments of labour – a differentiation whereby implements of a given sort acquire fixed shapes, adapted to each particular application, and by the specialisation of those instruments, giving to each special implement its full play only in the hands of a specific detail labourer. In Birmingham alone 500 varieties of hammers are produced, and not only is each adapted to one particular process, but several varieties often serve exclusively for the different operations in one and the same process. The manufacturing period simplifies, improves, and multiplies the implements of labour, by adapting them to the exclusively special functions of each detail labaourer. It thus creates at the same time one of the material conditions for the existence of machinery, which consists of a combination of simple instruments.

The detail labourer and his implements are the simplest elements of manufacture. Let us now turn to its aspect as a whole.

SECTION 3. THE TWO FUNDAMENTAL FORMS OF MANUFACTURE: HETEROGENEOUS MANUFACTURE, SERIAL MANUFACTURE

The organisation of manufacture has two fundamental forms which, in spite of occasional blending, are essentially different in kind, and, moreover, play very distinct parts in the subsequent transformation of manufacture into modern industry carried on by machinery. This double character arises from the nature of the article produced. This article either results from the mere mechanical fitting together of partial products made independently, or owes its completed shape to a series of connected processes and manipulations.

A locomotive, for instance, consists of more than 5,000 independent parts. It cannot, however, serve as an example of the first kind of genuine manufacture, for it is a structure produced by modern mechanical industry. But a watch can; and William Petty used it to illustrate the division of labour in manufacture. Formerly the individual work of a Nuremberg artificer, the watch has been transformed into the social product of an immense number of detail labourers, such as mainspring makers, dial makers, spiral spring makers, jewelled hole makers, ruby lever makers, hand makers, case makers, screw makers, gilders, with numerous subdivisions, such as wheel makers (brass and steel separate), pin makers, movement makers, *acheveur de pignon* (fixes the wheels on the axles, polishes the facets, etc), pivot makers, *planteur de finissage* (puts the wheels and springs in the works), *finisseur de barillet* (cuts teeth in the wheels, makes the holes of the right size, etc.), escapement makers, cylinder makers for cylinder escapements, escapement wheel makers, balance wheel makers, raquette makers (apparatus for regulating the watch), the *planteur d'échappement* (escapement maker proper); then the *repasseur de barillet* (finishes the box for the spring, etc.), steel polishers, wheel polishers, screw polishers, figure painters, dial enamellers (melt the enamel on the copper), *fabricant de pendants* (makes the ring by which the case is hung), *finisseur de charnière* (puts the brass hinge in the cover, etc.), *faiseur de secret* (puts in the springs that open the case), *graveur, ciseleur, polisseur de boîte*, etc. etc., and last of all the *repasseur*, who fits together the whole watch and hands it over in a going state. Only a few parts of the watch pass through several hands; and all these *membra disjecta* come together for the first time in the hand that binds them into one mechanical whole. This external relation between the finished product, and its various and diverse elements makes it, as well in this case as in the case of all similar finished articles, a matter of chance whether the detail labourers are brought together in one workshop or not. The detail operations may further be carried on like so many independent handicrafts, as they are in the Cantons of Vaud and Neufchâtel; while in Geneva there exist large watch manufactories where the detail labourers directly cooperate under the control of a single capitalist. And even in the latter case the dial, the springs, and the case, are seldom made in the factory itself. To carry on the trade as a manufacture, with concentration of workmen, is, in the watch trade, profitable only under exceptional conditions, because competition is greater between the labourers who desire to work at home, and because the splitting up of the work into a number of heterogeneous processes permits but little use of the instruments of labour in common, and the capitalist, by scattering the work, saves the outlay on workshops etc. Nevertheless the position of this detail labourer who, though he works at home, does so for a capitalist (manufacturer, *établisseur*), is very different from that of the independent artificer, who works for his own customers.

The second kind of manufacture, its perfected form, produces articles that go through connected phases of development, through a series of processes step by step, like the wire in the manufacture of needles, which passes through the hands of 72 and sometimes even 92 different detail workmen.

In so far as such a manufacture, when first started, combines scattered handicrafts, it lessens the space by which the various phases of production are separated from each other. The time taken in passing from one stage to another is shortened, so is the labour that effectuates this passage. In comparison with a handicraft, productive power is gained, and this gain is owing to the general cooperative character of manufacture. On the other hand, division of labour, which is the distinguishing principle of manufacture, requires the isolation of the various stages of production and their independence of each other. The establishment and maintenance of a connexion between the isolated functions necessitates the incessant transport of the article from one hand to another, and from one process to another. From the standpoint of modern mechanical industry, this necessity stands forth as a characteristic and costly disadvantage, and one that is immanent in the principle of manufacture.

If we confine our attention to some particular lot of raw materials, of rags, for instance, in paper manufacture, or of wire in needle manufacture, we perceive that it passes in succession through a series of stages in the hands of the various detail workmen until completion. On the other hand, if we look at the workshop as a whole, we see the raw material in all the stages of its production at the same time. The collective labourer, with one set of his many hands armed with one kind of tools, draws the wire, with another set, armed with different tools, he, at the same time, straightens it, with another, he cuts it, with another, points it, and so on. The different detail processes, which were successive in time, have become simultaneous, go on side by side in space. Hence, production of a greater quantum of finished commodities in a given time. This simultaneity, it is true, is due to the general cooperative form of the process as a whole; but manufacture not only finds the conditions for cooperation ready to hand, it also, to some extent, creates them by the subdivision of handicraft labour. On the other hand, it accomplishes this social organisation of the labour-process only by riveting each labourer to a single fractional detail.

Since the fractional product of each detail labourer is, at the same time, only a particular stage in the development of one and the same finished article, each labourer, or each group of labourers, prepares the raw material for another labourer or group. The result of the labour of the one is the starting-point for the labour of the other. The one workman therefore gives occupation directly to the other. The labour-time necessary in each partial process, for attaining the desired effect, is learnt by experience; and the mechanism of manufacture, as a whole, is based on the assumption that a given result will be obtained in a given time. It is only on this assumption that the various supplementary labour-processes can proceed uninterruptedly, simultaneously, and side by side. It is clear that this direct dependence of the operations, and therefore of the labourers, on each other, compels each one of them to spend on his work no more than the necessary time, and thus a continuity, uniformity, regularity, order, and even intensity of labour, of quite a different kind, is begotten than is to be found in an independent handicraft or even in simple cooperation. The rule, that the labour-time expended on a commodity should not exceed that which is socially necessary for its production, appears, in the production of commodities generally, to be established by the mere effect of competition; since, to express ourselves superficially, each single producer is obliged to sell his commodity at its market price. In manufacture, on the contrary, the turning out of a given quantum of product in a given time is a technical law of the process of production itself.

Different operations take, however, unequal periods, and yield therefore, in equal times unequal quantities of fractional products. If, therefore, the same labourer has, day after day, to perform the same operation, there must be a different number of labourers for each operation; for instance, in type manufacture, there are four founders and two breakers to one rubber: the founder casts 2,000 type an hour, the breaker breaks up 4,000, and the rubber polishes 8,000. Here we have again the principle of cooperation in its simplest form, the simultaneous employment of many doing the same thing; only now, this principle is the expression of an organic relation. The division of labour, as carried out in manufacture, not only simplifies and multiplies the qualitatively different parts of the social collective labourer, but also creates a fixed mathematical relation or ratio which regulates the quantitative extent of those parts – i.e. the relative number of labourers, or the relative size of the group of labourers, for each detail operation. It develops, along with the qualitative subdivision of the social labour-process, a quantitative rule and proportionality for that process.

When once the most fitting proportion has been experimentally established for the numbers of the detail labourers in the various groups when producing on a given scale, that scale can be extended only by employing a multiple of each particular group. There is this to boot, that the same individual can do certain kinds of work just as well on a large as on a small scale; for instance, the labour of superintendence, the carriage of the fractional product from one stage to the next, etc. The isolation of such functions, their allotment to a particular labourer, does not become advantageous till after an increase in the number of labourers employed; but this increase must affect every group proportionally.

The isolated group of labourers to whom any particular detail function is assigned, is made up of homogeneous elements, and is one of the constituent parts of the total mechanism. In many manufactures, however, the group itself is an organised body of labour, the total mechanism being a repetition or multiplication of these elementary organisms. Take, for instance, the manufacture of glass bottles. It may be resolved into three essentially different stages. First, the preliminary stage, consisting of the preparation of the components of the glass, mixing the sand and lime, etc. and melting them into a fluid mass of glass. Various detail labourers are employed in this first stage, as also in the final one of removing the bottles from the drying furnace, sorting and packing them, etc. In the middle, between these two stages, comes the glass melting proper, the manipulation of the fluid mass. At each mouth of the furnace, there works a group, called 'the hole', consisting of one bottlemaker or finisher, one blower, one gatherer, one putter-up or whetter-off, and one taker-in. These five detail workers are so many special organs of a single working organism that acts only as a whole, and therefore can operate only by the direct cooperation of the whole five. The whole body is paralysed if but one of its members be wanting. But a glass furnace has several openings (in England from 4 to 6), each of which contains an earthenware melting-pot full of molten glass, and employs a similar five-membered group of workers. The organisation of each group is based on division of labour, but the bond between the different groups is simple cooperation, which, by using in common one of the means of production, the furnace, causes it to be more economically consumed. Such a furnace, with its four to six groups, constitutes a glass house; and a glass manufactory comprises a number of such glass houses, together with the apparatus and workmen requisite for the preparatory and final stages.

Finally, just as manufacture arises in part from the combination of various handicrafts, so, too, it develops into a combination of various manufactures. The larger English glass manufacturers, for instance, make their own earthenware melting-pots, because on the quality of these depends, to a great extent, the success or failure of the process. The manufacture of one of the means of production is here united with that of the product. On the other hand, the manufacture of the product may be united with other manufactures, of which that product is the raw material, or with the products of which it is itself subsequently mixed. Thus we find the manufacture of flint glass combined with that of glass cutting and brass founding; the latter for the metal settings of various articles of glass. The various manufactures so combined form more or less separate departments of a larger manufacture, but are at the same time independent processes, each with its own division of labour. In spite of the many advantages offered by this combination of manufactures, it never grows into a complete technical system on its own foundation. That happens only on its transformation into an industry carried on by machinery.

The collective labourer, formed by the combination of a number of detail labourers, is the machinery specially characteristic of the manufacturing period. The various operations that are performed in turns by the producer of a commodity, and coalesce one with another during the progress of production, lay claim to him in various ways. In one operation he must exert more strength, in another more skill, in another more attention; and the same individual does not possess all these qualities in an equal degree. After manufacture has once separated, made independent, and isolated the various operations, the labourers are divided, classified, and grouped according to their predominating qualities. If their natural endowments are, on the one hand, the foundation on which the division of labour is built up, on the other hand, manufacture, once introduced, develops in them new powers that are by nature fitted only for limited and special functions. The collective labourer now possesses, in an equal degree of excellence, all the qualities requisite for production, and expends them in the most economical manner, by exclusively employing all his organs, consisting of particular labourers, or groups of labourers, in performing their special functions. The one-sidedness and the deficiencies of the detail labourer become perfections when he is a part of the collective labourer. The habit of doing only one thing converts him into a never failing instrument, while his connexion with the whole mechanism compels him to work with the regularity of the parts of a machine.

Since the collective labourer has functions, both simple and complex, both high and low, his members, the individual labour-powers, require different degrees of training, and must therefore have different values. Manufacture, therefore, develops a hierarchy of labour-powers, to which there corresponds a scale of wages. If, on the one hand, the individual labourers are appropriated and annexed for life by a limited function; on the other hand, the various operations of the hierarchy are parcelled out among the labourers according to both their natural and their acquired capabilities. Every process of production, however, requires certain simple manipulations, which every man is capable of doing. They too are now severed from their connexion with the more pregnant moments of activity, and ossified into exclusive functions of specially appointed labourers. Hence, manufacture begets, in every handicraft that it seizes upon, a class of so-called unskilled labourers, a class which handicraft industry strictly excluded. If it develops a one-sided speciality into a perfection, at the expense of the whole of a man's working capacity, it also begins to make a speciality of the absence of all development. Alongside of the hierarchic gradation there steps the simple separation of the labourers into skilled and unskilled. For the latter, the cost of apprenticeship vanishes; for the former, it diminishes, compared with that of artificers, in consequence of the functions being simplified. In both cases the value of labour-power falls. An exception to this law holds good whenever the decomposition of the labour-process begets new and comprehensive functions, that either had no place at all, or only a very modest one, in handicrafts. The fall in the value of labour-power, caused by the disappearance or diminution of the expenses of apprenticeship, implies a direct increase of surplus-value for the benefit of capital; for everything that shortens the necessary labour-time required for the reproduction of labour-power, extends the domain of surplus-labour.

SECTION 4. DIVISION OF LABOUR IN MANUFACTURE, AND DIVISION OF LABOUR IN SOCIETY

We first considered the origin of manufacture, then its simple elements, then the detail labourer and his implements, and finally, the totality of the mechanism. We shall now lightly touch upon the relation between the division of labour in manufacture, and the social division of labour, which forms the foundation of all production of commodities.

If we keep labour alone in view, we may designate the separation of social production into its main divisions or *genera* – viz., agriculture, industries, etc., as division of labour in general, and the splitting up of these families into species and sub-species, as division of labour in particular, and the division of labour within the workshop as division of labour in singular or in detail.

Division of labour in a society, and the corresponding tying down of individuals to a particular calling, develops itself, just as does the division of labour in manufacture, from opposite starting-points. Within a family, and after further development within a tribe, there springs up naturally a division of labour, caused by differences of sex and age, a division that is consequently based on a purely physiological foundation, which division enlarges its materials by the expansion of the community, by the increase of population, and more especially, by the conflicts between different tribes, and the subjugation of one tribe by another. On the other hand, as I have before remarked, the exchange of products springs up at the points where different families, tribes, communities, come in contact; for, in the beginning of civilisation, it is not private individuals but families, tribes, etc., that meet on an independent footing. Different communities find different means of production and different means of subsistence in their natural environment. Hence, their modes of production, and of living, and their products are different. It is this spontaneously developed difference which, when different communities come in contact, calls forth the mutual exchange of products, and the consequent gradual conversion of those products into commodities. Exchange does not create the differences between the spheres of production, but brings what are already different into relation, and thus converts them into more or less interdependent branches of the collective production of an enlarged society. In the latter case, the social division of labour arises from the exchange between spheres of production, that are originally distinct and independent of one another. In the former, where the physiological division of labour is the starting-point, the particular organs of a compact whole grow loose, and break off, principally owing to the exchange of commodities with foreign communities, and then isolate themselves so far, that the sole bond, still connecting the various kinds of work, is the exchange of the products as commodities. In the one case, it is the making dependent what was before independent; in the other case, the making independent what was before dependent.

The foundation of every division of labour that is well developed, and brought about by the exchange of commodities, is the separation between town and country. It may be said, that the whole economic history of society is summed up in the movement of this antithesis. We pass it over, however, for the present.

Just as a certain number of simultaneously employed labourers are the material prerequisites for division of labour in manufacture, so are the number and density of the population, which here correspond to the agglomeration in one workshop, a necessary condition for the division of labour in society. Nevertheless, this density is more or less relative. A relatively thinly populated country, with well developed means of communication, has a denser population than a more numerously populated country, with badly developed means of communication; and in this sense the Northern States of the American Union, for instance, are more thickly populated than India.

Since the production and the circulation of commodities are the general prerequisites of the capitalist mode of production, division of labour in manufacture demands that division of labour in society at large should previously have attained a certain degree of development. Inversely, the former division reacts upon and develops and multiplies the latter. Simultaneously, with the differentiation of the instruments of labour, the industries that produce these instruments become more and more differentiated. If the manufacturing system seize upon an industry which previously was carried on in connexion with others, either as a chief or as a subordinate industry, and by one producer, these industries immediately separate their connexion, and become independent. If it seize upon a particular stage in the production of a commodity, the other stages of its production become converted into so many independent industries. It has already been stated that where the finished article consists merely of a number of parts fitted together, the detail operations may reestablish themselves as genuine and separate handicrafts. In order to carry out more perfectly the division of labour in manufacture, a single branch of production is, according to the varieties of its raw material, or the various forms that one and the same raw material may assume, split up into numerous, and to some extent, entirely new manufactures. Accordingly, in France alone, in the first half of the eighteenth century, over 100 different kinds of silk stuffs were woven, and in Avignon it was law, that 'every apprentice should devote himself to only one sort of fabrication, and should not learn the preparation of several kinds of stuff at once.' The territorial division of labour, which confines special branches of production to special districts of a country, acquires fresh stimulus from the manufacturing system, which exploits every special advantage.

But, in spite of the numerous analogies and links connecting them, division of labour in the interior of a society, and that in the interior of a workshop, differ not only in degree, but also in kind. The analogy appears most indisputable where there is an invisible bond uniting the various branches of trade. For instance the cattle breeder produces hides, the tanner makes the hides into leather, and the shoemaker, the leather into boots. Here the thing produced by each of them is but a step towards the final form, which is the product of all their labours combined. There are, besides, all the various industries that supply the cattle breeder, the tanner, and the shoemaker with the means of production. Now it is quite possible to imagine, with Adam Smith, that the difference between the above social division of labour, and the division in manufacture, is merely subjective, exists merely for the observer, who, in a manufacture, can see with one glance all the numerous operations being performed on one spot, while in the instance given above, the spreading out of the work over great areas, and the great number of people employed in each branch of labour, obscure the connexion. But what is it that forms the bond between the independent labours of the cattle breeder, the tanner, and the shoemaker? It is the fact that their respective products are commodities. What, on the other hand, characterises division of labour in manufactures? The fact that the detail labourer produces no commodities. It is only the common product of all the detail labourers that becomes a commodity. Division of labour in society is brought about by the purchase and sale of the products of different branches of industry, while the connexion between the detail operations in a workshop, is due to the sale of the labour-power of several workmen to one capitalist, who applies it as combined labour-power. The division of labour in the workshop implies concentration of the means of production in the hands of one capitalist; the division of labour in society implies their dispersion among many independent producers of commodities. While within the workshop, the iron law of proportionality subjects definite numbers of workmen to definite functions, in the society outside the workshop, chance and caprice have full play in distributing the producers and their means of production among the various branches of industry. The different spheres of production, it is true, constantly tend to an equilibrium: for, on the one hand, while each producer of a commodity is bound to produce a use-value, to satisfy a particular social want, and while the extent of these wants differs quantitatively, still there exists an inner relation which settles their proportions into a regular system, and that system one of spontaneous growth; and, on the other hand, the law of the value of commodities ultimately determines how much of its disposable working-time society can expend on each particular class of commodities. But this constant tendency to equilibrium of the various spheres of production is exercised only in the shape of a reaction against the constant upsetting of this equilibrium. The *a priori* system on which the division of labour within the workshop is regularly carried out, becomes in the division of labour within the society, an *a posteriori*, nature-imposed necessity, controlling the lawless caprice of the producers, and perceptible in the barometrical fluctuations of the market prices. Division of labour within the workshop implies the undisputed authority of the capitalist over men, that are but parts of a mechanism that belongs to him. The division of labour within the society brings into contact independent commodity-producers, who acknowledge no other authority but that of competition, of the coercion exerted by the pressure of their mutual interests; just as in the animal kingdom, the *bellum omnium contra omnes* more or less preserves the conditions of existence of every species. The same bourgeois mind which praises division of labour in the workshop, life-long annexation of the labourer to a partial operation, and his complete subjection to capital, as being an organisation of labour that increases its productiveness – that same bourgeois mind denounces with equal vigour every conscious attempt to socially control and regulate the process of production as an inroad upon such sacred things as the rights of property, freedom and unrestricted play for the bent of the individual capitalist. It is very characteristic that the enthusiastic apologists of the factory system have nothing more damning to urge against a general organisation of the labour of society, than that it would turn all society into one immense factory.

If, in a society with capitalist production, anarchy in the social division of labour and despotism in that of the workshop are mutual conditions the one of the other, we find, on the contrary, in those earlier forms of society in which the separation of trades has been spontaneously developed, then crystallised, and finally made permanent by law, on the one hand, a specimen of the organisation of the labour of society, in accordance with an approved and authoritative plan, and on the other, the entire exclusion of division of labour in the workshop, or at all events a mere dwarflike or sporadic and accidental development of the same.

Those small and extremely ancient Indian communities, some of which have continued down to this day, are based on possession in common of the land, on the blending of agriculture and handicrafts, and on an unalterable division of labour, which serves, whenever a new community is started, as a plan and scheme ready cut and dried. Occupying areas of from 100 up to several thousand acres, each forms a compact whole producing all it requires. The chief part of the products is destined for direct use by the community itself, and does not take the form of a commodity. Hence, production here is independent of that division of labour brought about, in Indian society as a whole, by means of the exchange of commodities. It is the surplus alone that becomes a commodity, and a portion of even that, not until it has reached the hands of the state, into whose hands from time immemorial a certain quantity of these products has found its way in the shape of rent in kind. The constitution of these communities varies in different parts of India. In those of the simplest form, the land is tilled in common, and the produce divided among the members. At the same time, spinning and weaving are carried on in each family as subsidiary industries. Side by side with the masses thus occupied with one and the same work, we find the 'chief inhabitant', who is judge, police, and tax-gatherer in one; the book-keeper, who keeps the accounts of the tillage and registers everything relating thereto; another official, who prosecutes criminals, protects strangers travelling through and escorts them to the next village; the boundary man, who guards the boundaries against neighbouring communities; the water-overseer, who distributes the water from the common tanks for irrigation; the Brahmin, who conducts the religious services; the schoolmaster, who on the sand teaches the children reading and writing; the calendar-Brahmin, or astrologer, who makes known the lucky or unlucky days for seed-time and harvest, and for every other kind of agricultural work; a smith and a carpenter, who make and repair all the agricultural implements; the potter, who makes all the pottery of the village; the barber, the washerman, who washes clothes, the silversmith, here and there the poet, who in some communities replaces the silversmith, in others the schoolmaster. This dozen of individuals is maintained at the expense of the whole community. If the population increases, a new community is founded, on the pattern of the old one, on unoccupied land. The whole mechanism discloses a systematic division of labour; but a division like that in manufactures is impossible, since the smith and the carpenter, etc. find an unchanging market, and at the most there occur, according to the sizes of the villages, two or three of each, instead of one. The law that regulates the division of labour in the community acts with the irresistible authority of a law of Nature, at the same time that each individual artificer, the smith, the carpenter, and so on, conducts in his workshop all the operations of his handicraft in the traditional way, but independently, and without recognising any authority over him. The simplicity of the organisation for production in these self-sufficing communities that constantly reproduce themselves in the same form, and when accidentally destroyed, spring up again on the spot and with the same name – this simplicity supplies the key to the secret of the unchangeableness of Asiatic societies, an unchangeableness in such striking contrast with the constant dissolution and refounding of Asiatic States, and the never-ceasing changes of dynasty. The structure of the economic elements of society remains untouched by the storm-clouds of the political sky.

The rules of the guilds, as I have said before, by limiting most strictly the number of apprentices and journeymen that a single master could employ, prevented him from becoming a capitalist. Moreover, he could not employ his journeymen in any other handicrafts than the one in which he was a master. The guilds zealously repelled every encroachment by the capital of merchants, the only form of free capital with which they came in contact. A merchant could buy every kind of commodity, but labour as a commodity he could not buy. He existed only on sufferance, as a dealer in the products of the handicrafts. If circumstances called for a further division of labour, the existing guilds split themselves up into varieties, or founded new guilds by the side of the old ones; all this, however, without concentrating various handicrafts in a single workshop. Hence, the guild organisation, however much it may have contributed by separating, isolating, and perfecting the handicrafts, to create the material conditions for the existence of manufacture, excluded division of labour in the workshop. On the whole, the labourer and his means of production remained closely united, like the snail with its shell, and thus there was wanting the principal basis of manufacture, the separation of the labourer from his means of production, and the conversion of these means into capital.

While division of labour in society at large, whether such division be brought about or not by exchange of commodities, is common to economic formations of society the most diverse, division of labour in the workshop, as practised by manufacture, is a special creation of the capitalist mode of production alone.

SECTION 5. THE CAPITALISTIC CHARACTER OF MANUFACTURE

An increased number of labourers under the control of one capitalist is the natural starting-point, as well of cooperation generally, as of manufacture in particular. But the division of labour in manufacture makes this increase in the number of workmen a technical necessity. The minimum number that any given capitalist is bound to employ is here prescribed by the previously established division of labour. On the other hand, the advantages of further division are obtainable only by adding to the number of workmen, and this can be done only by adding multiples of the various detail groups. But an increase in the variable component of the capital employed necessitates an increase in its constant component, too, in the workshops, implements, etc., and in particular, in the raw material, the call for which grows quicker than the number of workmen. The quantity of it consumed in a given time by a given amount of labour increases in the same ratio as does the productive power of that labour in consequence of its division. Hence, it is a law based on the very nature of manufacture, that the minimum amount of capital, which is bound to be in the hands of each capitalist, must keep increasing; in other words, that the transformation into capital of the social means of production and subsistence must keep extending.

In manufacture, as well as in simple cooperation, the collective working organism is a form of existence of capital. The mechanism that is made up of numerous individual detail labourers belongs to the capitalist. Hence, the productive power resulting from a combination of labours appears to be the productive power of capital. Manufacture proper not only subjects the previously independent workman to the discipline and command of capital, but in addition, creates a hierarchic gradation of the workmen themselves. While simple cooperation leaves the mode of working by the individual for the most part unchanged, manufacture thoroughly revolutionises it, and seizes labour-power by its very roots. It converts the labourer into a crippled monstrosity, by forcing his detail dexterity at the expense of a world of productive capabilities and instincts; just as in the States of La Plata they butcher a whole beast for the sake of his hide or his tallow. Not only is the detail work distributed to the different individuals, but the individual himself is made the automatic motor of a fractional operation, and the absurd fable of Menenius Agrippa, which makes man a mere fragment of his own body, becomes realised. If at first the workman sells his labour-power to capital, because the material means of producing a commodity fail him, now his very labour-power refuses its services unless it has been sold to capital. Its functions can be exercised only in an environment that exists in the workshop of the capitalist after the sale. By nature unfitted to make anything independently, the manufacturing labourer develops productive activity as a mere appendage of the capitalist's workshop.

The knowledge, the judgement, and the will, which, though in ever so small a degree, are practised by the independent peasant or handicraftsman, in the same way as the savage makes the whole art of war consist in the exercise of his personal cunning – these faculties are now required only for the workshop as a whole. Intelligence in production expands in one direction, because it vanishes in many others. What is lost by the detail labourers is concentrated in the capital that employs them. It is a result of the division of labour in manufactures that the labourer is brought face to face with the intellectual potencies of the material process of production, as the property of another, and as a ruling power. This separation begins in simple cooperation, where the capitalist represents to the single workman, the oneness and the will of the associated labour. It is developed in manufacture which cuts down the labourer into a detail labourer. It is completed in modern industry, which makes science a productive force distinct from labour and presses it into the service of capital.

In manufacture, in order to make the collective labourer, and through him capital, rich in social productive power, each labourer must be made poor in individual productive powers.

> Ignorance is the mother of industry as well as of superstition. Reflection and fancy are subject to err; but a habit of moving the hand or the foot is independent of either. Manufactures, accordingly, prosper most where the mind is least consulted, and where the workshop may ... be considered as an engine, the parts of which are men. (A. Ferguson.)

As a matter of fact, some few manufacturers in the middle of the eighteenth century preferred, for certain operations that were trade secrets, to employ half-idiotic persons.

'The understandings of the greater part of men', says Adam Smith, 'are necessarily formed by their ordinary employments. The man whose whole life is spent in performing a few simple operations . . . has no occasion to exert his understanding. . . . He generally becomes as stupid and ignorant as it is possible for a human creature to become.' After describing the stupidity of the detail labourer he goes on:

> The uniformity of his stationary life naturally corrupts the courage of his mind. . . . It corrupts even the activity of his body and renders him incapable of exerting his strength with vigour and perseverance in any other employments than that to which he has been bred. His dexterity at his own particular trade seems in this manner to be acquired at the expense of his intellectual, social, and martial virtues. But in every improved and civilised society, this is the state into which the labouring poor, that is, the great body of the people, must necessarily fall.

For preventing the complete deterioration of the great mass of the people by division of labour, A. Smith recommends education of the people by the state, but prudently, and in homeopathic doses. G. Garnier, his French translator and commentator, who, under the first French Empire, quite naturally developed into a senator, quite as naturally opposes him on this point. Education of the masses, he urges, violates the first law of the division of labour, and with it 'our whole social system would be proscribed.' 'Like all other divisions of labour', he says,

> that between hand labour and head labour is more pronounced and decided in proportion as society [he rightly uses this word, for capital, landed property and their state] becomes richer. This division of labour, like every other, is an effect of past, and a cause of future progress . . . ought the government then to work in opposition to this division of labour, and to hinder its natural course? Ought it to expend a part of the public money in the attempt to confound and blend together two classes of labour, which are striving after division and separation?

Some crippling of body and mind is inseparable even from division of labour in society as a whole. Since, however, manufacture carries this social separation of branches of labour much further, and also, by its peculiar division, attacks the individual at the very roots of his life, it is the first to afford the materials for, and to give a start to, industrial pathology.

'To subdivide a man is to execute him, if he deserves the sentence, to assassinate him if he does not. . . . The subdivision of labour is the assassination of a people.' (David Urquhart)

Cooperation based on division of labour, in other words, manufacture, commences as a spontaneous formation. So soon as it attains some consistence and extension, it becomes the recognised methodical and systematic form of capitalist production. History shows how the division of labour peculiar to manufacture, strictly so called, acquires the best adapted form at first by experience, as it were behind the backs of the actors, and then, like the guild handicrafts, strives to hold fast that form when once found, and here and there succeeds in keeping it for centuries. Any alteration in this form, except in trivial matters, is solely owing to a revolution in the instruments of labour. Modern manufacture wherever it arises – I do not here allude to modern industry based on machinery – either finds the *disjecta membra poetae* ready to hand, and only waiting to be collected together, as is the case in the manufacture of clothes in large towns, or it can easily apply the principle of division, simply by exclusively assigning the various operations of a handicraft (such as book-binding) to particular men. In such cases, a week's experience is enough to determine the proportion between the numbers of the hands necessary for the various functions.

By decomposition of handicrafts, by specialisation of the instruments of labour, by the formation of detail labourers, and by grouping and combining the latter into a single mechanism, division of labour in manufacture creates a qualitative gradation and a quantitative proportion in the social process of production; it consequently creates a definite organisation of the labour of society, and thereby develops at the same time new productive forces in the society. In its specific capitalist form – and under the given conditions, it could take no other form than a capitalistic one – manufacture is but a particular method of begetting relative surplus-value, or of augmenting at the expense of the labourer the self-expansion of capital – usually called social wealth, 'Wealth of nations', etc. It increases the social productive power of labour, not only for the benefit of the capitalist instead of for that of the labourer, but it does this by crippling the individual labourers. It creates new conditions for the lordship of capital over labour. If, therefore, on the one hand, it presents itself historically as a progress and as a necessary phase in the economic development of society, on the other hand, it is a refined and civilised method of exploitation.

During the manufacturing period proper, i.e. the period during which manufacture is the predominant form taken by capitalist production, many obstacles are opposed to the full development of the peculiar tendencies of manufacture. Although manufacture creates, as we have already seen, a simple separation of the labourers into skilled and unskilled, simultaneously with their hierarchic arrangement in classes, yet the number of the unskilled labourers, owing to the preponderating influence of the skilled, remains very limited. Although it adapts the detail operations to the various degrees of maturity, strength, and development of the living instruments of labour, thus conducing to exploitation of women and children, yet this tendency as a whole is wrecked on the habits and the resistance of the male labourers. Although the splitting up of handicrafts lowers the cost of forming the workman, and thereby lowers his value, yet for the more difficult detail work, a longer apprenticeship is necessary, and even where it would be superfluous, is jealously insisted upon by the workmen. In England, for instance, we find the laws of apprenticeship, with their seven years' probation, in full force down to the end of the manufacturing period, and they are not thrown on one side till the advent of modern industry. Since handicraft skill is the foundation of manufacture, and since the mechanism of manufacture as a whole possesses no framework, apart from the labourers themselves, capital is constantly compelled to wrestle with the insubordination of the workmen. 'By the infirmity of human nature', says friend Ure, 'it happens that the more skilful the workman, the more self-willed and intractable he is apt to become, and of course the less fit a component of a mechanical system in which . . . he may do great damage to the whole.' Hence throughout the whole manufacturing period there runs the complaint of want of discipline among the workmen. And had we not the testimony of contemporary writers, the simple facts, that during the period between the sixteenth century and the epoch of modern industry, capital failed to become the master of the whole disposable working-time of the manufacturing labourers, that manufactures are short-lived, and change their locality from one country to another with the emigrating or immigrating workmen, these facts would speak volumes. 'Order must in one way or another be established', exclaims in 1770 the author of the *Essay on Trade and Commerce*. 'Order', re-echoes Dr Andrew Ure 66 years later, 'Order' was wanting in manufacture based on 'the scholastic dogma of division of labour', and 'Arkwright created order'.

At the same time manufacture was unable either to seize upon the production of society to its full extent, or to revolutionise that production to its very core. It towered up as an economic work of art, on the broad foundation of the town handicrafts and of the rural domestic industries. At a given stage in its development the narrow technical basis on which manufacture rested came into conflict with requirements of production that were created by manufacture itself.

One of its most finished creations was the workshop for the production of the instruments of labour themselves, including especially the complicated mechanical apparatus then already employed. A machine-factory, says Ure, 'displayed the division of labour in manifold gradations – the file, the drill, the lathe, having each its different workman in the order of skill'. This workshop, the product of the division of labour in manufacture, produced in its turn – machines. It is they that sweep away the handicraftsman's work as the regulating principle of social production. Thus, on the one hand, the technical reason for the life-long annexation of the workman to a detail function is removed. On the other hand, the fetters that this same principle laid on the dominion of capital fall away.

CHAPTER 15

Machinery and Modern Industry

SECTION 1. THE DEVELOPMENT OF MACHINERY

All fully developed machinery consists of three essentially different parts, the motor mechanism, the transmitting mechanism, and finally the tool or working machine. The motor mechanism is that which puts the whole in motion. It either generates its own motive power, like the steam engine, the caloric engine, the electromagnetic machine, etc. or it receives its impulse from some already existing natural force, like the waterwheel from a head of water, the windmill from wind, etc. The transmitting mechanism, composed of flywheels, shafting, toothed wheels, pullies, straps, ropes, bands, pinions, and gearing of the most varied kinds, regulates the motion, changes its form where necessary, as for instance, from linear to circular, and divides and distributes it among the working machines. These two first parts of the whole mechanism are there solely for putting the working machines in motion, by means of which motion the subject of labour is seized upon and modified as desired. The tool or working machine is that part of the machinery with which the industrial revolution of the eighteenth century started. And to this day it constantly serves as such a starting-point, whenever a handicraft, or a manufacture, is turned into an industry carried on by machinery.

The steam-engine itself, such as it was at its invention, during the manufacturing period at the close of the seventeenth century, and such as it continued to be down to 1780, did not give rise to any industrial revolution. It was, on the contrary, the invention of machines that made a revolution in the form of steam-engines necessary. As soon as man, instead of working with an implement on the subject of his labour, becomes merely the motive power of an implement-machine, it is a mere accident that motive power takes the disguise of human muscle; and it may equally well take the form of wind, water or steam.

Of course, this does not prevent such a change of form from producing great technical alterations in the mechanism that was originally constructed to be driven by man alone. Nowadays, all machines that have their way to make, such as sewing-machines, bread-making machines, etc. are, unless from their very nature their use on a small scale is excluded, constructed to be driven both by human and by purely mechanical motive power.

The machine, which is the starting-point of the industrial revolution, supersedes the workman, who handles a single tool, by a mechanism operating with a number of similar tools, and set in motion by a single motive power, whatever the form of that power may be. Here we have the machine, but only as an elementary factor of production by machinery.

Increase in the size of the machine, and in the number of its working tools, calls for a more massive mechanism to drive it; and this mechanism requires, in order to overcome its resistance, a mightier moving power than that of man, apart from the fact that man is a very imperfect instrument for producing uniform continued motion. But assuming that he is acting simply as a motor, that a machine has taken the place of his tool, it is evident that he can be replaced by natural forces. Of all the great motors handed down from the manufacturing period, horse-power is the worst, partly because a horse has a head of his own, partly because he is costly, and the extent to which he is applicable in factories is very restricted. Nevertheless the horse was extensively used during the infancy of modern industry. This is proved, as well by the complaints of contemporary agriculturists, as by the term 'horsepower', which has survived to this day as an expression for mechanical force.

Wind was too inconstant and uncontrollable, and besides, in England, the birthplace of modern industry, the use of water-power preponderated even during the manufacturing period. In the seventeenth century attempts had already been made to turn two pairs of millstones with a single waterwheel. But the increased size of the gearing was too much for the water-power, which had now become insufficient, and this was one of the circumstances that led to a more accurate investigation of the laws of friction. In the same way the irregularity caused by the motive power in mills that were put in motion by pushing and pulling a lever led to the theory, and the application, of the fly-wheel, which afterwards plays so important a part in modern industry. In this way, during the manufacturing period, were developed the first scientific and technical elements of modern mechanical industry. Arkwright's throstle-spinning mill was from the very first turned by water. But for all that, the use of water, as the predominant motive power, was beset with difficulties. It could not be increased at will, it failed at certain seasons of the year, and, above all, it was essentially local. Not till the invention of Watt's second and so-called double-acting steam-engine, was a prime mover found, that begot its own force by the consumption of coal and water, whose power was entirely under man's control, that was mobile and a means of locomotion, that was urban and not, like the waterwheel, rural, that permitted production to be concentrated in towns instead of, like the waterwheels, being scattered up and down the country, that was of universal technical application, and, relatively speaking, little affected in its choice of residence by local circumstances. The greatness of Watt's genius showed itself in the specification of the patent that he took out in April 1784. In that specification his steam-engine is described not as an invention for a specific purpose, but as an agent universally applicable in mechanical industry. In it he points out applications many of which, as for instance the steam-hammer, were not introduced till half a century later. Nevertheless he doubted the use of steam-engines in navigation. His successors, Boulton and Watt, sent to the exhibition of 1851 steam-engines of colossal size for ocean steamers.

As soon as tools had been converted from being manual implements of man into implements of a mechanical apparatus, of a machine, the motive mechanism also acquired an independent form, entirely emancipated from the restraints of human strength. Thereupon the individual machine, that we have hitherto been considering, sinks into a mere factor in production by machinery. One motive mechanism was now able to drive many machines at once. The motive mechanism grows with the number of the machines that are turned simultaneously, and the transmitting mechanism becomes a wide-spreading apparatus.

We now proceed to distinguish the cooperation of a number of machines of one kind from a complex system of machinery.

In the one case, the product is entirely made by a single machine, which performs all the various operations previously done by one handicraftsman with his tool; as, for instance, by a weaver with his loom; or by several handicraftsmen successively, either separately or as members of a system of manufacture. For example, in the manufacture of envelopes, one man folded the paper with the folder, another laid on the gum, a third turned the flap over, on which the device is impressed, a fourth embossed the device, and so on; and for each of these operations the envelope had to change hands. One single envelope machine now performs all these operations at once, and makes more than 3,000 envelopes in an hour. In the London exhibition of 1862 there was an American machine for making paper cornets. It cut the paper, pasted, folded, and finished 300 in a minute. Here the whole process, which, when carried on as manufacture, was split up into and carried out by, a series of operations, is completed by a single machine, working a combination of various tools. Now whether such a machine be merely a reproduction of a complicated manual implement or a combination of various simple implements specialised by manufacture, in either case, in the factory, i.e. in the workshop in which machinery alone is used, we meet again with simple cooperation; and, leaving the workman out of consideration for the moment, this cooperation presents itself to us, in the first instance, as the conglomeration in one place of similar and simultaneously acting machines. Thus, a weaving factory is constituted of a number of power-looms working side by side and a sewing factory of a number of sewing-machines all in the same building. But there is here a technical oneness in the whole system, owing to all the machines receiving their impulse simultaneously, and in an equal degree, from the pulsations of the common prime mover, by the intermediary of the transmitting mechanism; and this mechanism, to a certain extent, is also common to them all, since only particular ramifications of it branch off to each machine. Just as a number of tools, then, form the organs of a machine, so a number of machines of one kind constitute the organs of the motive mechanism.

A real machinery system, however, does not take the place of these independent machines, until the subject of labour goes through a connected series of detail processes, that are carried out by a chain of machines of various kinds, the one supplementing the other. Here we have again the cooperation by division of labour that characterises manufacture; only now, it is a combination of detail machines. The special tools of the various detail workmen, such as those of the beaters, combers, spinners, etc., in the woollen manufacture, are now transformed into the tools of specialised machines, each machine constituting a special organ with a special function in the system. In those branches of industry in which the machinery system is first introduced, manufacture itself furnishes, in a general way, the natural basis for the division, and consequent organisation, of the process of production. Nevertheless an essential difference at once manifests itself. In manufacture it is the workmen who, with their manual implements, must, either singly or in groups, carry on each particular detail process. If, on the one hand, the workman becomes adapted to the process, on the other, the process was previously made suitable to the workman. This subjective principle of the division of labour no longer exists in production by machinery. Here, the process as a whole is examined objectively in itself, that is to say without regard to the question of its execution by human hands it is analysed into its constituent phases; and the problem how to execute each detail process, and bind them all into a whole, is solved by the aid of machines, chemistry, etc. But of course in this case also, theory must be perfected by accumulated experience on a large scale. Each detail machine supplies raw material to the machine next in order; and since they are all working at the same time, the product is always going through the various stages of its fabrication, and is also constantly in a state of transition from one phase to another. Just as in manufacture, the direct cooperation of the detail labourers establishes a numerical proportion between the special groups, so in an organised system of machinery, where one detail machine is constantly kept employed by another, a fixed relation is established between their numbers, their size, and their speed. The collective machine, now an organised system of various kinds of single machines and of groups of single machines, becomes more and more perfect the more the process as a whole becomes a continuous one, i.e. the less the raw material is interrupted in its passage from its first phase to its last; in other words, the more its passage from one phase to another is effected, not by the hand of man, but by the machinery itself. In manufacture the isolation of each detail process is a condition imposed by the nature of division of labour, but in the fully developed factory the continuity of those processes is, on the contrary, imperative.

A system of machinery, whether it reposes on the mere cooperation of similar machines, as in weaving, or on a combination of different machines, as in spinning, constitutes in itself a huge automaton, whenever it is driven by a self-acting prime mover. But although the factory as a whole be driven by its steam-engine, yet either some of the individual machines may require the aid of the workman for some of their movements (such aid was necessary for the running in of the mule carriage, before the invention of the self-acting mule, and is still necessary in fine-spinning mills); or, to enable a machine to do its work, certain parts of it may require to be handled by the workman like a manual tool; this was the case in machine-makers' workshops, before the conversion of the slide rest into a self-actor. As soon as a machine executes, without man's help, all the movements requisite to elaborate the raw material, needing only attendance from him, we have an automatic system of machinery, and one that is susceptible of constant improvement in its details. Such improvements as the apparatus that stops a drawing frame, whenever a sliver breaks, and the self-acting stop, that stops the power-loom so soon as the shuttle bobbin is emptied of weft, are quite modern inventions. As an example, both of continuity of production, and of the carrying out of the automatic principle, we may take a modern paper mill. In the paper industry generally we may advantageously study in detail not only the distinctions between modes of production based on different means of production, but also the connexion of the social conditions of production with those modes: for the old German paper-making furnishes us with a sample of handicraft production; that of Holland in the seventeenth and of France in the eighteenth century with a sample of manufacturing in the strict sense; and that of modern England with a sample of automatic fabrication of this article. Besides these, there still exist, in India and China, two distinct antique Asiatic forms of the same industry.

An organised system of machines, to which motion is communicated by the transmitting mechanism from a central automaton, is the most developed form of production by machinery. Here we have, in the place of the isolated machine, a mechanical monster whose body fills whole factories, and whose demon power, at first veiled under the slow and measured motions of his giant limbs, at length breaks out into the fast and furious whirl of his countless working organs.

There were mules and steam-engines before there were any labourers, whose exclusive occupation it was to make mules and steam-engines; just as men wore clothes before there were such people as tailors. The inventions of Vaucanson, Arkwright, Watt, and others, were, however, practicable, only because those inventors found, ready to hand, a considerable number of skilled mechanical workmen, placed at their disposal by the manufacturing period. Some of those workmen were independent handicraftsmen of various trades, others were grouped together in manufactures, in which, as before-mentioned, division of labour was strictly carried out. As inventions increased in number, and the demand for the newly discovered machines grew larger, the machine-making industry split up, more and more, into numerous independent branches, and division of labour in these manufactures was more and more developed. Here, then, we see in manufacture the immediate technical foundation of modern industry. Manufacture produced the machinery by means of which modern industry abolished the handicraft and manufacturing systems in those spheres of production that it first seized upon. The factory system was therefore raised, in the natural course of things, on an inadequate foundation. When the system attained to a certain degree of development, it had to root up this ready-made foundation, which in the meantime had been elaborated on the old lines, and to build up for itself a basis that should correspond to its methods of production. Just as the individual machine retains a dwarfish character, so long as it is worked by the power of man alone, and just as no system of machinery could be properly developed before the steam-engine took the place of the earlier motive powers, animals, wind, and even water; so, too, modern industry was crippled in its complete development, so long as its characteristic instrument of production, the machine, owed its existence to personal strength and personal skill, and depended on the muscular development, the keenness of sight, and the cunning of hand, with which the detail workmen in manufactures, and the manual labourers in handicrafts, wielded their dwarfish implements. Thus, apart from the dearness of the machines made in this way, a circumstance that is ever present to the mind of the capitalist, the expansion of industries carried on by means of machinery, and the invasion by machinery of fresh branches of production, were dependent on the growth of a class of workmen, who, owing to the almost artistic nature of their employment, could increase their numbers only gradually, and not by leaps and bounds. But besides this, at a certain stage of its development modern industry became technologically incompatible with the basis furnished for it by handicraft and manufacture. The increasing size of the prime movers, of the transmitting mechanism, and of the machines proper, the greater complication, multiformity and regularity of the details of these machines, as they more and more departed from the model of those originally made by manual labour, and acquired a form, untrammelled except by the conditions under which they worked, the perfecting of the automatic system, and the use, every day more unavoidable, of a more refractory material, such as iron instead of wood – the solution of all these problems, which sprang up by the force of circumstances, everywhere met with a stumbling-block in the personal restrictions, which even the collective labourer of manufacture could not break through, except to a limited extent. Such machines as the modern hydraulic press, the modern power-loom, and the modern carding engine, could never have been furnished by manufacture.

A radical change in the mode of production in one sphere of industry involves a similar change in other spheres. This happens at first in such branches of industry as are connected together by being separate phases of a process, and yet are isolated by the social division of labour, in such a way that each of them produces an independent commodity. Thus spinning by machinery made weaving by machinery a necessity, and both together made the mechanical and chemical revolution that took place in bleaching, printing, and dyeing, imperative. So too, on the other hand, the revolution in cotton-spinning called forth the invention of the gin for separating the seeds from the cotton fibre; it was only by means of this invention, that the production of cotton became possible on the enormous scale at present required. But more especially, the revolution in the modes of production of industry and agriculture made necessary a revolution in the general conditions of the social process of production, i.e. in the means of communication and of transport. In a society whose pivot, to use an expression of Fourier, was agriculture on a small scale, with its subsidiary domestic industries, and the urban handicrafts, the means of communication and transport were so utterly inadequate to the productive requirements of the manufacturing period, with its extended division of social labour, its concentration of the instruments of labour, and of the workmen, and its colonial markets, that they became in fact revolutionised. In the same way the means of communication and transport handed down from the manufacturing period soon became unbearable trammels on modern industry, with its feverish haste of production, its enormous extent, its constant flinging of capital and labour from one sphere of production into another, and its newly-created connexions with the markets of the whole world. Hence, apart from the radical changes introduced in the construction of sailing vessels, the means of communication and transport became gradually adapted to the modes of production of mechanical industry, by the creation of a system of river steamers, railways, ocean steamers, and telegraphs. But the huge masses of iron that had now to be forged, to be welded, to be cut, to be bored, and to be shaped, demanded on their part cyclopean machines, for the construction of which the methods of the manufacturing period were utterly inadequate.

Modern industry had therefore itself to take in hand the machine, its characteristic instrument of production, and to construct machines by machines. It was not till it did this that it built up for itself a fitting technical foundation, and stood on its own feet. Machinery, simultaneously with the increasing use of it, in the first decades of this century, appropriated, by degrees, the fabrication of machines proper. But it was only during the decade preceding 1866 that the construction of railways and ocean steamers on a stupendous scale called into existence the cyclopean machines now employed in the construction of prime movers.

The most essential condition to the production of machines by machines was a prime mover capable of exerting any amount of force, and yet under perfect control. Such a condition was already supplied by the steam-engine. But at the same time it was necessary to produce the geometrically accurate straight lines, planes, circles, cylinders, cones, and spheres, required in the detail parts of the machines. This problem Henry Maudsley solved in the first decade of this century by the invention of the slide rest, a tool that was soon made automatic, and in a modified form was applied to other constructive machines besides the lathe, for which it was originally intended. This mechanical appliance replaces, not some particular tool, but the hand itself, which produces a given form by holding and guiding the cutting tool along the iron or other material operated upon. Thus it became possible to produce the forms of the individual parts of machinery 'with a degree of ease, accuracy, and speed, that no accumulated experience of the hand of the most skilled workman would give'.

If we now fix our attention on that portion of the machinery employed in the construction of machines, which constitutes the operating tool, we find the manual implements reappearing, but on a cyclopean scale. The operating part of the boring machine is an immense drill driven by a steam-engine; without this machine, on the other hand, the cylinders of large steam-engines and of hydraulic presses could not be made. The mechanical lathe is only a cyclopean reproduction of the ordinary foot-lathe; the planing machine, an iron carpenter, that works on iron with the same tools that the human carpenter employs on wood; the instrument that, on the London wharves, cuts the veneers, is a gigantic razor; the tool of the shearing machine, which shears iron as easily as a tailor's scissors cut cloth, is a monster pair of scissors; and the steam-hammer works with an ordinary hammer head, but of such a weight that not Thor himself could wield it. These steam-hammers are an invention of Nasmyth, and there is one that weighs over six tons and strikes with a vertical fall of seven feet, on an anvil weighing 36 tons. It is mere child's-play for it to crush a block of granite into powder, yet it is no less capable of driving, with a succession of light taps, a nail into a piece of soft wood.

The implements of labour, in the form of machinery, necessitate the substitution of natural forces for human force, and the conscious application of science, instead of rule of thumb. In manufacture, the organisation of the social labour-process is purely subjective; it is a combination of detail labourers; in its machinery system, modern industry has a productive organism that is purely objective, in which the labourer becomes a mere appendage to an already existing material condition of production. In simple cooperation, and even in that founded on division of labour, the suppression of the isolated by the collective workman still appears to be more or less accidental. Machinery, with a few exceptions to be mentioned later, operates only by means of associated labour, or labour in common. Hence the cooperative character of the labour-process is, in the latter case, a technical necessity dictated by the instrument of labour itself.

SECTION 2. THE VALUE TRANSFERRED BY MACHINERY TO THE PRODUCT

We saw that the productive forces resulting from cooperation and division of labour cost capital nothing. They are natural forces of social labour. So also physical forces, like steam, water, etc. when appropriated to productive processes, cost nothing. But just as a man requires lungs to breathe with, so he requires something that is work of man's hand, in order to consume physical forces productively. A waterwheel is necessary to exploit the force of water, and a steam-engine to exploit the elasticity of steam. Once discovered, the law of the deviation of the magnetic needle in the field of an electric current, or the law of the magnetisation of iron, around which an electric current circulates, cost never a penny. But the exploitation of these laws for the purposes of telegraphy, etc. necessitates a costly and extensive apparatus. The tool, as we have seen, is not exterminated by the machine. From being a dwarf implement of the human organism, it expands and multiplies into the implement of a mechanism created by man. Capital now sets the labourer to work, not with a manual tool, but with a machine which itself handles the tools. Although therefore it is clear at the first glance that, by incorporating both stupendous physical forces, and the natural sciences, with the process of production, modern industry raises the productiveness of labour to an extraordinary degree, it is by no means equally clear, that this increased productive force is not, on the other hand, purchased by an increased expenditure of labour. Machinery, like every other component of constant capital, creates no new value, but yields up its own value to the product that it serves to beget. In so far as the machine has value, and, in consequence, parts with value to the product, it forms an element in the value of that product. Instead of being cheapened, the product is made dearer in proportion to the value of the machine. And it is clear as noon-day that machines and systems of machinery, the characteristic instruments of labour of modern industry, are incomparably more loaded with value than the implements used in handicrafts and manufactures.

In the first place, it must be observed that the machinery, while always entering as a whole into the labour-process, enters into the value-begetting process only by bits. It never adds more value than it loses, on an average, by wear and tear. Hence there is a great difference between the value of a machine, and the value transferred in a given time by that machine to the product. The longer the life of the machine in the labour-process, the greater is that difference. It is true, no doubt, as we have already seen, that every instrument of labour enters as a whole into the labour-process, and only piece-meal, proportionally to its average daily loss by wear and tear, into the value-begetting process. But this difference between the instrument as a whole and its daily wear and tear, is much greater in a machine than in a tool, because the machine, being made from more durable material, has a longer life; because its employment, being regulated by strictly scientific laws, allows of greater economy in the wear and tear of its parts, and in the materials it consumes; and lastly, because its field of production is incomparably larger than that of a tool. After making allowance, both in the case of the machine and of the tool, for their average daily cost, that is for the value they transmit to the product by their average daily wear and tear, and for their consumption of auxiliary substance, such as oil, coal, and so on, they each do their work gratuitously, just like the forces furnished by Nature without the help of man. The greater the productive power of the machinery compared with that of the tool, the greater is the extent of its gratuitous service compared with that of the tool. In modern industry man succeeded for the first time in making the product of his past labour work on a large scale gratuitously, like the forces of Nature.

In treating of cooperation and manufacture, it was shown that certain general factors of production such as buildings are, in comparison with the scattered means of production of the isolated workman, economised by being consumed in common, and that they therefore make the product cheaper. In a system of machinery, not only is the framework of the machine consumed in common by its numerous operating implements, but the prime mover, together with a part of the transmitting mechanism, is consumed in common by the numerous operative machines.

Given the difference between the value of the machinery, and the value transferred by it in a day to the product, the extent to which this latter value makes the product dearer, depends in the first instance, upon the size of the product; so to say upon its area. Mr Baynes of Blackburn in a lecture published in 1858 estimates that 'each real mechanical horse-power will drive 450 self-acting mule spindles, with preparation, or 200 throstle spindles, or 15 looms for 40 inch cloth with the appliances for warping, sizing, etc.' In the first case, it is the day's product of 450 mule spindles, in the second, of 200 throstle spindles, in the third, of 15 power-looms, over which the daily cost of one horsepower, and the wear and tear of the machinery set in motion by that power, are spread; so that only a very minute value is transferred by such wear and tear to a pound of yarn or a yard of cloth. The same is the case with the steam-hammer mentioned above. Since its daily wear and tear, its coal-consumption, etc. are spread over the stupendous masses of iron hammered by it in a day, only a small value is added to a hundred weight of iron; but that value would be very great, if the cyclopean instrument were employed in driving in nails.

Given a machine's capacity for work, that is the number of its operating tools, or, where it is a question of force, their mass, the amount of its product will depend on the velocity of its working parts, on the speed for instance of the spindles, or on the number of blows given by the hammer in a minute. Many of these colossal hammers strike seventy times in a minute, and Ryder's patent machine for forging spindles with small hammers gives as many as 700 strokes per minute.

Given the rate at which machinery transfers its value to the product, the amount of value so transferred depends on the total value of the machinery. The less labour it contains, the less value it imparts to the product. The less value it gives up, so much the more productive it is, and so much the more its services approximate to those of natural forces. But the production of machinery by machinery lessens its value relatively to its extension and efficacy.

An analysis and comparison of the prices of commodities produced by handicrafts or manufactures, and of the prices of the same commodities produced by machinery, shows generally that, in the product of machinery, the value due to the instruments of labour increases relatively, but decreases absolutely. In other words, its absolute amount decreases, but its amount, relatively to the total value of the product, of a pound of yarn, for instance, increases.

It is evident that whenever it costs as much labour to produce a machine as is saved by the employment of that machine, there is nothing but a transposition of labour; consequently the total labour required to produce a commodity is not lessened or the productiveness of labour is not increased. It is clear however that the difference between the labour a machine costs and the labour it saves, in other words that the degree of its productiveness does not depend on the difference between its own value and the value of the implement it replaces. As long as the labour spent on a machine, and consequently the portion of its value added to the product, remains smaller than the value added by the workman to the product with his tool, there is always a difference of labour saved in favour of the machine. The productiveness of a machine is therefore measured by the human labour-power it replaces. According to Mr Baynes, 2½ operatives are required for the 450 mule spindles, inclusive of preparation machinery, that are driven by one horsepower; each self-acting mule spindle, working ten hours, produces 13 ounces of yarn (average number of thickness); consequently 2½ operatives spin weekly 365⅝ lb of yarn. Hence, leaving waste on one side, 366 lb of cotton absorb, during their conversion into yarn, only 150 hours' labour, or fifteen days' labour of ten hours each. But with a spinning-wheel, supposing the hand-spinner to produce thirteen ounces of yarn in sixty hours, the same weight of cotton would absorb 2,700 days' labour of ten hours each, or 27,000 hours' labour. Where blockprinting, the old method of printing calico by hand, has been superseded by machine printing, a single machine prints, with the aid of one man or boy, as much calico of four colours in one hour, as it formerly took 200 men to do. Before Eli Whitney invented the cotton gin in 1793, the separation of the seed from a pound of cotton cost an average day's labour. By means of his invention one negress was enabled to clean 100 lb daily; and since then, the efficacy of the gin has been considerably increased. A pound of cotton wool, previously costing 50 cents to produce, included after that invention more unpaid labour, and was consequently sold with greater profit, at 10 cents. In India they employ for separating the wool from the seed, an instrument, half machine, half tool, called a churka; with this one man and a woman can clean 28 lb daily. With the churka invented some years ago by Dr Forbes, one man and a boy produce 250 lb daily. If oxen, steam, or water be used for driving it, only a few boys and girls as feeders are required. Sixteen of these machines driven by oxen do as much work in a day as formerly 750 people did on an average.

As already stated, a steam-plough does as much work in one hour at a cost of threepence, as 66 men at a cost of 15 shillings. I return to this example in order to clear up an erroneous notion. The 15 shillings are by no means the expression in money of all the labour expended in one hour by the 66 men. If the ratio of surplus-labour to necessary labour were 100 per cent, these 66 men would produce in one hour a value of 30 shillings, although their wages, 15 shillings represent only their labour for half an hour. Suppose, then, a machine cost as much as the wages for a year of the 150 men it displaces, say £3,000; this £3,000 is by no means the expression in money of the labour added to the object produced by these 150 men before the introduction of the machine, but only of that portion of their year's labour which was expended for themselves and represented their wages. On the other hand, the £3,000, the money-value of the machine, expresses all the labour expended on its production, no matter in what proportion this labour constitutes wages for the workman, and surplus-value for the capitalist. Therefore, though a machine cost as much as the labour-power displaced by it costs, yet the labour materialised in it is even then much less than the living labour it replaces.

The use of machinery for the exclusive purpose of cheapening the product, is limited in this way, that less labour must be expended in producing the machinery than is displaced by the employment of that machinery. For the capitalist however, this use is still more limited. Instead of paying for the labour, he only pays the value of the labour-power employed; therefore, the limit to his using a machine is fixed by the difference between the value of the machine and the value of the labour-power replaced by it. Since the division of the day's work into necessary and surplus-labour differs in different countries, and even in the same country at different periods, or in different branches of industry; and further, since the actual wage of the labourer at one time sinks below the value of his labour-power, at another rises above it, it is possible for the difference between the price of the machinery and the price of the labour-power replaced by that machinery to vary very much, although the difference between the quantity of labour requisite to produce the machine and the total quantity replaced by it remain constant. (Hence in a communistic society there would be a very different scope for the employment of machinery than there can be in a bourgeois society.) But it is the former difference alone that determines the cost, to the capitalist, of producing a commodity, and, through the pressure of competition, influences his action. Hence the invention nowadays of machines in England that are employed only in North America; just as in the sixteenth and seventeenth centuries, machines were invented in Germany to be used only in Holland, and just as many a French invention of the eighteenth century was exploited in England alone. In the older countries, machinery, when employed in some branches of industry, creates such a redundancy of labour in other branches that in these latter the fall of wages below the value of labour-power impedes the use of machinery, and, from the standpoint of the capitalist whose profit comes not from a diminution of the labour employed, but of the labour paid for, renders that use superfluous and often impossible. In some branches of the woollen manufacture in England the employment of children has during recent years been considerably diminished, and in some cases has been entirely abolished. Why? Because the Factory Acts made two sets of children necessary, one working six hours, the other four, or each working five hours. But the parents refused to sell the 'half-timers' cheaper than the 'full-timers'. hence the substitution of machinery for the 'half-timers'. Before the labour of women and of children under ten years of age was forbidden in mines, capitalists considered the employment of naked women and girls, often in company with men, so far sanctioned by their moral code, and especially by their ledgers, that it was only after the passing of the Act that they had recourse to machinery. The Yankees have invented a stone-breaking machine. The English do not make use of it, because the wretch who does this work gets paid for such a small portion of his labour that machinery would increase the cost of production to the capitalist. In England women are still occasionally used instead of horses for hauling canal boats, because the labour required to produce horses and machines is an accurately known quantity, while that required to maintain the women of the surplus-population is below all calculation. Hence nowhere do we find a more shameful squandering of human labour-power for the most despicable purposes than in England, the land of machinery.

SECTION 3. THE PROXIMATE EFFECTS OF MACHINERY ON THE WORKMAN

The starting-point of modern industry is, as we have shown, the revolution in the instruments of labour, and this revolution attains its most highly developed form in the organised system of machinery in a factory. Before we inquire how human material is incorporated with this objective organism, let us consider some general effects of this revolution on the labourer himself.

a) Appropriation of Supplementary Labour-power by Capital. The Employment of Women and Children

In so far as machinery dispenses with muscular power, it becomes a means of employing labourers of slight muscular strength, and those whose bodily development is incomplete, but whose limbs are all the more supple. The labour of women and children was, therefore, the first thing sought for by capitalists who used machinery. That mighty substitute for labour and labourers was forthwith changed into a means for increasing the number of wage-labourers by enrolling, under the direct sway of capital, every member of the workman's family, without distinction of age or sex. Compulsory work for the capitalist usurped the place, not only of the children's play, but also of free labour at home within moderate limits for the support of the family.

The value of labour-power was determined, not only by the labour-time necessary to maintain the individual adult labourer, but also by that necessary to maintain his family. Machinery, by throwing every member of that family on to the labour-market, spreads the value of the man's labour-power over his whole family. It thus depreciates his labour-power. To purchase the labour-power of a family of four workers may, perhaps, cost more than it formerly did to purchase the labour-power of the head of the family, but in return, four days' labour takes the place of one, and their price falls in proportion to the excess of the surplus-labour of four over the surplus-labour of one. In order that the family may live, four people must now not only labour, but expend surplus-labour for the capitalist. Thus we see that machinery, while augmenting the human material that forms the principal object of capital's exploiting power at the same time raises the degree of exploitation.

Machinery also revolutionises out and out the contract between the labourer and the capitalist, which formally fixes their mutual relations. Taking the exchange of commodities as our basis, our first assumption was that capitalist and labourer met as free persons, as independent owners of commodities; the one possessing money and means of production, the other labour-power. But now the capitalist buys children and young persons under age. Previously, the workman sold his own labour-power, which he disposed of nominally as a free agent.

Now he sells wife and child. He has become a slave-dealer. The demand for children's labour often resembles in form the inquiries for negro slaves, such as were formerly to be read among the advertisements in American journals.

> My attention [says an English factory inspector] was drawn to an advertisement in the local paper of one of the most important manufacturing towns of my district, of which the following is a copy: Wanted, 12 to 20 young persons, not younger than what can pass for 13 years. Wages, 4 shillings a week. Apply etc.

The phrase 'what can pass for 13 years', has reference to the fact that by the Factory Act, children under 13 years may work only 6 hours. A surgeon officially appointed must certify their age. The manufacturer therefore asks for children who look as if they were already 13 years old. The decrease, often by leaps and bounds, in the number of children under 13 years employed in factories, a decrease that is shown in an astonishing manner by the English statistics of the last 20 years, was for the most part, according to the evidence of the factory inspectors themselves, the work of the certifying surgeons, who overstated the age of the children, agreeably to the capitalist's greed for exploitation, and the sordid trafficking needs of the parents. In the notorious district of Bethnal Green, a public market is held every Monday and Tuesday morning, where children of both sexes from 9 years of age upwards, hire themselves out to the silk manufacturers. 'The usual terms are 1s. 8d. a week [this belongs to the parents] and "2d. for myself and tea." The contract is binding only for the week. The scene and language while this market is going on are quite disgraceful.' It has also occurred in England that women have taken 'children from the workhouse and let anyone have them out for 2s. 6d. a week'. In spite of legislation, the number of boys sold in Great Britain by their parents to act as live chimney-sweeping machines (although there exist plenty of machines to replace them) exceeds 2,000. The revolution effected by machinery in the juridical relations between the buyer and the seller of labour-power causing the transaction as a whole to lose the appearance of a contract between free persons, afforded the English Parliament an excuse, founded on juridical principles, for the interference of the state with factories. Whenever the law limits the labour of children to six hours in industries not before interfered with, the complaints of the manufacturers are always renewed. They allege that numbers of the parents withdraw their children from the industry brought under the Act, in order to sell them where 'freedom of labour' still rules, i.e.

where children under 13 years are compelled to work like grown-up people, and therefore can be got rid of at a higher price. But since capital is by nature a leveller, since it exacts in every sphere of production equality in the conditions of the exploitation of labour, the limitation by law of children's labour, in one branch of industry, becomes the cause of its limitation in others.

We have already alluded to the physical deterioration as well of the children and young persons as of the women, whom machinery, first directly in the factories that shoot up on its basis, and then indirectly in all the remaining branches of industry, subjects to the exploitation of capital. In this place, therefore, we dwell only on one point, the enormous mortality during the first few years of their life of the children of the operatives. In sixteen of the registration districts into which England is divided, there are for every 100,000 children alive under the age of one year, only 9,000 deaths in a year on an average (in one district only 7,047); in 24 districts the deaths are over 10,000, but under 11,000; in 39 districts, over 11,000 but under 12,000; in 48 districts over 12,000, but under 13,000; in 22 districts over 20,000; in 25 districts over 21,000; in 17 over 22,000; in 11 over 23,000; in Hoo, Wolverhampton, Ashton-under-Lyme, and Preston, over 24,000; in Nottingham, Stockport, and Bradford, over 25,000; in Wisbeach, 26,000; and in Manchester, 26,125. As was shown by an official medical inquiry in the year 1861, the high death-rates are, apart from local causes, principally due to the employment of the mothers away from their homes, and to the neglect and maltreatment, consequent on her absence, such as, amongst others, insufficient nourishment, unsuitable food, and dosing with opiates; besides this, there arises an unnatural estrangement between mother and child, and as a consequence intentional starving and poisoning of the children. In those agricultural districts 'where a minimum in the employment of women exists, the death-rate is on the other hand very low.' The Inquiry Commission of 1861 led, however, to the unexpected result that in some purely agricultural districts bordering on the North Sea, the death-rate of children under one year old almost equalled that of the worst factory districts. Dr Julian Hunter was therefore commissioned to investigate this phenomenon on the spot. His report is incorporated with the *Sixth Report on Public Health*. Up to that time it was supposed that the children were decimated by malaria and other diseases peculiar to low-lying and marshy districts. But the inquiry showed the very opposite, namely, that the same cause which drove away malaria, the conversion of the land from a morass in winter and a scanty pasture in summer into fruitful corn land, created the exceptional death-rate of the infants. The 70 medical men whom Dr Hunter examined in that district, were 'wonderfully in accord' on this point. In fact, the revolution in the mode of cultivation had led to the introduction of the industrial system. Married women, who work in gangs along with boys and girls, are, for a stipulated sum of money placed at the disposal of the farmer by a man called the 'undertaker', who contracts for the whole gang.

> These gangs will sometimes travel many miles from their own village; they are to be met morning and evening on the roads, dressed in short petticoats, with suitable coats and boots, and sometimes trousers, looking wonderfully strong and healthy, but tainted with a customary immorality and heedless of the fatal results which their love of this busy and independent life is bringing on their unfortunate offspring who are pining at home.

Every phenomenon of the factory districts is here reproduced, including, but to a greater extent, ill-disguised infanticide, and dosing children with opiates. 'My knowledge of such evils', says Dr Simon, the medical officer of the Privy Council and editor in chief of the *Reports on Public Health*, 'may excuse the profound misgiving with which I regard any large industrial employment of adult women.' 'Happy indeed', exclaims Mr Baker, the factory inspector in his official report, 'happy indeed will it be for the manufacturing districts of England, when every married woman having a family is prohibited from working in any textile works at all.'

b) Prolongation of the Working Day

If machinery be the most powerful means for increasing the productiveness of labour, i.e. for shortening the working-time required in the production of a commodity, it becomes in the hands of capital the most powerful means, in those industries first invaded by it, for lengthening the working day beyond all bounds set by human nature. It creates, on the one hand, new conditions by which capital is enabled to give free scope to this its constant tendency, and on the other hand, new motives with which to whet capital's appetite for the labour of others.

In the first place, in the form of machinery, the implements of labour become automatic, things moving and working independent of the workman. They are thenceforth an industrial *perpetuum mobile*, that would go on producing forever, did it not meet with certain natural obstructions in the weak bodies and the strong wills of its human attendants. The automaton, as capital, and because it is capital, is endowed, in the person of the capitalist, with intelligence and will; it is therefore animated by the longing to reduce to a minimum the resistance offered by that repellent yet elastic natural barrier, man. This resistance is moreover lessened by the apparent lightness of machine work, and by the more pliant and docile character of the women and children employed on it.

The productiveness of machinery is, as we saw, inversely proportional to the value transferred by it to the product. The longer the life of the machine, the greater is the mass of the products over which the value transmitted by the machine is spread, and the less is the portion of that value added to each single commodity. The active lifetime of a machine is, however, clearly dependent on the length of the working day, or on the duration of the daily labour-process multiplied by the number of days for which the process is carried on.

The wear and tear of a machine is not exactly proportional to its working-time. And even if it were so, a machine working 16 hours daily for 7½ years covers as long a working period as, and transmits to the total product no more value than, the same machine would if it worked only 8 hours daily for 15 years. But in the first case the value of the machine would be reproduced twice as quickly as in the latter, and the capitalist would, by this use of the machine, absorb in 7½ years as much surplus-value as in the second case he would in 15.

The material wear and tear of a machine is of two kinds. The one arises from use, as coins wear away by circulating, the other from non-use, as a sword rusts when left in its scabbard. The latter kind is due to the elements. The former is more or less directly proportional, the latter to a certain extent inversely proportional, to the use of the machine.

But in addition to the material wear and tear, a machine also undergoes what we may call a moral depreciation. It loses exchange-value, either by machines of the same sort being produced cheaper than it, or by better machines entering into competition with it. In both cases, be the machine ever so young and full of life, its value is no longer determined by the labour actually materialised in it, but by the labour-time requisite to reproduce either it or the better machine. It has, therefore, lost value more or less. The shorter the period taken to reproduce its total value, the less is the danger of moral depreciation; and the longer the working day, the shorter is that period. When machinery is first introduced into an industry, new methods of reproducing it more cheaply follow blow upon blow, and so do improvements, that not only affect individual parts and details of the machine, but its entire build. It is, therefore, in the early days of the life of machinery that this special incentive to the prolongation of the working day makes itself felt most acutely.

Given the length of the working day, all other circumstances remaining the same, the exploitation of double the number of workmen demands, not only a doubling of that part of constant capital which is invested in machinery and buildings, but also of that part which is laid out in raw material and auxiliary substances. The lengthening of the working day, on the other hand, allows of production on an extended scale without any alteration in the amount of capital laid out on machinery and buildings. Not only is there therefore an increase of surplus-value, but the outlay necessary to obtain it diminishes. It is true that this takes place, more or less, with every lengthening of the working day; but in the case under consideration, the change is more marked, because the capital converted into the instruments of labour preponderates to a greater degree. The development of the factory system fixes a constantly increasing portion of the capital in a form, in which, on the one hand, its value is capable of continual self-expansion, and in which, on the other hand, it loses both use-value and exchange-value whenever it loses contact with living labour. 'When a labourer', said Mr Ashworth, a cotton magnate, 'lays down his spade, he renders useless, for that period, a capital worth eighteen pence. When one of our people leaves the mill, he renders useless a capital that has cost £100,000.' Only fancy! making 'useless' for a single moment, a capital that has cost £100,000! It is, in truth, monstrous that a single one of our people should ever leave the factory! The increased use of machinery makes a constantly increasing lengthening of the working day 'desirable'.

Machinery produces relative surplus-value; not only by directly depreciating the value of labour-power, and by indirectly cheapening the same through cheapening the commodities that enter into its reproduction, but also, when it is first introduced sporadically into an industry, by converting the labour employed by the owner of that machinery into labour of a higher degree and greater efficacy, by raising the social value of the article produced above its individual value, and thus enabling the capitalist to replace the value of a day's labour-power by a smaller portion of the value of a day's product. During this transition period, when the use of machinery is a sort of monopoly, the profits are therefore exceptional, and the capitalist endeavours to exploit thoroughly 'the sunny time of this his first love', by prolonging the working day as much as possible. The magnitude of the profit whets his appetite for more profit.

As the use of machinery becomes more general in a particular industry, the social value of the product sinks down to its individual value, and the law that surplus-value does not arise from the labour-power that has been replaced by the machinery, but from the labour-power actually employed in working with the machinery, asserts itself. Surplus-value arises from variable capital alone, and we saw that the amount of surplus-value depends on two factors, viz. the rate of surplus-value and the number of the workmen simultaneously employed. Given the length of the working day, the rate of surplus-value is determined by the relative duration of the necessary labour and of the surplus-labour in a day. The number of the labourers simultaneously employed depends, on its side, on the ratio of the variable to the constant capital. Now, however much the use of machinery may increase the surplus-labour at the expense of the necessary labour by heightening the productiveness of labour, it is clear that it attains this result, only by diminishing the number of workmen employed by a given amount of capital. It converts what was formerly variable capital, invested in labour-power, into machinery which, being constant capital, does not produce surplus-value. It is impossible, for instance, to squeeze as much surplus-value out of 2 as out of 24 labourers. If each of these 24 men gives only one hour of surplus-labour in 12, the 24 men give together 24 hours of surplus-labour, while 24 hours is the total labour of the two men. Hence, the application of machinery to the production of surplus-value implies a contradiction which is immanent in it, since of the two factors of the surplus-value created by a given amount of capital, one, the rate of surplus-value, cannot be increased, except by diminishing the other, the number of workmen. This contradiction comes to light as soon as by the general employment of machinery in a given industry, the value of the machine-produced commodity regulates the value of all commodities of the same sort; and it is this contradiction, that in its turn, drives the capitalist, without his being conscious of the fact, to excessive lengthening of the working day, in order that he may compensate the decrease in the relative number of labourers exploited by an increase not only of the relative, but of the absolute surplus-labour.

If then, the capitalistic employment of machinery, on the one hand, supplies new and powerful motives to an excessive lengthening of the working day, and radically changes, as well the methods of labour, as also the character of the social working organism, in such a manner as to break down all opposition to this tendency, on the other hand it produces, partly by opening out to the capitalist new strata of the working class, previously inaccessible to him, partly by setting free the labourers it supplants, a surplus working population, which is compelled to submit to the dictation of capital. Hence that remarkable phenomenon in the history of modern industry, that machinery sweeps away every moral and natural restriction on the length of the working day. Hence too, the economic paradox that the most powerful instrument for shortening labour-time becomes the most unfailing means for placing every moment of the labourer's time and that of his family at the disposal of the capitalist for the purpose of expanding the value of his capital. 'If', dreamed Aristotle, the greatest thinker of antiquity,

> if every tool, when summoned, or even of its own accord, could do the work that befits it, just as the creations of Daedalus moved of themselves, or the tripods of Hephaestos went of their own accord to their sacred work, if the weavers' shuttles were to weave of themselves, then there would be no need either of apprentices for the master workers, or of slaves for the lords.

And Antipatros, a Greek poet of the time of Cicero, hailed the invention of the waterwheel for grinding corn, an invention that is the elementary form of all machinery, as the giver of freedom to female slaves, and the bringer back of the golden age. Oh! those heathens! They understood nothing of political economy and Christianity. They did not, for example, comprehend that machinery is the surest means of lengthening the working day. They perhaps excused the slavery of one on the ground that it was a means to the full development of another. But to preach slavery of the masses, in order that a few crude and half-educated parvenus, might become 'eminent spinners', 'extensive sausage-makers', and 'influential shoe-black dealers', to do this, they lacked the bump of Christianity.

c) Intensification of Labour

The immoderate lengthening of the working day, produced by machinery in the hands of capital, leads to a reaction on the part of society, the very sources of whose life are menaced; and, thence, to a normal working day whose length is fixed by law. Thenceforth a phenomenon that we have already met with, namely, the intensification of labour, develops into great importance. Our analysis of absolute surplus-value had reference primarily to the extension or duration of the labour, its intensity being assumed as given. We now proceed to consider the substitution of a more intensified labour for labour of more extensive duration, and the degree of the former.

It is self-evident that in proportion as the use of machinery spreads, and the experience of a special class of workmen habituated to machinery accumulates, the rapidity and intensity of labour increase as a natural consequence. Thus in England, during half a century, lengthening of the working day went hand in hand with increasing intensity of factory labour. Nevertheless the reader will clearly see that where we have labour, not carried on by fits and starts, but repeated day after day with unvarying uniformity, a point must inevitably be reached where extension of the working day and intensity of the labour mutually exclude one another, in such a way that lengthening of the working day becomes compatible only with a lower degree of intensity, and a higher degree of intensity only with a shortening of the working day. So soon as the gradually surging revolt of the working class compelled Parliament to shorten compulsorily the hours of labour, and to begin by imposing a normal working day on factories proper, so soon consequently as an increased production of surplus-value by the prolongation of the working day was once for all put a stop to, from that moment capital threw itself with all its might into the production of relative surplus-value, by hastening on the further improvement of machinery. At the same time a change took place in the nature of relative surplus-value. Generally speaking, the mode of producing relative surplus-value consists in raising the productive power of the workman, so as to enable him to produce more in a given time with the same expenditure of labour. Labour-time continues to transmit as before the same value to the total product, but this unchanged amount of exchange-value is spread over more use-value; hence the value of each single commodity sinks. Otherwise, however, so soon as the compulsory shortening of the hours of labour takes place. The immense impetus it gives the development of productive power, and to economy in the means of production, imposes on the workman increased expenditure of labour in a given time, heightened tension of labour-power, and closer filling up of the pores of the working day, or condensation of labour to a degree that is attainable only within the limits of the shortened working day. This condensation of a greater mass of labour into a given period thenceforward counts for what it really is, a greater quantity of labour.

In addition to a measure of its extension, i.e. duration, labour now acquires a measure of its intensity or of the degree of its condensation or density. The denser hour of the ten hours' working day contains more labour, i.e. expended labour-power, than the more porous hour of the twelve hours' working day. The product therefore of one of the former hours has as much or more value than has the product of 1⅕ of the latter hours. Apart from the increased yield of relative surplus-value through the heightened productiveness of labour, the same mass of value is now produced for the capitalist say by 3⅓ hours of surplus-labour, and 6⅔ hours of necessary labour, as was previously produced by four hours of surplus-labour and eight hours of necessary labour.

We now come to the question: How is the labour intensified?

The first effect of shortening the working day results from the self-evident law, that the efficiency of labour-power is an inverse ratio to the duration of its expenditure. Hence, within certain limits what is lost by shortening the duration is gained by the increasing tension of labour-power. That the workman moreover really does expend more labour-power is ensured by the mode in which the capitalist pays him. In those industries such as potteries, where machinery plays little or no part, the introduction of the Factory Acts has strikingly shown that the mere shortening of the working day increases to a wonderful degree the regularity, uniformity, order, continuity, and energy of the labour. It seemed, however, doubtful whether this effect was produced in the factory proper, where the dependence of the workman on the continuous and uniform motion of the machinery had already created the strictest discipline. Hence, when in 1844 the reduction of the working day to less than twelve hours was being debated, the masters almost unanimously declared 'that their overlookers in the different rooms took good care that the hands lost no time', that 'the extent of vigilance and attention on the part of the workmen was hardly capable of being increased', and, therefore, that the speed of the machinery and other conditions remaining unaltered, 'to expect in a well-managed factory any important result from increased attention of the workmen was an absurdity'. This assertion was contradicted by experiments. Mr Robert Gardner reduced the hours of labour in his two large factories at Preston on and after the 20 April 1844 from twelve to eleven hours a day. The result of about a year's working was that 'the same amount of product for the same cost was received, and the workpeople as a whole earned in eleven hours as much wages as they did before in twelve.' I pass over the experiments made in the spinning and carding rooms, because they were accompanied by an increase of 2 per cent in the speed of the machines. But in the weaving department, where moreover many sorts of figured fancy articles were woven, there was not the slightest alteration in the conditions of the work. The result was: 'From 6 January to 20 April 1844, with a twelve hours' day, average weekly wages of each hand 10s. 1½d., from 20 April to 29 June 1844, with day of eleven hours, average weekly wages 10s. 3½d.' Here we have more produced in eleven hours than previously in twelve, and entirely in consequence of more steady application and economy of time by the workpeople. While they got the same wages and gained one hour of spare time, the capitalist got the same amount produced and saved the cost of coal, gas, and other such items, for one hour. Similar experiments, and with the like success, were carried out in the mills of Messrs Horrocks and Jackson.

The shortening of the hours of labour creates, to begin with, the subjective conditions for the condensation of labour, by enabling the workman to exert more strength in a given time. So soon as that shortening becomes compulsory, machinery becomes in the hands of capital the objective means, systematically employed for squeezing out more labour in a given time. This is effected in two ways: by increasing the speed of the machinery, and by giving the workman more machinery to tend. Improved construction of the machinery is necessary partly because without it greater pressure cannot be put on the workman, and partly because the shortened hours of labour force the capitalist to exercise the strictest watch over the cost of production. The improvements in the steam-engine have increased the piston speed, and at the same time have made it possible, by means of a greater economy of power, to drive with the same or even a smaller consumption of coal more machinery with the same engine. The improvements in the transmitting mechanism have lessened friction and, what so strikingly distinguishes modern from the older machinery, have reduced the diameter and weight of the shafting to a constantly decreasing minimum. Finally, the improvements in the operative machines have, while reducing their size, increased the speed and efficiency, as in the modern power-loom; or, while increasing the size of their framework, have also increased the extent and number of their working parts, as in spinning-mules, or have added to the speed of these working parts by imperceptible alterations of detail, such as those which ten years ago increased the speed of the spindles in self-acting mules by one-fifth.

The reduction of the working day to 12 hours dates in England from 1832. In 1836 a manufacturer stated:

> The labour now undergone in the factories is much greater than it used to be . . . compared with thirty or forty years ago . . . owing to the greater attention and activity required by the greatly increased speed which is given to the machinery.

In the year 1844, Lord Ashley, now Lord Shaftesbury, made in the House of Commons the following statements, supported by documentary evidence:

> The labour performed by those engaged in the processes of manufacture, is three times as great as in the beginning of such operations. Machinery has executed, no doubt, the work that would demand the sinews of millions of men; but it has also prodigiously multiplied the labour of those who are governed by its fearful movements. . . . In 1815, the labour of following a pair of mules spinning cotton of No. 40 – reckoning 12 hours to the working-day – involved a necessity of walking 8 miles. In 1832, the distance travelled in following a pair of mules, spinning cotton yarn of the same number, was 20 miles, and frequently more. In 1825 the spinner put up daily, on each of these mules, 820 stretches, making a total of 1,640 stretches in the course of the day. In 1832, the spinner put on each mule 2,200 stretches, making a total of 4,400. In 1844, 2,400 stretches, making a total of 4,800; and in some cases the amount of labour required is even still greater. ... I have another document sent to me in 1842, stating that the labour is progressively increasing – increasing not only because the distance to be travelled is greater, but because the quantity of goods produced is multiplied, while the hands are fewer in proportion than before; and, moreover, because an inferior species of cotton is now often spun, which it is more difficult to work. . . . In the carding-room there has also been a great increase of labour. One person there does the work formerly divided between two. In the weaving-room, where a vast number of persons are employed, and principally females . . . the labour has increased within the last few years fully 10 per cent, owing to the increased speed of the machinery in spinning. In 1838, the number of hanks spun per week was 18,000, in 1843 it amounted to 21,000. In 1819, the number of picks in power-loom-weaving per minute was 60 – in 1842 it was 140, showing a vast increase of labour.

In the face of this remarkable intensity of labour which had already been reached in 1844 under the Twelve Hours' Act, there appeared to be a justification for the assertion made at that time by the English manufacturers, that any further progress in that direction was impossible, and therefore that every further reduction of the hours of labour meant a lessened production. The apparent correctness of their reasons will be best known by the following contemporary statement by Leonard Horner, the factory inspector, their ever watchful censor.

> Now as the quantity produced must, in the main, be regulated by the speed of the machinery, it must be the interest of the mill-owner to drive it at the utmost rate of speed consistent with these following conditions, viz. the preservation of the machinery from too rapid deterioration; the preservation of the quality of the article manufactured; and the capability of the workman to follow the motion without a greater exertion than he can sustain for a constancy. One of the most important problems, therefore, which the owner of a factory has to solve is to find out the maximum speed at which he can run, with a due regard to the above conditions. It frequently happens that he finds he has gone too fast, that breakages and bad work more than counterbalance the increased speed, and that he is obliged to slacken his pace. I therefore concluded, that as an active and intelligent mill-owner would find out the safe maximum, it would not be possible to produce as much in eleven hours as in twelve. I further assumed that the operative paid by piece-work, would exert himself to the utmost consistent with the power of continuing at the same rate.

Horner, therefore, came to the conclusion that a reduction of the working hours below twelve would necessarily diminish production. He himself, ten years later, cites his opinion of 1845 in proof of how much he underestimated in that year the elasticity of machinery, and of man's labour-power, both of which are simultaneously stretched to an extreme by the compulsory shortening of the working day.

We now come to the period that follows the introduction of the Ten Hours' Act in 1847 into the English cotton, woollen, silk, and flax mills.

> The speed of the spindles has increased upon throstles 500, and upon mules 1,000 revolutions a minute, i.e. the speed of the throstle spindle, which in 1839 was 4,500 times a minute, is now (1862) 5,000; and of the mule spindle, that was 5,000, is now 6,000 times a minute, amounting in the former case to one-tenth, and in the second case to one-fifth additional increase.

James Nasmyth, the eminent civil engineer of Patricroft, near Manchester, explained in a letter to Leonard Horner, written in 1852, the nature of the improvements in the steam-engine that had been made between the years 1848 and 1852. After remarking that the horsepower of steam-engines, being always estimated in the official returns according to the power of similar engines in 1828, is only nominal, and can serve only as an index of their real power, he goes on to say:

> I am confident that from the same weight of steam-engine machinery, we are now obtaining at least 50 per cent more duty or work performed on the average, and that in many cases the identical steam-engines which in

the days of the restricted speed of 220 feet per minute, yielded 50 horsepower, are now yielding upwards of 100.

The modern steam-engine of 100 horse-power is capable of being driven at a much greater force than formerly, arising from improvements in its construction, the capacity and construction of the boilers, etc.

Although the same number of hands are employed in proportion to the horse-power as at former periods, there are fewer hands employed in proportion to the machinery.

In the year 1850, the factories of the United Kingdom employed 134,217 nominal horse-power to give motion to 25,638,716 spindles and 301,445 looms. The number of spindles and looms in 1856 was respectively 33,503,580 of the former, and 369,205 of the latter, which, reckoning the force of the nominal horse-power required to be the same as in 1850, would require a force equal to 175,000 horses, but the actual power given in the return for 1856 is 161,435, less by above 10,000 horses than, calculating upon the basis of the return of 1850, the factories ought to have required in 1856.

The facts thus brought out by the Return (of 1856) appear to be that the factory system is increasing rapidly; that although the same number of hands are employed in proportion to the horse-power as at former periods, there are fewer hands employed in proportion to the machinery; that the steam-engine is enabled to drive an increased weight of machinery by economy of force and other methods, and that an increased quantity of work can be turned off by improvements in machinery, and in methods of manufacture by increase of speed of the machinery, and by a variety of other causes.

The great improvements made in machines of every kind have raised their productive power very much. Without any doubt, the shortening of the hours of labour . . . gave the impulse to these improvements. The latter, combined with the more intense strain on the workman, have had the effect that at least as much is produced in the shortened (by two hours or one-sixth) working day as was previously produced during the longer one.

One fact is sufficient to show how greatly the wealth of the manufacturers increased along with the more intense exploitation of labour-power. From 1838 to 1850, the average proportional increase in English cotton and other factories was 32 per cent, while from 1850 to 1856 it amounted to 86 per cent.

But however great the progress of English industry had been during the 8 years from 1848 to 1856 under the influence of a working day of 10 hours, it was far surpassed during the next period of 6 years from 1856 to 1862. In silk factories for instance, there were in 1856, 1,093,799 spindles; in 1862, 1,388,544; in 1856, 9,260 looms; in 1862,

10,709. But the number of operatives in 1856 was 56,131; in 1862, 52,429. The increase in the spindles was therefore 26.9 per cent and in the looms 15.6 per cent, while the number of the operatives decreased 7 per cent. In the year 1850 there were employed in worsted mills 875,830 spindles; in 1856, 1,324,549 (increase 51.2 per cent), and in 1862, 1,289,172 (decrease 2.7 per cent). But if we deduct the doubling spindles that figure in the number for 1856, but not in those for 1862, it will be found that after 1856 the number of spindles remained nearly stationary. On the other hand, after 1850, the speed of the spindles and looms was in many cases doubled. The number of power-looms in worsted mills was in 1850, 32,617; in 1856, 38,956; in 1862, 43,048. The number of the operatives was in 1850, 79,737; in 1856, 87,794; in 1862, 86,063; included in these, however, the children under 14 years of age were, in 1850, 9,956; in 1856, 11,228; in 1862, 13,178. In spite, therefore, of the greatly increased number of looms in 1862 compared with 1856 the total number of the workpeople employed decreased, and that of the children exploited increased.

On the 27 April 1863, Mr Ferrand said in the House of Commons:

> I have been informed by delegates from 16 districts of Lancashire and Cheshire, in whose behalf I speak, that the work in the factories is, in consequence of the improvements in machinery, constantly on the increase. Instead of as formerly one person with two helps tenting two looms, one person now tents three looms without helps, and it is no uncommon thing for one person to tent four. Twelve hours' work, as is evident from the facts adduced, is now compressed into less than 10 hours. It is therefore self-evident, to what an enormous extent the toil of the factory operative has increased during the last 10 years.

Although therefore, the Factory Inspectors unceasingly and with justice, commend the results of the Acts of 1844 and 1850, yet they admit that the shortening of the hours of labour has already called forth such an intensification of the labour as is injurious to the health of the workman and to his capacity for work.

> In most of the cotton, worsted, and silk mills, an exhausting state of excitement necessary to enable the workers satisfactorily to mind the machinery, the motion of which has been greatly accelerated within the last few years, seems to me not unlikely to be one of the causes of that excess of mortality from lung disease, which Dr Greenhow has pointed out in his recent report on this subject.

There cannot be the slightest doubt that the tendency that urges capital, so soon as a prolongation of the hours of labour is once for all forbidden, to compensate itself by a systematic heightening of the intensity of labour, and to convert every improvement in machinery into a more perfect means of exhausting the workman, must soon lead to a state of things in which a reduction of the hours of labour will again be inevitable. On the other hand, the rapid advance of English industry between 1848 and the present time, under the influence of a day of ten hours, surpasses the advance made between 1833 and 1847, when the day was twelve hours long, by far more than the latter surpasses the advance made during the half century after the first introduction of the factory system, when the working day was without limits.

SECTION 4. THE FACTORY

At the commencement of this chapter we considered that which we may call the body of the factory, i.e. machinery organised into a system. We there saw how machinery, by annexing the labour of women and children, augments the number of human beings who form the material for capitalistic exploitation, how it confiscates the whole of the workman's disposable time by immoderate extension of the hours of labour, and how finally its progress, which allows of enormous increase of production in shorter and shorter periods, serves as a means of systematically getting more work done in a shorter time, or of exploiting labour-power more intensely. We now turn to the factory as a whole, and that in its most perfect form.

Dr Ure, the Pindar of the automatic factory, describes it, on the one hand, as 'Combined cooperation of many orders of workpeople, adult and young, in tending with assiduous skill, a system of productive machines, continuously impelled by a central power' (the prime mover); on the other hand, as 'a vast automaton, composed of various mechanical and intellectual organs, acting in uninterrupted concert for the production of a common object, all of them being subordinate to a self-regulated moving force.' These two descriptions are far from being identical. In one, the collective labourer, or social body of labour, appears as the dominant subject, and the mechanical automaton as the object; in the other, the automaton itself is the subject, and the workmen are merely conscious organs, coordinate with the unconscious organs of the automaton, and together with them, subordinated to the central moving-power. The first description is applicable to every possible employment of machinery on a large scale, the second is characteristic of its use by capital, and therefore of the modern factory system. Ure prefers therefore, to describe the central machine from which the motion comes, not only as an automaton, but as an autocrat. 'In these spacious halls the benignant power of steam summons around him his myriads of willing menials.'

Along with the tool, the skill of the workman in handling it passes over to the machine. The capabilities of the tool are emancipated from the restraints that are inseparable from human labour-power. Thereby the technical foundation on which is based the division of labour in manufacture is swept away. Hence, in the place of the hierarchy of specialised workmen that characterises manufacture, there steps, in the automatic factory, a tendency to equalise and reduce to one and the same level every kind of work that has to be done by the minders of the machines; in the place of the artificially produced differentiations of the detail workmen, step the natural differences of age and sex.

So far as division of labour reappears in the factory, it is primarily a distribution of the workmen among the specialised machines; and of masses of workmen, not however organised into groups, among the various departments of the factory, in each of which they work at a number of similar machines placed together; their cooperation, therefore, is only simple. The organised group, peculiar to manufacture, is replaced by the connexion between the head workman and his few assistants. The essential division is, into workmen who are actually employed on the machines (among whom are included a few who look after the engine), and into mere attendants (almost exclusively children) of these workmen. Among the attendants are reckoned more or less all 'feeders' who supply the machines with the material to be worked. In addition to these two principal classes, there is a numerically unimportant class of persons, whose occupation it is to look after the whole of the machinery and repair it from time to time; such as engineers, mechanics, joiners, etc. This is a superior class of workmen, some of them scientifically educated, others brought up to a trade; it is distinct from the factory operative class, and merely aggregated to it. This division of labour is purely technical.

To work at a machine, the workman should be taught from childhood, in order that he may learn to adapt his own movements to the uniform and unceasing motion of an automaton. When the machinery as a whole forms a system of manifold machines, working simultaneously and in concert, the cooperation based upon it requires the distribution of various groups of workmen among the different kinds of machines. But the employment of machinery does away with the necessity of crystallising this distribution after the manner of manufacture, by the constant annexation of a particular man to a particular function. Since the motion of the whole system does proceed from the workman, but from the machinery, a chang persons can take place at any time without an interruption of the w The most striking proof of this is afforded by the *relays system*, into operation by the manufacturers during their revolt f 1848-1850. Lastly, the quickness with which machine work is learn young people does away with the necessity of bringing up for exclu employment by machinery a special class of operatives. With regar the work of the mere attendants, it can, to some extent, be replace the mill by machines, and owing to its extreme simplicity, it allows rapid and constant change of the individuals burdened with drudgery.

Although then, technically speaking, the old system of divisio labour is thrown overboard by machinery, it hangs on in the facto a traditional habit handed down from manufacture, and is afterw systematically re-moulded and established in a more hideous forn capital, as a means of exploiting labour-power. The lifelong speci of handling one and the same tool, now becomes the lifelong speci of serving one and the same machine. Machinery is put to a wrong with the object of transforming the workman, from his childhood, into a part of a detail-machine. In this way, not only ar expenses of his reproduction considerably lessened, but at the s time his helpless dependence upon the factory as a whole, therefore upon the capitalist, is rendered complete. Her everywhere else, we must distinguish between the incre productiveness due to the development of the social proces production, and that due to the capitalist exploitation of that pro In handicrafts and manufacture, the workman makes use of a toc the factory, the machine makes use of him. There the movemen the instrument of labour proceed from him, here it is the movemen the machine that he must follow. In manufacture the workme parts of a living mechanism. In the factory we have a lif mechanism independent of the workman, who becomes its mere l appendage. At the same time that factory work exhausts the ner system to the uttermost, it does away with the many-sided play o muscles, and confiscates every atom of freedom, both in bodily intellectual activity. The lightening of the labour even becomes a of torture, since the machine does not free the labourer from work deprives the work of all interest. Every kind of capitalist productic so far as it is not only a labour-process, but also a process of cre surplus-value, has this in common, that it is not the workman employs the instruments of labour, but the instruments of labour that employ the workman. But it is only in the factory system that this inversion for the first time acquires technical and palpable reality. By means of its conversion into an automaton, the instrument of labour confronts the labourer, during the labour-process, in the shape of capital, of dead labour, that dominates, and pumps dry, living labour-power. The separation of the intellectual powers of production from the manual labour, and the conversion of those powers into the might of capital over labour, is, as we have already shown, finally completed by modern industry erected on the foundation of machinery. The special skill of each individual insignificant factory operative vanishes as an infinitesimal quantity before the science, the gigantic physical forces, and the mass of labour that are embodied in the factory mechanism and, together with that mechanism, constitute the power of the 'master'. This 'master', therefore, in whose brain the machinery and his monopoly of it are inseparably united, whenever he falls out with his 'hands', contemptuously tells them:

> The factory operatives should keep in wholesome remembrance the fact that theirs is really a low species of skilled labour; and that there is none which is more easily acquired, or of its quality more amply remunerated, or which by a short training of the least expert can be more quickly, as well as abundantly, acquired. . . . The master's machinery really plays a far more important part in the business of production than the labour and the skill of the operative, which six months' education can teach, and a common labourer can learn.

The technical subordination of the workman to the uniform motion of the instruments of labour, and the peculiar composition of the body of workpeople, consisting as it does of individuals of both sexes and of all ages, give rise to a barrack discipline which is elaborated into a complete system in the factory, and which fully develops the before mentioned labour of overlooking, thereby dividing the workpeople into operatives and overlookers, into private soldiers and sergeants of an industrial army.

> The main difficulty [in the automatic factory] . . . lay . . . above all in training human beings to renounce their desultory habits of work, and to identify themselves with the unvarying regularity of the complex automaton. To devise and administer a successful code of factory discipline, suited to the necessities of factory diligence, was the Herculean enterprise, the noble achievement of Arkwright! Even at the present day, when the system is perfectly organised and its labour lightened to the utmost it is found nearly impossible to convert persons past the age of puberty into useful factory hands. (Ure)

The factory code in which capital formulates, like a private legislator, and at his own good will, his autocracy over his workpeople, unaccompanied by that division of responsibility, in other matters so much approved of by the bourgeoisie, and unaccompanied by the still more approved representative system, this code is but the capitalistic caricature of that social regulation of the labour-process which becomes requisite in cooperation on a great scale, and in the employment in common, of instruments of labour and especially of machinery. The place of the slave-driver's lash is taken by the overlooker's book of penalties. All punishments naturally resolve themselves into fines and deductions from wages, and the law-giving talent of the factory Lycurgus so arranges matters, that a violation of his laws is, if possible, more profitable to him than the keeping of them. We shall here merely allude to the material conditions under which factory labour is carried on. Every organ of sense is injured in an equal degree by artificial elevation of the temperature, by the dust-laden atmosphere, by the deafening noise, not to mention danger to life and limb among the thickly crowded machinery, which, with the regularity of the seasons, issues its list of the killed and wounded in the industrial battle. Economy of the social means of production, matured and forced as in a hothouse by the factory system, is turned, in the hands of capital, into systematic robbery of what is necessary for the life of the workman while he is at work, robbery of space, light, air, and of protection to his person against the dangerous and unwholesome accompaniments of the productive process, not to mention the robbery of appliances for the comfort of the workman.

SECTION 5. THE STRIFE BETWEEN WORKMAN AND MACHINE

The contest between the capitalist and the wage-labourer dates back to the very origin of capital. It raged on throughout the whole manufacturing period. But only since the introduction of machinery has the workman fought against the instrument of labour itself, the material embodiment of capital. He revolts against this particular form of the means of production, as being the material basis of the capitalist mode of production.

In the seventeenth century nearly all Europe experienced revolts of the workpeople against the ribbon-loom, a machine for weaving ribbons and trimmings, called in Germany *Bandmühle, Schnurmühle*, and *Mühlenstuhl*. These machines were invented in Germany. Abbé

Lancellotti, in a work that appeared in Venice in 1636, but which was written in 1579, says as follows:

> Anthony Müller of Danzig saw about 50 years ago in that town, a very ingenious machine, which weaves 4 to 6 pieces at once. But the Mayor being apprehensive that this invention might throw a larger number of workmen on the streets, caused the inventor to be secretly strangled or drowned.

In Leyden, this machine was not used till 1629; there the riots of the ribbon-weavers at length compelled the Town Council to prohibit it. After making various decrees more or less prohibitive against this loom in 1632, 1639, etc. the States General of Holland at length permitted it to be used, under certain conditions, by the decree of 15 December 1661. It was also prohibited in Cologne in 1676, at the same time that its introduction into England was causing disturbances among the workpeople. By an imperial Edict of 19 February 1685, its use was forbidden throughout all Germany. In Hamburg it was burnt in public by order of the Senate. The Emperor Charles VI, on 9 February 1719, renewed the edict of 1685, and not till 1765 was its use openly allowed in the Electorate of Saxony. This machine, which shook Europe to its foundations, was in fact the precursor of the mule and the power-loom, and of the industrial revolution of the eighteenth century. It enabled a totally inexperienced boy to set the whole loom with all its shuttles in motion by simply moving a rod backwards and forwards, and in its improved form produced from 40 to 50 pieces at once.

About 1630, a wind-sawmill, erected near London by a Dutchman, succumbed to the excesses of the populace. Even as late as the beginning of the eighteenth century, sawmills driven by water overcame the opposition of the people, supported as it was by Parliament, only with great difficulty. No sooner had Everet in 1758 erected the first wool-shearing machine that was driven by water-power, than it was set on fire by 100,000 people who had been thrown out of work. Fifty thousand workpeople, who had previously lived by carding wool, petitioned Parliament against Arkwright's scribbling mills and carding engines. The enormous destruction of machinery that occurred in the English manufacturing districts during the first 15 years of this century, chiefly caused by the employment of the power-loom, and known as the Luddite movement, gave the anti-Jacobin governments of a Sidmouth, a Castlereagh, and the like, a pretext for the most reactionary and forcible measures. It took both time and experience before the workpeople learnt to distinguish between machinery and its employment by capital, and to direct their attacks, not against the material instruments of production, but against the mode in which they are used.

The contests about wages in manufacture presuppose manufacture, and are in no sense directed against its existence. The opposition against the establishment of new manufactures, proceeds from the guilds and privileged towns, not from the workpeople. Hence the writers of the manufacturing period treat the division of labour chiefly as a means of virtually supplying a deficiency of labourers, and not as a means of actually displacing those in work. This distinction is self-evident. If it be said that 100 millions of people would be required in England to spin with the old spinning-wheel the cotton that is now spun with mules by 500,000 people, this does not mean that the mules took the place of those millions who never existed. It means only this, that many millions of workpeople would be required to replace the spinning machinery. If, on the other hand, we say that in England the power-loom threw 800,000 weavers on the streets, we do not refer to existing machinery, that would have to be replaced by a definite number of workpeople, but to a number of weavers in existence who were actually replaced or displaced by the looms. During the manufacturing period, handicraft labour, altered though it was by division of labour, was yet the basis. The demands of the new colonial markets could not be satisfied owing to the relatively small number of town operatives handed down from the middle ages, and the manufactures proper opened out new fields of production to the rural population, driven from the land by the dissolution of the feudal system. At that time, therefore, division of labour and cooperation in the workshops, were viewed more from the positive aspect, that they made the workpeople more productive. Long before the period of modern industry, cooperation and the concentration of the instruments of labour in the hands of a few gave rise, in numerous countries where these methods were applied in agriculture, to great, sudden and forcible revolutions in the modes of production, and consequentially, in the conditions of existence, and the means of employment of the rural populations. But this contest at first takes place more between the large and the small landed proprietors, than between capital and wage-labour; on the other hand, when the labourers are displaced by the instruments of labour, by sheep, horses, etc., in this case force is directly resorted to in the first instance as the prelude to the industrial revolution. The labourers are first driven from the land, and then come the sheep. Land grabbing on a great scale, such as was perpetrated in England, is the first step in creating a field for the establishment of agriculture on a great scale. Hence this subversion of agriculture puts on, at first, more the appearance of a political revolution.

The instrument of labour, when it takes the form of a machine, immediately becomes a competitor of the workman himself. The self-expansion of capital by means of machinery is thenceforward directly proportional to the number of the workpeople whose means of livelihood have been destroyed by that machinery. The whole system of capitalist production is based on the fact that the workman sells his labour-power as a commodity. Division of labour specialises this labour-power, by reducing it to skill in handling a particular tool. So soon as the handling of this tool becomes the work of a machine, then, with the use-value, the exchange-value too of the workman's labour-power vanishes; the workman becomes unsaleable, like paper money thrown out of currency by legal enactment. That portion of the working class, thus by machinery rendered superfluous, i.e. no longer immediately necessary for the self-expansion of capital, either goes to the wall in the unequal contest of the old handicrafts and manufactures with machinery, or else floods all the more easily accessible branches of industry, swamps the labour-market, and sinks the price of labour-power below its value. It is impressed upon the workpeople, as a great consolation, first, that their sufferings are only temporary ('a temporary inconvenience'), secondly, that machinery acquires the mastery over the whole of a given field of production, only by degrees, so that the extent and intensity of its destructive effect is diminished. The first consolation neutralises the second. When machinery seizes on an industry by degrees, it produces chronic misery among the operatives who compete with it. Where the transition is rapid, the effect is acute and felt by great masses. History discloses no tragedy more horrible than the gradual extinction of the English hand-loom weavers, an extinction that was spread over several decades, and finally sealed in 1838. Many of them died of starvation, many with families vegetated for a long time on 2½d. a day. On the other hand, the English cotton machinery produced an acute effect in India. The Governor General reported 1834-35: 'The misery hardly finds a parallel in the history of commerce. The bones of the cotton-weavers are bleaching the plains of India.' No doubt, in turning them out of this 'temporal' world, the machinery caused them no more than 'a temporary inconvenience'. For the rest, since machinery is continually seizing upon new fields of production, its temporary effect is really permanent. Hence, the character of independence and estrangement which the capitalist mode of production as a whole gives to the instruments of labour and to the product, as against the workman, is developed by means of machinery into a thorough antagonism. Therefore, it is with the advent of machinery, that the workman for the first time brutally revolts against the instruments of labour.

The instrument of labour strikes down the labourer. This direct antagonism between the two comes out most strongly whenever newly introduced machinery competes with handicrafts or manufactures, handed down from former times. But even in modern industry the continual improvement of machinery, and the development of the automatic system, has an analogous effect.

> The object of improved machinery is to diminish manual labour, to provide for the performance of a process or the completion of a link in a manufacture by the aid of an iron instead of the human apparatus.
>
> The adaptation of power to machinery heretofore moved by hand, is almost of daily occurrence . . . the minor improvements in machinery having for their object economy of power, the production of better work, the turning off more work in the same time, or in supplying the place of a child, a female, or a man, are constant, and although sometimes apparently of no great moment, have somewhat important results.
>
> Whenever a process requires peculiar dexterity and steadiness of hand, it is withdrawn, as soon as possible, from the cunning workman, who is prone to irregularities of many kinds, and it is placed in charge of a peculiar mechanism, so self-regulating that a child can superintend it.
>
> On the automatic plan skilled labour gets progressively superseded.
>
> The effect of improvements in machinery, not merely in superseding the necessity for the employment of the same quantity of adult labour as before, in order to produce a given result, but in substituting one description of human labour for another, the less skilled for the more skilled, juvenile for adult, female for male, causes a fresh disturbance in the rate of wages.
>
> The effect of substituting the self-acting mule for the common mule, is to discharge the greater part of the men spinners, and to retain adolescents and children. (Ure)

The extraordinary power of expansion of the factory system owing to accumulated practical experience, to the mechanical means at hand, and to constant technical progress, was proved to us by the giant strides of that system under the pressure of a shortened working day. But who, in 1860, the zenith year of the English cotton industry, would have dreamt of the galloping improvements in machinery, and the corresponding displacement of working people, called into being during the following 3 years, under the stimulus of the American Civil War? A couple of examples from the Reports of the Inspectors of Factories will suffice on this point. A Manchester manufacturer states:

> We formerly had 75 carding engines, now we have 12, doing the same quantity of work. . . . We are doing with fewer hands by 14, at a saving in wages of £10 a-week. Our estimated saving in waste is about 10 per cent in the quantity of cotton consumed.
>
> In another fine-spinning mill in Manchester, I was informed that through increased speed and the adoption of some self-acting processes, a reduction had been made, in number, of a fourth in one department, and of above half in another, and that the introduction of the combing machine in place of the second carding, had considerably reduced the number of hands formerly employed in the carding-room.

Another spinning-mill is estimated to effect a saving of labour of 10 per cent. The Messrs Gilmour, spinners at Manchester, state:

> In our blowing-room department we consider our expense with new machinery is fully one-third less in wages and hands . . . in the jack-frame and drawing-frame room, about one-third less in expense, and likewise one-third less in hands; in the spinning-room about one-third less in expenses. But this is not all; when our yarn goes to the manufacturers, it is so much better by the application of our new machinery, that they will produce a greater quantity of cloth, and cheaper than from the yarn produced by old machinery.

Mr Redgrave further remarks in the same Report:

> The reduction of hands against increased production is, in fact, constantly taking place, in woollen mills the reduction commenced some time since, and is continuing; a few days since, the master of a school in the neighbourhood of Rochdale said to me, that the great falling off in the girls' school is not only caused by the distress, but by the changes of machinery in the woollen mills, in consequence of which a reduction of 70 short-timers had taken place.

The following table shows the total result of the mechanical improvements in the English cotton industry due to the American Civil War.

Number of Factories

	1857	*1861*	*1868*
England and Wales	2,046	2,715	2,405
Scotland	152	163	131
Ireland	12	9	13
United Kingdom	2,210	2,887	2,549

Number of Power-looms

	1857	*1861*	*1868*
England and Wales	275,590	368,125	344,719
Scotland	21,624	30,110	31,864
Ireland	1,633	1,757	2,746
United Kingdom	298,847	399,992	379,329

Number of Spindles

	1857	*1861*	*1868*
England and Wales	25,818,576	28,352,125	30,478,228
Scotland	2,041,129	1,915,398	1,397,546
Ireland	150,512	119,944	124,240
United Kingdom	28,010,217	30,387,467	32,000,014

Number of Persons Employed

	1857	*1861*	*1868*
England and Wales	341,170	407,598	357,052
Scotland	34,698	41,237	39,809
Ireland	3,345	2,734	4,203
United Kingdom	379,213	451,569	401,064

Hence, between 1861 and 1868, 338 cotton factories disappeared, in other words more productive machinery on a larger scale was concentrated in the hands of a smaller number of capitalists. The number of power-looms decreased by 20,663; but since their product increased in the same period, an improved loom must have yielded more than an old one. Lastly the number of spindles increased by 1,612,541, while the number of operatives decreased by 50,505. The 'temporary' misery inflicted on the workpeople by the cotton crisis was heightened, and from being temporary made permanent, by the rapid and persistent progress of machinery.

But machinery not only acts as a competitor who gets the better of the workman, and is constantly on the point of making him superfluous. It is also a power inimical to him, and as such capital proclaims it from the rooftops and as such makes use of it. It is the most powerful weapon for repressing strikes, those periodical revolts of the working class against the autocracy of capital. According to Gaskell, the steam-engine was from the very first an antagonist of human power, an antagonist that enabled the capitalist to tread under foot the growing claims of the workmen, who threatened the newly born factory system with a crisis. It would be possible to write quite a history of the inventions made since 1830 for the sole purpose of supplying capital with weapons against the revolts of the working class. At the head of these in importance, stands the self-acting mule, because it opened up a new epoch in the automatic system.

Nasmyth, the inventor of the steam-hammer, gives the following evidence before the Trades' Union Commission, with regard to the improvements made by him in machinery and introduced in consequence of the widespread and long strikes of the engineers of 1851.

> The characteristic feature of our modern mechanical improvements, is the introduction of self-acting tool machinery. What every mechanical workman has now to do, and what every boy can do, is not to work himself but to superintend the beautiful labour of the machine. The whole class of workmen that depend exclusively on their skill, is now done away with. Formerly, I employed four boys to every mechanic. Thanks to these new mechanical combinations, I have reduced the number of grown-up men from 1,500 to 750. The result was a considerable increase in my profits.

Ure says of a machine used in calico printing:

> At length capitalists sought deliverance from this intolerable bondage [namely the, in their eyes, burdensome terms of their contracts with the workmen] in the resources of science, and were speedily re-instated in their legitimate rule, that of the head over the inferior members. [Of an invention for dressing warps:] Then the combined malcontents, who fancied themselves impregnably intrenched behind the old lines of division of labour, found their flanks turned and their defences rendered useless by the new mechanical tactics, and were obliged to surrender at discretion. [Of the invention of the self-acting mule:] A creation destined to restore order among the industrious classes.... This invention confirms the great doctrine already propounded, that when capital enlists science into her service, the refractory hand of labour will always be taught docility.

Although Ure's work appeared 30 years ago, at a time when the factory system was comparatively but little developed, it still perfectly expresses the spirit of the factory, not only by its undisguised cynicism, but also by the naïvety with which it blurts out the stupid contradictions of the capitalist brain. For instance, after propounding the 'doctrine' stated above, that capital, with the aid of science taken into its pay, always reduces the refractory hand of labour to docility, he grows indignant because 'physico-mechanical science has been accused of lending itself to the rich capitalist as an instrument for harassing the poor'. After preaching a long sermon to show how advantageous the rapid development of machinery is to the working classes, he warns them that by their obstinacy and their strikes they hasten that development. 'Violent revulsions of this nature', he said, 'display short-sighted man in the contemptible character of a self-tormentor.' A few pages before he states the contrary. 'Had it not been for the violent collisions and interruptions resulting from erroneous views among the factory operatives, the factory system would have been developed still more rapidly and beneficially for all concerned.' Then he exclaims again: 'Fortunately for the state of society in the cotton districts of Great Britain, the improvements in machinery are gradual.'

> [Improvement in machinery] is said to lower the rate of earnings of adults by displacing a portion of them, and thus rendering their number superabundant as compared with the demand for their labour. It certainly augments the demand for the labour of children and increases the rate of *their* wages.

On the other hand, this same dispenser of consolation defends the lowness of the children's wages on the ground that it prevent parents from sending their children at too early an age into the factory. The whole of his book is a vindication of a working day of unrestricted length; that Parliament should forbid children of 13 years to be exhausted by working 12 hours a day, reminds his liberal soul of the darkest days of the middle ages. This does not prevent him from calling upon the factory operatives to thank Providence, who by means of machinery has given them the leisure to think of their 'immortal interests'.

SECTION 6. THE THEORY OF COMPENSATION AS REGARDS THE WORKPEOPLE DISPLACED BY MACHINERY

James Mill, MacCulloch, Torrens, Senior, John Stuart Mill, and a whole series besides, of bourgeois political economists, insist that all machinery that displaces workmen, simultaneously and necessarily sets free an amount of capital adequate to employ the same identical workmen.

The real facts, which are travestied by the optimism of economists, are as follows: The labourers, when driven out of the workshop by the machinery, are thrown upon the labour market, and there add to the number of workmen at the disposal of the capitalists. In Part VII of this book it will be seen that this effect of machinery, which as we have seen is represented to be a compensation to the working class, is on the contrary a most frightful scourge. For the present I will only say this: The labourers that are thrown out of work in any branch of industry can no doubt seek for employment in some other branch. If they find it, and thus renew the bond between them and the means of subsistence, this takes place only by the intermediary of a new and additional capital that is seeking investment; not at all by the intermediary of the capital that formerly employed them and was afterwards converted into machinery. And even should they find employment, what a poor look-out is theirs! Crippled as they are by division of labour, these poor devils are worth so little outside their old trade, that they cannot find admission into any industries, except a few of inferior kind, that are over-supplied with underpaid workmen. Further, every branch of industry attracts each year a new stream of men, who furnish a contingent from which to fill up vacancies, and to draw a supply for expansion. So soon as machinery sets free a part of the workmen employed in a given branch of industry, the reserve men are also diverted into new channels of employment, and become absorbed in other branches; meanwhile the original victims, during the period of transition, for the most part starve and perish.

Although machinery necessarily throws men out of work in those industries into which it is introduced, yet it may, notwithstanding this, bring about an increase of employment in other industries. This effect, however, has nothing in common with the so-called theory of compensation. Since every article produced by a machine is cheaper than a similar article produced by hand, we deduce the following infallible law: If the total quantity of the article produced by machinery be equal to the total quantity of the article previously produced by a handicraft or by manufacture, and now made by machinery, then the total labour expended is diminished. The new labour spent on the instruments of labour, on the machinery, on the coal, and so on, must necessarily be less than the labour displaced by the use of the machinery; otherwise the product of the machine would be as dear, or dearer, than the product of the manual labour. But, as a matter of fact, the total quantity of the article produced by machinery with a diminished number of workmen, instead of remaining equal to, by far exceeds the total quantity of the hand-made article that has been displaced. Suppose that 400,000 yards of cloth have been produced on power-looms by fewer weavers than could weave 100,000 yards by hand. In the quadrupled product there lies four times as much raw material. Hence the production of raw material must be quadrupled. But as regards the instruments of labour, such as buildings, coal, machinery, and so on, it is different; the limit up to which the additional labour required for their production can increase varies with the difference between the quantity of the machine-made article and the quantity of the same article that the same number of workmen could make by hand.

Hence, as the use of machinery extends in a given industry, the immediate effect is to increase production in the other industries that furnish the first with means of production. How far employment is thereby found for an increased number of men, depends, given the length of the working day and the intensity of labour, on the composition of the capital employed, i.e. on the ratio of its constant to its variable component. This ratio, in its turn, varies considerably with the extent to which machinery has already seized on, or is then seizing on, those trades. The number of the men condemned to work in coal and metal mines increased enormously owing to the progress of the English factory system; but during the last few decades this increase of number has been less rapid, owing to the use of new machinery in mining. A new type of workman springs into life along with the machine, namely, its maker. We have already learnt that machinery has possessed itself even of this branch of production on a scale that grows greater every day. As to raw material, there is not the least doubt that the rapid strides of cotton spinning not only pushed on with tropical luxuriance the growth of cotton in the United States, and with it the African slave trade, but also made the breeding of slaves the chief business of the border slave-states. When, in 1790, the first census of slaves was taken in the United States, their number was 697,000; in 1861 it had nearly reached four millions. On the other hand, it is no less certain that the rise of the English woollen factories, together with the gradual conversion of arable land into sheep pasture, brought about the superfluity of agricultural labourers that led to their being driven in masses into the towns. Ireland, having during the last twenty years reduced its population by nearly one half, is at this moment, undergoing the process of still further reducing the number of its inhabitants, so as exactly to suit the requirements of its landlords and of the English woollen manufacturers.

When machinery is applied to any of the preliminary or intermediate stages through which the subject of labour has to pass on its way to completion, there is an increased yield of material in those stages, and simultaneously an increased demand for labour in the handicrafts or manufactures supplied by the produce of the machines. Spinning by machinery, for example, supplied yarn so cheaply and so abundantly that the hand-loom weavers were, at first, able to work full time without increased outlay. Their earnings accordingly rose. Hence a flow of people into the cotton-weaving trade, till at length the 800,000 weavers, called into existence by the Jenny, the throstle and the mule, were overwhelmed by the power-loom. So also, owing to the abundance of clothing materials produced by machinery, the number of tailors, seamstresses and needlewomen went on increasing until the appearance of the sewing-machine.

In proportion as machinery, with the aid of a relatively small number of workpeople, increases the mass of raw materials, intermediate products, instruments of labour, etc., the working up of these materials and intermediate products becomes split up into numberless branches; social production increases in diversity. The factory system carries the social division of labour immeasurably further than does manufacture, for it increases the productiveness of the industries it seizes upon, in a far higher degree.

The immediate result of machinery is to augment surplus-value and the mass of products in which surplus-value is embodied. And, as the substances consumed by the capitalists and their dependants become more plentiful, so too do these orders of society. Their growing wealth, and the relatively diminished number of workmen required to produce the necessaries of life beget simultaneously with the rise of new and luxurious wants the means of satisfying those wants. A larger portion of the produce of society is changed into surplus-produce, and a larger part of the surplus-produce is supplied for consumption in a multiplicity of refined shapes. In other words, the production of luxuries increases. The refined and varied forms of the products are also due to new relations with the markets of the world, relations that are created by modern industry. Not only are greater quantities of foreign articles of luxury exchanged for home products, but a greater mass of foreign raw materials, ingredients and intermediate products are used as means of production in the home industries. Owing to these relations with the markets of the world, the demand for labour increases in the carrying trades, which split up into numerous varieties.

The increase of the means of production and subsistence, accompanied by a relative diminution in the number of labourers, causes an increased demand for labour in making canals, docks, tunnels, bridges and so on, works that can only bear fruit in the far future. Entirely new branches of production, creating new fields of labour, are also formed, as the direct result either of machinery or of the general industrial changes brought about by it. But the place occupied by these branches in the general production is, even in the most developed countries, far from important. The number of labourers that find employment in them is directly proportional to the demand created by those industries for the crudest form of manual labour. The chief industries of this kind are at present gas-works, telegraphs, photography, steam navigation and railways. According to the census of 1861 for England and Wales, we find in the gas industry (gas-works, production of mechanical apparatus, servants of the gas companies etc.) 15,211 persons; in telegraphy, 2,399; in photography, 2,366; steam navigation, 3,570; and in railways, 70,599, of whom the unskilled 'navvies', more or less permanently employed, and the whole administrative and commercial staff, make up about 28,000. The total number of persons, therefore, employed in these five new industries amounts to 94,145.

Lastly, the extraordinary productiveness of modern industry, accompanied as it is by both a more extensive and a more intense exploitation of labour-power in all other spheres of production, allows of the unproductive employment of a larger and larger part of the working class, and the consequent reproduction, on a constantly extending scale, of the ancient domestic slaves under the name of a servant class, including men-servants, women-servants, lackeys, etc. According to the census of 1861, the population of England and Wales was 20,066,244; of these, 9,776,259 males and 10,289,965 females. If we deduct from this population all who are too old or too young for work, all unproductive women, young persons and children, the 'ideological' classes, such as government officials, priests, lawyers, soldiers, etc.; further, all who have no occupation but to consume the labour of others in the form of rent, interest, etc.; and, lastly, paupers, vagabonds, and criminals, there remain in round numbers eight millions of the two sexes of every age, including in that number every capitalist who is in any way engaged in industry, commerce, or finance. Among these 8 millions are:

	Persons
Agricultural labourers (including shepherds, farm servants, and maidservants living in the houses of farmers)	1,098,261
All who are employed in cotton, woollen, worsted, flax, hemp, silk, and jute factories, in stocking making and lace making by machinery	642,607
All who are employed in coal mines and metal mines	565,835
All who are employed in metal works (blast-furnaces, rolling mills, etc.), and metal manufactures of every kind	396,998
The servant class	1,208,648

All the persons employed in textile factories and in mines, taken together, number, 1,208,442; those employed in textile factories and metal industries, taken together, number 1,039,605; in both cases less than the number of modern domestic slaves. What a splendid result of the capitalist exploitation of machinery!

SECTION 7. REPULSION AND ATTRACTION OF WORKPEOPLE BY THE FACTORY SYSTEM. CRISES IN THE COTTON TRADE

All political economists of any standing admit that the introduction of new machinery has a baneful effect on the workmen in the old handicrafts and manufactures with which this machinery at first competes. Almost all of them bemoan the slavery of the factory operative. And what is the great trump-card that they play? That machinery, after the horrors of the period of introduction and development have subsided, instead of diminishing in the long run increases the number of the slaves of labour! Yes, political economy revels in the hideous theory, hideous to every 'philanthropist' who believes in the eternal Nature-ordained necessity for capitalist production, that after a period of growth and transition, even its crowning success, the factory system based on machinery, grinds down more workpeople than on its first introduction it throws on the streets.

It is true that in some cases, as we saw from instances of English worsted and silk factories, an extraordinary extension of the factory system may, at a certain stage of its development, be accompanied not only by a relative but by an absolute decrease in the number of operatives employed. In the year 1860, when a special census of all the factories in the United Kingdom was taken by order of Parliament, the factories in those parts of Lancashire, Cheshire, and Yorkshire included in the district of Mr Baker the factory inspector, numbered 652; 570 of these contained 85,622 power-looms, 6,819,146 spindles (exclusive of doubling spindles), employed 27,439 horsepower (steam) and 1,390 (water) and 94,119 persons. In the year 1865, the same factories contained: looms 95,163, spindles 7,025,031, had a steam-power of 28,925 horses, and a water-power of 1,445 horses and employed 88,913 persons. Between 1860 and 1865, therefore, the increase in looms was 11 per cent, in spindles 3 per cent, and in engine-power 3 per cent, while the number of persons employed decreased 5½ per cent. Between 1852 and 1862 considerable extension of the English woollen manufacture took place, while the number of hands employed in it remained almost stationary, showing how greatly the introduction of new machines had superseded the labour of preceding periods. In certain cases, the increase in the number of hands employed is only apparent; that is, it is not due to the extension of the factories already established, but to the gradual annexation of connected trades; for instance, the increase in power-looms, and in the hands employed by them between 1838 and 1856, was in the cotton trade simply owing to the extension of this branch of industry; but in the other trades to the application of steam-power to the carpet-loom, to the ribbon-loom, and to the linen-loom, which previously had been worked by the power of men. Hence the increase of the hands in these latter trades was merely a symptom of a diminution in the total number employed. Finally, we have considered this question entirely apart from the fact that everywhere, except in the metal industries, young persons (under 18) and women and children form the preponderating element in the class of factory hands.

So long as, in a given branch of industry, the factory system extends itself at the expense of the old handicrafts or of manufacture, the result is as sure as is the result of an encounter between an army furnished with breach-loaders, and one armed with bows and arrows. This first period, during which machinery conquers its field of action, is of decisive importance owing to the extraordinary profits that it helps to produce. These profits not only form a source of accelerated accumulation, but also attract into the favoured sphere of production a large part of the additional social capital that is being constantly created, and is ever on the look-out for new investments. The special advantages of this first period of fast and furious activity are felt in every branch of production that machinery invades. So soon, however, as the factory system has gained a certain breadth of footing and a definite degree of maturity, and, especially, so soon as its technical basis, machinery, is itself produced by machinery; so soon as coal mining and iron mining, the metal industries and the means of transport have been revolutionised; so soon, in short, as the general conditions requisite for production by the modern industrial system have been established, this mode of production acquires an elasticity, a capacity for sudden extension by leaps and bounds that finds no hindrance except in the supply of raw material and in the disposal of the produce. On the one hand, the immediate effect of machinery is to increase the supply of raw material in the same way, for example, as the cotton gin augmented the production of cotton. On the other hand, the cheapness of the articles produced by machinery and the improved means of transport and communication furnish the weapons for conquering foreign markets. By ruining handicraft production in other countries, machinery forcibly converts them into fields for the supply of its raw material. In this way East India was compelled to produce cotton, wool, hemp, jute, and indigo for Great Britain. By constantly making a part of the hands 'supernumerary', modern industry, in all countries where it has taken root, gives a spur to emigration and to the colonisation of foreign lands which are thereby converted into settlements for growing the raw material of the mother country; just as Australia, for example, was converted into a colony for growing wool. A new and international division of labour, a division suited to the requirements of the chief centres of modern industry springs up, and converts one part of the globe into a chiefly agricultural field of production, for supplying the other part which remains a chiefly industrial field. This revolution hangs together with radical changes in agriculture which we need not here further inquire into.

The life of modern industry becomes a series of periods of moderate activity, prosperity, over-production, crisis and stagnation. The uncertainty and instability to which machinery subjects the employment, and consequently the conditions of existence, of the operatives become normal, owing to these periodic changes of the industrial cycle. Except in the periods of prosperity, there rages between the capitalists the most furious combat for the share of each in the markets. This share is directly proportional to the cheapness of the product. Besides the rivalry that this struggle begets in the application of improved machinery for replacing labour-power, and of new methods of production, there also comes a time in every industrial cycle when a forcible reduction of wages beneath the value of labour-power is attempted for the purpose of cheapening commodities.

A necessary condition therefore to the growth of the number of factory hands, is a proportionally much more rapid growth of the amount of capital invested in mills. This growth however is conditioned by the ebb and flow of the industrial cycle. It is, besides, constantly interrupted by the technical progress that at one time virtually supplies the place of new workmen, at another, actually displaces old ones. This qualitative change in mechanical industry continually discharges hands from the factory, or shuts its doors against the fresh stream of recruits, while the purely quantitative extension of the factories absorbs not only the men thrown out of work, but also fresh contingents. The workpeople are thus continually both repelled and attracted, hustled from pillar to post, while at the same time constant changes take place in the sex, age, and skill of the levies.

The lot of the factory operatives will be best depicted by taking a rapid survey of the course of the English cotton industry.

From 1770 to 1815 this trade was depressed or stagnant for 5 years only. During this period of 45 years the English manufacturers had a monopoly of machinery and of the markets of the world. From 1815 to 1821 depression; 1822 and 1823 prosperity; 1824 abolition of the laws against Trade Unions, great extension of factories everywhere; 1825 crisis; 1826 great misery and riots among the factory operatives; 1827 slight improvement; 1828 great increase in power-looms, and in exports; 1829 exports especially to India surpass all former years; 1830 glutted markets, great distress; 1831 to 1833 continued depression, the monopoly of the trade with India and China withdrawn from the East India Company; 1834 great increase of factories and machinery, shortness of hands. The new poor law furthers the migration of agricultural labourers into the factory districts. The country districts swept of children. White slave trade; 1835 great prosperity, contemporaneous starvation of the hand-loom weavers; 1836 great prosperity; 1837 and 1838 depression and crisis; 1839 revival; 1840 great depression, riots, calling out of the military; 1841 and 1842 frightful suffering among the factory operatives; 1842 the manufacturers lock the hands out of the factories in order to enforce the repeal of the Corn Laws. The operatives stream in thousands into the towns of Lancashire and Yorkshire, are driven back by the military, and their leaders brought to trial at Lancaster; 1843 great misery; 1844 revival; 1845 great prosperity; 1846 continued improvement at first, then reaction. Repeal of the Corn Laws; 1847 crisis, general reduction of wages by ten and more per cent in honour of the 'big loaf'; 1848 continued depression; Manchester under military protection; 1849 revival; 1850 prosperity; 1851 falling prices, low wages, frequent strikes; 1852 improvement begins, strikes continue, the manufacturers threaten to import foreign hands; 1853 increasing exports. Strike for 8 months, and great misery at Preston; 1854 prosperity, glutted markets; 1855 news of failures streams in from the United States, Canada, and the Eastern markets; 1856 great prosperity; 1857 crisis; 1858 improvement; 1859 great prosperity, increase in factories; 1860 zenith of the English cotton trade, the Indian, Australian, and other markets so glutted with goods that even in 1863 they had not absorbed the whole lot; the French Treaty of Commerce, enormous growth of factories and machinery; 1861 prosperity continues for a time, reaction, the American Civil War, cotton famine: 1862 to 1863 complete collapse.

SECTION 8. REVOLUTION EFFECTED IN MANUFACTURE, HANDICRAFTS, AND DOMESTIC INDUSTRY BY MODERN INDUSTRY

a) Overthrow of Cooperation Based on Handicraft and on the Division of Labour

We have seen how machinery does away with cooperation based on handicrafts, and with manufacture based on the division of handicraft labour. An example of the first sort is the mowing-machine; it replaces cooperation between mowers. A striking example of the second kind is the needle-making machine. According to Adam Smith, 10 men in his day made in cooperation over 48,000 needles a day. On the other hand, a single needle-machine makes 145,000 in a working day of 11 hours. One woman or one girl superintends four such machines, and so produces near upon 600,000 needles in a day, and upwards of 3,000,000 in a week. A single machine, when it takes the place of cooperation or of manufacture, may itself serve as the basis of an industry of a handicraft character. Still, such a return to handicrafts is but a transition to the factory system, which, as a rule, makes its appearance so soon as the human muscles are replaced, for the purpose of driving the machines, by a mechanical motive power, such as steam or water. Here and there, but in any case only for a time, an industry may be carried on, on a small scale, by means of mechanical power. This is effected by hiring steam-power, as is done in some of the Birmingham trades, or by the use of small caloric-engines, as in some branches of weaving. In the Coventry silk weaving industry the experiment of 'cottage factories' was tried. In the centre of a square surrounded by rows of cottages, an engine-house was built and the engine connected by shafts with the looms in the cottages. In all cases the power was hired at so much per loom. The rent was payable weekly, whether the looms worked or not. Each cottage held from two to six looms; some belonged to the weaver, some were bought on credit, some were hired. The struggle between these cottage factories and the factory proper lasted over twelve years. It ended with the complete ruin of the 300 cottage factories. Wherever the nature of the process did not involve production on a large scale, the new industries that have sprung up in the last few decades, such as envelope making, steel pen making, etc. have, as a general rule, first passed through the handicraft stage, and then the manufacturing stage, as short phases of transition to the factory stage. The transition is very difficult in those cases where the production of the article by manufacture consists, not of a series of graduated processes, but of a great number of disconnected ones. This circumstance formed a great hindrance to the establishment of steel pen factories. Nevertheless, about 15 years ago a machine was invented that automatically performed six separate operations at once. The first steel pens were supplied by the handicraft system in the year 1820, at £7 4s. the gross; in 1830 they were supplied by manufacture at 8s., and today the factory system supplies them to the trade at from 2s. to 6d. the gross.

b) Reaction of the Factory System on Manufacture and Domestic Industries

Along with the development of the factory system and of the revolution in agriculture that accompanies it, production in all the other branches of industry not only extends but alters its character. The principle carried out in the factory system of analysing the process of production into its constituent phases, and of solving the problems thus proposed by the application of mechanics, of chemistry, and of the whole range of the natural sciences, becomes the determining principle everywhere. Hence, machinery squeezes itself into the manufacturing industries first for one detail process, then for another. Thus the solid crystal of their organisation, based on the old division of labour, becomes dissolved, and makes way for constant changes. Independently of this, a radical change takes place in the composition of the collective labourer, a change of the persons working in combination. In contrast with the manufacturing period, the division of labour is thenceforth based, wherever possible, on the employment of women, of children of all ages, and of unskilled labourers, in one word, on cheap labour, as it is characteristically called in England. This is the case not only with all production on a large scale, whether employing machinery or not, but also with the so-called domestic industry, whether carried on in the houses of the workpeople or in small workshops. This modern so-called domestic industry has nothing, except the name, in common with the old-fashioned domestic industry, the existence of which presupposes independent urban handicrafts, independent peasant farming, and above all, a dwelling-house for the labourer and his family. That old-fashioned industry has now been converted into an outside department of the factory, the manufactory, or the warehouse. Besides the factory operatives, the manufacturing workmen and the handicraftsmen, whom it concentrates in large masses at one spot, and directly commands, capital also sets in motion, by means of invisible threads, another army; that of the workers in the domestic industries, who dwell in the large towns and are also scattered over the face of the country. An example: The shirt factory of Messrs Tillie at Londonderry, which employs 1,000 operatives in the factory itself, and 9,000 people spread up and down the country and working in their own houses.

The exploitation of cheap and immature labour-power is carried out in a more shameless manner in modern manufacture than in the factory proper. This is because the technical foundation of the factory system, namely, the substitution of machines for muscular power, and the light character of the labour, is almost entirely absent in manufacture, and at the same time women and over-young children are subjected, in a most unconscionable way, to the influence of poisonous or injurious substances. This exploitation is more shameless in the so-called domestic industry than in manufactures, and that because the power of resistance in the labourers decreases with their dissemination; because a whole series of plundering parasites insinuate themselves between the employer and the workman; because a domestic industry has always to compete either with the factory system, or with manufacturing in the same branch of production; because poverty robs the workman of the conditions most essential to his labour, of space, light and ventilation; because employment becomes more and more irregular; and, finally, because in these the last resorts of the masses made 'redundant' by modern industry and agriculture, competition for work attains its maximum. Economy in the means of production, first systematically carried out in the factory system, and there, from the very beginning, coincident with the most reckless squandering of labour-power, and robbery of the conditions normally requisite for labour – this economy now shows its antagonistic and murderous side more and more in a given branch of industry, the less the social productive power of labour and the technical basis for a combination of processes are developed in that branch.

c) *Modern Manufacture*

I now proceed, by a few examples, to illustrate the principles laid down above. As a matter of fact, the reader is already familiar with numerous instances given in the chapter on the working day. In the hardware manufactures of Birmingham and the neighbourhood, there are employed, mostly in very heavy work, 30,000 children and young persons, besides 10,000 women. There they are to be seen in the unwholesome brass foundries, button factories, enamelling, galvanising and lacquering works. Owing to the excessive labour of their workpeople, both adult and non-adult, certain London houses where newspapers and books are printed, have got the ill-omened name of 'slaughter-houses'. Similar excesses are practised in book-binding, where the victims are chiefly women, girls, and children; young persons have to do heavy work in rope-walks and night-work in salt mines, candle manufactories, and chemical works; young people are worked to death at turning the looms in silk weaving, when it is not carried on by machinery. One of the most shameful, the most dirty, and the worst paid kinds of labour, and one on which women and young girls are by preference employed, is the sorting of rags. It is well known that Great Britain, apart from its own immense store of rags, is the emporium for the rag trade of the whole world. They flow in from Japan, from the most remote States of South America, and from the Canary Islands. But the chief sources of their supply are Germany, France, Russia, Italy, Egypt, Turkey, Belgium, and Holland. They are used for manure, for making bedflocks, for shoddy, and they serve as the raw material of paper. The rag-sorters are the medium for the spread of small-pox and other infectious diseases, and they themselves are the first victims. A classical example of overwork, of hard and inappropriate labour, and of its brutalising effects on the workman from his childhood upwards, is afforded not only by coal-mining and miners generally, but also by tile and brick making, in which industry the recently invented machinery is, in England, used only here and there. Between May and September the work lasts from five in the morning till eight in the evening, and where the drying is done in the open air, it often lasts from four in the morning till nine in the evening. Work from five in the morning till seven in the evening is considered 'reduced' and 'moderate'. Both boys and girls of six and even of four years of age are employed. They work for the same number of hours, often longer, than the adults. The work is hard and the summer heat increases the exhaustion. In a certain tile-field at Mosley for example, a young woman, 24 years of age, was in the habit of making 2,000 tiles a day, with the assistance of 2 little girls, who carried the clay for her, and stacked the tiles. These girls carried daily 10 tons up the slippery sides of the clay pits. From a depth of 30 feet, and then for a distance of 210 feet.

> It is impossible for a child to pass through the purgatory of a tile-field without great moral degradation . . . the low language, which they are accustomed to hear from their tenderest years, the filthy, indecent, and

> shameless habits, amidst which, unknowing, and half wild, they grow up, make them in after-life lawless, abandoned, dissolute. . . . A frightful source of demoralisation is the mode of living. Each moulder, who is always a skilled labourer, and the chief of a group, supplies his 7 subordinates with board and lodging in his cottage. Whether members of his family or not, the men, boys and girls all sleep in the cottage, which contains generally two, exceptionally 3 rooms, all on the ground floor, and badly ventilated. These people are so exhausted after the day's hard work, that neither the rules of health, of cleanliness, nor of decency are in the least observed. Many of these cottages are models of untidiness, dirt, and dust. . . . The greatest evil of the system that employs young girls on this sort of work, consists in this, that, as a rule, it chains them fast from childhood for the whole of their after-life to the most abandoned rabble. They become rough, foul-mouthed boys, before Nature has taught them that they are women. Clothed in a few dirty rags, the legs naked far above the knees, hair and face besmeared with dirt, they learn to treat all feelings of decency and of shame with contempt. During meal-times they lie at full length in the fields, or watch the boys bathing in a neighbouring canal. Their heavy day's work at length completed, they put on better clothes, and accompany the men to the public houses.

That excessive insobriety is prevalent from childhood upwards among the whole of this class, is only natural. 'The worst is that the brickmakers despair of themselves. You might as well, said one of the better kind to a chaplain of Southallfield, try to raise and improve the devil as a brickie, sir!'

As to the manner in which capital effects an economy in the requisites of labour in modern manufacture (in which I include all workshops of larger size, except factories proper) official and most ample material bearing on it is to be found in the *Public Health Reports IV (1863)* and *VI (1864)*. The description of the workshops, more especially those of the London printers and tailors, surpasses the most loathsome phantasies of our romance writers. The effect on the health of the workpeople is self-evident. Dr Simon, the chief medical officer of the Privy Council and the official editor of the *Public Health Reports*, says:

> In my fourth Report (1863) I showed, how it is practically impossible for the workpeople to insist upon that which is their first sanitary right, viz., the right that, no matter what the work for which their employer brings them together, the labour, so far as it depends upon him, should be freed from all avoidably unwholesome conditions. I pointed out, that while the workpeople are practically incapable of doing themselves this sanitary justice, they are unable to obtain any effective support from the paid

administrations of the sanitary police. . . . The life of myriads of workmen and workwomen is now uselessly tortured and shortened by the never-ending physical suffering that their mere occupation begets.

In illustration of the way in which the workrooms influence the state of health Dr Simon gives the following table of mortality.

Number employed	*Industries compared*	*Death-rate per 100,000*		
		Age 25-35	*Age 35-45*	*Age 45-55*
958,265	Agriculture in England & Wales	743	805	1,145
22,301 men 12,379 women	London tailors	958	1,262	2,093
13,803	London printers	894	1,747	2,367

d) Passage of Modern Manufacture and Domestic Industry into Modern Mechanical Industry. The Hastening of This Revolution by the Application of the Factory Acts to Those Industries

The cheapening of labour-power by sheer abuse of the labour of women and children, by sheer robbery of every normal condition requisite for working and living, and by the sheer brutality of over-work and night-work, meets at last with natural obstacles that cannot be overstepped. So also, when based on these methods, do the cheapening of commodities and capitalist exploitation in general. So soon as this point is at last reached – and it takes many years – the hour has struck for the introduction of machinery, and for the thenceforth rapid conversion of the scattered domestic industries and also of manufactures into factory industries.

An example on the most colossal scale of this movement is afforded by the production of wearing apparel. This industry, according to the classification of the Children's Employment Commission, comprises straw hat makers, ladies' hat makers, cap-makers, tailors, milliners and dressmakers, shirt-makers, corset-makers, glove-makers, shoemakers, besides many minor branches, such as the making of neck-ties, collars, etc. In 1861, the number of females employed in these industries in England and Wales amounted to 586,299. Of these 115,242 at the least were under 20, and 16,650 under 15 years of age. The number of these workwomen in the United Kingdom in 1861, was 750,334. The number of males employed in England and Wales, in hat-making, shoemaking, glove-making and tailoring was 437,969; of these 14,964 under 15 years, 89,285 between 15 and 20, and 333,117 over 20 years. Many of the smaller branches are not included in these figures. But take the figures as they stand; we then have for England and Wales alone, according to the census of 1861, a total of 1,024,277 persons, about as many as are absorbed by agriculture and cattle breeding. We begin to understand what becomes of the immense quantities of goods conjured up by the magic of machinery, and of the enormous masses of workpeople which that machinery sets free.

The production of wearing apparel is carried on partly in manufactories in whose workrooms there is but a reproduction of that division of labour, the *membra disjecta* of which were found ready to hand; partly by small master-handicraftsmen; these, however, do not, as formerly, work for individual consumers, but for manufactories and warehouses, and to such an extent that often whole towns and stretches of country carry on certain branches, such as shoemaking, as a speciality; finally, on a very great scale by the so-called domestic workers, who form an external department of the manufactories, warehouses, and even of the workshops of the smaller masters.

The raw material, etc. is supplied by mechanical industry, the mass of cheap human material (*taillable à merci et miséricorde*) is composed of the individuals 'liberated' by mechanical industry and improved agriculture. The manufactures of this class owed their origin chiefly to the capitalist's need of having at hand an army ready equipped to meet any increase of demand. These manufactures nevertheless allowed the scattered handicrafts and domestic industries to continue to exist as a broad foundation. The great production of surplus-value in these branches of labour, and the progressive cheapening of their articles, were and are chiefly due to the minimum wages paid, no more than requisite for a miserable vegetation, and to the extension of working-time up to the maximum endurable by the human organism. It was in fact by the cheapness of the human sweat and the human blood, which were converted into commodities, that the markets were constantly being extended, and continue daily to be extended; more especially was this the case with England's colonial markets, where, besides, English tastes and habits prevail. At last the critical point was reached. The basis of the old method, sheer brutality in the exploitation of the workpeople, accompanied more or less by a systematic division of labour, no longer sufficed for the extending markets and for the still more rapidly extending competition of the capitalists. The hour struck for the advent of machinery. The decisively revolutionary machine, the machine which attacks in an equal degree the whole of the numberless branches of this sphere of production, dressmaking, tailoring, shoemaking, sewing, hat-making, and many others, is the sewing-machine.

Its immediate effect on the workpeople is like that of all machinery, which, since the rise of modern industry, has seized upon new branches of trade. Children of too tender an age are sent adrift. The wage of the machine hands rises compared with that of the house-workers, many of whom belong to the poorest of the poor. That of the better situated handicraftsmen, with whom the machine competes, sinks. The new machine-hands are exclusively girls and young women. With the help of mechanical force, they destroy the monopoly that male labour had of the heavier work, and they drive off from the lighter work numbers of old women and very young children. The overpowering competition crushes the weakest of the manual labourers. The fearful increase in death from starvation during the last ten years in London runs parallel with the extension of machine sewing. The new workwomen turn the machines by hand and foot, or by hand alone, sometimes sitting, sometimes standing, according to the weight, size, and special make of the machine, and expend a great deal of labour-power. Their occupation is unwholesome, owing to the long hours, although in most cases they are not so long as under the old system. Wherever the sewing-machine locates itself in narrow and already over-crowded workrooms, it adds to the unwholesome influences. 'The effect', says Mr Lord,

> on entering low-ceiled workrooms in which 30 to 40 machine hands are working is unbearable. . . . The heat, partly due to the gas stoves used for warming the irons, is horrible. . . . Even when moderate hours of work, i.e. from 8 in the morning till 6 in the evening, prevail in such places, yet three or four persons fall into a swoon regularly every day.

The revolution in the industrial methods which is the necessary result of the revolution in the instruments of production is effected by a medley of transition forms. These forms vary according to the extent to which the sewing-machine has become prevalent in one branch of industry or the other, to the time during which it has been in operation, to the previous condition of the workpeople, to the preponderance of manufacture, of handicrafts or of domestic industry, to the rent of the workrooms, etc. In dressmaking, for instance, where the labour for the most part was already organised, chiefly by simple cooperation, the sewing-machine at first formed merely a new factor in that manufacturing industry. In tailoring, shirtmaking, shoemaking, etc. all the forms are intermingled. Here the factory system proper. There middlemen receive the raw material from the capitalist *en chef*, and group around their sewing-machines, in 'chambers' and 'garrets', from 10 to 50 or more workwomen. Finally, as is always the case with machinery when not organised into a system, and when it can also be used in dwarfish proportions, handicraftsmen and domestic workers, along with their families, or with a little extra labour from without, make use of their own sewing-machines. The system actually prevalent in England is that the capitalist concentrates a large number of machines on his premises, and then distributes the produce of those machines for further manipulation amongst the domestic workers. The variety of the transition forms, however, does not conceal the tendency to conversion into the factory system proper. This tendency is nurtured by the very nature of the sewing-machine, the manifold uses of which push on the concentration, under one roof, and one management, of previously separated branches of a trade. It is also favoured by the circumstance that preparatory needlework, and certain other operations, are most conveniently done on the premises where the machine is at work; as well as by the inevitable expropriation of the hand sewers, and of the domestic workers who work with their own machines. This fate has already in part overtaken them. The constantly increasing amount of capital invested in sewing-machines gives the spur to the production of, and gluts the markets with, machine-made articles, thereby giving the signal to the domestic workers for the sale of their machines. The overproduction of sewing-machines themselves causes their producers, in bad want of a sale, to let them out for so much a week, thus crushing by their deadly competition the small owners of machines. Constant changes in the construction of the machines, and their ever-increasing cheapness, depreciate day by day the older makes, and allow of their being sold in great numbers, at absurd prices, to large capitalists, who alone can thus employ them at a profit. Finally, the substitution of the steam-engine for man gives in this, as in all similar revolutions, the finishing blow. At first, the use of steam power meets with mere technical difficulties, such as unsteadiness in the machines, difficulty in controlling their speed, rapid wear and tear of the lighter machines, etc. all of which are soon overcome by experience. If on the one hand the concentration of many machines in large manufactories leads to the use of steam power, on the other hand, the competition of steam with human muscles hastens on the concentration of workpeople and machines in large factories. Thus England is at present experiencing, not only in the colossal industry of making wearing apparel, but in most of the other trades mentioned above, the conversion of manufacture, of handicrafts, and of domestic work into the factory system, after each of those forms of production, totally changed and disorganised under the influence of modern industry, has long ago reproduced, and even overdone, all the horrors of the factory system, without participating in any of the elements of social progress it contains.

This industrial revolution which takes place spontaneously is artificially helped on by the extension of the Factory Acts to all industries in which women, young persons and children are employed. The compulsory regulation of the working day as regards its length, pauses, beginning and end, the system of relays of children, the exclusion of all children under a certain age, etc. necessitate on the one hand more machinery and the substitution of steam as a motive power in the place of muscles. On the other hand, in order to make up for the loss of time, an expansion occurs of the means of production used in common, of the furnaces, buildings, etc., in one word, greater concentration of the means of production and a correspondingly greater concourse of workpeople. The chief objection, repeatedly and passionately urged on behalf of each manufacture threatened with the Factory Act, is in fact this, that in order to continue the business on the old scale a greater outlay of capital will be necessary. But as regards labour in the so-called domestic industries and the intermediate forms between them and manufacture, so soon as limits are put to the working day and to the employment of children, those industries go to the wall. Unlimited exploitation of cheap labour-power is the sole foundation of their power to compete.

One of the essential conditions for the existence of the factory system, especially when the length of the working day is fixed, is certainty in the result, i.e. the production in a given time of a given quantity of commodities, or of a given useful effect. The statutory pauses in the working day, moreover, imply the assumption that periodical and sudden cessation of the work does no harm to the article undergoing the process of production. This certainty in the result, and this possibility of interrupting the work are, of course, easier to be attained in the purely mechanical industries than in those in which chemical and physical processes play a part; as, for instance, in the earthenware trade, in bleaching, dyeing, baking, and in most of the metal industries. Wherever there is a working day without restriction as to length, wherever there is night-work and unrestricted waste of human life, there the slightest obstacle presented by the nature of the work to a change for the better is soon looked upon as an everlasting barrier erected by Nature. No poison kills vermin with more certainty than the Factory Act removes such everlasting barriers. No one made a greater outcry over 'impossibilities' than our friends the earthenware manufacturers. In 1864 however, they were brought under the Act, and within sixteen months every 'impossibility' had vanished. 'The improved method' called forth by the Act,

> of making slip by pressure instead of by evaporation, the newly-constructed stoves for drying the ware in its green state, etc., are each events of great importance in the pottery art, and mark an advance which the preceding century could not rival. . . . It has even considerably reduced the temperature of the stoves themselves with a considerable saving of fuel, and with a readier effect on the ware.

In spite of every prophecy, the cost-price of earthenware did not rise, but the quantity produced did, and to such an extent that the export for the twelve months ending December 1865 exceeded in value by £138,628 the average of the preceding three years. In the manufacture of matches it was thought to be an indispensable requirement that boys, even while bolting their dinner, should go on dipping the matches in melted phosphorus, the poisonous vapour from which rose into their faces. The Factory Act (1864) made the saving of time a necessity, and so forced into existence a dipping machine, the vapour from which could not come in contact with the workers. So, at the present time, in those branches of the lace manufacture not yet subject to the Factory Act, it is maintained that the mealtimes cannot be regular owing to the different periods required by the various kinds of lace for drying, which periods vary from three minutes up to an hour and more. To this the Children's Employment Commissioners answer:

> The circumstances of this case are precisely analogous to that of the paper-stainers, dealt with in our first report. Some of the principal manufacturers in the trade urged that in consequence of the nature of the materials used, and their various processes, they would be unable, without serious loss, to stop for meal-times at any given moment. But it was seen from the evidence that, by due care and previous arrangement, the apprehended difficulty would be got over; and accordingly, by clause six of section six of the Factory Acts Extension Act, passed during this Session of Parliament, an interval of eighteen months is given to them

> from the passing of the Act before they are required to conform to the meal hours, specified by the Factory Acts.

Hardly had the Act been passed when our friends the manufacturers found out:

> The inconveniences we expected to arise from the introduction of the Factory Acts into our branch of manufacture, I am happy to say, have not arisen. We do not find the production at all interfered with; in short, we produce more in the same time.

It is evident that the English legislature, which certainly no one will venture to reproach with being overdosed with genius, has been led by experience to the conclusion that a simple compulsory law is sufficient to enact away all the so-called impediments, opposed by the nature of the process, to the restriction and regulation of the working day. Hence, on the introduction of the Factory Act into a given industry, a period varying from six to eighteen months is fixed within which it is incumbent on the manufacturers to remove all technical impediments to the working of the Act. But though the Factory Acts thus artificially ripen the material elements necessary for the conversion of the manufacturing system into the factory system, yet at the same time, owing to the necessity they impose for greater outlay of capital, they hasten on the decline of the small masters, and the concentration of capital.

Besides the purely technical impediments that are removable by technical means, the irregular habits of the workpeople themselves obstruct the regulation of the hours of labour. This is especially the case where piece-wage predominates, and where loss of time in one part of the day or week can be made good by subsequent overtime, or by night-work, a process which brutalises the adult workman, and ruins his wife and children. Although this absence of regularity in the expenditure of labour-power is a natural and rude reaction against the tedium of monotonous drudgery, it originates also to a much greater degree from anarchy in production, anarchy that in its turn presupposes unbridled exploitation of labour-power by the capitalist. Besides the general periodic changes of the industrial cycle, and the special fluctuations in the markets to which each industry is subject, we may also reckon what is called 'the season', dependent either on the periodicity of favourable seasons of the year for navigation; or on fashion, and the sudden placing of large orders that have to be executed in the shortest possible time. The habit of giving such orders becomes more frequent with the extension of railways and telegraphs.

> The extension of the railway system throughout the country has tended very much to encourage giving short notice. Purchasers now come up from Glasgow, Manchester, and Edinburgh once every fortnight or so to the wholesale city warehouses which we supply, and give small orders requiring immediate execution, instead of buying from stock as they used to do. Years ago we were always able to work in the slack times, so as to meet demand of the next season, but now no one can say beforehand what will be the demand then.

In those factories and manufactories that are not yet subject to the Factory Acts, the most fearful over-work prevails periodically during what is called the season, in consequence of sudden orders. In the outside department of the factory, of the manufactory, and of the warehouse, the so-called domestic workers, whose employment is at the best irregular, are entirely dependent for their raw material and their orders on the caprice of the capitalist, who in this industry is not hampered by any regard for depreciation of his buildings and machinery, and risks nothing by a stoppage of work, but the skin of the worker himself. Here then he sets himself systematically to work to form an industrial reserve force that shall be ready at a moment's notice; during one part of the year he decimates this force by the most inhuman toil, during the other part, he lets it starve for want of work.

> The employers avail themselves of the habitual irregularity in the homework, when any extra work is wanted at a push, so that the work goes on till 11, and 12 p.m. or 2 a.m., or as the usual phrase is, 'all hours', and that in localities where 'the stench is enough to knock you down, you go to the door, perhaps, and open it, but shudder to go further.' 'They are curious men,' said one of the witnesses, a shoemaker, speaking of the masters, 'they think it does a boy no harm to work too hard for half the year, if he is nearly idle for the other half.'

In the same way as technical impediments, so, too, those 'usages which have grown with the growth of trade' were and still are proclaimed by interested capitalists as obstacles due to the nature of the work. This was a favourite cry of the cotton lords at the time they were first threatened with the Factory Acts. Although their industry more than any other depends on navigation, yet experience has given them the lie. Since then, every pretended obstruction to business has been treated by the Factory inspectors as a mere sham. The thoroughly conscientious investigations of the Children's Employment Commission prove that the effect of the regulation of the hours of work, in some industries, was to spread the mass of labour previously employed more evenly over the whole year; that this regulation was the first rational bridle on the murderous, meaningless caprices of fashion, caprices that consort so badly with the system of modern industry; that the development of ocean navigation and of the means of communication generally, has swept away the technical basis on which season-work was really supported, and that all other so-called unconquerable difficulties vanish before larger buildings, additional machinery, increase in the number of workpeople employed, and the alterations caused by all these in the mode of conducting the wholesale trade. But for all that, capital never becomes reconciled to such changes – and this is admitted over and over again by its own representatives – except 'under the pressure of a General Act of Parliament' for the compulsory regulation of the hours of labour.

SECTION 9. THE FACTORY ACTS. EDUCATIONAL CLAUSES OF THE SAME. THEIR GENERAL EXTENSION IN ENGLAND

Factory legislation, that first conscious and methodical reaction of society against the spontaneously developed form of the process of production, is, as we have seen, just as much the necessary product of modern industry as cotton yarn, self-actors, and the electric telegraph.

Paltry as the education clauses of the Act appear on the whole, yet they proclaim elementary education to be an indispensable condition to the employment of children. The success of those clauses proved for the first time the possibility of combining education and gymnastics with manual labour, and, consequently, of combining manual labour with education and gymnastics. The factory inspectors soon found out by questioning the schoolmasters that the factory children, although receiving only one half the education of the regular day scholars, yet learnt quite as much and often more.

> This can be accounted for by the simple fact that, with only being at school for one half of the day, they are always fresh, and nearly always ready and willing to receive instruction. The system on which they work, half manual labour, and half school, renders each employment a rest and a relief to the other; consequently, both are far more congenial to the child, than would be the case were he kept constantly at one. It is quite clear that a boy who has been at school all the morning, cannot (in hot weather particularly) cope as well as one who comes fresh and bright from his work.

Further information on this point will be found in Senior's speech at the Social Science Congress at Edinburgh in 1863. He there shows, amongst other things, how the monotonous and uselessly long school hours of the children of the upper and middle classes uselessly add to the labour of the teacher, 'while he not only fruitlessly but absolutely injuriously, wastes the time, health, and energy of the children'. From the factory system budded, as Robert Owen has shown us in detail, the germ of the education of the future, an education that will, in the case of every child over a given age, combine productive labour with instruction and gymnastics, not only as one of the methods of adding to the efficiency of production, but as the only method of producing fully developed human beings.

Modern industry, as we have seen, sweeps away by technical means the manufacturing division of labour, under which each man is bound hand and foot for life to a single detail-operation. At the same time, the capitalistic form of that industry reproduces this same division of labour in a still more monstrous shape; in the factory proper, by converting the workman into a living appendage of the machine; and everywhere outside the factory, partly by the sporadic use of machinery and machine workers, partly by re-establishing the division of labour on a fresh basis by the general introduction of the labour of women and children, and of cheap unskilled labour.

The antagonism between the manufacturing division of labour and the methods of modern industry makes itself forcibly felt. It manifests itself, amongst other ways, in the frightful fact that a great part of the children employed in modern factories and manufactures, are from their earliest years riveted to the most simple manipulations, and exploited for years, without being taught a single sort of work that would afterwards make them of use, even in the same manufactory or factory. In the English letter-press printing trade, for example, there existed formerly a system, corresponding to that in the old manufactures and handicrafts, of advancing the apprentices from easy to more and more difficult work. They went through a course of teaching till they were finished printers. To be able to read and write was for every one of them a requirement of their trade. All this was changed by the printing machine. It employs two sorts of labourers, one grown up, tenters, the other, boys mostly from 11 to 17 years of age whose sole business is either to spread the sheets of paper under the machine, or to take from it the printed sheets. They perform this weary task, in London especially, for 14, 15, and 16 hours at a stretch, during several days in the week, and frequently for 36 hours, with only two hours' rest for meals and sleep. A great part of them cannot read, and they are, as a rule, utter savages and very extraordinary creatures.

> To qualify them for the work which they have to do, they require no intellectual training; there is little room in it for skill, and less for judgment; their wages, though rather high for boys, do not increase proportionately as they grow up, and the majority of them cannot look for advancement to the better paid and more responsible post of machine minder, because while each machine has but one minder, it has at least two, and often four boys attached to it.

As soon as they get too old for such child's work, that is about 17 at the latest, they are discharged from the printing establishments. They become recruits of crime. Several attempts to procure them employment elsewhere, were rendered of no avail by their ignorance and brutality, and by their mental and bodily degradation.

As with the division of labour in the interior of the manufacturing workshops, so it is with the division of labour in the interior of society. So long as handicraft and manufacture form the general groundwork of social production, the subjection of the producer to one branch exclusively, the breaking up of the multifariousness of his employment, is a necessary step in the development. On that groundwork each separate branch of production acquires empirically the form that is technically suited to it, slowly perfects it, and, so soon as a given degree of maturity has been reached, rapidly crystallises that form. The only thing, that here and there causes a change, besides new raw material supplied by commerce, is the gradual alteration of the instruments of labour. But their form, too, once definitely settled by experience, petrifies, as is proved by their being in many cases handed down in the same form by one generation to another during thousands of years. A characteristic feature is that, even down into the eighteenth century, the different trades were called 'mysteries' (*mystères*); into their secrets none but those duly initiated could penetrate. Modern industry rent the veil that concealed from men their own social process of production, and that turned the various, spontaneously divided branches of production into so many riddles, not only to outsiders, but even to the initiated. The principle which it pursued, of resolving each process into its constituent movements, without any regard to their possible execution by the hand of man, created the new modern science of technology. The varied, apparently unconnected, and petrified forms of the industrial processes now resolved themselves into so many conscious and systematic applications of natural science to the attainment of given useful effects. Technology also discovered the few main fundamental forms of motion, which, despite the diversity of the instruments used, are necessarily taken by every productive action of the human body; just as the science of mechanics sees in the most complicated machinery nothing but the continual repetition of the simple mechanical powers.

Modern industry never looks upon and treats the existing form of a process as final. The technical basis of that industry is therefore revolutionary, while all earlier modes of production were essentially conservative. By means of machinery, chemical processes and other methods, it is continually causing changes not only in the technical basis of production, but also in the functions of the labourer, and in the social combinations of the labour-process. At the same time, it thereby also revolutionises the division of labour within the society, and incessantly launches masses of capital and of workpeople from one branch of production to another. But if modern industry by its very nature therefore necessitates variation of labour, fluency of function, universal mobility of the labourer, on the other hand, in its capitalistic form, it reproduces the old division of labour with its ossified particularisations. We have seen how this absolute contradiction between the technical necessities of modern industry, and the social character inherent in its capitalistic form, dispels all fixity and security in the situation of the labourer; how it constantly threatens, by taking away the instruments of labour, to snatch from his hands his means of subsistence, and, by suppressing his detail-function, to make him superfluous. We have seen too, how this antagonism vents its rage in the creation of that monstrosity, an industrial reserve army, kept in misery in order to be always at the disposal of capital; in the incessant human sacrifices from among the working class, in the most reckless squandering of labour-power, and in the devastation caused by a social anarchy which turns every economic progress into a social calamity. This is the negative side. But if, on the one hand, variation of work at present imposes itself after the manner of an overpowering natural law, and with the blindly destructive action of a natural law that meets with resistance at all points, modern industry on the other hand, through its catastrophes imposes the necessity of recognising, as a fundamental law of production, variation of work, consequently fitness of the labourer for varied work, consequently the greatest possible development of his varied aptitudes. It becomes a question of life and death for society to adapt the mode of production to the normal functioning of this law. Modern industry indeed compels society, under penalty of death, to replace the detail-worker of today, crippled by life-long repetition of one and the same trivial operation, and thus reduced to the mere fragment of a man, by the fully developed individual, fit for a variety of labours, ready to face any change of production, and to whom the different social functions he performs, are but so many modes of giving free scope to his own natural and acquired powers.

One step already spontaneously taken towards effecting this revolution is the establishment of technical and agricultural schools, and of '*écoles d'enseignement professionel*', in which the children of the working-men receive some little instruction in technology and in the practical handling of the various implements of labour. Though the Factory Act, that first and meagre concession wrung from capital, is limited to combining elementary education with work in the factory, there can be no doubt that when the working class comes into power, as inevitably it must, technical instruction, both theoretical and practical, will take its proper place in the working-class schools. There is also no doubt that such revolutionary ferments, the final result of which is the abolition of the old division of labour, are diametrically opposed to the capitalistic form of production, and to the economic status of the labourer corresponding to that form. But the historical development of the antagonisms immanent in a given form of production, is the only way in which that form of production can be dissolved and a new form established.

So long as factory legislation is confined to regulating the labour in factories, manufactories, etc. it is regarded as a mere interference with the exploiting rights of capital. But when it comes to regulating the so-called 'home-labour', it is immediately viewed as a direct attack on the *patria potestas*, on parental authority. The tender-hearted English Parliament long affected to shrink from taking this step. The force of facts, however, compelled it at last to acknowledge that modern industry, in overturning the economic foundation on which was based the traditional family, and the family labour corresponding to it, had also unloosened all traditional family ties. The rights of the children had to be proclaimed. The final report of the Ch. Empl. Comm. of 1866 states: 'It is unhappily, to a painful degree, apparent throughout the whole of the evidence, that against no persons do the children of both sexes so much require protection as against their parents.' The system of unlimited exploitation of children's labour in general and the so-called home-labour in particular is

> maintained only because the parents are able, without check or control, to exercise this arbitrary and mischievous power over their young and tender offspring. . . . Parents must not possess the absolute power of making their children mere 'machines to earn so much weekly wage. . . .' The

> children and young persons, therefore, in all such cases may justifiably claim from the legislature, as a natural right, that an exemption should be secured to them, from what destroys prematurely their physical strength, and lowers them in the scale of intellectual and moral beings.

It was not, however, the misuse of parental authority that created the capitalistic exploitation, whether direct or indirect, of children's labour; but, on the contrary, it was the capitalistic mode of exploitation which, by sweeping away the economic basis of parental authority, made its exercise degenerate into a mischievous misuse of power. However terrible and disgusting the dissolution, under the capitalist system, of the old family ties may appear, nevertheless modern industry, by assigning as it does an important part in the process of production, outside the domestic sphere, to women, to young persons, and to children of both sexes, creates a new economic foundation for a higher form of the family and of the relations between the sexes. It is, of course, just as absurd to hold the Teutonic-Christian form of the family to be absolute and final as it would be to apply that character to the ancient Roman, the ancient Greek, or the Eastern forms which moreover taken together form a series in historical development. Moreover, it is obvious that the fact of the collective working group being composed of individuals of both sexes and all ages, must necessarily, under suitable conditions, become a source of humane development; although in its spontaneously developed, brutal, capitalistic form, where the labourer exists for the process of production, and not the process of production for the labourer, that fact is a pestiferous source of corruption and slavery.

The necessity for a generalisation of the Factory Acts, for transforming them from an exceptional law relating to mechanical spinning and weaving – those first creations of machinery – into a law affecting social production as a whole, arose, as we have seen, from the mode in which modern industry was historically developed. In the rear of that industry, the traditional form of manufacture, of handicraft, and of domestic industry, is entirely revolutionised; manufactures are constantly passing into the factory system, and handicrafts into manufactures; and lastly, the spheres of handicraft and of the domestic industries become, in a, comparatively speaking, wonderfully short time, dens of misery in which capitalistic exploitation obtains free play for the wildest excesses. There are two circumstances that finally turn the scale: first, the constantly recurring experience that capital, so soon as it finds itself subject to legal control at one point, compensates itself all the more recklessly at other points; secondly, the cry of the capitalists for equality in the conditions of competition, i.e. for equal restraint on all exploitation of labour. On this point let us listen to two heartbroken cries. Messrs Cooksley of Bristol, nail and chain, etc., manufacturers, spontaneously introduced the regulations of the Factory Act into their business.

> As the old irregular system prevails in neighbouring works, the Messrs Cooksley are subject to the disadvantage of having their boys enticed to continue their labour elsewhere after 6 p.m. 'This,' they naturally say, 'is an unjustice and loss to us, as it exhausts a portion of the boy's strength, of which we ought to have the full benefit.'

Mr J. Simpson (paper box and bagmaker, London) states before the commissioners of the Ch. Empl. Comm.: 'He would sign any petition for it [legislative interference]. . . . As it was, he always felt restless at night, when he had closed his place, lest others should be working later than him and getting away his orders.' Summarising, the Ch. Empl. Comm. says:

> It would be unjust to the larger employers that their factories should be placed under regulation, while the hours of labour in the smaller places in their own branch of business were under no legislative restriction. And to the injustice arising from the unfair conditions of competition, in regard to hours, that would be created if the smaller places of work were exempt, would be added the disadvantage to the larger manufacturers, of finding their supply of juvenile and female labour drawn off to the places of work exempt from legislation. Further, a stimulus would be given to the multiplication of the smaller places of work, which are almost invariably the least favourable to the health, comfort, education, and general improvement of the people.

In its final report the Commission proposes to subject to the Factory Act more than 1,400,000 children, young persons and women, of which number about one half are exploited in small industries and by the so-called home-work. It says,

> But if it should seem fit to Parliament to place the whole of that large number of children, young persons and females under the protective legislation above adverted to . . . it cannot be doubted that such legislation would have a most beneficent effect, not only upon the young and the feeble, who are its more immediate objects, but upon the still larger body of adult workers, who would in all these employments, both directly and indirectly, come immediately under its influence. It would enforce upon them regular and moderate hours; it would lead to their places of work being kept in a healthy and cleanly state; it would therefore husband and improve that store of physical strength on which their own well-being and

> that of the country so much depends; it would save the rising generation from that over-exertion at an early age which undermines their constitutions and leads to premature decay; finally, it would ensure them – at least up to the age of 13 – the opportunity of receiving the elements of education, and would put an end to that utter ignorance . . . so faithfully exhibited in the Reports of our Assistant Commissioners, and which cannot be regarded without the deepest pain, and a profound sense of national degradation.

In the Speech from the Throne on 5 February 1867, the Tory Cabinet of the day announced the introduction of Bills founded on the final recommendations of the Commission which had completed its labours in 1866.

On 15 August 1867, the Factory Acts Extension Act, and on 21 August, the Workshops' Regulation Act received the Royal Assent; the former Act having reference to large industries, the latter to small.

The Workshops' Regulation Act, wretched in all its details, remained a dead letter in the hands of the municipal and local authorities who were charged with its execution. When in 1871 Parliament withdrew from them this power, in order to confer it on the Factory Inspectors, to whose province it thus added by a single stroke more than one hundred thousand workshops, and three hundred brickworks, care was taken at the same time not to add more than eight assistants to their already undermanned staff.

What strikes us then in the English legislation of 1867 is, on the one hand, the necessity imposed on the Parliament of the ruling classes of adopting in principle measures so extraordinary, and on so great a scale, against the excesses of capitalistic exploitation; and on the other hand, the hesitation, the repugnance and the bad faith with which it lent itself to the task of carrying those measures into practice.

If the general extension of factory legislation to all trades for the purpose of protecting the working class both in mind and body has become inevitable, on the other hand as we have already pointed out, that extension hastens on the general conversion of numerous isolated small industries into a few combined industries carried on upon a large scale; it therefore accelerates the concentration of capital and the exclusive predominance of the factory system. It destroys both the ancient and the transitional forms, behind which the dominion of capital is still in part concealed, and replaces them by the direct and open sway of capital; but thereby it also generalises the direct opposition to this sway. While in each individual workshop it enforces uniformity, regularity, order, and economy, it increases by the immense spur which the limitation and regulation of the working day give to technical improvement, the anarchy and the catastrophes of capitalist production as a whole, the intensity of labour, and the competition of machinery with the labourer. By the destruction of petty and domestic industries it destroys the last resort of the 'redundant population', and with it the sole remaining safety-valve of the whole social mechanism. By maturing the material conditions, and the combination on a social scale of the processes of production, it matures the contradictions and antagonisms of the capitalist form of production, and thereby provides, along with the elements for the formation of a new society, the forces for exploding the old one.

SECTION 10. MODERN INDUSTRY AND AGRICULTURE

The revolution called forth by modern industry in agriculture, and in the social relations of agricultural producers, will be investigated later on. In this place we shall merely indicate a few results by way of anticipation. If the use of machinery in agriculture is for the most part free from the injurious physical effect it has on the factory operative, its action in superseding the labourers is more intense, and finds less resistance, as we shall see later in detail. In the counties of Cambridge and Suffolk for example, the area of cultivated land has extended very much within the last 20 years (up to 1868), while in the same period the rural population has diminished not only relatively but absolutely. In the United States it is as yet only virtually that agricultural machines replace labourers; in other words, they allow of the cultivation by the farmer of a larger surface, but do not actually expel the labourers employed. In 1861 the number of persons occupied in England and Wales in the manufacture of agricultural machines was 1,034, whilst the number of agricultural labourers employed in the use of agricultural machines and steam-engines did not exceed 1,205.

In the sphere of agriculture, modern industry has a more revolutionary effect than elsewhere, for this reason, that it annihilates the peasant, that bulwark of the old society, and replaces him by the wage-labourer. Thus the desire for social changes, and the class antagonisms are brought to the same level in the country as in the towns. The irrational, old-fashioned methods of agriculture are replaced by scientific ones. Capitalist production completely tears asunder the old bond of union which held together agriculture and manufacture in their infancy. But at the same time it creates the material conditions for a higher synthesis in the future, viz. the union of agriculture and industry on the basis of the more perfected forms they have each acquired during their temporary separation. Capitalist production, by collecting the population in great centres, and causing an ever-increasing preponderance of town population, on the one hand concentrates the historical motive power of society; on the other hand, it disturbs the circulation of matter between man and the soil, i.e. prevents the return to the soil of its elements consumed by man in the form of food and clothing; it therefore violates the conditions necessary to lasting fertility of the soil. By this action it destroys at the same time the health of the town labourer and the intellectual life of the rural labourer. But while upsetting the naturally grown conditions for the maintenance of that circulation of matter, it imperiously calls for its restoration as a system, as a regulating law of social production, and under a form appropriate to the full development of the human race. In agriculture as in manufacture, the transformation of production under the sway of capital means, at the same time, the martyrdom of the producer; the instrument of labour becomes the means of enslaving, exploiting, and impoverishing the labourer; the social combination and organisation of labour-processes is turned into an organised mode of crushing out the workman's individual vitality, freedom, and independence. The dispersion of the rural labourers over large areas breaks their power of resistance while concentration increases that of the town operatives. In modern agriculture, as in the urban industries, the increased productiveness and quantity of the labour set in motion are bought at the cost of laying waste and consuming by disease labour-power itself. Moreover, all progress in capitalistic agriculture is a progress in the art not only of robbing the labourer but of robbing the soil; all progress in increasing the fertility of the soil for a given time, is a progress towards ruining the lasting sources of that fertility. The more a country starts its development on the foundation of modern industry, like the United States for example, the more rapid is this process of destruction. Capitalist production therefore develops technology and the combining together of various processes into a social whole only by sapping the original sources of all wealth – the soil and the labourer.

PART V
THE PRODUCTION OF ABSOLUTE AND OF RELATIVE SURPLUS-VALUE

CHAPTER 16

ABSOLUTE AND RELATIVE SURPLUS-VALUE

In considering the labour-process, we began (see Chapter 7) by treating it in the abstract, apart from its historical forms, as a process between man and Nature. We there stated: 'If we examine the whole process from the point of view of its result, the product, it is plain that both the instruments and the subject of labour are means of production, and that the labour itself is productive labour.' And we further added: 'This method of determining, from the standpoint of the labour-process alone, what is productive labour, is by no means directly applicable to the case of the capitalist process of production.' We now proceed to the further development of this subject.

So far as the labour-process is purely individual, one and the same labourer unites in himself all the functions that later on become separated. When an individual appropriates natural objects for his livelihood, no one controls him but himself. Afterwards he is controlled by others. A single man cannot operate upon Nature without calling his own muscles into play under the control of his own brain. As in the natural body head and hand wait upon each other, so the labour-process unites the labour of the hand with that of the head. Later on they part company and even become deadly foes. The product ceases to be the direct product of the individual, and becomes a social product, produced in common by a collective labourer, i.e. by a combination of workmen, each of whom takes only a part, greater or less, in the manipulation of the subject of their labour. As the cooperative character of the labour-process becomes more and more marked, so, as a necessary consequence, does our notion of productive labour, and of its agent the productive labourer, become extended. In order to labour productively, it is no longer necessary for you to do manual work yourself; enough, if you are an organ of the collective labourer, and perform one of its subordinate functions. The first definition given above of productive labour, a definition deduced from the very nature of the production of material objects, still remains correct for the collective labourer, considered as a whole. But it no longer holds good for each member taken individually.

On the other hand, however, our notion of productive labour becomes narrowed. Capitalist production is not merely the production of commodities, it is essentially the production of surplus-value. The labourer produces not for himself, but for capital. It no longer suffices, therefore, that he should simply produce. He must produce surplus-value. That labourer alone is productive who produces surplus-value for the capitalist, and thus works for the self-expansion of capital. If we may take an example from outside the sphere of production of material objects, a schoolmaster is a productive labourer, when, in addition to belabouring the heads of his scholars, he works like a horse to enrich the school proprietor. That the latter has laid out his capital in a teaching factory, instead of in a sausage factory, does not alter the relation. Hence the notion of a productive labourer implies not merely a relation between work and useful effect, between labourer and product of labour, but also a specific, social relation of production, a relation that has sprung up historically and stamps the labourer as the direct means of creating surplus-value. To be a productive labourer is therefore not a piece of luck, but a misfortune.

The prolongation of the working day beyond the point at which the labourer would have produced just an equivalent for the value of his labour-power, and the appropriation of that surplus-labour by capital, this is production of absolute surplus-value. It forms the general groundwork of the capitalist system, and the starting-point for the production of relative surplus-value. The latter presupposes that the working day is already divided into two parts, necessary labour and surplus-labour. In order to prolong the surplus-labour, the necessary labour is shortened by methods whereby the equivalent for the wages is produced in less time. The production of absolute surplus-value turns exclusively upon the length of the working day; the production of relative surplus-value revolutionises out and out the technical processes of labour, and the composition of society. It therefore presupposes a specific mode, the capitalist mode of production, a mode which, along with its methods, means, and conditions, arises and develops itself spontaneously on the foundation afforded by the formal subjection of labour to capital. In the course of this development, the formal subjection is replaced by the real subjection of labour to capital.

If the labourer wants all his time to produce the necessary means of subsistence for himself and his race, he has no time left in which to work gratis for others. Without a certain degree of productiveness in his labour, he has no such superfluous time at his disposal; without such superfluous time, no surplus-labour, and therefore no capitalists, no slave-owners, no feudal lords, in one word, no class of large proprietors.

Thus we may say that surplus-value rests on a natural basis; but this is permissible only in the very general sense, that there is no natural obstacle absolutely preventing one man from disburdening himself of the labour requisite for his own existence, and burdening another with it, any more, for instance, than unconquerable natural obstacles prevent one man from eating the flesh of another. No mystical ideas must in any way be connected, as sometimes happens, with this historically developed productiveness of labour. It is only after men have raised themselves above the rank of animals, when therefore their labour has been to some extent socialised, that a state of things arises in which the surplus-labour of the one becomes a condition of existence for the other. At the dawn of civilisation the productiveness acquired by labour is small, but so too are the wants which develop with and by the means of satisfying them. Further, at that early period, the portion of society that lives on the labour of others is infinitely small compared with the mass of direct producers. Along with the progress in the productiveness of labour, that small portion of society increases both absolutely and relatively. Besides, capital with its accompanying relations springs up from an economic soil that is the product of a long process of development. The productiveness of labour that serves as its foundation and starting-point, is a gift, not of Nature, but of a history embracing thousands of centuries.

Favourable natural conditions alone give us only the possibility, never the reality, of surplus-labour, nor, consequently, of surplus-value and a surplus-product. The result of difference in the natural conditions of labour is this, that the same quantity of labour satisfies, in different countries, a different mass of requirements, consequently, that under circumstances in other respects analogous, the necessary labour-time is different. These conditions affect surplus-labour only as natural limits, i.e. by fixing the points at which labour for others can begin. In proportion as industry advances, these natural limits recede.

CHAPTER 17

CHANGES OF MAGNITUDE IN THE PRICE OF LABOUR-POWER AND IN SURPLUS-VALUE

The value of labour-power is determined by the value of the necessaries of life habitually required by the average labourer. The quantity of these necessaries is known at any given epoch of a given society, and can therefore be treated as a constant magnitude. What changes is the value of this quantity. There are besides two other factors that enter into the determination of the value of labour-power. One, the expenses of developing that power, which expenses vary with the mode of production; the other, its natural diversity, the difference between the labour-power of men and women, of children and adults. The employment of these different sorts of labour-power, an employment which is, in its turn, made necessary by the mode of production, makes a great difference in the cost of maintaining the family of the labourer, and in the value of the labour-power of the adult male. Both these factors however are excluded in the following investigation.

I assume (1) that commodities are sold at their value; (2) that the price of labour-power rises occasionally above its value, but never sinks below it.

On this assumption we have seen that the relative magnitudes of surplus-value and of price of labour-power are determined by three circumstances; (1) the length of the working day, or the extensive magnitude of labour; (2) the normal intensity of labour, its intensive magnitude, whereby a given quantity of labour is expended in a given time; (3) the productiveness of labour, whereby the same quantum of labour yields, in a given time, a greater or less quantum of product, dependent on the degree of development in the conditions of production. Very different combinations are clearly possible, according as one of the three factors is constant and two variable, or two constant and one variable or lastly all three simultaneously variable. In what follows the chief combinations alone are considered.

(1) LENGTH OF THE WORKING DAY AND INTENSITY OF LABOUR CONSTANT. PRODUCTIVENESS OF LABOUR VARIABLE

On these assumptions the value of labour-power and the magnitude of surplus-value are determined by three laws.

(1) A working day of given length always creates the same amount of value, no matter how the productiveness of labour, and, with it, the mass of the product, and the price of each single commodity produced, may vary.

If the value created by a working day of twelve hours be, say six shillings, then, although the mass of the articles produced varies with the productiveness of labour, the only result is that the value represented by six shillings is spread over a greater or less number of articles.

(2) Surplus-value and the value of labour-power vary in opposite directions. A variation in the productiveness of labour, its increase or diminution, causes a variation in the opposite direction in the value of labour-power, and in the same direction in surplus-value.

The value created by a working day of twelve hours is a constant quantity, say six shillings. This constant quantity is the sum of the surplus-value plus the value of the labour-power, which latter value the labourer replaces by an equivalent. It is self-evident, that if a constant quantity consists of two parts, neither of them can increase without the other diminishing. Let the two parts at starting be equal; three shillings value of labour-power, three shillings surplus-value. Then the value of the labour-power cannot rise from three shillings to four, without the surplus-value falling from three shillings to two; and the surplus-value cannot rise from three shillings to four, without the value of labour-power falling from three shillings to two. Under these circumstances, therefore, no change can take place in the absolute magnitude, either of the surplus-value, or of the value of labour-power, without a simultaneous change in their relative magnitudes, i.e. relatively to each other. It is impossible for them to rise or fall simultaneously.

Further, the value of labour-power cannot fall, and consequently surplus-value cannot rise, without a rise in the productiveness of labour. For instance, in the above case, the value of the labour-power cannot sink from three shillings to two, unless an increase in the productiveness of labour makes it possible to produce in four hours the same quantity of necessaries as previously required six hours to produce.

(3) Increase or diminution of surplus-value is always consequent on, and never the cause of, the corresponding diminution or increase in the value of labour-power.

According to the third law, a change in the magnitude of surplus-value presupposes a movement in the value of labour-power, which movement is brought about by a variation in the productiveness of labour.

The value of labour-power is determined by the value of a given quantity of necessaries. It is the value and not the mass of these necessaries that varies with the productiveness of labour. It is, however, possible that, owing to an increase of productiveness, both the labourer and the capitalist may simultaneously be able to appropriate a greater quantity of these necessaries without any change in the price of labour-power or in surplus-value. If the value of labour-power be three shillings, and the necessary labour-time amount to six hours, if the surplus-value likewise be three shillings, and the surplus-labour six hours, then if the productiveness of labour were doubled without altering the ratio of necessary labour to surplus-labour, there would be no change of magnitude in surplus-value and price of labour-power. The only result would be that each of them would represent twice as many use-values as before; these use-values being twice as cheap as before. Although labour-power would be unchanged in price, it would be above its value. If however the price of labour-power had fallen not to 1s. 6d., the lowest possible point consistent with its new value, but to 2s. 10d. or 2s. 6d., still this lower price would represent an increased mass of necessaries. In this way it is possible with an increasing productiveness of labour for the price of labour-power to keep on falling, and yet this fall to be accompanied by a constant growth in the mass of the labourer's means of subsistence. But even in such case, the fall in the value of labour-power would cause a corresponding rise of surplus-value, and thus the abyss between the labourer's position and that of the capitalist would keep widening.

(2) INCREASING INTENSITY AND PRODUCTIVENESS OF LABOUR WITH SIMULTANEOUS SHORTENING OF THE WORKING DAY

Increased productiveness and greater intensity of labour both have a like effect. They both augment the mass of articles produced in a given time. Both therefore shorten that portion of the working day which the labourer needs to produce his means of subsistence or their equivalent. The minimum length of the working day is fixed by this necessary but contractile portion of it. If the whole working day were to shrink to the length of this portion, surplus-labour would vanish, a consummation utterly impossible under the regime of capital. Only by suppressing the capitalist form of production could the length of the working day be reduced to the necessary labour-time. But, even in that case, the latter would extend its limits. On the one hand, because the notion of 'means of subsistence' would considerably expand, and the labourer would lay claim to an altogether different standard of life. On the other hand, because a part of what is now surplus-labour, would then count as necessary labour; I mean the labour of forming a fund for reserve and accumulation.

The more the productiveness of labour increases, the more can the working day be shortened; and the more the working day is shortened, the more can the intensity of labour increase. From a social point of view, the productiveness increases in the same ratio as the economy of labour, which, in its turn, includes not only economy of the means of production, but also the avoidance of all useless labour. The capitalist mode of production while on the one hand enforcing economy in each individual business, on the other hand begets, by its anarchical system of competition, the most outrageous squandering of labour-power and of the social means of production, not to mention the creation of a vast number of employments, at present indispensable, but in themselves superfluous.

The intensity and productiveness of labour being given, the time which society is bound to devote to material production is shorter, and as a consequence, the time at its disposal for the free development, intellectual and social, of the individual is greater, in proportion as the work is more and more evenly divided among all the able-bodied members of society, and as a particular class is more and more deprived of the power to shift the natural burden of labour from its own shoulders to those of another layer of society. In this direction, the shortening of the working day finds at last a limit in the generalisation of labour. In capitalist society spare time is acquired for one class by converting the whole lifetime of the masses into labour-time.

PART VI
WAGES

CHAPTER 19

THE TRANSFORMATION OF THE VALUE (AND RESPECTIVELY THE PRICE) OF LABOUR-POWER INTO WAGES

On the surface of bourgeois society the wage of the labourer appears as the price of labour, a certain quantity of money that is paid for a certain quantity of labour. Thus people speak of the value of labour and call its expression in money its necessary or natural price. On the other hand they speak of the market-prices of labour, i.e. prices oscillating above or below its natural price.

But what is the value of a commodity? The objective form of the social labour expended in its production. And how do we measure the quantity of this value? By the quantity of the labour contained in it. How then is the value, for example of a twelve hours' working day to be determined? By the twelve working-hours contained in a working day of twelve hours, which is an absurd tautology.

In order to be sold as a commodity in the market, labour must at all events exist before it is sold. But could the labourer give it an independent objective existence, he would sell a commodity and not labour.

Apart from these contradictions, a direct exchange of money, i.e. of realised labour, with living labour would either do away with the law of value which only begins to develop itself freely on the basis of capitalist production, or do away with capitalist production itself, which rests directly on wage-labour. The working day of twelve hours embodies itself for example in a money-value of 6s. Either equivalents are exchanged and then the labourer receives 6s. for twelve hours' labour; the price of his labour would be equal to the price of his product. In this case he produces no surplus-value for the buyer of his labour, the 6s. are not transformed into capital, the basis of capitalist production vanishes. But it is on this very basis that he sells his labour and that his labour is wage-labour. Or else he receives for twelve hours' labour less than 6s., i.e. less than twelve hours' labour. Twelve hours' labour are exchanged against ten, six, etc. hours' labour. This equalisation of unequal quantities not merely does away with the determination of value. Such a self-destructive contradiction cannot be in any way even enunciated or formulated as a law.

It is of no avail to deduce the exchange of more labour against less from their difference of form, the one being realised, the other living. This is the more absurd as the value of a commodity is determined not by the quantity of labour actually realised in it, but by the quantity of living labour necessary for its production. A commodity represents, say six working-hours. If an invention is made by which it can be produced in three hours, the value, even of the commodity already produced, falls by half. It represents now three hours of social labour instead of the six formerly necessary. It is the quantity of labour required for its production, not the realised form of that labour, by which the amount of value of a commodity is determined.

That which comes directly face to face with the possessor of money on the market is in fact not labour, but the labourer. What the latter sells is his labour-power. As soon as his labour actually begins, it has already ceased to belong to him; it can therefore no longer be sold by him. Labour is the substance and the immanent measure of value, but *has itself no value*.

In the expression 'value of labour', the idea of value is not only completely obliterated, but actually reversed. It is an expression as imaginary as the value of the earth. These imaginary expressions, arise however, from the relations of production themselves. They are categories for the phenomenal forms of essential relations. That in their appearance things often represent themselves in inverted form is pretty well known in every science except political economy.

Classical political economy borrowed from everyday life the category 'price of labour' without further criticism, and then simply asked the question, how is this price determined? It soon recognised that the change in the relations of demand and supply explained in regard to the price of labour, as of all other commodities, nothing except its changes, i.e. the oscillations of the market-price above or below a certain mean. If demand and supply balance, the oscillation of prices ceases, all other conditions remaining the same. But then demand and supply also cease to explain anything. The price of labour, at the moment when demand and supply are in equilibrium, is its natural price, determined independently of the relation of demand and supply. And how this price is determined is just the question. Or a larger period of oscillations in the market-price is taken, for example, a year, and they are found to cancel one the other, leaving a mean average quantity, a relatively constant magnitude. This had naturally to be determined otherwise than by its own compensating variations. This price which always finally predominates over the accidental market-prices of labour and regulates them, this 'necessary price' (physiocrats) or 'natural price' of labour (Adam Smith) can, as with all other commodities, be nothing else than its value expressed in money. In this way political economy expected to penetrate athwart the accidental prices of labour, to the value of labour. As with other commodities, this value was determined by the cost of production. But what is the cost of production – of the labourer, i.e. the cost of producing or reproducing the labourer himself? This question unconsciously substituted itself in political economy for the original one; for the search after the cost of production of labour as such turned in a circle and never left the spot. What economists therefore call value of labour is in fact the value of labour-power, as it exists in the personality of the labourer, which is as different from its function, labour, as a machine is from the work it performs. Occupied with the difference between the market-price of labour and its so-called value, with the relation of this value to the rate of profit, and to the values of the commodities produced by means of labour, etc., they never discovered that the course of the analysis had led not only from the market-prices of labour to its presumed value, but had led to the resolution of this value of labour itself into the value of labour-power. Classical economy never arrived at a consciousness of the results of its own analysis; it accepted uncritically the categories 'value of labour', 'natural price of labour', etc. as final and as adequate expressions for the value-relation under consideration, and was thus led, as will be seen later, into inextricable confusion and contradiction, while it offered to the vulgar economists a secure basis of operations for their shallowness, which on principle worships appearances only.

Let us next see how value (and price) of labour-power present themselves in this transformed condition as wages.

We know that the daily value of labour-power is calculated upon a certain length of the labourer's life, to which, again, corresponds a certain length of working day. Assume the habitual working day as twelve hours, the daily value of labour-power as 3s., the expression in money of a value that embodies six hours of labour. If the labourer receives 3s., then he receives the value of his labour-power functioning through twelve hours. If, now, this value of a day's labour-power is expressed as the value of a day's labour itself, we have the formula: Twelve hours' labour has a value of 3s. The value of labour-power thus determines the value of labour, or expressed in money, its necessary price. If on the other hand, the price of labour-power differs from its value, in like manner the price of labour differs from its so-called value.

As the value of labour is only an irrational expression for the value of labour-power it follows, of course, that the value of labour must always be less than the value it produces, for the capitalist always makes labour-power work longer than is necessary for the reproduction of its own value. In the above example, the value of the labour-power that functions through twelve hours is 3s., a value for the reproduction of which six hours are required. The value which the labour-power produces is, on the other hand 6s., because it in fact functions during twelve hours, and the value it produces depends, not on its own value, but on the length of time it is in action. Thus, we have a result absurd at first sight – that labour which creates a value of 6s. possesses a value of 3s.

We see further: The value of 3s. by which a part only of the working day, i.e. six hours' labour, is paid for, appears as the value or price of the whole working day of twelve hours, which thus includes six hours unpaid for. The wage-form thus extinguishes every trace of the division of the working day into necessary labour and surplus-labour, into paid and unpaid labour. All labour appears as paid labour. In the *corvée*, the labour of the worker for himself, and his compulsory labour for his lord, differ in space and time in the clearest possible way. In slave-labour, even that part of the working day in which the slave is only replacing the value of his own means of existence, in which, therefore, in fact he works for himself alone, appears as labour for his master. All the slave's labour appears as unpaid labour. In wage-labour, on the contrary, even surplus-labour, or unpaid labour, appears as paid. There the property-relation conceals the labour of the slave for himself; here the money-relation conceals the unrequited labour of the wage-labourer.

Hence we may understand the decisive importance of the transformation of value and price of labour-power into the form of wages, or into the value and price of labour itself. This phenomenal form, which makes the actual relation invisible and indeed shows the direct opposite of that relation, forms the basis of all the juridical notions of both labourer and capitalist, of all the mystifications of the capitalistic mode of production, of all its illusions as to liberty, of all the apologetic shifts of the vulgar economists.

If history took a long time to get at the bottom of the mystery of wages, nothing, on the other hand, is more easy to understand than the necessity, the *raison d'être*, of this phenomenon.

The exchange between capital and labour at first presents itself to the mind in the same guise as the buying and selling of all other commodities. The buyer gives a certain sum of money, the seller an article of a nature different from money.

Further. Exchange-value and use-value, being intrinsically incommensurable magnitudes, the expressions 'value of labour', 'price of labour', do not seem more irrational than the expressions 'value of cotton', 'price of cotton'. Moreover, the labourer is paid after he has given his labour. In its function of means of payment money realises subsequently the value or price of the article supplied, i.e. in this particular case, the value or price of the labour supplied. Finally, the use-value supplied by the labourer to the capitalist is not in fact his labour-power, but its function, some definite useful labour, the work of tailoring, shoemaking, spinning, etc. That this same labour is, on the other hand, the universal value-creating element, and thus possesses a property by which it differs from all other commodities, is beyond the cognisance of the ordinary mind.

Let us put ourselves in the place of the labourer who receives for twelve hours' labour, say the value produced by six hours' labour, say 3s. For him, in fact, his twelve hours' labour is the means of buying the 3s. The value of his labour-power may vary, with the value of his usual means of subsistence, from 3 to 4 shillings, or from 3 to 2 shillings; or, if the value of his labour-power remains constant, its price may, in consequence of changing relations of demand and supply, rise to 4s. or fall to 2s. He always gives twelve hours of labour. Every change in the amount of the equivalent that he receives appears to him, therefore, necessarily as a change in the value or price of his twelve hours' work.

Let us consider, on the other hand, the capitalist. He wishes to receive as much labour as possible for as little money as possible. Practically therefore the only thing that interests him is the difference between the price of labour-power and the value which its function creates. But then, he tries to buy all commodities as cheaply as possible, and always accounts for his profit by simple cheating, by buying under and selling over the value. Hence, he never comes to see that if such a thing as the value of labour really existed, and he really paid this value, no capital would exist, his money would not be turned into capital.

Moreover, the actual movement of wages presents phenomena which seem to prove that not the value of labour-power is paid, but the value of its function, of labour itself. We may reduce these phenomena to two great classes: (1) Change of wages with the changing length of the working day. One might as well conclude that not the value of a machine is paid, but that of its working, because it costs more to hire a machine for a week than for a day. (2) The individual difference in the wages of different labourers who do the same kind of work. We find this individual difference, but are not deceived by it, in the system of slavery, where, frankly and openly, without any circumlocution, labour-power itself is sold. Only, in the slave system, the advantage of a labour-power above the average, and the disadvantage of a labour-power below the average, affects the slave-owner; in the wage-labour system it affects the labourer himself, because his labour-power is, in the one case, sold by himself, in the other, by a third person.

For the rest, in respect to the phenomenal form, 'value and price of labour', or 'wages', as contrasted with the essential relation manifested therein, viz. the value and price of labour-power, the same difference holds that holds in respect to all phenomena and their hidden substratum. The former appear directly and spontaneously as current modes of thought; the latter must first be discovered by science. Classical political economy nearly touches the true relation of things, without, however, consciously formulating it. This it cannot so long as it sticks in its bourgeois skin.

CHAPTER 22

NATIONAL DIFFERENCES IN WAGES

In the comparison of the wages in different nations, we must take into account all the factors that determine changes in the amount of the value of labour-power; the price and the extent of the prime necessaries of life as naturally and historically developed, the cost of training the labourers, the part played by the labour of women and children, the productiveness of labour, its extensive and intensive magnitude. Even the most superficial comparison requires the reduction first of the average day-wage for the same trades, in different countries, to a uniform working day. After this reduction to the same terms of the day-wages, time-wage must again be translated into piece-wage, as the latter only can be a measure both of the productivity and the intensity of labour.

In every country there is a certain average intensity of labour, below which the labour for the production of a commodity requires more than the socially necessary time, and therefore does not reckon as labour of normal quality. Only a degree of intensity above the national average affects, in a given country, the measure of value by the mere duration of the working-time. This is not the case on the universal market, whose integral parts are the individual countries. The average intensity of labour changes from country to country; here it is greater, there less. These national averages form a scale whose unit of measure is the average unit of universal labour. The more intense national labour therefore, as compared with the less intense, produces in the same time more value, which expresses itself in more money.

But the law of value in its international application is yet more modified by this, that on the world market the more productive national labour reckons also as the more intense, so long as the more productive nation is not compelled by competition to lower the selling price of its commodities to the level of their value.

In proportion as capitalist production is developed in a country, in the same proportion do the national intensity and productivity of labour there rise above the international level. The different quantities of commodities of the same kind produced in different countries in the same working-time, have, therefore, unequal international values, which are expressed in different prices, i.e. in sums of money varying according to international values. The relative value of money will therefore be less in the nation with more developed capitalist mode of production than in the nation with less developed. It follows then that the nominal wages, the equivalent of labour-power expressed in money, will also be higher in the first nation than in the second; which does not at all prove that this holds also for the real wages, i.e. for the means of subsistence placed at the disposal of the labourer.

PART VII
THE ACCUMULATION OF CAPITAL

The conversion of a sum of money into means of production and labour-power is the first step taken by the quantum of value that is going to function as capital. This conversion takes place in the market, within the sphere of circulation. The second step, the process of production, is complete so soon as the means of production have been converted into commodities whose value exceeds that of their component parts, and therefore contains the capital originally advanced plus a surplus-value. These commodities must then be thrown into circulation. They must be sold, their value realised in money, this money afresh converted into capital, and so over and over again. This circular movement, in which the same phases are continually gone through in succession, forms the circulation of capital.

The first condition of accumulation is that the capitalist must have contrived to sell his commodities and to reconvert into capital the greater part of the money so received. In the following pages we shall assume that capital circulates in its normal way.

The capitalist who produces surplus-value, i.e. who extracts unpaid labour directly from the labourers and fixes it in commodities, is indeed the first appropriator, but by no means the ultimate owner, of this surplus-value. He has to share it with capitalists, with landowners etc. who fulfil other functions in the complex of social production. Surplus-value, therefore, splits up into various parts. Its fragments fall to various categories of persons, and take various forms, independent the one of the other, such as profit, interest, merchants' profit, rent, etc.

On the one hand, then, we assume that the capitalist sells at their value the commodities he has produced, without concerning ourselves either about the new forms that capital assumes while in the sphere of circulation, or about the concrete conditions of reproduction hidden under these forms. On the other hand, we treat the capitalist producer as owner of the entire surplus-value, or better perhaps as the representative of all the sharers with him in the booty. We, therefore, first of all consider accumulation from an abstract point of view, i.e. as a mere phase in the actual process of production.

CHAPTER 23

SIMPLE REPRODUCTION

Whatever the form of the process of production in a society, it must be a continuous process, must continue to go periodically through the same phases. A society can no more cease to produce than it can cease to consume. When viewed therefore as a connected whole, and as flowing on with incessant renewal, every social process of production is at the same time a process of reproduction.

The conditions of production are also those of reproduction. No society can go on producing, in other words, no society can reproduce, unless it constantly reconverts a part of its products into means of production, or elements of fresh products. All other circumstances remaining the same, the only mode by which it can reproduce its wealth, and maintain it at one level, is by replacing the means of production – the instruments of labour, the raw material and the auxiliary substances consumed in the course of the year – by an equal quantity of the same kind of articles; these must be separated from the mass of the yearly products, and thrown afresh into the process of production. Hence a definite portion of each year's product belongs to the domain of production. Destined for productive consumption from the very first, this portion exists, for the most part, in the shape of articles totally unfitted for individual consumption.

If production be capitalistic in form, so too will be reproduction. Just as in the former the labour-process figures but as a means towards the self-expansion of capital, so in the latter it figures but as a means of reproducing as capital, i.e. as self-expanding value, the value advanced. It is only because his money constantly functions as capital that the economic guise of a capitalist attaches to a man. If, for instance, a sum of £100 has this year been converted into capital, and produced a surplus-value of £20, it must continue during next year, and subsequent years, to repeat the same operation. As a periodic increment of the capital advanced, or periodic fruit of capital in process, surplus-value acquires the form of a revenue flowing out of capital.

If this revenue serve the capitalist only as a fund to provide for his consumption, and be spent as periodically as it is gained, then *ceteris paribus*, simple reproduction will take place. And although this reproduction is a mere repetition of the process of production on the old scale, yet this mere repetition, or continuity, gives a new character to the process, or, rather, causes the disappearance of some apparent characteristics which it possessed as an isolated discontinuous process.

The purchase of labour-power for a fixed period is the prelude to the process of production; and this prelude is constantly repeated when the stipulated term comes to an end, when a definite period of production, such as a week or a month, has elapsed. But the labourer is not paid until after he has expended his labour-power, and realised in commodities not only its value, but surplus-value. He has therefore produced not only surplus-value, which we for the present regard as a fund to meet the private consumption of the capitalist, but he has also produced, before it flows back to him in the shape of wages, the fund out of which he himself is paid, the variable capital; and his employment lasts only so long as he continues to reproduce this fund. What flows back to the labourer in the shape of wages is a portion of the product that is continuously reproduced by him. The capitalist, it is true, pays him in money, but this money is merely the transmuted form of the product of his labour. While he is converting a portion of the means of production into products, a portion of his former product is being turned into money. It is his labour of last week, or of last year, that pays for his labour-power this week or this year. The illusion begotten by the intervention of money vanishes immediately, if, instead of taking a single capitalist and a single labourer, we take the class of capitalists and the class of labourers as a whole. The capitalist class is constantly giving to the labouring class order-notes, in the form of money, on a portion of the commodities produced by the latter and appropriated by the former. The labourers give these order-notes back just as constantly to the capitalist class, and in this way get their share of their own product. The transaction is veiled by the commodity-form of the product and the money-form of the commodity.

Variable capital is therefore only a particular historical form of appearance of the fund for providing the necessaries of life, or the labour fund which the labourer requires for the maintenance of himself and family, and which, whatever be the system of social production, he must himself produce and reproduce. If the labour fund constantly flows to him in the form of money that pays for his labour, it is because the product he has created moves constantly away from him in the form of capital. But all this does not alter the fact that it is the labourer's own labour, realised in a product, which is advanced to him by the capitalist. Let us take a peasant liable to do compulsory service for his lord. He works on his own land with his own means of production for say three days a week. The three other days he does forced work on the lord's domain. He constantly reproduces his own labour fund, which never, in his case, takes the form of a money payment for his labour, advanced by another person. But in return, his unpaid forced labour for the lord, on its side, never acquires the character of voluntary paid labour. If one fine morning the lord appropriates to himself the land, the cattle, the seed, in a word, the means of production of this peasant, the latter will thenceforth be obliged to sell his labour-power to the lord. He will, *ceteris paribus*, labour six days a week as before, three for himself, three for his lord, who thenceforth becomes a wages-paying capitalist. As before, he will use up the means of production as means of production, and transfer their value to the product. As before, a definite portion of the product will be devoted to reproduction. But from the moment that the forced labour is changed into wage-labour, from that moment the labour fund, which the peasant himself continues as before to produce and reproduce, takes the form of a capital advanced in the form of wages by the lord. The bourgeois economist whose narrow mind is unable to separate the form of appearance from the thing that appears, shuts his eyes to the fact that it is but here and there on the face of the earth that even nowadays the labour fund crops up in the form of capital.

Variable capital, it is true, only then loses its character of a value advanced out of the capitalist's funds when we view the process of capitalist production in the flow of its constant renewal. But that process must have had a beginning of some kind. From our present standpoint it therefore seems likely that the capitalist once upon a time became possessed of money, by some accumulation that took place independently of the unpaid labour of others, and that this was, therefore, how he was enabled to frequent the market as a buyer of labour-power. However this may be, the mere continuity of the process, the simple reproduction, brings about some other wonderful changes, which affect not only the variable, but the total capital.

If a capital of £1,000 beget yearly a surplus-value of £200, and if this surplus-value be consumed every year, it is clear that at the end of 5 years the surplus-value consumed will amount to 5 × £200 or the £1,000 originally advanced. If only a part, say one half, were consumed, the same result would follow at the end of 10 years, since 10

× £100 = £1,000. General Rule: The value of the capital advanced divided by the surplus-value annually consumed, gives the number of years, or reproduction periods, at the expiration of which the capital originally advanced has been consumed by the capitalist and has disappeared. The capitalist thinks that he is consuming the produce of the unpaid labour of others, i.e. the surplus-value, and is keeping intact his original capital; but what he thinks cannot alter facts. After the lapse of a certain number of years, the capital value he then possesses is equal to the sum total of the surplus-value appropriated by him during those years, and the total value he has consumed is equal to that of his original capital. It is true he has in hand a capital whose amount has not changed, and of which a part, viz. the buildings, machinery, etc. were already there when the work of his business began. But what we have to do with here, is not the material elements but the value of that capital. When a person gets through all his property by taking upon himself debts equal to the value of that property, it is clear that his property represents nothing but the sum total of his debts. And so it is with the capitalist; when he has consumed the equivalent of his original capital, the value of his present capital represents nothing but the total amount of the surplus-value appropriated by him without payment. Not a single atom of the value of his old capital continues to exist.

Apart then from all accumulation, the mere continuity of the process of production, in other words simple reproduction, sooner or later, and of necessity, converts every capital into accumulated capital, or capitalised surplus-value. Even if that capital was originally acquired by the personal labour of its employer, it sooner or later becomes value appropriated without an equivalent, the unpaid labour of others materialised either in money or in some other object. We saw in Chapters 4–6 that in order to convert money into capital something more is required than the production and circulation of commodities. We saw that on the one side the possessor of value or money, on the other, the possessor of the value-creating substance; on the one side, the possessor of the means of production and subsistence, on the other, the possessor of nothing but labour-power, must confront one another as buyer and seller. The separation of labour from its product, of subjective labour-power from the objective conditions of labour, was therefore the real foundation in fact, and the starting-point of capitalist production.

But that which at first was but a starting-point, becomes, by the mere continuity of the process, by simple reproduction, the peculiar result, constantly renewed and perpetuated, of capitalist production.

On the one hand, the process of production incessantly converts material wealth into capital, into means of creating more wealth and means of enjoyment for the capitalist. On the other hand, the labourer, on quitting the process, is what he was on entering it, a source of wealth, but devoid of all means of making that wealth his own. Since, before entering on the process, his own labour has already been alienated from himself by the sale of his labour-power, has been appropriated by the capitalist and incorporated with capital, it must during the process be realised in a product that does not belong to him. Since the process of production is also the process by which the capitalist consumes labour-power, the product of the labourer is incessantly converted not only into commodities, but into capital, into value that sucks up the value-creating power, into means of subsistence that buy the person of the labourer, into means of production that command the producers. The labourer therefore constantly produces material, objective wealth, but in the form of capital, of an alien power that dominates and exploits him: and the capitalist as constantly produces labour-power, but in the form of a subjective source of wealth, separated from the objects in and by which it can alone be realised; in short he produces the labourer, but as a wage-labourer. This incessant reproduction, this perpetuation of the labourer, is the *sine qua non* of capitalist production.

The labourer consumes in a two-fold way. While producing he consumes by his labour the means of production, and converts them into products with a higher value than that of the capital advanced. This is his productive consumption. It is at the same time consumption of his labour-power by the capitalist who bought it. On the other hand, the labourer turns the money paid to him for his labour-power into means of subsistence: this is his individual consumption. The labourer's productive consumption and his individual consumption are therefore totally distinct. In the former he acts as the motive power of capital, and belongs to the capitalist. In the latter, he belongs to himself, and performs his necessary vital functions outside the process of production. The result of the one is that the capitalist lives; of the other, that the labourer lives.

The matter takes quite another aspect when we contemplate not the single capitalist and the single labourer, but the capitalist class and the labouring class, not an isolated process of production, but capitalist production in full swing, and on its actual social scale. By converting part of his capital into labour-power, the capitalist augments the value of his entire capital. He kills two birds with one stone. He profits not only by what he receives from but by what he gives to the labourer. The capital given in exchange for labour-power is converted into necessaries, by the consumption of which the muscles, nerves, bones, and brains of existing labourers are reproduced, and new labourers are begotten. Within the limits of what is strictly necessary, the individual consumption of the working class is, therefore, the reconversion of the means of subsistence given by capital in exchange for labour-power into fresh labour-power at the disposal of capital for exploitation. It is the production and reproduction of that means of production so indispensable to the capitalist: the labourer himself. The individual consumption of the labourer, whether it proceed within the workshop or outside it, whether it be part of the process of production or not, forms therefore a factor of the production and reproduction of capital; just as cleaning machinery does, whether it be done while the machinery is working or while it is standing. The fact that the labourer consumes his means of subsistence for his own purposes, and not to please the capitalist, has no bearing on the matter. The consumption of food by a beast of burden is none the less a necessary factor in the process of production because the beast enjoys what it eats. The maintenance and reproduction of the working class is, and must ever be, a necessary condition to the reproduction of capital. But the capitalist may safely leave its fulfilment to the labourer's instincts of self-preservation and of propagation. All the capitalist cares for is to reduce the labourer's individual consumption as far as possible to what is strictly necessary.

Hence both the capitalist and his ideological representative, the political economist, consider that part alone of the labourer's individual consumption to be productive, which is requisite for the perpetuation of the class, and which therefore must take place in order that the capitalist may have labour-power to consume; what the labourer consumes for his own pleasure beyond that part is unproductive consumption. If the accumulation of capital were to cause a rise of wages and an increase in the labourer's consumption, unaccompanied by increase in the consumption of labour-power by capital, the additional capital would be consumed unproductively. In reality, the individual consumption of the labourer is unproductive as regards himself, for it reproduces nothing but the needy individual: it is productive to the capitalist and to the state since it is the production of the power that creates their wealth.

From a social point of view, therefore, the working class, even when not directly engaged in the labour-process, is just as much an appendage of capital as the ordinary instruments of labour. Even its individual consumption is, within certain limits, a mere factor in the process of production. That process, however, takes good care to prevent these self-conscious instruments from leaving it in the lurch, for it removes their product, as fast as it is made, from their pole to the opposite pole of capital. Individual consumption provides, on the one hand, the means for their maintenance and reproduction: on the other hand, it secures by the annihilation of the necessaries of life, the continued re-appearance of the workman in the labour-market. The Roman slave was held by fetters: the wage-labourer is bound to his owner by invisible threads. The appearance of independence is kept up by means of a constant change of employers, and by the *fictio juris* of a contract.

Capitalist production therefore of itself reproduces the separation between labour-power and the means of labour. It thereby reproduces and perpetuates the condition for exploiting the labourer. It incessantly forces him to sell his labour-power in order to live, and enables the capitalist to purchase labour-power in order that he may enrich himself. It is no longer a mere accident, that capitalist and labourer confront each other in the market as buyer and seller. It is the process itself that incessantly hurls back the labourer on to the market as a vendor of his labour-power, and that incessantly converts his own product into a means by which another man can purchase him. In reality, the labourer belongs to capital before he has sold himself to capital. His economic bondage is both brought about and concealed by the periodic sale of himself, by his change of masters, and by the oscillations in the market-price of labour-power.

Capitalist production therefore, under its aspect of a continuous connected process, of a process of reproduction, produces not only commodities, not only surplus-value, but it also produces and reproduces the capitalist relation; on the one side the capitalist, on the other the wage-labourer.

CHAPTER 24

Conversion of Surplus-value into Capital

SECTION 1. CAPITALIST PRODUCTION ON A PROGRESSIVELY INCREASING SCALE. TRANSITION OF THE LAWS OF PROPERTY THAT CHARACTERISE PRODUCTION OF COMMODITIES INTO LAWS OF CAPITALIST APPROPRIATION

Hitherto we have investigated how surplus-value emanates from capital; we have now to see how capital arises from surplus-value. Employing surplus-value as capital, reconverting it into capital, is called accumulation of capital.

First let us consider this transaction from the standpoint of the individual capitalist. Suppose a spinner to have advanced a capital of £10,000, of which four-fifths (£8,000) are laid out in cotton, machinery, etc., and one-fifth (£2,000) in wages. Let him produce 240,000 lb of yarn annually, having a value of £12,000. The rate of surplus-value being 100 per cent, the surplus-value lies in the surplus or net product of 40,000 lb of yarn, one-sixth of the gross product, with a value of £2,000 which will be realised by a sale. £2,000 is £2,000. We can neither see nor smell in this sum of money a trace of surplus-value. When we know that a given value is surplus-value, we know how its owner came by it; but that does not alter the nature either of value or of money.

In order to convert this additional sum of £2,000 into capital, the master-spinner will, all circumstances remaining as before, advance four-fifths of it (£1,600) in the purchase of cotton etc. and one-fifth (£400) in the purchase of additional spinners, who will find in the market the necessaries of life whose value the master has advanced to them. Then the new capital of £2,000 functions in the spinning-mill, and brings in, in its turn, a surplus-value of £400.

The capital-value was originally advanced in the money-form. The surplus-value on the contrary is, originally, the value of a definite portion of the gross product. If this gross product be sold, converted into money, the capital-value regains its original form. From this moment the capital-value and the surplus-value are both of them sums of money, and their reconversion into capital takes place in precisely the same way. The one, as well as the other, is laid out by the capitalist in the purchase of commodities that place him in a position to begin afresh the fabrication of his goods, and this time on an extended scale. But in order to be able to buy those commodities, he must find them ready in the market.

His own yarns circulate only because he brings his annual product to market, as all other capitalists likewise do with their commodities. But these commodities, before coming to market, were part of the general annual product, part of the total mass of objects of every kind, into which the sum of the individual capitals, i.e. the total capital of society, had been converted in the course of the year, and of which each capitalist had in hand only an aliquot part. The transactions in the market effectuate only the interchange of the individual components of this annual product, transfer them from one hand to another, but can neither augment the total annual production, nor alter the nature of the objects produced. Hence the use that can be made of the total annual product, depends entirely upon its own composition, but in no way upon circulation.

The annual production must in the first place furnish all those objects (use-values) from which the material components of capital, used up in the course of the year, have to be replaced. Deducting these there remains the net or surplus-product, in which the surplus-value lies. And of what does this surplus-product consist? Only of things destined to satisfy the wants and desires of the capitalist class, things which, consequently, enter into the consumption-fund of the capitalists? Were that the case, the cup of surplus-value would be drained to the very dregs, and nothing but simple reproduction would ever take place.

To accumulate it is necessary to convert a portion of the surplus-product into capital. But we cannot, except by a miracle, convert into capital anything but such articles as can be employed in the labour-process (i.e. means of production), and such further articles as are suitable for the sustenance of the labourer (i.e. means of subsistence). Consequently, a part of the annual surplus-labour must have been applied to the production of additional means of production and subsistence over and above the quantity of these things required to replace the capital advanced. In one word, surplus-value is convertible into capital solely because the surplus-product whose value it is already comprises the material elements of new capital.

Now in order to allow of these elements actually functioning as capital, the capitalist class requires additional labour. If the exploitation of the labourers already employed does not increase either extensively or intensively then additional labour-power must be found. For this the mechanism of capitalist production provides beforehand, by converting the working class into a class dependent on wages, a class whose ordinary wages suffice not only for its maintenance but for its increase. It is only necessary for capital to incorporate this additional labour-power, annually supplied by the working class in the shape of labourers of all ages, with the surplus means of production comprised in the annual produce, and the conversion of surplus-value into capital is complete. From a concrete point of view, accumulation resolves itself into the reproduction of capital on a progressively increasing scale. The circle in which simple reproduction moves alters its form, and, to use Sismondi's expression, changes into a spiral.

Let us now return to our illustration. It is the old story: Abraham begat Isaac, Isaac begat Jacob, and so on. The original capital of £10,000 brings in a surplus-value of £2,000, which is capitalised. The new capital of £2,000 brings in a surplus-value of £400, and this, too, is capitalised, converted into a second additional capital, which, in its turn, produces a further surplus-value of £80. And so the ball rolls on.

We here leave out of consideration the portion of the surplus-value consumed by the capitalist. Just as little does it concern us for the moment, whether the additional capital is joined on to the original capital, or is separated from it to function independently; whether the same capitalist, who accumulated it, employs it, or whether he hands it over to another. This only we must not forget, that by the side of the newly-formed capital, the original capital continues to reproduce itself, and to produce surplus-value, and that this is also true of all accumulated capital, and the additional capital engendered by it.

The original capital was formed by the advance of £10,000. How did the owner become possessed of it? 'By his own labour and that of his forefathers', answer unanimously the spokesmen of political economy. And in fact their supposition appears the only one consonant with the laws of the production of commodities.

But it is quite otherwise with regard to the additional capital of £2,000. How that originated we know perfectly well. There is not one single atom of its value that does not owe its existence to unpaid labour. The means of production with which the additional labour-power is incorporated, as well as the necessaries with which the labourers are sustained, are nothing but component parts of the surplus-product, of the tribute annually exacted from the working class by the capitalist class. Though the latter with a portion of that tribute purchases the additional labour-power even at its full price, so that equivalent is exchanged for equivalent, yet the transaction is for all that only the old dodge of every conqueror who buys commodities from the conquered with the money he has robbed them of.

If the additional capital employs the person who produced it, this producer must not only continue to augment the value of the original capital, but must buy back the fruits of his previous labour with more labour than they cost. When viewed as a transaction between the capitalist class and the working class, it makes no difference that additional labourers are employed by means of the unpaid labour of the previously employed labourers. The capitalist may even convert the additional capital into a machine that throws the producers of that capital out of work, and that replaces them by a few children. In every case the working class creates by the surplus-labour of one year the capital destined to employ additional labour in the following year. And this is what is called: creating capital out of capital.

The accumulation of the first additional capital of £2,000 presupposes a value of £10,000 belonging to the capitalist by virtue of his 'primitive labour', and advanced by him. The second additional capital of £400 presupposes, on the contrary, only the previous accumulation of the £2,000, of which the £400 is the surplus-value capitalised. The ownership of past unpaid labour is thenceforth the sole condition for the appropriation of living unpaid labour on a constantly increasing scale. The more the capitalist has accumulated, the more is he able to accumulate.

In so far as the surplus-value, of which the additional capital, no. 1, consists, is the result of the purchase of labour-power with part of the original capital, a purchase that conformed to the laws of the exchange of commodities, and that from a legal standpoint presupposes nothing beyond the free disposal, on the part of the labourer, of his own capacities, and on the part of the owner of money or commodities, of the values that belong to him; in so far as the additional capital, no. 2 etc. is the mere result of no. 1, and therefore a consequence of the above conditions; in so far as each single transaction invariably conforms to the laws of the exchange of commodities, the capitalist buying labour-power, the labourer selling it, and we will assume at its real value; in so far as all this is true, it is evident that the laws of appropriation or of private property, laws that are based on the production and circulation of commodities, become by their own inner and inexorable dialectic changed into their very opposite. The exchange of equivalents, the original operation with which we started, has now become turned round in such a way that there is only an apparent exchange. This is owing to the fact first that the capital which is exchanged for labour-power is itself but a portion of the product of others' labour appropriated without an equivalent; and secondly, that this capital must not only be replaced by its producer, but replaced together with an added surplus. The relation of exchange subsisting between capitalist and labourer becomes a mere semblance appertaining to the process of circulation, a mere form, foreign to the real nature of the transaction, and only mystifying it. The ever repeated purchase and sale of labour-power is now the mere form; what really takes place is this – the capitalist again and again appropriates, without equivalent, a portion of the previously materialised labour of others, and exchanges it for a greater quantity of living labour. At first the rights of property seemed to us to be based on a man's own labour. At least, some such assumption was necessary since only commodity-owners with equal rights confronted each other, and the sole means by which a man could become possessed of the commodities of others was by alienating his own commodities; and these could be replaced by labour alone. Now, however, property turns out to be the right, on the part of the capitalist, to appropriate the unpaid labour of others or its product, and to be the impossibility, on the part of the labourer, of appropriating his own product. The separation of property from labour has become the necessary consequence of a law that apparently originated in their identity.

Therefore however much the capitalist mode of appropriation may seem to fly in the face of the original laws of commodity production, it nevertheless arises, not from a violation but on the contrary from the application of these laws. Let us make this clear once more by briefly reviewing the consecutive phases of motion whose culminating point is capitalist accumulation.

We saw in the first place that the original conversion of a sum of values into capital was achieved in complete accordance with the laws of exchange. One party to the contract sells his labour-power, the other buys it. The former receives the value of his commodity, whose use-value – labour – is thereby alienated to the buyer. Means of production which already belong to the latter are then transformed by him, with the aid of labour equally belonging to him, into a new product which is likewise lawfully his.

The value of this product includes first, the value of the used-up means of production. Useful labour cannot consume these means of production without transferring their value to the new product, but to be saleable, labour-power must be capable of supplying useful labour in the branch of industry in which it is to be employed.

The value of the new product further includes the equivalent of the value of the labour-power together with a surplus-value. This is so because the value of the labour-power – sold for a definite length of time, say a day, a week, etc. – is less than the value created by its use during that time. But the worker has received payment for the exchange-value of his labour-power and by so doing has alienated its use-value – this being the case in every sale and purchase.

The fact that this particular commodity, labour-power, possesses the peculiar use-value of supplying labour, and therefore of creating value, cannot affect the general law of commodity production. If therefore the magnitude of value advanced in wages is not merely found again in the product, but is found there augmented by a surplus-value, this is not because the seller has been defrauded, for he has really received the value of his commodity; it is due solely to the fact that this commodity has been used up by the buyer.

The law of exchange requires equality only between the exchange-values of the commodities given in exchange for one another. From the very outset it presupposes even a difference between their use-values and it has nothing whatever to do with their consumption, which only begins after the deal is closed and executed.

Thus the original conversion of money into capital is achieved in the most exact accordance with the economic laws of commodity production and with the right of property derived from them. Nevertheless its result is:

(1) that the product belongs to the capitalist and not to the worker;
(2) that the value of this product includes, besides the value of the capital advanced, a surplus-value which costs the worker labour but the capitalist nothing, and which none the less becomes the legitimate property of the capitalist;
(3) that the worker has retained his labour-power and can sell it anew if he can find a buyer.

Simple reproduction is only the periodical repetition of this first operation; each time money is converted afresh into capital. Thus the law is not broken; on the contrary, it is merely enabled to operate continuously.

Nor does it matter if simple reproduction is replaced by reproduction on an extended scale, by accumulation. In the former case the capitalist squanders the whole surplus-value in dissipation, in the latter he demonstrates his bourgeois virtue by consuming only a portion of it and converting the rest into money.

The surplus-value is his property; it has never belonged to anyone else. If he advances it for the purpose of production, the advances made come from his own funds, exactly as on the day when he first entered the market. The fact that on this occasion the funds are derived from the unpaid labour of his workers makes absolutely no difference. If worker B is paid out of the surplus-value which worker A produced, then, in the first place, A furnished that surplus-value without having the just price of his commodity cut by a halfpenny, and, in the second place, the transaction is no concern of B's whatever. What B claims, and has a right to claim, is that the capitalist should pay him the value of his labour-power.

To be sure, the matter looks quite different if we consider capitalist production in the uninterrupted flow of its renewal, and if, in place of the individual capitalist and the individual worker, we view in their totality the capitalist class and the working class confronting each other. But in so doing we should be applying standards entirely foreign to commodity production.

Only buyer and seller, mutually independent, face each other in commodity production. The relations between them cease on the day when the term stipulated in the contract they concluded expires. If the transaction is repeated, it is repeated as the result of a new agreement which has nothing to do with the previous one and which only by chance brings the same seller together again with the same buyer.

If, therefore, commodity production, or one of its associated processes, is to be judged according to its own economic laws, we must consider each act of exchange by itself, apart from any connexion with the act of exchange preceding it and that following it. And since sales and purchases are negotiated solely between particular individuals, it is not admissible to seek here for relations between whole social classes.

However long a series of periodical reproductions and preceding accumulations the capital functioning today may have passed through, it always preserves its original virginity. So long as the laws of exchange are observed in every single act of exchange the mode of appropriation can be completely revolutionised without in any way affecting the property rights which correspond to commodity production. These same rights remain in force both at the outset, when the product belongs to its producer, who, exchanging equivalent for equivalent, can enrich himself only by his own labour, and also in the period of capitalism, when social wealth becomes to an ever-increasing degree the property of those who are in a position to appropriate continually and ever afresh the unpaid labour of others.

This result becomes inevitable from the moment there is a free sale, by the labourer himself, of labour-power as a commodity. But it is also only from then onwards that commodity production is generalised and becomes the typical form of production; it is only from then onwards that, from the first, every product is produced for sale and all wealth produced goes through the sphere of circulation. Only when and where wage-labour is its basis does commodity production impose itself upon society as a whole; but only then and there also does it unfold all its hidden potentialities. To say that the supervention of wage-labour adulterates commodity production is to say that commodity production must not develop if it is to remain unadulterated. To the extent that commodity production, in accordance with its own inherent laws, develops further, into capitalist production, the property laws of commodity production change into the laws of capitalist appropriation.

SECTION 3. SEPARATION OF SURPLUS-VALUE INTO CAPITAL AND REVENUE

In the last preceding chapter, we treated surplus-value (or the surplus-product) solely as a fund for supplying the individual consumption of the capitalist. In this chapter we have, so far, treated it solely as a fund for accumulation. It is, however, neither the one nor the other, but is both together. One portion is consumed by the capitalist as revenue, the other is employed as capital, is accumulated.

Given the mass of surplus-value, then, the larger the one of these parts, the smaller is the other. *Ceteris paribus*, the ratio of these parts determines the magnitude of the accumulation. But it is by the owner of the surplus-value, by the capitalist alone, that the division is made. It is his deliberate act. That part of the tribute exacted by him which he accumulates, is said to be saved by him, because he does not eat it, i.e. because he performs the function of a capitalist, and enriches himself.

Except as personified capital, the capitalist has no historical value, and no right to that historical existence which, to use an expression of the witty Lichnowsky, 'hasn't got no date'. And so far only is the necessity for his own transitory existence implied in the transitory necessity for the capitalist mode of production. But, so far as he is personified capital, it is not values in use and the enjoyment of them, but exchange-value and its augmentation, that spur him into action. Fanatically bent on making value expand itself, he ruthlessly forces the human race to produce for production's sake; he thus forces the development of the productive powers of society, and creates those material conditions, which alone can form the real basis of a higher form of society, a society in which the full and free development of every individual forms the ruling principle. Only as personified capital is the capitalist respectable. As such, he shares with the miser the passion for wealth as wealth. But that which in the miser is a mere idiosyncrasy is, in the capitalist, the effect of the social mechanism, of which he is but one of the wheels. Moreover, the development of capitalist production makes it constantly necessary to keep increasing the amount of the capital laid out in a given industrial undertaking, and competition makes the immanent laws of capitalist production to be felt by each individual capitalist, as external coercive laws. It compels him to keep constantly extending his capital in order to preserve it, but extend it he cannot except by means of progressive accumulation.

So far, therefore, as his actions are a mere function of capital – endowed as capital is, in his person, with consciousness and a will – his own private consumption is a robbery perpetrated on accumulation, just as in book-keeping by double entry, the private expenditure of the capitalist is placed on the debtor side of his account against his capital. To accumulate is to conquer the world of social wealth, to increase the mass of human beings exploited by him, and thus to extend both the direct and the indirect sway of the capitalist.

But original sin is at work everywhere. As capitalist production, accumulation and wealth, become developed, the capitalist ceases to be the mere incarnation of capital. He has a fellow-feeling for his own Adam, and his education gradually enables him to smile at the rage for asceticism as a mere prejudice of the old-fashioned miser. While the capitalist of the classical type brands individual consumption as a sin against his function, and as 'abstinence' from accumulating, the modernised capitalist is capable of looking upon accumulation as 'abstinence' from pleasure.

At the historical dawn of capitalist production – and every capitalist upstart has personally to go through this historical stage – avarice, and desire to get rich, are the ruling passions. But the progress of capitalist production not only creates a world of delights; it lays open, in speculation and the credit system, a thousand sources of sudden enrichment. When a certain stage of development has been reached, a conventional degree of prodigality, which is also an exhibition of wealth, and consequently a source of credit, becomes a business necessity to the 'unfortunate' capitalist. Luxury enters into capital's expenses of representation. Moreover, the capitalist gets rich not like the miser, in proportion to his personal labour and restricted consumption, but at the same rate as he squeezes out the labour-power of others, and enforces on the labourer abstinence from all life's enjoyments. Although, therefore, the prodigality of the capitalist never possesses the *bona fide* character of the open-handed feudal lord's prodigality, but, on the contrary, has always lurking behind it the most sordid avarice and the most anxious calculation, yet his expenditure grows with his accumulation, without the one necessarily restricting the other. But along with this growth, there is at the same time developed in his breast, a Faustian conflict between the passion for accumulation and the desire for enjoyment.

Dr Aikin says in a work published in 1795: 'The trade of Manchester may be divided into four periods. First, when manufacturers were obliged to work hard for their livelihood.' They enriched themselves chiefly by robbing the parents, whose children were bound as apprentices to them; the parents paid a high premium, while the apprentices were starved. On the other hand, the average profits were low, and to accumulate, extreme parsimony was requisite. They lived like misers, and were far from consuming even the interest on their capital. 'The second period, when they had begun to acquire little fortunes, but worked as hard as before' – for direct exploitation of labour costs labour, as every slave-driver knows

> and lived in as plain a manner as before. . . . The third, when luxury began, and the trade was pushed by sending out riders for orders into every market town in the Kingdom. . . . It is probable that few or no capitals of £3,000 to £4,000 acquired by trade, existed here before 1690. However, about that time, or a little later, the traders had got money beforehand, and began to build modern brick houses, instead of those of wood and plaster.

Even in the early part of the eighteenth century, a Manchester manufacturer, who placed a pint of foreign wine before his guests, exposed himself to the remarks and headshakings of all his neighbours.

Before the rise of machinery, a manufacturer's evening expenditure at the public house where they all met, never exceeded sixpence for a glass of punch, and a penny for a screw of tobacco. It was not till 1758, and this marks an epoch, that a person actually engaged in business was seen with an equipage of his own. 'The fourth period', the last 30 years of the eighteenth century, 'is that in which expense and luxury have made great progress, and was supported by a trade extended by means of riders and factors through every part of Europe.' What would the good Dr Aiken say if he could rise from his grave and see the Manchester of today?

Accumulate, accumulate! That is Moses and the prophets! Therefore, save, save, i.e. reconvert the greatest possible portion of surplus-value, or surplus-product into capital! Accumulation for accumulation's sake, production for production's sake: by this formula classical economy expressed the historical mission of the bourgeoisie, and did not for a single instant deceive itself over the birth-throes of wealth. But what avails lamentation in the face of historical necessity? If to classical economy, the proletarian is but a machine for the production of surplus-value; on the other hand, the capitalist is in its eyes only a machine for the conversion of this surplus-value into additional capital.

CHAPTER 25

THE GENERAL LAW OF CAPITALIST ACCUMULATION

SECTION 1. THE INCREASED DEMAND FOR LABOUR-POWER THAT ACCOMPANIES ACCUMULATION, THE COMPOSITION OF CAPITAL REMAINING THE SAME

In this chapter we consider the influence of the growth of capital on the lot of the labouring class. The most important factor in this inquiry is the composition of capital and the changes it undergoes in the course of the process of accumulation.

The composition of capital is to be understood in a twofold sense. On the side of value, it is determined by the proportion in which it is divided into constant capital or value of the means of production, and variable capital or value of labour-power, the sum total of wages. On the side of material, as it functions in the process of production, all capital is divided into means of production and living labour-power. This latter composition is determined by the relation between the mass of the means of production employed, on the one hand, and the mass of labour necessary for their employment on the other. I call the former the *value-composition*, the latter the *technical composition* of capital. Between the two there is a strict correlation. To express this, I call the value-composition of capital, in so far as it is determined by its technical composition and mirrors the change of the latter, the *organic composition* of capital. Wherever I refer to the composition of capital, without further qualification, its organic composition is always understood.

The many individual capitals invested in a particular branch of production have, one with another, more or less different compositions. The average of their individual compositions gives us the composition of the total capital in this branch of production. Lastly, the average of these averages, in all branches of production, gives us the composition of the total social capital of a country, and with this alone are we, in the last resort, concerned in the following investigation.

Growth of capital involves growth of its variable constituent or of the part invested in labour-power. A part of the surplus-value turned into additional capital must always be re-transformed into variable capital, or additional labour fund. If we suppose that, all other circumstances remaining the same, the composition of capital also remains constant (i.e. that a definite mass of means of production constantly needs the same mass of labour-power to set it in motion), then the demand for labour and the subsistence-fund of the labourers clearly increase in the same proportion as the capital, and the more rapidly, the more rapidly the capital increases. Since the capital produces yearly a surplus-value, of which one part is yearly added to the original capital; since this increment itself grows yearly along with the augmentation of the capital already functioning; since lastly, under special stimulus to enrichment, such as the opening of new markets, or of new spheres for the outlay of capital in consequence of newly developed social wants etc., the scale of accumulation may be suddenly extended merely by a change in the division of the surplus-value or surplus-product into capital and revenue, the requirements of accumulating capital may exceed the increase of labour-power or of the number of labourers; the demand for labourers may exceed the supply, and, therefore, wages may rise. This must, indeed, ultimately be the case if the conditions supposed above continue. For since in each year more labourers are employed than in its predecessor, sooner or later a point must be reached at which the requirements of accumulation begin to surpass the customary supply of labour, and, therefore, a rise of wages takes place. A lamentation on this score was heard in England during the whole of the fifteenth, and the first half of the eighteenth centuries. The more or less favourable circumstances in which the wage-working class supports and multiplies itself in no way alter the fundamental character of capitalist production. As simple reproduction constantly reproduces the capital-relation itself, i.e. the relation of capitalists on the one hand, and wage-workers on the other, so reproduction on a progressive scale, i.e. accumulation, reproduces the capital-relation on a progressive scale, more capitalists or larger capitalists at this pole more wage-workers at that. The reproduction of a mass of labour-power, which must incessantly re-incorporate itself with capital for that capital's self-expansion; which cannot get free from capital, and whose enslavement to capital is only concealed by the variety of individual capitalists to whom it sells itself, this reproduction of labour-power forms, in fact, an essential of the reproduction of capital itself. Accumulation of capital is, therefore, increase of the proletariat.

Under the conditions of accumulation supposed thus far, which conditions are those most favourable to the labourers, their relation of dependence upon capital takes on a form endurable or, as Eden says: 'easy and liberal'. Instead of becoming more intensive with the growth of capital, this relation of dependence only becomes more extensive, i.e. the sphere of capital's exploitation and rule merely extends with its own dimensions and the number of its subjects. A larger part of their own surplus-product, always increasing and continually transformed into additional capital, comes back to them in the shape of means of payment, so that they can extend the circle of their enjoyment; can make some additions to their consumption-fund of clothes, furniture, etc. and can lay by small reserve-funds of money. But just as little as better clothing, food, and treatment, and a larger peculium, do away with the exploitation of the slave, so little do they set aside that of the wage-worker. A rise in the price of labour as a consequence of accumulation of capital only means, in fact, that the length and weight of the golden chain the wage-worker has already forged for himself allow of a relaxation of the tension of it. In the controversies on this subject the chief fact has generally been overlooked, viz. the *differentia specifica* of capitalistic production. Labour-power is sold today, not with a view of satisfying, by its service or by its product, the personal needs of the buyer. His aim is augmentation of his capital, production of commodities containing more labour than he pays for, containing therefore a portion of value that costs him nothing, and that is nevertheless realised when the commodities are sold. Production of surplus-value is the absolute law of this mode of production. Labour-power is only saleable so far as it preserves the means of production in their capacity of capital, reproduces its own value as capital, and yields in unpaid labour a source of additional capital. The conditions of its sale, whether more or less favourable to the labourer, include therefore the necessity of its constant re-selling, and the constantly extended reproduction of all wealth in the shape of capital. Wages, as we have seen, by their very nature, always imply the performance of a certain quantity of unpaid labour on the part of the labourer. Altogether, irrespective of the case of a rise of wages with a falling price of labour etc., such an increase only means at best a quantitative diminution of the unpaid labour that the worker has to supply. This diminution can never reach the point at which it would threaten the system itself. Apart from violent conflicts as to the rate of wages (and Adam Smith has already shown that in such a conflict, taken on the whole, the master is always master), a rise in the price of labour resulting from accumulation of capital implies the following alternative:

Either the price of labour keeps on rising, because its rise does not interfere with the progress of accumulation. In this there is nothing wonderful, for, says Adam Smith, 'after these [profits] are diminished, stock may not only continue to increase, but to increase much faster than before. . . . A great stock, though with small profits, generally increases faster than a small stock with great profits.' In this case it is evident that a diminution in the unpaid labour in no way interferes with the extension of the domain of capital. – Or, on the other hand, accumulation slackens in consequence of the rise in the price of labour, because the stimulus of gain is blunted. The rate of accumulation lessens; but with its lessening, the primary cause of that lessening vanishes, i.e. the disproportion between capital and exploitable labour-power. The mechanism of the process of capitalist production removes the very obstacles that it temporarily creates. The price of labour falls again to a level corresponding with the needs of the self-expansion of capital, whether the level be below, the same as, or above the one which was normal before the rise of wages took place. We see thus: In the first case, it is not the diminished rate either of the absolute, or of the proportional, increase in labour-power, or labouring population, which causes capital to be in excess, but conversely the excess of capital that makes exploitable labour-power insufficient. In the second case, it is not the increased rate either of the absolute, or of the proportional, increase in labour-power, or labouring population, that makes capital insufficient; but, conversely, the relative diminution of capital that causes the exploitable labour-power, or rather its price, to be in excess. It is these absolute movements of the accumulation of capital which are reflected as relative movements of the mass of exploitable labour-power, and therefore seem produced by the latter's own independent movement.

The law of capitalist production that is at the bottom of the pretended 'natural law of population', reduces itself simply to this: The correlation between accumulation of capital and rate of wages is nothing else than the correlation between the unpaid labour transformed into capital, and the additional paid labour necessary for the setting in motion of this additional capital. It is therefore in no way a relation between two magnitudes, independent one of the other: on the one hand, the magnitude of the capital; on the other, the number of the labouring population; it is rather, at bottom, only the relation between the unpaid and the paid labour of the same labouring population. If the quantity of unpaid labour supplied by the working class, and accumulated by the capitalist class, increases so rapidly that its conversion into capital requires an extraordinary addition of paid labour, then wages rise, and, all other circumstances remaining equal, the unpaid labour diminishes in proportion. But as soon as this diminution touches the point at which the surplus-labour that nourishes capital is no longer supplied in normal quantity, a reaction sets in: a smaller part of revenue is capitalised, accumulation lags, and the movement of rise in wages receives a check. The rise of wages therefore is confined within limits that not only leave intact the foundations of the capitalistic system, but also secure its reproduction on a progressive scale. The law of capitalistic accumulation, metamorphosed by economists into pretended law of Nature, in reality merely states that the very nature of accumulation excludes every diminution in the degree of exploitation of labour, and every rise in the price of labour, which could seriously imperil the continual reproduction, on an ever-enlarging scale, of the capitalistic relation. It cannot be otherwise in a mode of production in which the labourer exists to satisfy the needs of self-expansion of existing values, instead of, on the contrary, material wealth existing to satisfy the needs of development on the part of the labourer. As in religion man is governed by the products of his own brain, so in capitalistic production, he is governed by the products of his own hand.

SECTION 2. RELATIVE DIMINUTION OF THE VARIABLE PART OF CAPITAL SIMULTANEOUSLY WITH THE PROGRESS OF ACCUMULATION AND OF THE CONCENTRATION THAT ACCOMPANIES IT

According to the economists themselves, it is neither the actual extent of social wealth, nor the magnitude of the capital already functioning, that lead to a rise of wages, but only the constant growth of accumulation and the degree of rapidity of that growth. So far, we have only considered one special phase of this process, that in which the increase of capital occurs along with a constant technical composition of capital. But the process goes beyond this phase.

Once given the general basis of the capitalistic system then, in the course of accumulation, a point is reached at which the development of the productivity of social labour becomes the most powerful lever of accumulation.

Apart from natural conditions, such as fertility of the soil etc., and from the skill of independent and isolated producers (shown rather qualitatively in the goodness than quantitatively in the mass of their products) the degree of productivity of labour in a given society is expressed in the relative extent of the means of production that one labourer, during a given time, with the same tension of labour-power, turns into products. The mass of the means of production which he thus transforms increases with the productiveness of his labour. But those means of production play a double part. The increase of some is a consequence, that of the others a condition of the increasing productivity of labour. For example with the division of labour in manufacture, and with the use of machinery, more raw material is worked up in the same time, and, therefore, a greater mass of raw material and auxiliary substances enter into the labour-process. That is the consequence of the increasing productivity of labour. On the other hand, the mass of machinery, beasts of burden, mineral manures, drain-pipes, etc. is a condition of the increasing productivity of labour. So also is it with the means of production concentrated in buildings, furnaces, means of transport, etc. But whether condition or consequence, the growing extent of the means of production as compared with the labour-power incorporated with them, is an expression of the growing productiveness of labour. The increase of the latter appears therefore in the diminution of the mass of labour in proportion to the mass of means of production moved by it, or in the diminution of the subjective factor of the labour-process as compared with the objective factor.

This change in the technical composition of capital, this growth in the mass of means of production as compared with the mass of the labour-power that vivifies them, is reflected again in its value-composition, by the increase of the constant constituent of capital at the expense of its variable constituent. There may be e.g., originally 50 per cent of a capital laid out in means of production, and 50 per cent in labour-power; later on, with the development of the productivity of labour, 80 per cent in means of production, 20 per cent in labour-power, and so on. This law of the progressive increase in constant capital in proportion to the variable, is confirmed at every step (as already shown) by the comparative analysis of the prices of commodities, whether we compare different economic epochs or different nations in the same epoch. The relative magnitude of the element of price which represents the value of the means of production only, or the constant part of capital consumed, is in direct, the relative magnitude of the other element of price that pays labour (the variable part of capital) is in inverse proportion to the advance of accumulation.

This diminution in the variable part of capital as compared with the constant, or the altered value-composition of the capital, however, only shows approximately the change in the composition of its material constituents. If e.g., the capital-value employed today in spinning is ⅞ constant and ⅛ variable, whilst at the beginning of the eighteenth century it was ½ constant and ½ variable, on the other hand, the mass of raw material, instruments of labour, etc. that a certain quantity of spinning labour consumes productively today, is many hundred times greater than at the beginning of the century. The reason is simply that, with the increasing productivity of labour, not only does the mass of the means of production consumed by it increase, but their value compared with their mass diminishes. Their value therefore rises absolutely, but not in proportion to their mass. The increase of the difference between constant and variable capital is therefore much less than that of the difference between the mass of the means of production into which the constant, and the mass of the labour-power into which the variable, capital is converted. The former difference increases with the latter, but in a smaller degree.

But if the progress of accumulation lessens the relative magnitude of the variable part of capital, it by no means, in doing this, excludes the possibility of a rise in its absolute magnitude. Suppose that a capital-value at first is divided into 50 per cent of constant and 50 per cent of variable capital; later into 80 per cent of constant and 20 per cent of variable. If in the meantime the original capital, say £6,000, has increased to £18,000, its variable constituent has also increased. It was £3,000, it is now £3,600. But whereas formerly an increase of capital by 20 per cent would have sufficed to raise the demand for labour 20 per cent, now this latter rise requires a tripling of the original capital.

In Part IV it was shown how the development of the productiveness of social labour presupposes cooperation on a large scale; how it is only upon this supposition that division and combination of labour can be organised, and the means of production economised by concentration on a vast scale; how instruments of labour which from their very nature are only fit for use in common, such as a system of machinery, can be called into being; how huge natural forces can be pressed into the service of production; and how the transformation can be effected of the process of production into a technological application of science. On the basis of the production of commodities, where the means of production are the property of private persons, and where the artisan therefore either produces commodities, isolated from and independent of others, or sells his labour-power as a commodity, because he lacks the means for independent industry, cooperation on a large scale can realise itself only in the increase of individual capitals, only in proportion as the means of social production and the means of subsistence are transformed into the private property of capitalists. The basis of the production of commodities can admit of production on a large scale in the capitalistic form alone. A certain accumulation of capital in the hands of individual producers of commodities forms therefore the necessary preliminary of the specifically capitalistic mode of production. We had, therefore, to assume that this occurs during the transition from handicraft to capitalistic industry. It may be called primitive accumulation, because it is the historic basis instead of the historic result of specifically capitalist production. How it itself originates we need not here inquire as yet. It is enough that it forms the starting-point. But all methods for raising the social productive power of labour that are developed on this basis are at the same time methods for the increased production of surplus-value or surplus-product, which in its turn is the formative element of accumulation. They are, therefore, at the same time methods of the production of capital by capital, or methods of its accelerated accumulation. The continual re-transformation of surplus-value into capital now appears in the shape of the increasing magnitude of the capital that enters into the process of production. This in turn is the basis of an extended scale of production, of the methods for raising the productive power of labour that accompany it, and of accelerated production of surplus-value. If, therefore, a certain degree of accumulation of capital appears as a condition of the specifically capitalist mode of production, the latter causes conversely an accelerated accumulation of capital. With the accumulation of capital, therefore, the specifically capitalistic mode of production develops, and with the capitalist mode of production the accumulation of capital. Both these economic factors bring about, in the compound ratio of the impulses they reciprocally give one another, that change in the technical composition of capital by which the variable constituent becomes always smaller and smaller as compared with the constant.

Every individual capital is a larger or smaller concentration of means of production, with a corresponding command over a larger or smaller labour-army. Every accumulation becomes the means of new accumulation. With the increasing mass of wealth which functions as capital, accumulation increases the concentration of that wealth in the hands of individual capitalists, and thereby widens the basis of production on a large scale and of the specific methods of capitalist production. The growth of social capital is effected by the growth of many individual capitals. All other circumstances remaining the same, individual capitals, and with them the concentration of the means of production, increase in such proportion as they form aliquot parts of the total social capital. At the same time portions of the original capitals disengage themselves and function as new independent capitals. Besides other causes, the division of property, within capitalist families, plays a great part in this. With the accumulation of capital, therefore, the number of capitalists grows to a greater or less extent. Two points characterise this kind of concentration which grows directly out of, or rather is identical with, accumulation. First: the increasing concentration of the social means of production in the hands of individual capitalists is, other things remaining equal, limited by the degree of increase of social wealth. Second: the part of social capital domiciled in each particular sphere of production is divided among many capitalists who face one another as independent commodity-producers competing with each other. Accumulation and the concentration accompanying it are, therefore, not only scattered over many points, but the increase of each functioning capital is thwarted by the formation of new and the sub-division of old capitals. Accumulation, therefore, presents itself on the one hand as increasing concentration of the means of production, and of the command over labour; on the other, as repulsion of many individual capitals one from another.

This splitting-up of the total social capital into many individual capitals or the repulsion of its fractions one from another, is counteracted by their attraction. This last does not mean that simple concentration of the means of production and of the command over labour, which is identical with accumulation. It is concentration of capitals already formed, destruction of their individual independence, expropriation of capitalist by capitalist, transformation of many small into few large capitals. This process differs from the former in this, that it only presupposes a change in the distribution of capital already to hand, and functioning; its field of action is therefore not limited by the absolute growth of social wealth, by the absolute limits of accumulation. Capital grows in one place to a huge mass in a single hand, because it has in another place been lost by many. This is centralisation proper, as distinct from accumulation and concentration.

The laws of this centralisation of capitals, or of the attraction of capital by capital, cannot be developed here. A brief hint at a few facts must suffice. The battle of competition is fought by cheapening of commodities. The cheapness of commodities depends, *ceteris paribus*, on the productiveness of labour, and this again on the scale of production. Therefore, the larger capitals beat the smaller. It will further be remembered that, with the development of the capitalist mode of production, there is an increase in the minimum amount of individual capital necessary to carry on a business under its normal conditions. The smaller capitals, therefore, crowd into spheres of production which modern industry has only sporadically or incompletely got hold of. Here competition rages in direct proportion to the number, and in inverse proportion to the magnitudes, of the antagonistic capitals. It always ends in the ruin of many small capitalists, whose capitals partly pass into the hands of their conquerors, partly vanish. Apart from this, with capitalist production an altogether new force comes into play – the credit system, which in its first stages furtively creeps in as the humble assistant of accumulation; drawing into the hands of individual or associated capitalists by invisible threads the money resources which lie scattered over the surface of society in larger or smaller amounts; but it soon becomes a new and terrible weapon in the battle of competition and is finally transformed into an enormous social mechanism for the centralisation of capitals.

Commensurately with the development of capitalist production and accumulation there develop the two most powerful levers of centralisation – competition and credit. At the same time the progress of accumulation increases the material amenable to centralisation, i.e. the individual capitals, whilst the expansion of capitalist production creates on the one hand the social want and on the other, the technical means necessary for those immense industrial undertakings which require a previous centralisation of capital for their accomplishment. Today, therefore, the force of attraction, drawing together individual capitals, and the tendency to centralisation are stronger than ever before. But if the relative extension and energy of the movement towards centralisation is determined in a certain degree by the magnitude of capitalist wealth and superiority of economic mechanism already attained, progress in centralisation does not in any way depend upon a positive growth in the magnitude of social capital. And this is the specific difference between centralisation and concentration, the latter being only another name for reproduction on an extended scale.

Centralisation may result from a mere change in the distribution of capitals already existing, from a simple alteration in the quantitative grouping of the component parts of social capital. Here capital can grow into powerful masses in a single hand because there it has been withdrawn from many individual hands. In any given branch of industry centralisation would reach its extreme limit if all the individual capitals invested in it were fused into a single capital. In a given society the limit would be reached only when the entire social capital was united in the hands of either a single capitalist or a single capitalist company.

Centralisation completes the work of accumulation by enabling industrial capitalists to extend the scale of their operations. Whether this latter result is the consequence of accumulation or centralisation, whether centralisation is accomplished by the violent method of annexation – when certain capitals become such preponderant centres of attraction for others that they shatter the individual cohesion of the latter and then draw the separate fragments to themselves – or whether the fusion of a number of capitals already formed or in process of formation takes place by the smoother process of organising joint-stock companies – the economic effect remains the same. Everywhere the increased scale of industrial establishments is the starting-point for a more comprehensive organisation of the collective work of many, for a wider development of their material motive forces – in other words, for the progressive transformation of isolated processes of production, carried on by customary methods, into processes of production socially combined and scientifically arranged.

But accumulation, the gradual increase of capital by reproduction as it passes from the circular to the spiral form, is clearly a very slow procedure compared with centralisation, which has only to change the quantitative groupings of the constituent parts of social capital. The world would still be without railways if it had had to wait until accumulation had got a few individual capitals far enough to be adequate for the construction of a railway. Centralisation, on the contrary, accomplished this in the twinkling of an eye by means of joint-stock companies. And whilst centralisation thus intensifies and accelerates the effects of accumulation, it simultaneously extends and speeds those revolutions in the technical composition of capital which raise its constant portion at the expense of its variable portion, thus diminishing the relative demand for labour.

The masses of capital fused together overnight by centralisation reproduce and multiply as the others do, only more rapidly, thereby becoming new and powerful levers in social accumulation. Therefore when we speak of the progress of social accumulation we tacitly include – today – the effects of centralisation.

The additional capitals formed in the normal course of accumulation serve particularly as vehicles for the exploitation of new inventions and discoveries, and industrial improvements in general. But in time the old capital also reaches the moment of renewal from top to toe, when it sheds its skin and is reborn like the others in a perfected technical form, in which a smaller quantity of labour will suffice to set in motion a larger quantity of machinery and raw materials. The absolute reduction in the demand for labour which necessarily follows from this is obviously so much the greater the higher the degree in which the capitals undergoing this process of renewal are already massed together by virtue of the centralisation movement.

On the one hand, therefore, the additional capital formed in the course of accumulation attracts fewer and fewer labourers in proportion to its magnitude. On the other hand, the old capital periodically reproduced with change of composition, repels more and more of the labourers formerly employed by it.

SECTION 3. PROGRESSIVE PRODUCTION OF A RELATIVE SURPLUS-POPULATION OR INDUSTRIAL RESERVE ARMY

The accumulation of capital, though originally appearing as its quantitative extension only, is effected, as we have seen, under a progressive qualitative change in its composition, under a constant increase of its constant at the expense of its variable constituent.

The specifically capitalist mode of production, the development of the productive power of labour corresponding to it, and the change thence resulting in the organic composition of capital, do not merely keep pace with the advance of accumulation, or with the growth of social wealth. They develop at a much quicker rate, because mere accumulation, the absolute increase of the total social capital, is accompanied by the centralisation of the individual capitals of which that total is made up; and because the change in the technological composition of the additional capital goes hand in hand with a similar change in the technological composition of the original capital. With the advance of accumulation therefore, the proportion of constant to variable capital changes. If it was originally say 1:1, it now becomes successively 2:1, 3:1, 4:1, 5:1, 7:1, etc. so that, as the capital increases, instead of $\frac{1}{2}$ of its total value, only $\frac{1}{3}$, $\frac{1}{4}$, $\frac{1}{5}$, $\frac{1}{6}$, $\frac{1}{8}$, etc. is transformed into labour-power, and on the other hand, 2/3, 3/4, 4/5, 5/6, 7/8 into means of production. Since the demand for labour is determined not by the amount of capital as a whole, but by its variable constituent alone, that demand falls progressively with the increase of the total capital, instead of, as previously assumed, rising in proportion to it. It falls relatively to the magnitude of the total capital, and at an accelerated rate, as this magnitude increases. With the growth of the total capital, its variable constituent or the labour incorporated in it, also does increase, but in a constantly diminishing proportion. The intermediate pauses are shortened, in which accumulation works as simple extension of production, on a given technical basis. It is not merely that an accelerated accumulation of total capital, accelerated in a constantly growing progression, is needed to absorb an additional number of labourers, or even, on account of the constant metamorphosis of old capital, to keep employed those already functioning. In its turn, this increasing accumulation and centralisation becomes a source of new changes in the composition of capital, of a more accelerated diminution of its variable as compared with its constant constituent. This accelerated relative diminution of the variable constituent that goes along with the accelerated increase of the total capital, and moves more rapidly than this increase, takes the inverse form at the other pole of an apparently absolute increase of the labouring population, an increase always moving more rapidly than that of the variable capital or the means of employment. But in fact it is capitalistic accumulation itself that constantly produces, and produces in the direct ratio of its own energy and extent, a relatively redundant population of labourers, i.e. a population of greater extent than suffices for the average needs of the self-expansion of capital, and therefore a surplus-population.

Consider the social capital in its totality, the movement of its accumulation now causes periodical changes, affecting it more or less as a whole, now distributes its various phases simultaneously over the different spheres of production. In some spheres a change in the composition of capital occurs without increase of its absolute magnitude, as a consequence of simple centralisation; in others the absolute growth of capital is connected with absolute diminution of its variable constituent, or of the labour-power absorbed by it; in others again, capital continues growing for a time on its given technical basis, and attracts additional labour-power in proportion to its increase, while at other times it undergoes organic change, and lessens its variable constituent; in all spheres, the increase of the variable part of capital, and therefore of the number of labourers employed by it, is always connected with violent fluctuations and transitory production of surplus-population, whether this takes the more striking form of the repulsion of labourers already employed, or the less evident but not less real form of the more difficult absorption of the additional labouring population through the usual channels. With the magnitude of social capital already functioning, and the degree of its increase, with the extension of the scale of production, and the mass of the labourers set in motion, with the development of the productiveness of their labour, with the greater breadth and fulness of all sources of wealth, there is also an extension of the scale on which greater attraction of labourers by capital is accompanied by their greater repulsion; the rapidity of the change in the organic composition of capital, and in its technical form increases, and an increasing number of spheres of production becomes involved in this change, now simultaneously, now alternately. The labouring population therefore produces, along with the accumulation of capital produced by it, the means by which it itself is made relatively superfluous, is turned into a relative surplus-population; and it does this to an always increasing extent. This is a law of population peculiar to the capitalist mode of production; and in fact every special historic mode of production has its own special laws of population, historically valid within its limits alone. An abstract law of population exists for plants and animals only, and only in so far as man has not interfered with them.

But if a surplus labouring population is a necessary product of accumulation or of the development of wealth on a capitalist basis, this surplus-population becomes,. conversely, the lever of capitalist accumulation, nay, a condition of existence of the capitalist mode of production. It forms a disposable industrial reserve army, that belongs to capital quite as absolutely as if the latter had bred it at its own cost. Independently of the limits of the actual increase of population, it creates, for the changing needs of the self-expansion of capital, a mass of human material always ready for exploitation. With accumulation, and the development of the productiveness of labour that accompanies it, the power of sudden expansion of capital grows also; it grows not merely because the elasticity of the capital already functioning increases, not merely because the absolute wealth of society expands, of which capital only forms an elastic part, not merely because credit, under every special stimulus, at once places an unusual part of this wealth at the disposal of production in the form of additional capital; it grows also because the technical conditions of the process of production themselves – machinery, means of transport etc. – now admit of the rapidest transformation of masses of surplus-product into additional means of production. The mass of social wealth, overflowing with the advance of accumulation, and transformable into additional capital, thrusts itself frantically into old branches of production, whose market suddenly expands, or into newly formed branches, such as railways etc. the need for which grows out of the development of the old ones. In all such cases, there must be the possibility of throwing great masses of men suddenly on the decisive points without injury to the scale of production in other spheres. Overpopulation supplies these masses. The course characteristic of modern industry, viz. a decennial cycle (interrupted by smaller oscillations), of periods of adverse activity, production at high pressure, crisis and stagnation, depends on the constant formation, the greater or less absorption, and the re-formation of the industrial reserve army or surplus-population. In their turn, the varying phases of the industrial cycle recruit the surplus-population, and become one of the most energetic agents of its reproduction. This peculiar course of modern industry, which occurs in no earlier period of human history, was also impossible in the childhood of capitalist production. The composition of capital changed but very slowly. With its accumulation, therefore, there kept pace on the whole a corresponding growth in the demand for labour. Slow as was the advance of accumulation compared with that of more modern times, it found a check in the natural limits of the exploitable labouring population, limits which could only be got rid of by forcible means to be mentioned later. The expansion by fits and starts of the scale of production is the preliminary to its equally sudden contraction; the latter again evokes the former, but the former is impossible without disposable human material, without an increase in the number of labourers independently of the absolute growth of the population. This increase is effected by the simple process that constantly 'sets free' a part of the labourers; by methods which lessen the number of labourers employed in proportion to the increased production. The whole form of the movement of a modern industry depends, therefore, upon the constant transformation of a part of the labouring population into unemployed or half-employed hands.

Capitalist production can by no means content itself with the quantity of disposable labour-power which the natural increase of population yields. It requires for its free play an industrial reserve army independent of these natural limits.

Up to this point it has been assumed that the increase or diminution of the variable capital corresponds rigidly with the increase or diminution of the number of labourers employed.

The number of labourers commanded by capital may remain the same, or even fall, while the variable capital increases. This is the case if the individual labourer yields more labour, and therefore his wages increase, and this although the price of labour remains the same or even falls, only more slowly than the mass of labour rises. Increase of variable capital in this case becomes an index of more labour, but not of more labourers employed. It is the absolute interest of every capitalist to press a given quantity of labour out of a smaller, rather than a greater number of labourers, if the cost is about the same. In the latter case, the outlay of constant capital increases in proportion to the mass of labour set in action; in the former that increase is much smaller. The more extended the scale of production, the stronger this motive. Its force increases with the accumulation of capital.

We have seen that the development of the capitalist mode of production and of the productive power of labour – at once the cause and effect of accumulation – enables the capitalist, with the same outlay of variable capital, to set in action more labour by greater exploitation (extensive or intensive) of each individual labour-power. We have further seen that the capitalist buys with the same capital a greater mass of labour-power, as he progressively replaces skilled labourers by less skilled, mature labour-power by immature, male by female, that of adults by that of young persons or children.

On the one hand, therefore, with the progress of accumulation, a larger variable capital sets more labour in action without enlisting more labourers; on the other, a variable capital of the same magnitude sets in action more labour with the same mass of labour-power; and, finally, a greater number of inferior labour-powers by displacement of higher.

The production of a relative surplus-population, or the setting free of labourers, goes on therefore yet more rapidly than the technical revolution of the process of production that accompanies, and is accelerated by, the advance of accumulation; and more rapidly than the corresponding diminution of the variable part of capital as compared with the constant. If the means of production, as they increase in extent and effective power, become to a less extent means of employment of labourers, this state of things is again modified by the fact that in proportion as the productiveness of labour increases, capital increases its supply of labour more quickly than its demand for labourers. The overwork of the employed part of the working class swells the ranks of the reserve, whilst conversely the greater pressure that the latter by its competition exerts on the former forces these to submit to overwork and to subjugation under the dictates of capital. The condemnation of one part of the working class to enforced idleness by the overwork of the other part, and the converse, becomes a means of enriching the individual capitalists, and accelerates at the same time the production of the industrial reserve army on a scale corresponding with the advance of social accumulation. How important is this element in the formation of the relative surplus-population is shown by the example of England. Her technical means for saving labour are colossal. Nevertheless, if tomorrow morning labour generally were reduced to a rational amount, and proportioned to the different sections of the working class according to age and sex, the working population to hand would be absolutely insufficient for the carrying on of national production on its present scale. The great majority of the labourers now 'unproductive' would have to be turned into 'productive' ones.

Taking them as a whole, the general movements of wages are exclusively regulated by the expansion and contraction of the industrial reserve army, and these again correspond to the periodic changes of the industrial cycle. They are, therefore, not determined by the variations of the absolute number of the working population, but by the varying proportions in which the working class is divided into active and reserve army, by the increase or diminution in the relative amount of the surplus-population, by the extent to which it is now absorbed, now set free. For modern industry with its decennial cycles and periodic phases, which, moreover, as accumulation advances, are complicated by irregular oscillations following each other more and more quickly, that would indeed be a beautiful law, which pretends to make the action of capital dependent on the absolute variation of the population, instead of regulating the demand and supply of labour by the alternate expansion and contraction of capital, the labour market now appearing relatively under-full, because capital is expanding, now again over-full, because it is contracting. Yet this is the dogma of the economists. According to them, wages rise in consequence of accumulation of capital. The higher wages stimulate the working population to more rapid multiplication, and this goes on until the labour market becomes too full, and therefore capital, relatively to the supply of labour, becomes insufficient. Wages fall, and now we have the reverse of the medal. The working population is little by little decimated as the result of the fall in wages, so that capital is again in excess relatively to them, or, as others explain it, falling wages and the corresponding increase in the exploitation of the labourer again accelerates accumulation, whilst, at the same time, the lower wages hold the increase of the working class in check. Then comes again the time when the supply of labour is less than the demand, wages rise, and so on. A beautiful mode of motion this for developed capitalist production! Before, in consequence of the rise of wages, any positive increase of the population really fit for work could occur, the time would have been passed again and again during which the industrial campaign must have been carried through, the battle fought and won.

Between 1849 and 1859, a rise of wages practically insignificant, though accompanied by falling prices of corn, took place in the English agricultural districts. In Wiltshire for example, the weekly wages rose from 7s. to 8s.; in Dorsetshire from 7s. to 8s., to 9s. etc. This was the result of an unusual exodus of the agricultural surplus-population caused by the demands of war, the vast extension of railroads, factories, mines, etc. The lower the wages, the higher is the proportion in which ever so insignificant a rise of them expresses itself. If the weekly wage e.g., is 20s. and it rises to 22s., that is a rise of 10 per cent; but if it is only 7s. and it rises to 9s., that is a rise of $28\frac{4}{9}$ per cent, which sounds very fine. Everywhere the farmers were howling, and the London *Economist*, with reference to these starvation wages, prattled quite seriously of 'a general and substantial advance'. What did the farmers do now? Did they wait until, in consequence of this brilliant remuneration, the agricultural labourers had so increased and multiplied that their wages must fall again, as prescribed by the dogmatic economic brain? They introduced more machinery, and in a moment the labourers were redundant again in a proportion satisfactory even to the farmers. There was now 'more capital' laid out in agriculture than before, and in a more productive form. With this the demand for labour fell not only relatively, but absolutely.

The above economic fiction confuses the laws that regulate the general movement of wages, or the ratio between the working class – i.e. the total labour-power – and the total social capital, with the laws that distribute the working population over the different spheres of production. If, in consequence of favourable circumstances, accumulation in a particular sphere of production becomes especially active, and profits in it, being greater than the average profits, attract additional capital, of course the demand for labour rises and wages also rise. The higher wages draw a larger part of the working population into the more favoured sphere, until it is glutted with labour-power, and wages at length fall again to their average level or below it, if the pressure is too great. Then, not only does the immigration of labourers into the branch of industry in question cease; it gives place to their emigration. Here the political economist thinks he sees the why and wherefore of an absolute increase of workers accompanying an increase in wages, and of a diminution of wages accompanying an absolute increase of labourers. But he sees really only the local oscillation of the labour market in a particular sphere of production – he sees only the phenomena accompanying the distribution of the working population into the different spheres of outlay of capital, according to its varying needs.

The industrial reserve army, during the period of stagnation and average prosperity, weighs down the active labour-army; during the periods of over-production and paroxysm, it holds its pretensions in check. Relative surplus-population is therefore the pivot upon which the law of demand and supply of labour works. It confines the field of action of this law within the limits absolutely convenient to the activity of exploitation and to the domination of capital.

As soon therefore as the labourers learn the secret, how it comes to pass that in the same measure as they work more, as they produce more wealth for others, and as the productive power of their labour increases, so in the same measure even their function, as a means of the self-expansion of capital becomes more and more precarious for them; as soon as they discover that the degree of intensity of the competition among themselves depends wholly on the pressure of the relative surplus-population; as soon as, by trade unions etc. they try to organise a regular cooperation between employed and unemployed in order to destroy or to weaken the ruinous effects of this natural law of capitalistic production on their class, so soon capital and its sycophant, political economy, cry out at the infringement of the 'eternal' and so to say 'sacred' law of supply and demand. Every combination of employed and unemployed disturbs the 'harmonious' action of this law. But, on the other hand, as soon as (in the colonies, for example) adverse circumstances prevent the creation of an industrial reserve army and with it, the absolute dependence of the working class upon the capitalist class, capital, along with its commonplace Sancho Panza, rebels against the 'sacred' law of supply and demand, and tries to check its inconvenient action by forcible means and state interference.

SECTION 4. DIFFERENT FORMS OF THE RELATIVE SURPLUS-POPULATION. THE GENERAL LAW OF CAPITALISTIC ACCUMULATION

The relative surplus-population exists in every possible form. Every labourer belongs to it during the time when he is only partially employed or wholly unemployed. Not taking into account the great periodically recurring forms that the changing phases of the industrial cycle impress on it, now an acute form during the crisis, then again a chronic form during dull times – it has always three forms, the floating, the latent, the stagnant.

In the centres of modern industry – factories, manufactures, ironworks, mines, etc. – the labourers are sometimes repelled, sometimes attracted again in greater masses, the numbers of those employed increasing on the whole, although in a constantly decreasing proportion to the scale of production. Here the surplus-population exists in the floating form.

In the automatic factories, as in all the great workshops, where machinery enters as a factor, or where only the modern division of labour is carried out, large numbers of boys are employed up to the age of maturity. When this term is once reached, only a very small number continue to find employment in the same branches of industry, whilst the majority are regularly discharged. This majority forms an element of the floating surplus-population, growing with the extension of those branches of industry. Part of them emigrates, following in fact capital that has emigrated. One consequence is that the female population grows more rapidly than the male, *teste* England. That the natural increase of the number of labourers does not satisfy the requirements of the accumulation of capital, and yet all the time is in excess of them, is a contradiction inherent to the movement of capital itself. It wants larger number of youthful labourers, a smaller number of adults. The contradiction is not more glaring than that other one that there is a complaint of the want of hands, while at the same time many thousands are out of work, because the division of labour chains them to a particular branch of industry.

The consumption of labour-power by capital is, besides, so rapid that the labourer, half-way through his life, has already more or less completely lived himself out. He falls into the ranks of the supernumeraries, or is thrust down from a higher to a lower step in the scale. It is precisely among the workpeople of modern industry that we meet with the shortest duration of life. Dr Lee, Medical Officer of

Health for Manchester, stated

> that the average age at death of the Manchester . . . upper middle class was 38 years, while the average age at death of the labouring class was 17; while at Liverpool those figures were represented as 35 against 15. It thus appeared that the well-to-do classes had a lease of life which was more than double the value of that which fell to the lot of the less favoured citizens.

In order to conform to these circumstances, the absolute increase of this section of the proletariat must take place under conditions that shall swell their numbers, although the individual elements are used up rapidly. Hence, rapid renewal of the generations of labourers (this law does not hold for the other classes of the population). This social need is met by early marriages, a necessary consequence of the conditions in which the labourers of modern industry live, and by the premium that the exploitation of children sets on their production.

As soon as capitalist production takes possession of agriculture, and in proportion to the extent to which it does so, the demand for an agricultural labouring population falls absolutely, while the accumulation of the capital employed in agriculture advances, without this repulsion being, as in non-agricultural industries, compensated by a greater attraction. Part of the agricultural population is therefore constantly on the point of passing over into an urban or manufacturing proletariat, and on the look-out for circumstances favourable to this transformation. (Manufacture is used here in the sense of all non-agricultural industries.) This source of relative surplus-population is thus constantly flowing. But the constant flow towards the towns presupposes, in the country itself, a constant latent surplus-population, the extent of which becomes evident only when its channels of outlet open to exceptional width. The agricultural labourer is therefore reduced to the minimum of wages, and always stands with one foot already in the swamp of pauperism.

The third category of the relative surplus-population, the stagnant, forms a part of the active labour army, but with extremely irregular employment. Hence it furnishes to capital an inexhaustible reservoir of disposable labour-power. Its conditions of life sink below the average normal level of the working class; this makes it at once the broad basis of special branches of capitalist exploitation. It is characterised by maximum of working-time, and minimum of wages. We have learnt to know its chief form under the rubric of 'domestic industry'. It recruits itself constantly from the supernumerary forces of modern industry and agriculture, and specially from those decaying branches of industry where handicraft is yielding to manufacture, manufacture to machinery. Its extent grows, as with the extent and energy of accumulation, the creation of a surplus-population advances. But it forms at the same time a self-reproducing and self-perpetuating element of the working class, taking a proportionally greater part in the general increase of that class than the other elements. In fact, not only the number of births and deaths, but the absolute size of the families stand in inverse proportion to the height of wages, and therefore to the amount of means of subsistence of which the different categories of labourers dispose. This law of capitalistic society would sound absurd to savages, or even civilised colonists. It calls to mind the boundless reproduction of animals individually weak and constantly hunted down.

The lowest sediment of the relative surplus-population finally dwells in the sphere of pauperism. Exclusive of vagabonds, criminals, prostitutes, in a word the 'dangerous' classes, this layer of society consists of three categories. First, those able to work. One need only glance superficially at the statistics of English pauperism to find that the quantity of paupers increases with every crisis, and diminishes with every revival of trade. Second, orphans and pauper children. These are candidates for the industrial reserve army, and are, in times of great prosperity, as 1860 for example, speedily and in large numbers enrolled in the active army of labourers. Third, the demoralised and ragged, and those unable to work, chiefly people who succumb to their incapacity for adaptation, due to the division of labour; people who have passed the normal age of the labourer; the victims of industry, whose number increases with the increase of dangerous machinery, of mines, chemical works, etc., the mutilated, the sickly, the widows, etc. Pauperism is the hospital of the active labour-army and the dead weight of the industrial reserve army. Its production is included in that of the relative surplus-population, its necessity in theirs; along with the surplus-population, pauperism forms a condition of capitalist production, and of the capitalist development of wealth. It enters into the *faux frais* of capitalist production; but capital knows how to throw these, for the most part, from its own shoulders on to those of the working class and the lower middle class.

The greater the social wealth, the functioning capital, the extent and energy of its growth, and, therefore, also the absolute mass of the proletariat and the productiveness of its labour, the greater is the industrial reserve army. The same causes which develop the expansive power of capital develop also the labour-power at its disposal. The relative mass of the industrial reserve army increases therefore with the potential energy of wealth. But the greater this reserve army in proportion to the active labour-army, the greater is the mass of a consolidated surplus-population, whose misery is in inverse ratio to its torment of labour. The more extensive, finally, the lazarus-layers of the working class and the industrial reserve army, the greater is official pauperism. *This is the absolute general law of capitalist accumulation.* Like all other laws it is modified in its working by many circumstances, the analysis of which does not concern us here.

The folly is now patent of the economic wisdom that preaches to the labourers the accommodation of their number to the requirements of capital. The mechanism of capitalist production and accumulation constantly effects this adjustment. The first word of this adaptation is the creation of a relative surplus-population, or industrial reserve army. Its last word is the misery of constantly extending strata of the active army of labour, and the dead weight of pauperism.

The law by which a constantly increasing quantity of means of production, thanks to the advance in the productiveness of social labour, may be set in movement by a progressively diminishing expenditure of human power, this law, in a capitalist society – where the labourer does not employ the means of production, but the means of production employ the labourer – undergoes a complete inversion and is expressed thus: the higher the productiveness of labour, the greater is the pressure of the labourers on the means of employment, the more precarious, therefore, becomes their condition of existence, viz. the sale of their own labour-power for the increasing of another's wealth, or for the self-expansion of capital. The fact that the means of production and the productiveness of labour increase more rapidly than the productive population, expresses itself, therefore, capitalistically in the inverse form that the labouring population always increases more rapidly than the conditions under which capital can employ this increase for its own self-expansion.

We saw in Part IV when analysing the production of relative surplus-value: within the capitalist system all methods for raising the social productiveness of labour are brought about at the cost of the individual labourer; all means for the development of production transform themselves into means of domination over, and exploitation of, the producers; they mutilate the labourer into a fragment of a man, degrade him to the level of an appendage of a machine, destroy every remnant of charm in his work and turn it into a hated toil; they estrange from him the intellectual potentialities of the labour-process in the same proportion as science is incorporated in it as an independent power; they distort the conditions under which he works, subject him during the labour-process to a despotism the more hateful for its meanness; they transform his life-time into working-time, and drag his wife and child beneath the wheels of the Juggernaut of capital. But all methods for the production of surplus-value are at the same time methods of accumulation; and every extension of accumulation becomes again a means for the development of those methods. It follows therefore that in proportion as capital accumulates, the lot of the labourer, be his payment high or low, must grow worse. The law, finally, that always equilibrates the relative surplus-population, or industrial reserve army, to the extent and energy of accumulation, this law rivets the labourer to capital more firmly than the wedges of Vulcan did Prometheus to the rock. It establishes an accumulation of misery, corresponding with accumulation of capital. Accumulation of wealth at one pole is, therefore, at the same time accumulation of misery, agony of toil, slavery, ignorance, brutality, mental degradation, at the opposite pole, i.e. on the side of the class that produces its own product in the form of capital.

PART VIII

THE SO-CALLED PRIMITIVE ACCUMULATION

CHAPTER 26

The Secret of Primitive Accumulation

We have seen how money is changed into capital; how through capital surplus-value is made, and from surplus-value more capital. But the accumulation of capital presupposes surplus-value; surplus-value presupposes capitalist production; capitalist production presupposes the pre-existence of considerable masses of capital and of labour-power in the hands of producers of commodities. The whole movement, therefore, seems to turn in a vicious circle, out of which we can only get by supposing a primitive accumulation ('previous accumulation' of Adam Smith) preceding capitalistic accumulation; an accumulation not the result of the capitalist mode of production, but its starting-point.

In themselves money and commodities are no more capital than are the means of production and of subsistence. They want transforming into capital. But this transformation itself can only take place under certain circumstances that centre in this, viz. that two very different kinds of commodity-possessors must come face to face and into contact: on the one hand, the owners of money, means of production, means of subsistence, who are eager to increase the sum of values they possess by buying other people's labour-power; on the other hand, free labourers, the sellers of their own labour-power, and therefore the sellers of labour. Free labourers, in the double sense that neither they themselves form part and parcel of the means of production, as in the case of slaves, bondsmen, etc., nor do the means of production belong to them, as in the case of peasant proprietors; they are, therefore, free from, unencumbered by, any means of production of their own. With this polarisation of the market for commodities, the fundamental conditions of capitalist production are given. The capitalist system presupposes the complete separation of the labourers from all property in the means by which they can realise their labour. As soon as capitalist production is once on its own legs, it not only maintains this separation, but reproduces it on a continually extending scale. The process therefore that clears the way for the capitalist system, can be none other than the process which takes away from the labourer the possession of his means of production; a process that transforms on the one hand the social means of subsistence and of production into capital, on the other the immediate producers into wage-labourers. The so-called primitive accumulation, therefore, is nothing else than the historical process of divorcing the producer from the means of production. It appears as primitive, because it forms the prehistoric stage of capital and of the mode of production corresponding with it.

The economic structure of capitalist society has grown out of the economic structure of feudal society. The dissolution of the latter set free the elements of the former.

The immediate producer, the labourer, could only dispose of his own person after he had ceased to be attached to the soil and ceased to be the slave, serf, or bondsman of another. To become a free seller of labour-power, who carries his commodity wherever he finds a market, he must further have escaped from the regime of the guilds, their rules for apprentices and journeymen, and the impediments of their labour regulations. Hence, the historical movement which changes the producers into wage-workers, appears, on the one hand, as their emancipation from serfdom and from the fetters of the guilds, and this side alone exists for our bourgeois historians. But, on the other hand, these new freedmen became sellers of themselves only after they had been robbed of all their own means of production, and of all the guarantees of existence afforded by the old feudal arrangements. And the history of this, their expropriation, is written in the annals of mankind in letters of blood and fire.

CHAPTER 27

EXPROPRIATION OF THE AGRICULTURAL POPULATION FROM THE LAND

In England, serfdom had practically disappeared in the last part of the fourteenth century. The immense majority of the population consisted then, and to a still larger extent, in the fifteenth century, of free peasant proprietors, whatever was the feudal title under which their right of property was hidden. In the larger seignorial domains, the old bailiff, himself a serf, was displaced by the free farmer. The wage-labourers of agriculture consisted partly of peasants, who utilised their leisure time by working on the large estates, partly of an independent special class of wage-labourers, relatively and absolutely few in numbers. The latter also were practically at the same time peasant farmers, since, besides their wages, they had allotted to them arable land to the extent of four or more acres, together with their cottages. Besides they, with the rest of the peasants, enjoyed the usufruct of the common land, which gave pasture to their cattle, furnished them with timber, firewood, turf, etc. In all countries of Europe, feudal production is characterised by division of the soil amongst the greatest possible number of sub-feudatories. The might of the feudal lord, like that of the sovereign, depended not on the length of his rent-roll, but on the number of his subjects, and the latter depended on the number of peasant proprietors. Although, therefore, the English land, after the Norman conquest, was distributed in gigantic baronies, one of which often included some 900 of the old Anglo-Saxon lordships, it was bestrewn with small peasant properties, only here and there interspersed with great seignorial domains. Such conditions, together with the prosperity of the towns so characteristic of the fifteenth century, allowed of that wealth of the people which Chancellor Fortescue so eloquently paints in his *Laudes legum Angliae*; but it excluded the possibility of capitalist wealth.

The prelude of the revolution that laid the foundation of the capitalist mode of production was played in the last third of the fifteenth and the first decade of the sixteenth century. A mass of free proletarians was hurled on the labour market by the breaking up of the bands of feudal retainers, who, as Sir James Steuart well says, 'everywhere uselessly filled house and castle'. Although the royal power, itself a product of bourgeois development, in its strife after absolute sovereignty forcibly hastened on the dissolution of these bands of retainers, it was by no means the sole cause of it. In insolent conflict with king and Parliament, the great feudal lords created an incomparably larger proletariat by the forcible driving of the peasantry from the land, to which the latter had the same feudal right as the lord himself, and by the usurpation of the common lands. The rapid rise of the Flemish wool manufacturers, and the corresponding rise in the price of wool in England, gave the direct impulse to these evictions. The old nobility had been devoured by the great feudal wars. The new nobility was the child of its time, for which money was the power of all powers. Transformation of arable land into sheep-walks was, therefore, its cry.

The process of forcible expropriation of the people received in the sixteenth century a new and frightful impulse from the Reformation, and from the consequent colossal spoliation of the church property. The Catholic church was, at the time of the Reformation, feudal proprietor of a great part of the English land. The suppression of the monasteries etc. hurled their inmates into the proletariat. The estates of the church were to a large extent given away to rapacious royal favourites, or sold at a nominal price to speculating farmers and citizens, who drove out *en masse* the hereditary sub-tenants and threw their holdings into one. The legally guaranteed property of the poorer folk in a part of the church's tithes was tacitly confiscated. '*Pauper ubique jacet*', cried Queen Elizabeth after a journey through England. In the 43rd year of her reign the nation was obliged to recognise pauperism officially by the introduction of a poor-rate. 'The authors of this law seem to have been ashamed to state the grounds of it, for [contrary to traditional usage] it has no preamble whatever.' By the 16th of Charles I, Ch. 4, it was declared perpetual, and in fact only in 1834 did it take a new and harsher form. These immediate results of the Reformation were not its most lasting ones. The property of the church formed the religious bulwark of the traditional conditions of landed property. With its fall these were no longer tenable.

Even in the last decade of the seventeenth century, the yeomanry, the class of independent peasants, were more numerous than the class of farmers. They had formed the backbone of Cromwell's strength, and even according to the confession of Macaulay, stood in favourable contrast to the drunken squires and to their servants, the country clergy, who had to marry their masters' cast-off mistresses. About 1750, the yeomanry had disappeared, and so had, in the last decade of the eighteenth century, the last trace of the common land of the agricultural labourer. We leave on one side here the purely economic causes of the agricultural revolution. We deal only with the forcible means employed.

After the restoration of the Stuarts, the landed proprietors carried by legal means, an act of usurpation, effected everywhere on the Continent without any legal formality. They abolished the feudal tenure of land, i.e. they got rid of all its obligations to the state, 'indemnified' the state by taxes on the peasantry and the rest of the mass of the people, vindicated for themselves the rights of modern private property in estates to which they had only a feudal title, and finally, passed those laws of settlement which *mutatis mutandis* had the same effect on the English agricultural labourer as the edict of the Tartar Boris Godunof on the Russian peasantry.

The 'glorious Revolution' brought into power, along with William of Orange, the landlord and capitalist appropriators of surplus-value. They inaugurated the new era by practising on a colossal scale thefts of state lands, thefts that had been hitherto managed more modestly. These estates were given away, sold at a ridiculous figure, or even annexed to private estates by direct seizure. All this happened without the slightest observation of legal etiquette. The Crown lands thus fraudulently appropriated, together with the robbery of the Church estates, as far as these had not been lost again during the republican revolution, form the basis of the today princely domains of the English oligarchy. The bourgeois capitalists favoured the operation with the view, among others, to promoting free trade in land, to extending the domain of modern agriculture on the large farm system, and to increasing their supply of the free agricultural proletarians ready to hand. Besides, the new landed aristocracy was the natural ally of the new bankocracy, of the newly-hatched *haute finance*, and of the large manufacturers, then depending on protective duties. The English bourgeoisie acted for its own interest quite as wisely as did the Swedish bourgeoisie who, reversing the process hand in hand with their economic allies the peasantry, helped the kings in the forcible resumption of the Crown lands from the oligarchy. This happened since 1604 under Charles X and Charles XI.

Communal property – always distinct from the state property just dealt with – was an old Teutonic institution which lived on under cover of feudalism. We have seen how the forcible usurpation of this, generally accompanied by the turning of arable into pasture land, begins at the end of the fifteenth and extends into the sixteenth century. But at that time the process was carried on by means of individual acts of violence against which legislation, for a hundred and fifty years, fought in vain. The advance made by the eighteenth century shows itself in this, that the law itself becomes now the instrument of the theft of the people's land, although the large farmers make use of their little independent methods as well. The parliamentary form of the robbery is that of Acts for enclosures of commons, in other words, decrees by which the landlords grant themselves the people's land as private property, decree of expropriation of the people.

Whilst the place of the independent yeoman was taken by tenants at will, small farmers on yearly leases, a service rabble dependent on the pleasure of the landlords, the systematic robbery of the communal lands helped especially, next to the theft of the state domains, to swell those large farms, that were called in the eighteenth century capital farms or merchant farms, and to 'set free' the agricultural population as proletarians for manufacturing industry.

The eighteenth century, however, did not yet recognise as fully as the nineteenth the identity between national wealth and the poverty of the people. Hence the most vigorous polemic in the economic literature of that time on the 'enclosure of commons'. From the mass of materials that lie before me, I give a few extracts that will throw a strong light on the circumstances of the time. 'In several parishes of Hertfordshire', writes one indignant person, '24 farms, numbering on the average 50–150 acres, have been melted up into three farms.'

> In Northamptonshire and Leicestershire the enclosure of common lands has taken place on a very large scale, and most of the new lordships, resulting from the enclosure, have been turned into pasturage, in consequence of which many lordships have not now 50 acres ploughed yearly, in which 1,500 were ploughed formerly. The ruins of former dwelling-houses, barns, stables, etc. [are the sole traces of the former inhabitants.] An hundred houses and families have in some open-field villages . . . dwindled to eight or ten. . . . The landholders in most parishes that have been enclosed only 15 or 20 years are very few in comparison of the numbers who occupied them in their open-field state. It is no uncommon thing for 4 or 5 wealthy graziers to engross a large enclosed lordship which was before in the hands of 20 or 30 farmers, and as many

> smaller tenants and proprietors. All these are hereby thrown out of their livings with their families and many other families who were chiefly employed and supported by them.

It was not only the land that lay waste, but often land cultivated either in common or held under a definite rent paid to the community that was annexed by the neighbouring landlords under pretext of enclosure.

> I have here in view enclosures of open fields and lands already improved. It is acknowledged by even the writers in defence of enclosures that these diminished villages increase the monopolies of farms, raise the prices of provisions, and produce depopulation . . . and even the enclosure of waste lands (as now carried on) bears hard on the poor, by depriving them of a part of their subsistence, and only goes towards increasing farms already too large.

'When', says Dr Price 'this land gets into the hands of a few great farmers, the consequence must be that the little farmers' (earlier designated by him 'a multitude of little proprietors and tenants, who maintain themselves and families by the produce of the ground they occupy by sheep kept on a common, by poultry, hogs, etc. and who therefore have little occasion to purchase any of the means of subsistence')

> will be converted into a body of men who earn their subsistence by working for others, and who will be under a necessity of going to market for all they want. . . . There will, perhaps, be more labour, because there will be more compulsion to it. . . . Towns and manufacturers will increase, because more will be driven to them in quest of places and employment. This is the way in which the engrossing of farms naturally operates. And this is the way in which, for many years, it has been actually operating in this kingdom.

He sums up the effect of the enclosure thus:

> Upon the whole, the circumstances of the lower ranks of men are altered in almost every respect for the worse. From little occupiers of land, they are reduced to the state of day-labourers and hirelings; and, at the same time, their subsistence in that state has become more difficult.

In fact, usurpation of the common lands and the revolution in agriculture accompanying this told so acutely on the agricultural labourers that, even according to Eden, between 1765 and 1780 their wages began to fall below the minimum, and to be supplemented by official poor-law relief. Their wages, he says, 'were not more than enough for the absolute necessaries of life'.

Let us hear for a moment a defender of enclosures and an opponent of Dr Price.

> Nor is it a consequence that there must be depopulation, because men are not seen wasting their labour in the open field. . . . If, by converting the little farmers into a body of men who must work for others, more labour is produced, it is an advantage which the nation [to which, of course, the 'converted' ones do not belong] should wish for . . . the produce being greater when their joint labours are employed on one farm, there will be a surplus for manufacturers, and by this means manufactures, one of the mines of the nation, will increase, in proportion to the quantity of corn produced.

In the nineteenth century, the very memory of the connexion between the agricultural labourer and the communal property had of course vanished. To say nothing of more recent times, have the agricultural population received a farthing of compensation for the 3,511,770 acres of common land which between 1801 and 1831 were stolen from them and by parliamentary devices presented to the landlords by the landlords?

The last process of wholesale expropriation of the agricultural population from the soil is, finally, the so-called clearing of estates, i.e. the sweeping men off them. All the English methods hitherto considered culminated in 'clearing'. As we saw in the picture of modern conditions given in a former chapter, where there are no more independent peasants to get rid of, the 'clearing' of cottages begins; so that the agricultural labourers do not find on the soil cultivated by them even the spot necessary for their own housing. But what 'clearing of estates' really and properly signifies, we learn only in the promised land of modern romance, the Highlands of Scotland. There the process is distinguished by its systematic character, by the magnitude of the scale on which it is carried out at one blow (in Ireland landlords have gone to the length of sweeping away several villages at once; in Scotland areas as large as German principalities are dealt with), finally by the peculiar form of property, under which the embezzled lands were held.

The Highland Celts were organised in clans, each of which was the owner of the land on which it was settled. The representative of the clan, its chief or 'great man', was only the titular owner of this property, just as the Queen of England is the titular owner of all the national soil. When the English government succeeded in suppressing the intestine wars of these 'great men', and their constant incursions into the Lowland plains, the chiefs of the clans by no means gave up their time-honoured trade as robbers; they only changed its form. On their own authority they transformed their nominal right into a right of private property, and as this brought them into collision with their clansmen, resolved to drive them out by open force. 'A king of England might as well claim to drive his subjects into the sea,' says Professor Newman. This revolution, which began in Scotland after the last rising of the followers of the Pretender, can be followed through its first phases in the writings of Sir James Steuart and James Anderson. In the eighteenth century the hunted-out Gaels were forbidden to emigrate from the country, with a view to driving them by force to Glasgow and other manufacturing towns. As an example of the method obtaining in the nineteenth century, the 'clearing' made by the Duchess of Sutherland will suffice here. This person, well instructed in economy, resolved, on entering upon her government, to effect a radical cure, and to turn the whole country, whose population had already been by earlier processes of the like kind reduced to 15,000, into a sheep-walk. From 1814 to 1820 these 15,000 inhabitants, about 3,000 families, were systematically hunted and rooted out. All their villages were destroyed and burnt, all their fields turned into pasturage. British soldiers enforced this eviction, and came to blows with the inhabitants. One old woman was burnt to death in the flames of the hut, which she refused to leave. Thus this fine lady appropriated 794,000 acres of land that had from time immemorial belonged to the clan. She assigned to the expelled inhabitants about 6,000 acres on the sea-shore – 2 acres per family. The 6,000 acres had until this time lain waste, and brought in no income to their owners. The Duchess, in the nobility of her heart, actually went so far as to let these at an average rent of 2s. 6d. per acre to the clansmen, who for centuries had shed their blood for her family. The whole of the stolen clanland she divided into 29 great sheep farms, each inhabited by a single family, for the most part imported English farm-servants. In the year 1835 the 15,000 Gaels were already replaced by 131,000 sheep. The remnant of the aborigines flung on the sea-shore tried to live by catching fish. They became amphibious and lived, as an English author says, half on land and half on water, and withal only half on both.

But the brave Gaels must expiate yet more bitterly their idolatry, romantic and of the mountains, for the 'great men' of the clan. The smell of their fish rose to the noses of the great men. They scented some profit in it, and let the sea-shore to the great fishmongers of London. For the second time the Gaels were hunted out.

The spoliation of the church's property, the fraudulent alienation of the state domains, the robbery of the common lands, the usurpation of feudal and clan property, and its transformation into modern private property under circumstances of reckless terrorism, were just so many idyllic methods of primitive accumulation. They conquered the field for capitalistic agriculture, made the soil part and parcel of capital, and created for the town industries the necessary supply of a 'free' and outlawed proletariat.

CHAPTER 28

Bloody Legislation Against the Expropriated, From the End of the Fifteenth Century

The proletariat created by the breaking up of the bands of feudal retainers and by the forcible expropriation of the people from the soil, this 'free' proletariat could not possibly be absorbed by the nascent manufacturers as fast as it was thrown upon the world. On the other hand, these men, suddenly dragged from their wonted mode of life, could not as suddenly adapt themselves to the discipline of their new condition. They were turned *en masse* into beggars, robbers, vagabonds, partly from inclination, in most cases from stress of circumstances. Hence at the end of the fifteenth and during the whole of the sixteenth century, throughout Western Europe a bloody legislation against vagabondage. The fathers of the present working class were chastised for their enforced transformation into vagabonds and paupers. Legislation treated them as 'voluntary' criminals, and assumed that it depended on their own good will to go on working under the old conditions that no longer existed.

Thus were the agricultural people first forcibly expropriated from the soil, driven from their homes, turned into vagabonds, and then whipped, branded, tortured by laws grotesquely terrible, into the discipline necessary for the wage system.

It is not enough that the conditions of labour are concentrated in a mass, in the shape of capital, at the one pole of society, while at the other are grouped masses of men, who have nothing to sell but their labour-power. Neither is it enough that they are compelled to sell it voluntarily. The advance of capitalist production develops a working class, which by education, tradition, habit, looks upon the conditions of that mode of production as self-evident laws of Nature. The organisation of the capitalist process of production, once fully developed, breaks down all resistance. The constant generation of a relative surplus-population keeps the law of supply and demand of labour, and therefore keeps wages, in a rut that corresponds with the wants of capital. The dull compulsion of economic relations completes the subjection of the labourer to the capitalist. Direct force, outside economic conditions, is of course still used, but only exceptionally. In the ordinary run of things, the labourer can be left to the 'natural laws of production', i.e. to his dependence on capital, a dependence springing from, and guaranteed in perpetuity by, the conditions of production themselves. It is otherwise during the historic genesis of capitalist production. The bourgeoisie, at its rise, wants and uses the power of the state to 'regulate' wages, i.e. to force them within the limits suitable for surplus-value making, to lengthen the working day and to keep the labourer himself in the normal degree of dependence. This is an essential element of the so-called primitive accumulation.

Coalition of the labourers is treated as a heinous crime from the fourteenth century to 1825, the year of the repeal of the laws against trade unions. The provisions of the labour statutes as to contracts between master and workman, as to giving notice and the like, which only allow of a civil action against the contract-breaking master, but on the contrary permit a criminal action against the contract-breaking workman, are to this hour (1873) in full force. The barbarous laws against trade unions fell in 1825 before the threatening bearing of the proletariat. Despite this, they fell only in part. Certain beautiful fragments of the old statute vanished only in 1859. Finally, the Act of Parliament of 29 June 1871 made a pretence of removing the last traces of this class of legislation by legal recognition of trade unions. But an Act of Parliament of the same date (an act to amend the criminal law relating to violence, threats, and molestation), re-established, in point of fact, the former state of things in a new shape. By this parliamentary *escamotage* the means which the labourers could use in a strike or lock-out were withdrawn from the laws common to all citizens, and placed under exceptional penal legislation, the interpretation of which fell to the masters themselves in their capacity as justices of the peace. Two years earlier, the same House of Commons and the same Mr Gladstone in the well-known straightforward fashion brought in a bill for the abolition of all exceptional penal legislation against the working class. But this was never allowed to go beyond the second reading, and the matter was thus protracted until at last the 'great Liberal party', by an alliance with the Tories, found courage to turn against the very proletariat that had carried it into power. Not content with this treachery, the 'great Liberal party' allowed the English judges, ever complaisant in the service of the ruling classes, to dig up again the earlier laws against 'conspiracy', and to apply them to coalitions of labourers. We see that only against its will and under the pressure of the masses did the English Parliament give up the laws against strikes and trade unions, after it had itself, for 500 years, held, with shameless egoism, the position of a permanent trade union of the capitalists against the labourers.

During the very first storms of the Revolution, the French bourgeoisie dared to take away from the workers the right of association but just acquired. By a decree of 14 June 1791, they declared all coalition of the workers as 'an attempt against liberty and the declaration of the rights of man', punishable by a fine of 500 livres, together with deprivation of the rights of an active citizen for one year. This law which, by means of state compulsion, confined the struggle between capital and labour within limits comfortable for capital, has outlived revolutions and changes of dynasties. Even the Reign of Terror left it untouched. It was but quite recently struck out of the Penal Code.

CHAPTER 32

HISTORICAL TENDENCY OF CAPITALIST ACCUMULATION

What does the primitive accumulation of capital, i.e. its historical genesis, resolve itself into? In so far as it is not immediate transformation of slaves and serfs into wage-labourers, and therefore a mere change of form, it only means the expropriation of the immediate producers, i.e. the dissolution of private property based on the labour of its owner. Private property, as the antithesis to social, collective property, exists only where the means of labour and the external conditions of labour belong to private individuals. But according as these private individuals are labourers or not labourers, private property has a different character. The numberless shades that it at first sight presents correspond to the intermediate stages lying between these two extremes. The private property of the labourer in his means of production is the foundation of petty industry, whether agricultural, manufacturing, or both; petty industry again is an essential condition for the development of social production and of the free individuality of the labourer himself. Of course this petty mode of production exists also under slavery, serfdom, and other states of dependence. But it flourishes, it lets loose its whole energy, it attains its adequate classical form, only where the labourer is the private owner of his own means of labour set in action by himself: the peasant of the land which he cultivates, the artisan of the tool which he handles as a virtuoso. This mode of production presupposes parcelling of the soil, and scattering of the other means of production. As it excludes the concentration of these means of production, so also it excludes cooperation, division of labour within each separate process of production, the control over, and the productive application of the forces of Nature by society, and the free development of the social productive powers. It is compatible only with a system of production and a society moving within narrow and more or less primitive bounds. To perpetuate it would be, as Pecqueur rightly says, 'to decree universal mediocrity'. At a certain stage of development it brings forth the material agencies for its own dissolution. From that moment new forces and new passions spring up in the bosom of society; but the old social organisation fetters them and keeps them down. It must be annihilated; it is annihilated. Its annihilation, the transformation of the individualised and scattered means of production into socially concentrated ones, of the pigmy property of the many into the huge property of the few, the expropriation of the great mass of the people from the soil, from the means of subsistence, and from the means of labour, this fearful and painful expropriation of the mass of the people forms the prelude to the history of capital. It comprises a series of forcible methods, of which we have passed in review only those that have been epoch-making as methods of the primitive accumulation of capital. The expropriation of the immediate producers was accomplished with merciless vandalism, and under the stimulus of passions the most infamous, the most sordid, the pettiest, the most meanly odious. Self-earned private property that is based, so to say, on the fusing together of the isolated, independent labouring-individual with the conditions of his labour, is supplanted by capitalistic private property, which rests on exploitation of the nominally free labour of others, i.e. on wage-labour.

As soon as this process of transformation has sufficiently decomposed the old society from top to bottom, as soon as the labourers are turned into proletarians, their means of labour into capital, as soon as the capitalist mode of production stands on its own feet, then the further socialisation of labour and further transformation of the land and other means of production into socially exploited and therefore common means of production, as well as the further expropriation of private proprietors, takes a new form. That which is now to be expropriated is no longer the labourer working for himself, but the capitalist exploiting many labourers. This expropriation is accomplished by the action of the immanent laws of capitalistic production itself, by the centralisation of capital. One capitalist always kills many. Hand in hand with this centralisation, or this expropriation of many capitalists by few, develop, on an ever-extending scale, the cooperative form of the labour-process, the conscious technical application of science, the methodical cultivation of the soil, the transformation of the instruments of labour into instruments of labour only usable in common, the economising of all means of production by their use as the means of production of combined, socialised labour, the entanglement of all peoples in the net of the world market, and with this, the international character of the capitalist régime. Along with the constantly diminishing number of the magnates of capital, who usurp and monopolise all advantages of this process of transformation, grows the mass of misery, oppression, slavery, degradation, exploitation; but with this too grows the revolt of the working class, a class always increasing in numbers, and disciplined, united, organised by the very mechanism of the process of capitalist production itself. The monopoly of capital becomes a fetter upon the mode of production which has sprung up and flourished along with and under it. Centralisation of the means of production and socialisation of labour at last reach a point where they become incompatible with their capitalist integument. This integument is burst asunder. The knell of capitalist private property sounds. The expropriators are expropriated.

The capitalist mode of appropriation, the result of the capitalist mode of production, produces capitalist private property. This is the first negation of individual private property, as founded on the labour of the proprietor. But capitalist production begets with the inexorability of a law of Nature its own negation. It is the negation of negation. This does not re-establish private property for the producer, but gives him individual property based on the acquisitions of the capitalist era: i.e. on cooperation and the possession in common of the land and of the means of production.

The transformation of scattered private property arising from individual labour into capitalist private property is, naturally, a process incomparably more protracted, violent, and difficult than the transformation of capitalistic private property, already practically resting on socialised production, into socialised property. In the former case, we had the expropriation of the mass of the people by a few usurpers; in the latter, we have the expropriation of a few usurpers by the mass of the people.

> The advance of industry, whose involuntary promoter is the bourgeoisie, replaces the isolation of the labourers, due to competition, by their revolutionary combination, due to association. The development of modern industry, therefore, cuts from under its feet, the very foundation on which the bourgeoisie produces and appropriates products. What the bourgeoisie, therefore, produces, above all, are its own grave-diggers. Its fall and the victory of the proletariat are equally inevitable. (Karl Marx und Friedrich Engels, *Manifest der Kommunistischen Partei*, London, 1848).

Index